CRIME INC.

by the same author

THE KURDS

THE FALL OF SCOTLAND YARD

CRIME INC.

The Story of Organized Crime

Martin Short

THAMES METHUEN
LONDON

First published in Great Britain 1984 by Methuen London Ltd
11 New Fetter Lane, London EC4P 4EE
in association with Thames Television International Ltd
149 Tottenham Court Road, London W1P 9LL

Printed in Great Britain by
Richard Clay (The Chaucer Press) Ltd,
Bungay, Suffolk

British Library Cataloguing in Publication Data

Short, Martin
Crime Inc.
1. Organized Crime – United States – History
I. Title
364.1′06′073 HV6446

ISBN 0–423–01040–9
ISBN 0–423–01120–0 Pbk

CONTENTS

ILLUSTRATIONS

ACKNOWLEDGEMENTS

My thanks are due to literally thousands of Americans and scores of American law enforcement agencies for allowing me to take up their valuable time, pillage their memories and their files, and ask them questions which may often have struck them as naive.

This book could not have been written, nor could the television series have been made, without the help and support of the FBI, the DEA and the Organized Crime and Racketeering Section of the Department of Justice. Within these agencies I especially thank the FBI's offices in Cleveland, Las Vegas and New York and its public affairs unit in Washington; the DEA in Miami; the Strike Forces in Boston, Brooklyn, Chicago, Cleveland, Kansas City and Newark; and the US Attorneys' offices in the Southern and Eastern districts of New York. I also thank the US Customs and Coastguard in Miami and the Bureau of Alcohol, Tobacco and Firearms.

For help in relation to Federal witnesses in the care of the Witness Security Program, I thank the US Marshals' Service and Howard Safir. I also thank the US Bureau of Prisons.

Among numerous state and city forces, I was greatly aided by the New York Police Department, the Florida Department of Law Enforcement, Dade County Public Safety (Homicide), the Broward County Strike Force and the Essex County (New Jersey) Narcotics Squad. On gambling issues, the New Jersey Division of Gaming Enforcement was particularly helpful.

In the conception and execution of this entire project I owe my deepest debt to the New Jersey State Police, through the goodwill and endless co-operation of Colonel Justin Dintino and Lieutenant Freddie Martens.

The work of the Pennsylvania Crime Commission was an

inspiration, personified by one of its investigators, Gino Lazzari. The same is true of that unique group of concerned citizens, the Chicago Crime Commission, under its past and present directors, Virgil Peterson and Pat Healy.

I thank all those people who consented to being interviewed on film (over 100 in all). Those whose help went beyond the call of public service and courtesy to foreign inquisitors included Edgar Croswell (the man who proved that the Mafia did exist in 1957), John Cusack, Pete Donohue, Remo Franceschini, Louis Freeh, Jack Key, Aaron Kohn, Bob Kortenhaus, Vincent Piersante, Bill Roemer and Joe Yablonsky.

For academic perspectives and overviews I thank Professors Robert Blakey, Charles Rogovin (who is still expecting me to show up with a film crew!), Francis Ianni and Elizabeth Reuss-Ianni.

Other experts who helped me greatly were Nick Akerman, Christopher Andreoff, Judge Charles Breitel, Thomas Coon, Steve del Corso, Denny Debbaudt, Mike Defeo, Orange Dickey, Donald Gray, Bill Lambie, Paul Kelly, Bill Lambie, John Olszewski, Joe Quarequio, Max Renner, Ray Shryock, John Sopko, Lou Spalla, Ed Stier, Geoffrey L. Thomas and my dear friend John Bassett.

I have relied greatly on the work and support of many authors, reporters and writers, notably Ed Barnes, Ned Day, Ovid Demaris, Ron Koziol, Jon Kwitny, Ron Labreque, Bruce Locklin, Mike Mallowe, Paul Meskil, Dan Moldea, John O'Brien, Nic Pileggi, Tom Renner, Allen Richardson and Tony DeStefano, Sandy Smith, Ned Whelan, Clyde Weiss and Maire-Jane Woge. Among television reporters and producers, my greatest debt is to John Drummond and J. P. Stadius of CBS in Chicago.

There are many more people in law enforcement who helped me despite the rules of their organizations and whose identities must therefore remain confidential. For even more obvious reasons, I cannot publicly thank those people within the Mafia, including several crime family bosses, who talked to me in confidence.

Much of this book, and even more of the television series, is based on the testimony of the federal witnesses who agreed to go face-to-camera and name names. Wherever they may be now, I offer my deepest gratitude, my best wishes and my prayers.

Among archive sources I thank the Chicago Historical Society, Henry Scheafer of Chicago, the Historic New Orleans Collection, the Louisiana Historical Centre, the New York Municipal Archives (Ken Cobb) and the Central Archives for the History of the Jewish People in Jerusalem, for access to the records of the Bureau of Social Morals (Hadassah Assouline).

I thank Thames Television for backing the idea I brought to its documentaries department more than four years ago, and I am indebted to numerous Thames executives, past and present, who played a part in getting that idea onto the screen. My thanks are due in particular to the production team: ace researchers Helen Dickinson and Dai Richards, film researcher extraordinaire Adrian Wood, directors Ken Craig and Ian Stuttard, cameraman Ted Adcock, sound engineer Ron Thomas, production assistant Betty Kenworthy, graphic designer Lester Halhed, Jenny Holt, editors Howard Bradburn and George Smith (the long-suffering troglodytes who serve without glory, EDM magician Alan Ritchie, and series producer John Edwards. I thank Mary Fox for her help on the photographs and for her three years looking after us all. Our manager Roy English is another unsung hero who fought many battles on our behalf. It is probably because of him that 'I still have my earlobes'. Similarly, Angela Doyle has shielded me from the wrath of numerous lending libraries.

Credited on the series as 'consultant' was Frank Pulley. This ill describes the Scotland Yard detective who quit the Metropolitan Police after twenty-seven years' service for the turbulent waters of the television industry. As *compare* and *consigliere*, Frank has remained a tireless ally and, I trust, a friend of mine, if not a friend of ours! He also dreamed up the title.

I must thank Nic Jones at Thames for commissioning this book. At Methuen, accolades and garlands are due to Ann Mansbridge for her unending patience in the face of my pleas that the TV series must always have first claim on my time. There were many occasions when she must have felt she was never going to get a complete manuscript. Thanks also to Alex Bennion and text editor Diana Levinson.

For more than two years, my wife and children tolerated my prolonged absences in America. They then had to put up with my mental absence for another year at home as I worked seven days and nights a week on both the series and the book. I hope they will think it has all been worthwhile.

INTRODUCTION

Organized crime is America's biggest business. According to some estimates, its profits are greater than those of *Fortune* magazine's top 500 business and industrial corporations added together. One estimate accepted by the US Senate in 1979 assessed major crime revenues in America at over $160 billion a year. The annual retail value of illegal narcotics alone may be anything between $50 billion and $100 billion. But what is organized crime?

I appropriate here two attempts at a definition of organized crime. The shorter version comes from Ralph Salerno, the eminent former New York detective:

> Organized crime is a self-perpetuating, continuing criminal conspiracy, for profit and power, using fear and corruption and seeking immunity from the law.

A longer definition comes from the Task Force *Report on Organized Crime*, published in 1967:

> Organized crime is a society that seeks to operate outside the control of the American people and their governments. It involves thousands of criminals, working within structures as complex as those of legitimate governments. Its actions are not impulsive but rather the result of intricate conspiracies, carried on over many years and aimed at gaining control over whole fields of activity in order to amass huge profits.
>
> The core of organized crime activity is the supply of illegal goods and services – gambling, loansharking, narcotics and other forms of vice – to countless numbers of citizen customers. But organized crime is also extensively involved in legitimate business and in labor unions. Here it employs illegitimate methods – monopolization, terrorism, extortion,

tax evasion – to drive out or control lawful ownership and leadership to exact illegal profits from the public. And to carry on its many activities secure from governmental interference, organized crime corrupts public officials.

I have tried to write a study of organized crime which will be of interest to the general reader, the television viewer and the student. I hope the book can be read both as a companion work to the television series and by itself. This has been a difficult objective and I trust that I have neither short-changed the experts nor befuddled the newcomer with too many names and numbers.

I can foresee that there may be places where a torrent of concentrated fact might confuse the general reader. This seems most likely when I refer to the five Mafia crime families of New York. I attempt a summary here. What began in 1931 as the Lucky Luciano family is now known as the Vito *Genovese* family. What is known today as the Carlo *Gambino* family was originally led by the Mangano brothers and then by Albert Anastasia until he was murdered in 1957. The three smaller families are the Joe *Colombo* family (formerly led by Joes Profaci and Magliocco), the Joe *Bonanno* family (named after its founder boss, who is still alive in exile in Arizona and now in prison) and the Tommy *Lucchese* family, founded by Jack Gagliano. The families are now led by men with different surnames but all five families have retained the names of their bosses in the 1960s. These names are, of course, accorded by law enforcement rather than by the mafiosi themselves.

This book is not a chronological history but an attempt to interweave the past and the present theme by theme. For those who wish to read the book in conjunction with the television series the following chapters correspond to each of the seven episodes:

1 to 5	1. All in the Family
6 to 12	2. The Making of the Mob
13 to 15	3. Racketbusters
16 to 19	4. The Birthright of Gangsters
20 to 22	5. The Mob at Work

23 to 26	6. Make it Legitimate
27	7. New Rivals, Old Connections

Most of the quotations, unless otherwise attributed, are taken from my filmed interviews for the series. However, much of this book deals with areas of organized crime which we found we could not satisfactorily illustrate on film. Such rackets, which in this sense are invisible, are no less menacing to American society than those which we were able to portray on television.

My use of the word 'Mafia' throughout the text may not be true to a strict interpretation of the word, meaning a purely Sicilian organization. This the Mafia in America today is certainly not. However, Mafia is the only term which can adequately convey the true power and awesome strength of this octopoid conspiracy. Euphemisms like La Cosa Nostra or Traditional Organized Crime are best left to law enforcement and politicians.

I use the term 'racket' to describe any crooked manipulation of a legitimate or outwardly legitimate business or activity. Sometimes I have applied it to wholly illegal operations such as narcotics. The word apparently originates from the Saturday night dances or soirées, known as rackets, held at Tammany Hall in the nineteenth century. They were called rackets because of the appalling noise made by the carousers who attended. Since most of them were crooked politicians and their criminal friends, it was not long before the words 'racket' and 'racketeer' acquired their corrupt meaning. The noise of those long-gone Tammany celebrations is still ringing in our ears.

1

The City of Brotherly Love

On a March evening in one of America's largest cities the boss of the Mafia crime family was shotgunned to death outside his home.

Four weeks later the family's *consigliere* (elder statesman) was found dead in the trunk of a stolen car. Tortured, stabbed and repeatedly shot, his body was surrounded with torn $20 notes to symbolize that he was killed for being greedy. The same day his brother-in-law was found shotgunned to death. Naked, brutally tortured, bound hand and foot and stuffed in an undertaker's body bag he had been dumped on a deserted street.

In September the body of a capo (a lieutenant in the crime family) was discovered near an isolated landfill. He had been shot three times in the back of the head.

That October another victim was found, also shot in the head: the family's chief loanshark, the boss of its extortionate moneylending business. His body was bound with his hands behind his back and stuffed inside two green plastic rubbish bags. He had $500 in his pockets and was still wearing his gold watch. In Mafia language this denotes that he was killed not in some casual mugging but for crimes against the family.

In December a florist's delivery man called at the home of a union boss corruptly involved with the crime family. The poinsettias he carried concealed his real gift: six bullets with which he shot the union man in the face and head in front of his victim's wife.

Twelve months after the old boss's murder his successor met his death on his front porch. His killers detonated a massive bomb packed with finishing nails from across the street.

Chicago in the 1920s? New York in the 1930s? No. Philadelphia in the 1980s. Since March 1980 more than twenty Philadelphia mobsters have been slaughtered in a civil war of such violence that nothing in America compares with it since the repeal of Prohibition in 1933.

To most Americans, and indeed to any Britons who recall the late revolution in the colonies, Philadelphia means the Liberty Bell and Independence Hall. It is the city of Benjamin Franklin and the city where the Founding Fathers signed the Declaration of Independence in 1776. When W. C. Fields visited Philadelphia he found that it was closed. On balance, however, he said he would rather be there than dead. If you belong to the Philadelphia Mafia there is no such choice. Either way, you're dead.

If a Mafia necrophile goes to Philadelphia he should head for south Philly where, if he has a strong stomach, he should dine at a restaurant known until recently as Cous' Little Italy. Cous' (pronounced Cuzz'es and named after its former superb chef) has had to change its name. It was developing a reputation for losing customers – not because they didn't like the food but because they died soon after eating there.

The Philadelphia mob war began after a meal at Cous'. On the evening of 21 March 1980 Angelo Bruno, boss of the city's crime family, left the restaurant and climbed into the front passenger seat of a car belonging to John Stanfa, his driver and bodyguard. Stanfa drove Bruno the few blocks to his home at 934 Snyder Avenue where at 9.50 p.m. he double-parked. He then wound down the window on Bruno's side. A man stepped out from behind a parked car, thrust a sawn-off shotgun through the window, put it behind Bruno's right ear and fired. Nobody saw a thing.

Angelo Bruno died instantly. In Mafia language his was an honourable death: painless, without mutilation and taking place in public outside his own home. Understandably his wife Sue did not feel this way. Photographers arrived to capture the Don's grotesque appearance in death for the world's press the following day. The indignity continued. Bruno was left in the car for hours while neighbours gawked and television crews gathered their footage. Finally the neighbours, who were mostly Italian, realized his indignity was also theirs, shouting, 'Take him away, take him away,' until he was finally removed to the morgue.

Philadelphians reacted in widely differing ways to the killing, revealing America's schizophrenic attitude towards the Mafia. Neighbours were interviewed on local television. 'A wonderful person. He couldn't be any better,' said one woman. 'He was a peaceful man, he wasn't violent,' said another. 'We all play numbers, we all go to the racetrack, know what I mean?' explained a man. 'We all cheat a little bit, but this man didn't play narcotics and that's why he's dead today.'

Most south Philadelphians seemed to think of Bruno more as a grandfather than a godfather. Their attitude is typical. Just as millions of drinking Americans do not condemn those who sold liquor in Prohibition, people who gamble see little wrong in those who run illegal lotteries and betting shops. To them the racketeer is a public servant, not a public enemy.

A Jesuit priest went much further in his column in the *Daily News* when Bruno died, writing:

> Do you think he was any more ruthless than a David Rockefeller, onetime chairman of Chase Manhattan Bank, who called in many a loan on strapped businessmen? What about the people Mafia hit men blow away? . . . . I'll say this, take all the men the Mafia may have liquidated over the last half-century and they're like a drop of blood compared to the legalized murders sanctioned by President Nixon and Henry Kissinger and the CIA.

Mike Chitwood, a veteran Philadelphia policeman, was working in the homicide squad when Bruno was killed. Chitwood grew up among the Italians of south Philadelphia and knows the way they feel. 'Angelo Bruno? You could never find anybody say a bad word about him. Because they [the Mafia] always were, "nice to the people". People needed help – they couldn't pay their gas bill, electric bill, whatever – these guys would pick up the tab.

'Angelo Bruno had a reputation for being a gentleman, a family man, close to his wife and children. He was a respected member of the community and with his intelligence and business sense he could probably have been a financier or industrialist. I think he was so well-liked because he was non-violent and he wouldn't involve himself in the drug trade. A lot of people respect that.'

Press and television took up the theme of non-violence, praising Bruno as the 'gentle' or 'docile Don'. Yet there was glee in the way reporters were anticipating 'more mob rubouts soon'. They seem to regard organized crime as an amusing sideshow and the death of a top mafioso is deemed to have no impact on the rest of society. Such slaughter is irrelevant to the world at large because the mafiosi 'only kill each other'.

The police, the FBI and the Pennsylvania Crime Commission, however, realized Bruno's importance. They knew him to be one of the most powerful crime bosses in America, not simply the head of the Philadelphia family but a member of the nine-man 'National Commission' that was alleged to govern the Mafia's affairs from coast to coast. He was on the 'board of directors' of the most profitable corporation in America.

Angelo Bruno Anneloro was born in Sicily in 1910. Brought to America as a child it seems that he soon joined the network of immigrants who were rapidly becoming the most powerful force in the country's underworld. The police first picked him up in 1928 for reckless driving. He was later arrested many times but convicted only twice: for gambling and operating a still. In American law such offences are called 'misdemeanours' and are not viewed as serious crimes or felonies. Because Bruno was never convicted of a felony the Catholic church granted him a Christian burial. When he did go to jail in October 1970 it was for contempt. He had refused to answer questions asked by New Jersey's Commission of Investigation. He stayed in jail for thirty-two months and was freed only on medical grounds. Despite this imprisonment he hailed America as the best country in the world. On the Fourth of July he hung out flags.

His daughter Jeanne recalled him: 'They never pinned anything on him. They couldn't prove he did anything wrong. He never dealt in drugs, he never dealt in prostitution, pornography or murder. Even his speech was clean.' Jeanne remembers her father as a jolly man with a fine singing voice, who could play the violin and piano. She still finds it difficult to believe what organized-crime experts say about her father.

As far back as the 1950s Bruno was identified by the Federal Bureau of Narcotics as 'one of the upper echelon of the Mafia organization in the Philadelphia area' who held a policy-making role. Yet not even the FBN said that he was involved in drugs.

His Mafia career took off in 1959 when Joe Ida, then Philadelphia's boss, fled to Italy to avoid arrest. The National

Commission entrusted the family to the care of Ida's under boss, Antonio Pollina, until a successor was chosen. Pollina wanted the job permanently so he ordered the murder of his main rival, Angelo Bruno. The man entrusted with killing told Bruno of Pollina's plot. Bruno complained to the National Commission which made him boss and authorized him to execute Pollina. But Bruno refused and for this non-violence he was first dubbed the 'gentle Don'.

It seems inconceivable that so benign a man should rise to the top of the Mafia, yet Bruno was not an enforcer. He was a moneymaker and above all else organized crime exists to make money. He oversaw the rackets that were fundamental to the mob – illegal gambling and loansharking – in greater Philadelphia, an area of more than 6 million inhabitants. He also controlled the rackets in vacation towns on the south New Jersey shore, notably Atlantic City, the one-time 'queen of the resorts', only 60 miles from Philadelphia.

For many years Bruno owned legitimate businesses, starting with a grocery store. By the 1950s hc ran one company which dealt in aluminium goods and another ambiguously named Atlas Extermination. Later he moved into vending machines and cigarettes. He owned land in Florida which, he said, accounted for most of his wealth. He had bought when land in the sunshine state was very cheap and had benefited like many other investors from its huge real estate boom. Bruno told his daughter, 'Anybody who makes money illegally these days must be crazy. There are so many opportunities to make money the right way.'

Police experts argue that when mafiosi like Bruno buy up businesses or land it does not mean they are really 'legitimate' or reformed characters. They use these assets to 'launder' or disguise their criminal income or as fronts for further criminal activity. This way they gain a spurious respectability which, in Bruno's case, protected him from public hostility. Behind his veneer of good citizenship Bruno was, say the police, little better than his murderous Mafia *compares*. He may have played the part of the 'gentle Don' but in the four years before he died his crime family murdered at least seven people. They included a cigarette smuggler, a professional arsonist who had turned witness against a Philadelphia mobster, a gambler who had a fight with another family member, a shady judge and three drug traffickers. None of the dead were themselves mafiosi but each had upset the interests of the Bruno crime family.

Theories as to why Bruno was executed abound. The one most to his credit is that he abhorred drug-trafficking of any sort. Drugs had become the Mafia's biggest moneymaker. The families have little if any control over America's cocaine or marijuana trade but they dominate the heroin market in the north-eastern states. A huge market had also built up in Philadelphia for methamphetamine, PCP or 'angel dust', and quaaludes. The younger mafiosi wanted to muscle in on the market but Bruno would have none of it.

'My father got to be too good for his own good,' says Jeanne Bruno. 'People were into drugs . . . and my father was against it. A lot of people wanted to make money, most likely, and they were dissatisfied because my father stuck to his beliefs. . . .'

Other experts say that Bruno was killed over Atlantic City. For years this rundown resort had not been worth fighting over but in November 1976 the state of New Jersey made it the only place outside Nevada where casino gambling was legal. Organized-crime figures from all over America wanted this piece of Bruno territory. New York's five families, especially the huge Gambino and Genovese outfits, were not going to sit back while Philadelphia ran the lucrative rackets which are always part of 'legitimate' casino business. Henceforth Atlantic City would be an open city, like Las Vegas and Miami, with New York taking the lion's share. According to one theory Bruno was killed by his own followers for surrendering to New York. According to another he was killed by a New York family because he had told them to keep out.[1]

There is a simpler explanation. Bruno stood in the way of younger men. Philadelphia's 'Young Turks' killed off the old Don just as an earlier generation of New York mafiosi had wiped out the old 'Moustache Petes' from Sicily in 1931. Philadelphia's Young Turks were hardly young. The entire family was ageing and the oldest of them realized that if they did not remove Bruno soon they might die before he did.

Phil Testa, Bruno's under-boss, was particularly aggrieved. 'Chicken Man' as he was known (he once ran a chicken business) felt Bruno did not confide in him. He complained about this to other family members in a conversation in November 1977 at a business bizarrely named the Tyrone Denittis Talent Agency. None of them knew the FBI was listening.

TESTA: So what's going to happen Harry? Did you hear anything about the new *consigliere*?

HARRY 'THE HUNCHBACK' RICCOBENE (a caporegime): Not a thing. Not one thing!

FRANK 'CHICKIE' NARDUCCI: he [Bruno] never says nothing to us. I'm capi [caporegime] and I don't know. I presume he [Testa] don't know either.

TESTA: No.

RICCOBENE: What the hell, he don't know! How are we gonna know?

NICODEMUS 'NICKY' SCARFO: And he's the 'under' [under-boss]!

RICCOBENE: If I ask him [Bruno] the first thing he might say is 'What's the interest? What's your interest in knowing?'

NARDUCCI: Well, don't they have to ask us anyway?

RICCOBENE: No.

* * *

NARDUCCI: You know who I think would get it? This is off my head, just thinking. I would think your uncle, Nicky [Nicolo Piccolo] . . . because he's up there. He's no kid. He's about 75 ain't he? He's not a young man.

SCARFO: Well, that's just it. I mean . . . just keeps it up in the old age bracket. . . . Not that I'm against old age, but I know now if I lived to be 75 I don't think I want no headaches. I'd leave it to the younger generation.

* * *

TESTA: I'm going to tell you something. This is in my heart. I know who is qualified but I know he [Scarfo] will never get it because there is too much opposition right now. . . . He knows this fucking thing better than a lot of guys. I'm talking about the young generation. . . . He's got smarts. He's not a kid you know. He's 48, I mean . . . how old do you have to be to, ah . . . get somewhere. . . ? How old are you Nick?

SCARFO: 48. I'll be 49.

TESTA: I think you're old enough. I don't . . . understand. They look at us like we was kids. [Testa was 52.]

* * *

RICCOBENE: Well, see nobody can take the initiative in this thing.

TESTA: Why not?

RICCOBENE: Because you can be ostracized.

TESTA: Ostracized? What the hell is that? That word I don't understand.

RICCOBENE (laughing): You become an outlaw. . . . You need backing. . . . You see, it isn't like it used to be, where everybody was invited. Today . . . they are only gonna invite certain people. And the certain people are going to be the ones that are gonna give him [Bruno] the vote. . . .

If it could be like the old days, then you could go around him a little . . . you know, use the power. You talk to all your potential close associates. Then you . . . nominate somebody. You propose him! 'I propose this guy!' And somebody seconds the motion. And then there is a vote between them. If nobody goes against the guy that is selected, it's all over.

NARDUCCI: Over here [meaning the USA in comparison with Italy] he's not even bounded by the 'Cigars' [the Mafia chieftains]. He just proposes 'A' and that's it. Whatever he says.

* * *

Testa then guesses that Bruno will choose Nicolo Piccolo because he has to keep a balance between Calabrians and Sicilians in the family and Piccolo is a Calabrian.

TESTA: . . . because he's looking at it not as La Cosa Nostra. He looks at it like it's two factions. Let's face it. So he wants to satisfy . . . a faction.

SCARFO: Which is very wrong.

TESTA: Of course it's wrong. . . . You're supposed to look at this thing, La Cosa Nostra . . . that's the end of it.

Under-boss Philip 'Chicken Man' Testa had been sore with Bruno since 1975 feeling he had held on too tight and too long to the reins of power. In addition Bruno favoured old and weak advisers whom he could control rather than younger, stronger men. The family was also split about the use of violence, both for external business reasons and as a means of enforcing internal discipline. Bruno was against it, Testa was in favour. As Testa said on the Tyrone Denittis tape, 'Let's face it . . . he's not a gangster. He's political.'

Even so it was not Testa who ordered the hit on Bruno but the family's *consigliere*, Antonio Caponigro – 'Tony Bananas'. Following meetings in New York he thought he had the backing of the Genovese family in the enterprise. He would certainly not have done it without outside support. If such support ever existed it did not last. Caponigro and his brother-in-law, Alfred Salerno, were found murdered in the Bronx, New York only four weeks after Bruno was killed.

Phil Testa was the immediate beneficiary of Caponigro's treachery for he now took over the family. Five months later he seems to have decided he had to show he was boss and what kind of family he was running. On 18 September 1980 Johnny Simone, Bruno's cousin and a capo in the family, was killed, as was Frank Sindone, another ally of Bruno's, at the end of October.

Sindone's story gives some insight into the lives of the mafiosi. As the family's top loanshark he made a fortune threatening unfortunates who could not pay their debts with torture and death. In April 1976 the FBI bugged a meeting between Sindone and two cronies at his south Philly restaurant, Frank's Cabana Steaks.

'You watch,' said Sindone. 'I'll get the fuck out . . . I want to get a nice ranch, with some grapes on it, you know. Make a little wine. Sell the wine, get a couple of horses, oranges. About 40 or 50 acres. Change my name. This way they can't call me no more.'

But, he claimed, Bruno would not set him free. 'He says, "What do you want in California? . . . . What do you want with that big house of your own?"

'I said, "I try to tell you, maybe you'll understand. I was poor all my fucking life. I didn't have nothing. My mother and father wasn't rich people. Whatever I have I had to steal. I had to make it on my own. My father used to sell fish, like a fucking Indian. So now I got a money. I'm getting old fast and I'm almost 50. I want to enjoy the fucking money. . . ."

'Chuck, see . . . I love this guy [Bruno]! This guy has been good to me! But he's got them old fucking ways. . . . Those guys, I don't know, I don't understand them. It's just get the money! Get the money! Don't spend it! What the fucking good is it? I mean, you know, that's all he says to me! He's gonna die and he is gonna leave all his money to . . . his kids. And what are his kids going to do with it? They gonna play horses. . . .'

Sindone never dared to leave Philadelphia because Bruno never released him. He suspected that 'sooner or later they are gonna knock my fucking socks off!' and his prediction came true. He was killed six months after Bruno, apparently on Phil Testa's orders.

Testa now turned his attention to Atlantic City. One of Bruno's allies was John McCullough, the Roofer's Union president in Philadelphia. He was also Bruno's labour representative in Atlantic City where Testa had his own man, Nicodemus 'Nicky' Scarfo. Testa and Scarfo realized that a lot of money could be made by threatening to bring building workers out on strike before the casinos were completed. For every day the opening of a casino was held up the owners would lose $500,000 profit as well as incurring hundreds of thousands of dollars' additional interest on the money they had borrowed to build. Testa gave McCullough orders to shut down construction on the Golden Nugget casino. The Irishman refused.[2]

It was McCullough who was killed by the florist's delivery man at his Philadelphia home a few days before Christmas 1980. This was the first murder in Philadelphia's mob war to be formally solved. In July 1982 Willard Moran admitted that he had shot McCullough. He claimed he had killed on the orders of Albert Daidone, another Atlantic City union boss, and Raymond 'Long John' Martorano, a member of the Philadelphia family. Both men were allies of Testa and Scarfo.

Sadly for the 'Chicken Man' he did not live long to enjoy the fruits of office. On 15 March 1981 at 4.15 in the morning Testa parked his car near his home at 2117 Porter Street. As he walked up to his front door two men sitting in a nearby truck detonated a bomb, blowing out the front of Testa's house. He was peppered with nails and shotgun shell. Astonishingly he survived but died a few hours later in hospital.

As usual there were many theories as to why Testa was killed. It was the Pagans motorcycle gang settling an old score. It was because Testa had ordered McCullough's murder. It was tied in with the IRA because McCullough was an Irish-American and bombing by remote control is a well-tried IRA technique in Northern Ireland. Solving mob killings is never simple.

The man who stepped into Testa's shoes was his Atlantic City acolyte, Nicky Scarfo, a man with a frightening reputation for violence. Convicted of manslaughter in 1963, he has since been suspected of several murders but has never been convicted. His rise to the top of the Philadelphia family coincided with the deaths of all his rivals. Since he took over there have been at least another dozen killings. The bodies have been found in woods and on streets but usually in the boots of cars. Only one was symbolically embellished. On 14 March 1982 Rocco Marinucci was found with multiple gunshot wounds. His mouth was stuffed with three large unexploded firecrackers. Mafia soothsayers say this shows he was murdered for detonating the bomb that killed Testa.

Outsiders also fall victim to the Philadelphia hit men. A Greek loanshark, Steve Bouras, was shot while dining at a restaurant with friends. The gunmen also killed his girlfriend. When gunmen came for another loanshark, 60-year-old Vincent 'Tippy' Panetta, they caught him in bed with his 19-year-old girlfriend. Both were hideously beaten and strangled. Maybe the killers condemned the girl as a degenerate. It is more likely that she died because she knew who they were.

Dining at Cous' Little Italy did not get any safer. In October 1981 John Calabrese, a mobster with the same name as the broccoli they used to serve, was shot to death as he left the restaurant. Cous' is under new management. It is now called Torano's, short for Martorano, the name of the mobster whose wife has taken it over. There is no guarantee that it is any safer, however. Anthony 'Long John' Martorano is a soldier in the family with a list of narcotics convictions stretching back to 1955. He controlled the city's methamphetamine market until he was jailed for ten years in

July 1982. In August 1984 he was convicted of conspiring to murder John McCullough.

What about the man who now heads this murderous mob? 'If Nicky Scarfo's intellect were rated on a scale of 1 to 10, I'd have to give him about 1.5,' says Colonel Justin Dintino of the New Jersey State police. 'On his propensity towards violence I'd rate him 9.5. I consider him an imbecile but his indiscriminate use of violence has projected him into the top spot. Maybe we're back to the 1930s. Violence always wins out over intellect.

'I would disagree that Bruno was too gentle or had gone soft. Among organized-crime leaders Bruno was a professional. He knew how to avoid pressure from law enforcement by maintaining a low profile. What Scarfo has done by the succession of homicides that have occurred during his leadership is attract enormous pressure on the family. Eventually it's going to weaken, maybe destroy the family altogether. He's already lost the independence Bruno had. He owes his position to the Genovese family of New York. They wanted a bigger slice of the pie in the Atlantic City area and they have probably got it.'

In 1981 Scarfo was convicted of illegally possessing a firearm and jailed for not staying away from his Mafia friends. While he was 1500 miles away in a Texas prison south Philadelphia's death rate slowed. When he was about to be freed the killing started again. On 6 December 1983 Robert Riccobene, half-brother to Harry 'the Hunchback', was shot dead. Since Scarfo seized power only the Riccobenes have had the courage to oppose him. Four days later gunmen tried to kill Salvatore Testa, Phil Testa's son and an ally of Scarfo's. The handsome young Testa was not hit, unlike in July 1982 when he was shot eight times but survived. This latest attempt seems to have been in retaliation for Robert Riccobene's murder.

After another four days the Testa–Riccobene war claimed its saddest victim. Enrico Riccobene, the 27-year-old nephew of Harry and Robert, ran a jeweller's in south Philadelphia. For days mafiosi had been making sure he saw them hanging around his shop. Police would park nearby to identify the loitering mobsters. They warned Enrico that he might be the next victim of his uncles' enemies. The tension was too great. On 14 December Enrico sent his sister home early. He went to the walk-in safe at the back of the shop, pulled the heavy door behind him, but a pistol to his left temple and fired. He had been literally frightened to death.

A few minutes before Enrico's suicide police stopped a Cadillac near his shop. Inside were Sal Testa and two men who in 1980 had been tried for murder with Scarfo: Lawrence Merlino and Philip Leonetti (they were all acquitted). In January 1984 Testa, Merlino and Leonetti were at the city's airport to meet a man freed from a Texas jail. Philadelphia's *Daily News* devoted its entire front page to a picture of the group as it left the terminal. The banner headline read, 'Nicky's home'. No one needed to ask, 'Nicky who?'

Maybe now, says detective Mike Chitwood, people will realize what organized crime is about. 'These nice-guy number-writers are not as nice and as gentle as everybody thought. They're vicious. They're animals. They'll kill at the drop of a dime.'

Jeanne Bruno grew up with many of the people murdered in south Philadelphia in the last few years. 'It's very sad for the people's families and their children. I remember at my father's funeral I refused to show any grief, so as not to give anybody satisfaction. . . . Maybe some people were glad that he was dead. Evidently some people were or they wouldn't have killed him. There's a saying, "God protect me from my friends." Well, you don't know who they are at a time like that.'

In south Philadelphia today that is how many people feel.

2

La Mala Vita

In 1265 Charles of Anjou, brother of the King of France, called himself King of Sicily with the blessing of the Pope. Now all he had to do to gain power was oust Sicily's crowned King Manfred, son of the German emperor and the Pope's excommunicated enemy. In 1266 Charles defeated Manfred's armies and Manfred was killed. The Frenchman soon became the undisputed ruler of the kingdom which included not just Sicily but all of Italy south of Rome.

To Sicilians he was just the latest conqueror in a line 1500 years long. Phoenicians, Greeks, Romans, Vandals, Ostrogoths, Arabs, Normans and Germans had all invaded and plundered the island. The new king slaughtered all who resisted him, seized the great estates and destroyed the power of the local barons. He taxed them so heavily that in 1282 they rebelled, supported by yet another foreigner, the Spanish King of Aragon.

For most Sicilians life went on as usual. In Palermo parishioners at the Church of the Holy Spirit observed Holy Week and then enjoyed their traditional Easter Monday festival. To their disgust they were joined by some drunken French soldiers. As people gathered for the evening service Vespers rang out all over the city. A newly married girl attracted the unwelcome attention of a Frenchman, Sergeant Pierre Drouet. He molested the bride, dragged her away and tried to rape her. She broke free but her shoe became trapped in the slate paving. She fell, hitting her head against the church wall, and died instantly.

The girl's husband ran to help her. In a fury he stabbed Drouet to death. '*Morte alla Francia*,' he cried, 'Death to France.' In the uproar which followed the local menfolk massacred every French soldier at the festival. Immediately the entire city was in revolt. The men of Palermo avenged the honour of both the girl and all Sicily by slaying the entire French garrison, to the chant 'Death to France is Italy's Cry'.

For three days and nights Palermitans continued their vendetta in what became known as the Sicilian Vespers. Thousands of French civilians and their families perished along with the military. Sicilian women married to Frenchmen were also slaughtered. Soon almost the entire island rebelled. The French were forced to surrender all of Sicily and the few who remained fled for their lives. In the long run the uprising made little difference since within six months Palermo was hailing the King of Aragon as the island's new overlord. All those Sicilians who had joined together to overthrow the French, however, founded a secret society. Its password was 'MAFIA', from the initials of their victory: '*Morte Alla Francia Italia Anela*'. Seven hundred years later that secret society still exists.

Some people say that is how both the society and its name were born, but it is unlikely that the Mafia had such a romantic or patriotic beginning. In the thirteenth century Sicilians did not speak Italian. The rebels did not shout '*Morte alla Francia*' but, in their Sicilian dialect, '*Moranu li Franchiski*'. The islanders did not even consider themselves Italians. Indeed the idea of Italy as a nation gained little support anywhere for another five hundred years.

'Mafia' is not strictly an Italian word. It is Sicilian, originating in the Palermo dialect, and probably has an Arabic root. The word has been traced back to the Ma'afir, an Arab tribe which once settled in Palermo, and to the Arabic name for the caves on the western edge of the island where for many centuries bands of rebels have sheltered from Sicily's rulers.

In 1947 Benedict Pocoroba, an American narcotics agent born in Sicily, recalled that: 'The word Mafia and its derivations as I have heard them used in my youth imply grace, beauty, perfection and excellence, the best that there is in any form of life. A Sicilian trying to describe the most beautiful horse he had ever seen would say "*un cavaddu mafiusu*" or "*un cavaddu di la mafia*". A fruit vendor would chant at the top of his voice "*ficu* (figs) *di la mafia*" or "*racina* (grapes) *di la mafia*". A handsome girl, well dressed, stylish, striking, was said to be "*mafiusa*". The word "*mafiusu*" as applied to a man meant more than mere physical attractions. It meant a man conscious of being a man and acting a man's part. One who could display true courage without any bravado, arrogance or truculence. A "*mafiusu*" did not aspire to create fear, or to rob and kill merely to satisfy his brutal instincts."

The word *mafiusu*, or *mafioso* in Italian, only came to mean a member of a sect or secret society around 1863 when Giuseppe Rizzuto, a playwright born and raised in Palermo wrote *I Mafiusi di la Vicarria di Palermu – (The Braves of Palermo Jail)*. In this melodrama Rizzuto portrayed the prisoners as men of courage who fought duels with knives. The piece played to packed houses and Rizzuto was lionized in his double role as author and actor. He expanded '*I Mafiusi*' from two to four acts and, despite the Palermitan dialogue, it was performed more than 3000 times all over Italy. Only with the play's success did the words Mafia and Mafioso/i find their way into general use and Italian dictionaries.

Whether the Mafia started as a liberation movement in medieval times or as a prison gang nearly six hundred years later, this secret society seems always to have had a criminal side. Subjected to thousands of years of foreign rule, Sicilians have learned to hate all forms of government. In a country of peasants nothing was more likely to induce lawlessness than foreign absentee landlords owning huge tracts of neglected farmland. Usually there was no such thing as justice, only the tyrannical laws of invaders arbitrarily enforced by their own secret police or by Sicilian stooges. The Bourbon kingdom of the Two Sicilies (Naples and Sicily) which lasted from 1738 to 1860 was a police state and the police were the only government employees most Sicilians ever encountered.

Bourbon rule was overthrown by a secret society of sorts: not the Mafia but Giuseppe Garibaldi's Redshirts. In 1860 Garibaldi conquered Sicily and proclaimed it part of the northern Italian kingdom of Piedmont. His ramshackle army of 1000 volunteers was augmented by gangs of bandits and brigands. Together they liberated Sicily from the foreign oppressor but the gangs Garibaldi had embraced now exploited the anarchy of the times to expand their traditional criminal activities. They stole crops and livestock. They extorted money by chopping down fruit trees, cutting off water supplies and setting fire to sulphur awaiting shipment at the mines. They robbed and kidnapped, they eliminated rival brigands and settled ancient vendettas by killing their enemies.

All these rackets had existed under Bourbon rule but in the new Italy crime became far more lucrative. Bourbon governors would crush the bandits from time to time with arbitrary executions but Italy's new liberal democracy was committed to a system of fair trials. The gangs soon realized that the new judges and juries could be bought or bullied into acquitting. It was also far easier to intimidate rulers chosen by local elections than those imposed by a despot in a far-off land. The brutality and injustice of life after unification provoked two northern investigators to observe that. 'Violence is the only prosperous industry in Sicily': the violence of revolutionaries against the rich, of the rich against the poor, and of criminal secret societies against everyone else.

At first there was no one society called the Mafia but many separate fraternities existed. In Monreale and the province of Palermo there were the Stoppaglieri and the Fratuzzi (Little Brothers). The province of Messina was blessed with the Beati Paoli. In central Sicily around Caltanissetta the Fratellanza (Brotherhood) flourished. Each society had a code with similar rules. Poor members and their families had to be helped against rich oppressors. Each member had to aid any other member who asked for help. All members had to swear absolute obedience to the chief. Any offence committed against one member was an offence against the entire association and had to be avenged at any cost. Justice was never to be sought from the state. The secrets of the society and its members' names were never to be revealed to outsiders.

The societies developed the techniques of rural gangsterism, practised by mountain brigands for centuries, into a continuing system of retributive justice and organized criminal revenue. They used terrorist methods to avenge the insults and injustices of the rick, kidnapping noblemen for ransom and vandalising vineyards, orchards, citrus and olive groves. They stole cattle and other livestock and transported them for sale to other parts of Sicily where the animals would not be recognized. To build the necessary underground network, societies co-operated with others in nearby provinces and eventually merged. Their members were now no longer only peasants but also sulphur miners, artisans, priests and even those landowners whom the societies had once regarded as their oppressors.

People who did not belong to the secret societies regarded them all as *La Mala Vita*: the evil life, the underworld. They existed not just in Sicily but throughout southern Italy. They had long since lost whatever 'Robin Hood' qualities they may ever have possessed and were now as oppressive as the tyrants they claimed to fight. In cities like Palermo they were nothing better than protection rackets, *cosche*, parasites each bleeding a specific area of urban life and killing anyone who stood in their way.

By 1886 one society had emerged sufficiently above all the others to merit investigation by Palermo's chief of police. Commissioner Giuseppe Alongi, born and raised in Sicily, wrote a book in which he described the initiation rituals of 'La Mafia', based on what Mafia informers had told him over the years. A candidate would be approached to join only after his conduct and character had been scrutinized for some years. Then two members who knew him well would bring before a council of Mafia leaders for initiation.

> He walks into the room and halts in front of a table on which is displayed the paper image of a saint. He offers his right hand to his two friends who draw enough blood from it to wet the effigy, on which he swears this oath:
>
> > I pledge my honour to be faithful to the Mafia, as the Mafia is faithful to me. As this saint and a few drops of my blood were burned, so will I give all my blood for the Mafia, when my ashes and my blood will return to their original condition.
>
> The novice then burns the effigy with the flame of a candle. From that moment he is a member indissolubly tied to the association and he will be chosen to carry out the next killing ordered by the council.

For every ten members there was a group leader, a 'capo di diecina'. This was not only for discipline but, as in any underground movement or secret society, to make sure that no one member could know the full extent of the Mafia's illegal activities.

Alongi obviously had great experience of dealing with informers. He confessed that he could not guarantee the truth of what Mafia members had told him. Yet his account disclosed secrets identical to those which astonished American senators seventy-seven years later.

Sicily was not the only part of Italy where secret societies flourished. In the sixteenth century officials of the Spanish monarchy, which ruled Naples for 350 years, transplanted their own brotherhood, the Garduna, to Naples. Its members initiated Neapolitan collaborators, who in turn created a hybrid society, the Camorra. The Camorra's laws were like those of the Sicilian brotherhoods: blood-initiation rituals, mutual aid until death and full membership only when a candidate had carried out a murder ordered by the society. Within the Camorra were small cells each led by a caporegima, who in turned belonged to the Camorra Grand Council. Despite its courtly origins the Camorra soon found most of its recruits in the jails of Naples.

By the nineteenth century camorristi controlled gambling and moneylending in Naples. They levied their own taxes from farmers and food shops, fishermen and ship owners, cab-drivers, factory owners and even the city's infant stockmarket. Legitimate businessmen found they had to have Camorra protection: Bourbon police were incapable of curbing crime or recovering stolen goods. Indeed, the police subcontracted the job of controlling crime to the Camorra's bosses, elevating their unofficial status as Naples' second government almost to a royal command.

In 1859 the Bourbon police jailed 300 Camorra members for spying on behalf of Italian unification but in June 1860 that movement liberated Naples. Camorra prisoners were set free and clubbed to death any police they could find. They then incited Neapolitans to riot and loot. The new government was forced to follow Spain's example and hire camorristi to police Naples and collect taxes. By 1863 the government realized the camorristi were pocketing the money themselves and sent in Italy's new royal army to fight them. The Camorra was crushed and reduced to a small gang of extortioners. Yet by 1911 the brotherhood was again large enough for thirty-five of its leaders, including its grand master, to be jailed for murder.

In the new united Italy the criminal secret societies incited Sicilian peasants to feel that government from Rome was just as foreign and oppressive as that from Bourbon Spain had been. Life did not get any easier. Local government remained as corrupt as ever and when central government tried to clean it up the secret societies made sure it did not succeed. Their chokehold on society stemmed in part from this corruption. If the government were honest, if justice were swift and fair, no one would ever turn to the Mafia for redress. The Mafia won the respect of ordinary folk by claiming to be the only force that could fight social evils so it had to make sure those social evils did not disappear.

In November 1877 a crime was perpetrated in Sicily which brought the Mafia worldwide notoriety. John Forester Rose, a young Edinburgh banker, was travelling to visit estates and sulphur mines owned by his family. He was kidnapped 20 miles south of Palermo by one Leone, an illiterate peasant who was allegedly Sicily's Mafia boss. Mrs Rose was sent a note demanding a huge ransom. She wrote back saying she had no such money. Leone replied that if she did not pay, her husband would lose his ears. Mrs Rose then received two letters from Sicily each containing one of Rose's ears. The next letter contained a slice of his nose. British newspapers raised half the sum demanded which satisfied Leone who then released his mutilated victim.

By this time the British government had forced Italy to hunt down Leone by threatening to land an army of its own. It took the Italian army a year and many of its soldiers' lives to capture Leone in a rocky citadel outside Palermo. Leone was tried in Rome and jailed for life but he soon escaped to Algeria where he died. His lieutenant, Giuseppe Esposito, had escaped even before his captors could get him out of Sicily. By 1878 he and six other fugitives were in New York. They scrutinized the big city's rackets and the competition. Esposito decided there were easier pickings in New Orleans. The Mafia had arrived in the New World.

3

The Land of Opportunity

Sicilians first emigrated to America in the 1840s. By the 1890s they were arriving in tens of thousands but the real rush came from 1902 to 1913 when over 100,000 entered the United States each year. In the 1880s the most popular destination was not New York but New Orleans. Its climate was like the old country's. More important, there were jobs to be had.

After the disastrous Civil War, the South with its sugar and cotton industries was booming. Railroads reached the Mississippi Delta in 1873. At last its rich soil could be farmed commercially but there was a labour shortage. Slavery had been abolished and blacks were not prepared to work in the fields for low wages, preferring to migrate north or west. Plantation owners soon realized that Sicilians were ideal replacements for blacks. They were far more productive because they were willing to work longer hours seven days a week without supervision. Men and boys arrived first, living cheaply in overcrowded shacks to save money fast and bring across the rest of their families. Soon they had saved enough money to buy land of their own to grow the vegetables and fruit they grew back home in far less productive soil.

By 1890 Sicilians made up more than 10 per cent of the population of New Orleans and were a major economic force. They turned the celebrated 'French market' into an Italian-dominated market which it remains to this day. Sicilians now controlled for the most part New Orleans' supply of fruit, vegetables, fish, meat, flowers and cheap clothing. International shipping on the Mississippi was becoming a Sicilian domain. In less than a generation the immigrants had risen from agricultural labourers to independent farmers, prominent businessmen and industrialists. They feared only two things. One was the hostility of the white establishment. The other was the Mafia which had crossed the Atlantic with them.

Giuseppe Esposito, joint-kidnapper of John Rose, set himself up in style as soon as he arrived in New Orleans in the spring of 1879. He took the name Vincenzo Rebello and was soon well known as the boss of the city's infant Mafia. He married a Sicilian girl and they had a son despite the fact that he already had a wife and five children in Sicily. Someone in the Sicilian community in New Orleans betrayed him to the Italian authorities who were still diplomatically obliged to put him on trial because of the Rose affair. The city's police chief handed the task of recapturing him to David Hennessey, a rising young detective. The intrepid Hennessey arrested Esposito on 5 July 1881 in broad daylight without a struggle. He shipped him off to New York for extradition. The story goes that Joseph Macheca, a steamship magnate and New Orleans' leading Sicilian businessman, now offered Hennessey $50,000 to say at the extradition hearings that the arrested 'Rebello' was not Esposito after all. The policeman refused. Esposito was extradited to Rome where he was convicted of six murders and died in jail.

Hennessey became a national hero. The son of a New Orleans policeman murdered by robbers in 1867, he was flash and ambitious. He wanted to become chief of police but found that Joseph Macheca was gaining his revenge. Macheca allegedly ensured that William Devereaux was appointed chief over Hennessey. The two policemen hated each other and on 13 October 1881 they quarrelled. In the gunfight that ensued Mike Hennessey – David's cousin and also a policeman – was wounded and David shot Devereaux dead. The cousins were tried for murder and although they were acquitted they lost their jobs. David Hennessey became a private detective and allied himself with the city's reform movement. Its leader, Joseph Shakspeare, was elected mayor in 1888. He made Hennessey chief of police. The new chief declared his main task was to destroy the Mafia. Within a year he announced that he had dossiers on ninety-four murders committed in the city since 1868 and made public his intention to crush one man above all, Joseph Macheca.

At 11.15 p.m. on Wednesday, 15 October 1890 Hennessey left his office with his friend Bill O'Connor, the captain of a private police force almost as big as Hennessey's. After a meal at an oyster bar they parted at Girod Street where Hennessey lived alone with his mother. Hennessey was only a few doors from his home when five men appeared firing shotguns, hitting him six times. He drew his revolver and fired back. Conflicting accounts state that the gunmen either continued to fire, forcing Hennessey back down the street, or that Hennessey's shots made his assailants flee in all directions. Hennessey shouted out for O'Connor who had heard the shooting and ran to his aid with some patrolmen.

'Who gave it to you, Dave?'

'Put your ear down here,' Hennessey whispered. 'The Dagoes.'

Hennessey was lifted into a wagon and taken to Charity Hospital. Within minutes New Orleans was in uproar. Crowds gathered at the scene as police searched the locality. Exploiting O'Connor's story that Hennessey blamed the 'Dagoes' the mayor ordered police to 'Scour the whole neighbourhood. Arrest every Italian you run across.' One hundred Italians were promptly arrested and locked up in the parish prison. Strangely, no one bothered to ask Hennessey if he could name his attackers even though he was conscious and talking for most of the night. At 9 a.m. the next morning he died. Even before the shooting Hennessey was the most famous policeman in America. His death, at only 32, made him a national martyr and nearly caused a war with Italy.

Some detectives thought that the names of Hennessey's killers would be in his dossier of the ninety-four Mafia murders allegedly committed in New Orleans since 1868. He had known that the city's Mafia was split into two factions. The more powerful faction was led by Charles Matranga and backed by Hennessey's enemy, Joseph Macheca. The weaker faction was led by an old-timer, Joe Provenzano. Matranga's strength lay in the backing not of the Mafia itself but of the Stoppaglieri, the brotherhood which ran crime in his home town of Monreale in Sicily. More than 300 Stoppaglieri had emigrated to New Orleans when the Mafia's increasing strength in Palermo threatened to overwhelm them. In New Orleans they outnumbered Provenzano's small Mafia crew by six to one.

Hennessey knew that one of Matranga's strengths was his ability to find jobs for immigrants, especially those who had come in illegally. He was a '*padrone*'. He could get them street pedlars' permits, find them somewhere to live and sort out any problems with American authorities. Matranga wanted sole patronage over jobs in the New Orleans docks and fought with Provenzano over who was to hire labour to work the steamships on the Mississippi waterfront. In 1889 the factions began killing each other.

First Joe Provenzano sent a man to negotiate peace with the Matrangas. They split his head open with an axe. Provenzano then murdered one of Matranga's lieutenants. Hennessey called both men together and told them to settle their differences. They agreed but there was to be no peace. The Provenzanos, backed by Hennessey, got their blow in first. Before dawn on 6 April 1890 they ambushed a wagonload of Matranga's men on their way to work in the docks. No one died and only two were wounded. Hennessey was obliged to arrest the Provenzanos but he was only going through the motions. He knew Italian crooks were sworn never to seek justice in the courts. So he was astonished when the Matrangas named the Provenzanos as their attackers.

Hennessey was in trouble. Joe Provenzano was a personal friend. They socialized at an exclusive club which the Italian was able to join only because Hennessey sponsored him. When the Provenzanos went on trial twenty of Hennessey's men perjured themselves by swearing the defendants were boozing in another part of town when the attack happened. The jury did not believe them and convicted. Pressure was brought to bear on the judge overnight and the next day he rejected the verdict on the grounds that the Provenzanos had not been positively identified. A new trial was ordered.

Hennessey now stated publicly that he would discredit the Matrangas by revealing their criminal activities. Joseph Macheca responded by telling the newspapers: 'Hennessey is investigating the Provenzano case the wrong way and he will pay for it.' His murder took place five days before the Provenzanos were due to be re-tried.

Nineteen Sicilians were charged with the killing, ten for murder. Among the other nine charged with conspiring to kill Hennessey were Matranga and Macheca. Mayor Shakspeare publicly blamed 'stiletto societies' (*stilo* means dagger in Italian) for Hennessey's death. He was 'the victim of Sicilian vengeance . . . because he was seeking to break up the fierce vendettas that have so often stained our streets with blood'.

The Provenzanos had an incontrovertible alibi: they were still in prison awaiting trial. Three days later in an interview with a reporter Joe Provenzano blamed Matranga for the murder, on the grounds that Hennessey would have been a witness for the Provenzanos. He then volunteered that Matranga was head of the Stoppaglieri. Asked about the Mafia he said, 'They've got the Mafia society everywhere, in San Francisco, St Louis, Chicago, New York and here.' Accused of being boss of the Mafia he denied even being a member. 'We had a labourers' association when we had the stevedore business and never let any greenhorns in it. All our men were Italians who were raised here. They were Americans.' Provenzano thus saved himself and dished his enemies, a wise move because Hennessey's murder was causing riots against Italians in every American city where they lived in large numbers. He was soon cleared and released.

His enemies were locked in the same jail. So was Frank Dimaio, a private detective pretending to be a Sicilian gangster, who insinuated himself into their confidence. He subsequently claimed that one of the defendants, Joe Polizzi, had told him Matranga and Macheca had ordered Hennessey's murder.

There were two murder trials. The first, on the main conspiracy charges, started on 16 February 1891. During the trial stories appeared in the newspapers that the Mafia had raised $75,000 for the defence and had fixed the jury. On 13 March the jury reported that it could not come to a verdict on three defendants, and cleared the other six who included Macheca. Other charges remained so all the defendants were returned to prison.

New Orleans erupted. Within hours of the verdict sixty-one men had signed a notice for publication in the morning newspapers. It called on 'all good citizens' to attend a mass meeting that morning to 'remedy the failure of justice in the Hennessey case. Come prepared for action.' A crowd of 8000 people turned out. They were addressed by William Parkerson, a young lawyer who was Mayor Shakspeare's campaign manager. He asked what protection there would be if Hennessey's Mafia assassins were turned loose on the community. 'The time has come for the people of New Orleans to say whether they are going to stand for these outrages by organized bands of assassins. Are you going to let it continue? Are there men enough here to set aside the verdict of that infamous jury, every one of whom is a perjurer and a scoundrel? Men and citizens of New Orleans, follow me. I will be your leader!'

Armed with an assortment of clubs, rifles and shotguns the citizens promptly headed for the prison. Locked out, they smashed down a side door and found Macheca and two others crouched behind a pillar. They were shot at point-blank range and killed. Six others huddled against a wall in the yard. They begged for their lives but their pleas went unheeded. Thousands of people outside had been deprived of the spectacle. They wanted to make their own contribution so two men were dragged out for a public execution that was both messy and brutal. Parkerson emerged from the prison, carried shoulder high by the triumphant crowd. The lynch-mob had killed eleven Italians. Three of them had been cleared, the jury had not reached a verdict on three others and the remaining five had not even been tried. Eight survived, including Charles Matranga who had hidden under the floorboards in the women's part of the prison. The events were celebrated in the *States* newspaper that afternoon:

> Citizens of New Orleans! You have, in one righteous upheaval, in one fateful gust of mighty wrath, vindicated your laws, heretofore desecrated and trampled underfoot by oath-bound aliens who had thought to substitute Murder for Justice and the suborner's gold for the Freeman's honest verdict. Your vengeance is consecrated in the forfeited blood of the assassins!

Newspapers across America applauded the lynching or condoned it as a social obligation. Editorials condemning the Mafia assumed both that the dead belonged to it and that they were guilty of Hennessey's murder. Even the London *Times* approved. The Italian government was not so enthusiastic and protested. America now fell victim to a war scare. Italy had more than 2 million soldiers. The USA had only 128,000. Italy had a large modern navy. America had only three tiny warships. Fortunately for America the Italian government's coffers were empty and it could not afford a war. It later accepted a sum of $25,000 to be distributed among the victims' families. The King of Italy expressed his profound thanks.

In New Orleans it became clear that the lynching had not been a spontaneous outburst of public wrath but the work of an execution squad. A grand jury was sworn in to investigate the incident but in its report it indicted no one and exonerated the unknown executioners. The lynching was dismissed in a few lines. Since so many people took part, it said, it was impossible to pinpoint guilt. The grand jury was much more concerned to convict the lynch-mob's victims and digressed completely to give a study of the Mafia, claiming hundreds of mafiosi were living in New Orleans.

Mayor Shakspeare had not finished with the 'Dagoes'. He backed the city's 'white' establishment by banning all Italians from running businesses or labour unions on the waterfront. He singled out Joe Provenzano, telling him: 'You have not learned the lesson taught your race by the people of New Orleans. I want you to go home and tell your friends that if you make any more trouble, the police and the mayor of this city will not consider themselves responsible for the lives of you and yours.'

His conduct showed breathtaking hypocrisy. In the wide-open city over which he presided the illegal trades of prostitution and gambling were rampant. Bordellos and casinos were shut down only if they failed to pay off the politicians or the police. In 1881 Shakspeare himself set up an illegal system of licensing some casinos while forcing others to close, establishing a segregated gambling quarter where some sixteen elite casinos operated without police interference. In return they paid him a total of $30,000 a year, most of which went to his own charity: the Shakspeare Almshouse. After a few years the system collapsed. When the Italians were lynched, scores of casinos were flourishing in the heart of the city.

In the 1890s New Orleans, a city of 200,000, boasted 2000 prostitutes and 200 brothels. Shakspeare had a personal connection with the city's favourite whore, Abbie Reed. He sold his home to this lubricious blonde who turned it into a high-class bordello. The brothels corruptly escaped the city's property taxes. By 1898 vice was so pervasive that a segregated prostitution district was established. Storyville, as it became known, was soon the most famous and best-patronized red-light district in America.

Towering over every other racket was the Louisiana Lottery Company which had ruled politics in New Orleans and the entire state of Louisiana since the Civil War. In 1868 the state's corruptible carpetbagger legislature granted the lottery a monopoly charter exempting it from all state laws and taxation. In return the lottery agreed to give $40,000 a year to the New Orleans Charity Hospital. This was hardly a good deal for the state since the lottery was soon taking $1 million a year out of the pockets of Louisiana's citizens. The deal was secured by annual bribes to the legislature of at least as much money again as went to the hospital for twenty-five years.

The lottery draw may have been straight but it was also a fraud in that the odds against winning were more than 75,000 to 1. With this kind of margin the lottery's owners cleared at least £13 million a year and were so rich they were able to buy off all opposition. The lottery was the strongest economic force in New Orleans, controlling banks, sugar refineries, cotton presses and the waterworks company. In 1890 Mayor Shakspeare was grateful for a gift of $50,000 from the lottery to help prevent a flood from engulfing the low-lying city. Such politically motivated charity did not prevent the lottery from becoming America's longest-running scandal. Exempt from the law of Louisiana it still abused United States law by illegally sending its tickets all over America. In 1890 President Harrison charged that it 'debauched and defrauded' the people of all states. It was not suppressed until 1893 when the Supreme Court upheld the postal law.

Shakspeare's New Orleans was thus dominated by organized crime: the casinos, the whorehouses and the lottery. It is difficult to see how a few Sicilian crooks could have made the place any more evil that it already was. But the lynching had its desired effect. Those who survived kept their heads down. Joe Provenzano and Charles Matranga lived on, Matranga till 1943 when he died a rich man. For a decade lynching Italians became a national pastime, second only to lynching blacks. In the 1890s six more were lynched in Louisiana and the habit spread to five other states. It became open season for racial slurs on Italians. Three weeks after the massacre the *Illustrated American* published photographs and sketches of Italians in New Orleans with lurid captions. 'Travel through the Italian Quarter of any big city, and you may find yourself in the midst of a Camorra or Mafia.' A knife-grinder at work was said to be 'sharpening the stiletto of a New Orleans assassin.' The Italians' resentment at such treatment was justified, yet in the decades following the New Orleans massacre evidence piled up that many southern Italians, and Sicilians in particular, belonged to violent criminal societies. For the next thirty years the group that caught the American imagination was not the Mafia or the Camorra but La Mano Nera – the 'Black Hand'.

Nothing was more frightening for an Italian immigrant than to receive an anonymous letter from the Black Hand:

> Most Gentle Mr Silvani,
>
> Hoping that the present will not impress you too much, you will be so good as to send me $2000 if your life is dear to you. So I beg you warmly to put them on the door within four days. But if not I swear this week's time not even the dust of your family will exist. With regards, believe me to be your friend.

The letter would be embellished with bloodcurdling illustrations such as a skull and crossbones or a dagger and always a black hand, either drawn or in the form of an inky palm and fingerprint. The language would usually be a mockingly deferential form of Sicilian, but sometimes the message was more bluntly expressed:

> You got some cash. I need $1000. You place the $100 bills in an envelope and place it underneath a board in the north-east corner of 69th Street and Euclid Avenue at eleven o'clock tonight. If you place the money there you will live. If you don't, you die. If you report this to the police, I'll kill you when I get out. They may save you the money but they won't save your life.

Both those letters were sent to people in Chicago but Black Hand threats were common to all America's Little Italys. The extortioners preferred rich targets but would shake down any immigrant cowed by the traditions of the Old World or too scared to trust the police in the New. Author Frederick Sondern spoke to an old Sicilian vegetable grower who had come to America at the turn of the century. His father was sent a Black Hand letter.

'Then my father would pay. He would say, "Giuseppe, you see it is the same as at home. The Mafia is always with us." Then I would plead with him to go to the police. After all we were in America. "No, Mother of God, no," he would shout. "The police here cannot do even as much as the police at home. They do not know the Mafia. We get put out of business or killed and no one will ever know why. They do not understand the Mafia and they never will".'[1]

From 1910 to 1912 Chicago's Black Handers were credited with nearly 100 murders. The *Daily News* estimated that for every Italian living in the 'Spaghetti Zone' who reported a Black Hand threat ten more did not. In the first three months of 1913 fifty-five bombs were detonated against people who would not pay. Using the 10 to 1 yardstick, the *News* said some 550 victims must have got the message in both senses and given in. Black Handers were picking up at least $500,000 a year in Chicago. Law-abiding Italians set up a 'White Hand' organization in 1907 to combat the Black Hand but six years later they decided the task was hopeless and disbanded.

Occasionally police successfully followed up a complaint and a Black Hander went on trial. Most victims and witnesses, however, suffered a strange amnesia in the witness box. As cronies of the accused showed up to wave red handkerchieves, make throat-cutting gestures or point trigger fingers at their temples they would fall silent or claim mistaken identity. The prosecution's case would collapse and the extortioner go free. In such a climate most victims naturally decided there wasn't much of a future in resisting the Black Hand.

The Black Hand was not a single organization. The threats usually came from freelance hoodlums who found it easier to shelter behind the symbols of a feared if mythical society than to invent a new one. Even members of the Mafia and Camorra extorted in the name of the Mano Nera. For quick payoffs no emblem was more effective.

One New York cop declared a lone war on the Black Hand, the Mafia and *La Mala Vita* in general. Lieutenant Joseph Petrosino was born in 1860 in Calabria, southern Italy, a province which had its own criminal societies. He joined the police at a time when dozens of men were being killed in New York in a Mafia–Camorra war and became famous by crushing gangs of Sicilian and Neapolitan thugs single-handed. He was made head of a new detective team known as the Italian Squad, formed to fight what would later be called organized crime. He specialized in identifying Italian felons as soon as they landed and shipping them back to Italy. In 1908 Raffaele Palizzolo – a member of Italy's parliament until a murder conviction forced his resignation – sailed into New York to a welcome from hundreds of cheering supporters. He was about to become the leader of the Mafia in America. Petrosino promptly moved to deport him. Palizzolo chose to sail home again before he suffered that indignity.

In the early 1900s the term Black Hand was used by police and press to describe not only freelance extortioners but also Mafia racketeers. Petrosino himself said that, 'The Black Hand, as a large organization, does not exist.' Ignazio Saietta, known as 'Lupo the Wolf', was one of Petrosino's prime targets. He was sometimes named as boss of the Black Hand and sometimes as Mafia boss of New York's Little Italy. Either way Petrosino showed him no respect. In 1908 he heard that Saietta was bragging that he was going to kill him. The detective was enraged. He burst into the Wolf's lair, knocked him down and trampled all over him. If Lupo was ever a top mafioso he lost his place in 1910 when he was jailed for thirty years for fake currency dealing. Wags said he should have stuck to what he was good at: killing people.

In another act of bravura Petrosino seized three Black Handers, roped them together, dragged them down four flights of stairs and across two blocks of Mulberry Street to a police station, all the time hurling abuse at the cowardly denizens of Little Italy who were too scared to accept his invitation to spit on their oppressors. One of them turned out to be Enrico Alfano, the grand master of the Camorra of Naples whom Petrosino soon deported to face murder charges back home.

In 1909 New York police commissioner, Theodore Bingham, gave Petrosino his most important assignment: to travel to Italy and establish full liaison with police there 'so that the Camorra and Mafia may be watched on both sides of the ocean'. His voyage was meant to be a secret but before he had even arrived in Rome the *New York Herald* published an editorial revealing that Bingham had set up a secret service squad to crush the Black Hand. 'As a first step Lieut. Petrosino has gone to Italy and Sicily where he will procure important information about Italian criminals who have come to this country.' The *Herald* explained he was to collect the criminal records of many New York-based hoods who could be deported only on firm evidence. For those mafiosi who could not read English the same report appeared in New York's Italian newspapers.

By the time he arrived in Palermo every mafioso in Sicily must have known he was coming. Hundreds knew him by sight for he had got them deported from the USA. With his stocky, muscular physique he was easily recognized. Anyone who could read knew of Petrosino as Italy's Sherlock Holmes. His exploits had been immortalized in bestselling paperbacks. In Palermo he registered at his hotel under a false name. He was exhausted by travel and influenza. His judgement was failing and he naively revealed the itinerary of his planned trip through the region's most notorious Mafia towns to the local police.

On 12 March he returned to Palermo to meet an informer in the Piazza Marina. He was probably set up for when he arrived in the square that evening the usual crowds and police patrols were absent. He had been standing for a while at the foot of a statue of Garibaldi when two men shot him in the back and head. A third man shot him in the face. Petrosino died instantly.

One of his killers is alleged to have been Don Vito Cascio Ferro who was to become the Sicilian Mafia's boss of bosses. The others were New Orleans-based mafiosi who had left America after Petrosino but reached Palermo well ahead of him. Many top hoods later claimed credit for the murder, including Lupo the Mafia boss and Alfano the Camorra grand master. No detective could ever have had so distinguished an assortment of would-be assassins yet no one was ever tried for his murder.

Back in New York Petrosino was given a hero's funeral with a mile-long procession. A memorial fund raised $10,000 for his widow and infant son. Mrs Petrosino was also granted $1000 a year pension. His assassins had definitely murdered the right man. With Petrosino dead American law enforcement lost sight of the Mafia for almost fifty years.

4

What is this Thing Called Thing?

When the Mafia turned up once again in American police files nobody gave it a name. On 6 December 1928 at the Statler Hotel in Cleveland police arrested twenty-one men from six states. Most of them were armed and they were each fined $50. All were Sicilians. No Cleveland policeman seems to have known of the existence of a crime confederation, nor did the police forces of the cities from which most of the mobsters came (Cleveland, Chicago, New York and St Louis) pool their knowledge. Outside the New York Police no one gathered or analyzed 'criminal intelligence'. America had to wait almost thirty years before a dedicated state trooper proved that there was a Mafia and that it operated from coast to coast.

For thirteen years Sergeant Edgar Croswell of the New York State Police had stalked Joseph Barbara, a businessmen much respected in Endicott, a town 150 miles north-west of New York City. Barbara owned a Canada Dry bottling plant but Croswell realized that this was no ordinary soft drinks' salesman when he learned Barbara had taken over the plant by intimidating the previous owner. He also found out that Barbara had twice been cleared of attempted murder in nearby Pennsylvania. In one case a dying man claimed Barbara had shot him. Much to his surprise the victim recovered. He recanted his testimony, leaving Barbara in the clear.

On 13 November 1957 Sergeant Croswell and another trooper were investigating a dud cheque at a local motel when they spotted Jo Barbara Jun., the old gangster's son, making reservations for a Canada Dry convention. The troopers thought this odd so they visited the Barbara home just outside the village of Apalachin. There they checked the number plates on visitors' cars and found out that the cars belonged not to soft drinks salesmen but to hoodlums.

Early next day Croswell took several detectives back to the house where they found many more limousines. They were taking down licence numbers when suddenly men swarmed out of the house and scattered in all directions, some into cars and others into the woods. There was only one road out so Croswell's men set up a roadblock. They identified the passengers in the first car and let it through but then decided to take everyone else to the police station and check them out with their home-town police.

Croswell was tickled by the high fashion in which the men had dressed for their trip to the country: tailored suits, grey fedoras and pointed embroidered shoes. Most of them had Italian accents. Several could speak no English. They said they had come to see their old friend Joe Barbara because he was sick. Croswell could not prove they were lying. Merely by meeting together they had not broken the law. They were not even carrying guns so they all had to be released.

At first Croswell had no real idea who these people were or why they were all at Barbara's. He soon realized that he had broken up a meeting of the warlords of organized crime, the leaders of the Mafia in America. Most of their names meant little to him and nothing at all to most detectives, but they were some of the most powerful and violent criminals in the nation. As Croswell later found out the men were '14-carat hoodlums. Strictly lived by breaking the law, preying on honest people, taking over businesses, killing each other, killing other people that got in their way.'

Top of the list was Vito Genovese, the most powerful mafioso in New York. Born in Naples in 1897, he had fled to Italy from America in 1937 to avoid a murder charge. He spent most of the Second World War close to Mussolini but when the Allies reached Naples in 1943 he turned up in the service of the Allied military governor of Italy. Genovese worked as his most trusted interpreter at the same time as he controlled the huge black market. He developed a remarkably effective way of keeping the rackets to himself by exposing rival thieves to his employers, from whom he himself was stealing. Despite his position he was arrested for black-market activities and taken back to New York in 1945 to face the murder charge he had fled eight years earlier.[1]

Suddenly the main witness was murdered. Genovese was free again in New York just in time to take over from his *compare*, Lucky Luciano. Born in Sicily, Luciano had built up the most powerful crime syndicate in America. His career was interrupted when he spent ten years in jail for controlling prostitution and was deported to Italy in 1946 (see Chapter 14). His organization was steadily taken over by Genovese and in 1957 the Mafia chieftains met at Apalachin partly to anoint him *Il Capo di Tutti Capi*, 'boss of bosses'. It was Genovese who overturned the Mafia's formal ban on drug-trafficking. Not that anyone had ever observed it – least of all Genovese.

Also at Apalachin were Joe Profaci and his brother-in-law, Joe Magliocco. Born within nine months of each other in Villabate, Sicily they had come to America in the 1920s. In 1957 they claimed to be legitimate businessmen in olive oil, liquor and the garment industry. In reality they led another powerful Mafia faction.

Other Sicilians visiting Barbara were 'labour consultant' Carlo Gambino and his brother-in-law, Paul Castellano, probably the most powerful man in New York's wholesale meat business. Only three weeks earlier Gambino had taken over the criminal organization of Albert Anastasia, shot to death in a barber's chair in New York's Park Sheraton Hotel. On the Apalachin agenda was the belated ratification of old Albert's murder.

Also at Apalachin were two more Sicilian-born New York bosses, Joe Bonanno of Brooklyn and Vinnie Rao of Italian East Harlem. New York City dominated the Apalachin summit but there were top mafiosi from upstate New York, from Philadelphia and north-east Pennsylvania, from Boston, Cleveland, Kansas City, from New Jersey, Illinois, Texas, Colorado, California and even Havana.

Sixty-two Italian-American mobsters are known to have gathered at Apalachin. Forty more may have got away or had not arrived by the time Croswell struck. It was the largest mob gathering ever discovered by American police and it would be the last meeting of its size. Never again would the Mafia risk so humiliating a capture. Twenty men were convicted of obstructing justice. They were cleared on appeal but their real conviction was by the media. After more than sixty years' argument over whether the Mafia really existed in America the Mafia itself had supplied the proof.

Yet even Apalachin failed to reveal the structure of the Mafia. 'At the time,' says Ed Croswell today, 'there was no such thing as organized-crime charts or rosters of families or even family heads. They were just known as hoodlums in their own communities. The state of intelligence was very unsophisticated. You didn't have computer checks where you can get information in three minutes. Then it would take you days – you would probably never get it – it would get lost in the files or the mail. Each individual policeman who was interested in organized crime was a voice in the wilderness and that worked both ways: there was nobody to listen and he didn't know what he was talking about.'

After Apalachin many 'experts' emerged, most of whom certainly did not know what they were talking about. The most coherent interpretation came from the Federal Bureau of Narcotics. Its main witness at New York State's subsequent inquiry was John Cusack. Looking back twenty-five years he says that Apalachin was 'a bombshell' in that it proved conclusively that some form of organization did exist. Yet, 'We didn't know with precision the existence of the five families of New York. We knew there were affiliations but we had conflicting information as to who was who in the organization. We talked to one informant and he would describe Tommy 'Three Fingers' Brown [Tommy Lucchese] as the head of the Mafia in New York. Someone else would tell us it was Frank Costello, another informant would absolutely swear it was Joe Bonanno or Joe Profaci or Vincent Mangano. We later learned that each informer was telling us that their man was the head of a family, which to them meant being head of the Mafia.'

The first mafioso to turn public informer and betray the true structure of the Mafia in America was Joseph Valachi, a thirty-year veteran of organized crime. Serving twenty years for narcotics in Atlanta Penitentiary, he became convinced that his Mafia boss, Vito Genovese, had given him the kiss of death. Genovese, who by this time was also in Atlanta for a narcotics offence, ordered another inmate to kill him. Valachi mistook another prisoner for his would-be assassin and clubbed him to death. When he realized he had killed the wrong man he became so consumed with fear and remorse that he turned government witness and informed on the Mafia. Ironically it was only because Genovese wrongly believed

Valachi already to be an informer that he decided to have him killed. That at least was Valachi's story.

In September 1963 Valachi began to testify before the US Senate Permanent Sub-committee On Investigations. His account of the structure and history of an organization which he called not the Mafia but 'La Cosa Nostra' – 'Our Thing' or 'Our Family' – was breathtaking.

Valachi revealed that the Mafia was not a loose confederation of mobsters working under a few big shots but a structured army of 'families', each ruling organized crime in their respective cities. Only one city had more than one crime family: New York which had five. Valachi identified these families by the names of their leaders at the time: Vito Genovese, Carlo Gambino, Tommy Lucchese, Joe Magliocco and Joe Bonanno. Valachi revealed that the head of each La Cosa Nostra family is called the 'boss'. Under him is the 'under-boss'. Equal with the under-boss is the '*consigliere*', a counsellor or adviser to the boss who is also the family's representative at large. Beneath the under-boss are 'caporegimes' – captains or lieutenants who each command a crew of 'soldiers'. Although soldiers hold the lowest rank in the family, they are often major criminals in their own right and may be worth millions of dollars.

At the top of this pyramid is the 'National Commission'. In Valachi's day all the most powerful bosses in the country were on the Commission but he was not sure who they were. He assumed all the New York bosses were members. Attorney-General Robert Kennedy told the senators that the 'national crime syndicate' was headed by a commission of nine to twelve members. It made policy decisions, settled disputes and allocated territories and businesses between the families. Later the FBI stated there were twenty-five to twenty-seven crime families across America, each structured in the way Valachi had disclosed. Nationwide there were between 2000 and 5000 'made men' who had ten times as many professional criminal associates.

Valachi explained that he had joined La Cosa Nostra in 1930 in a ritual identical to that written down by Palermo Police Commissioner Alongi in 1886. Thirty-five high-ranking members had assembled in a large room in upstate New York into which the novitiates were summoned one by one. 'When I came in they were at the edge of a long table and there was a gun and a knife on the table. They sat me down at the edge of the table with Maranzano [the boss] doing the talking. I repeated some words they told me, but I couldn't explain what he meant. I could repeat the words but they were in Italian, Sicilian. Maranzano went on to explain that they lived by the gun and by the knife and you die by the gun and by the knife.

'Then he gave me a piece of paper and I was to burn it . . . the piece of paper is burning, and it is lighted and in your hand, you say – again they give you words in Italian but I knew what it meant – "This is the way I burn if I expose this organization." '

Then a godfather to be responsible for Valachi was chosen at random. It was Joe Bonanno who would still be boss of one of New York's families when Valachi testified thirty-three years later. 'The godfather pricks your finger with a needle and he makes a little blood come out. That is the expression, the blood relationship. It is supposed to be like brothers. Then everybody gets up and shakes hands and they say a few more words together, also in Italian. I never bothered finding out what it meant. I had an idea: we are all tied up – we are all together.'

Valachi also revealed the code with which one member introduces another. If someone is in La Cosa Nostra he is introduced as 'a friend of ours'. If not, he is introduced as a 'a friend of mine'. To prevent conflict over each other's women no member may violate the wife, sisters or daughters of another member.

Valachi then spoke of the fate that awaited him: 'Can I say something? What I am telling you, what I am exposing to you and to the press and everybody. This is my doom. This is the promise I am breaking. Even if I talked I should never talk about this.'

The Genovese family to which he had belonged had 450 to 500 members. Gambino's family was about the same size. Valachi did not know everyone in his family. As a soldier he belonged to a 'regime' of only thirty members. In Sicily the regime had evolved to improve secrecy and limit damage if a member turned informer. Yet at the Senate hearings Valachi named hundreds of members. He identified all but ten of 141 Genovese members displayed on a huge chart. He also identified members of all the other New York families, claiming to know 289 out of 338 mafiosi on all five family charts. Single-handed he had blown La Cosa Nostra wide open. Twenty years on John Cusack said of his testimony: 'Valachi for the first time, in a very organized way, answered all our questions. . . . He gave us a perfect understanding of the Mafia organization in America.'

Joe had known a lot about the Mafia from the moment he joined. In 1930 the New York crime families were fighting a civil war. They needed new members as gunmen. Valachi said that between forty and sixty men had been killed in fourteen months although the Senate investigators could confirm only a few of these. All these cases were still 'active', an oddly dynamic word to describe murders unsolved for thirty years. Valachi gave precise accounts of the murders in which he had been directly involved. What he said was confirmed by what was still on file in New York police files. Either he was telling the truth or he had been brilliantly coached.

According to Valachi the war was fought over who should control the New York underworld. In 1930 the principal warriors were two Sicilians: Joe 'the Boss' Masseria from Trapani and Salvatore Maranzano from Castellamare del Golfo. Joe Masseria was the better established, having come to America many years earlier. An unprepossessing figure of a man, he was now New York's biggest bootlegger and controlled many leading non-Italian racketeers. In contrast, Maranzano had arrived in America in the 1920s and was already over 50. In his home town he was a Mafia boss. When he came to America he assumed the leadership of all the mafiosi from Castellamare who were already there or who arrived soon after. They included Joe Profaci, Joe Bonanno and Carlo Gambino. Masseria felt threatened by this rapidly growing clan and condemned all Castellamarese to death.

On 26 February 1930 Masseria struck his first blow by ordering the murder of Tom Reina, a boss allied to Maranzano. Tom Gagliano now took over Reina's family, inducting Valachi with Maranzano's participation. Gagliano was not from Castellamare but he shared Castellamarese hatred of Masseria.

They now struck back by killing several of Masseria's top men. He lost face and his supporters began to desert. He sued for peace and offered to work as a soldier if Maranzano would spare him.

Maranzano refused. Masseria thought he could still survive with the help of some of his able 'Young Turks', notably Vito Genovese and Lucky Luciano. On 15 April 1931 he went to a restaurant in Coney Island to meet Luciano, Genovese and Ciro Terranova, the 'Artichoke King'. But Masseria's underlings had set him up. As he sat down he was shot six times in the back and the head. His murder was never solved.

Maranzano blossomed like the Roman emperors he so admired. He summoned a meeting to announce his peace terms. Valachi was there. 'It was around Washington Avenue in the Bronx. There were about 400 to 500 people in this big hall. Maranzano was standing on the platform when he got up to speak. He explained about Masseria and his groups killing people without just cause.

' "Now it is going to be different," he said. "First, we are going to have the boss of all bosses, which is myself. Then we have the boss and then we have an under-boss under the boss. Then we have the caporegima." He explained all the rules.'

Maranzano explained that the soldiers would now be divided between Gagliano and himself. Valachi chose to go with Maranzano for whom he had already carried out murders. Maranzano then held a banquet lasting five nights at which gangsters gave $115,000 in tribute to the self-styled boss of bosses. The money was not all for Maranzano. His soldiers were each meant to get a share. Despite his loyalty, Valachi lamented, 'I never got a nickel out of that, senator.'

Valachi worked for Maranzano from his office on Park Avenue. Aggrieved though he was about the money, he still trusted his boss to look after him. One day he found Luciano and Genovese with Maranzano. Not long after the boss told him, 'We have to go to the mattress again.' Valachi explained to the senators. 'The "mattress" means we have to go back to war. He told me he can't get along with Charlie and Vito. He gave me a list. "We have to get rid of these people." On the list: Al Capone, Frank Costello, Charley Lucky, Vito Genovese, Vincent Mangano, Joe Adonis, Dutch Schultz. These are all important names at the time.'

The next day, 10 September 1932, Maranzano was to meet Luciano and Genovese again at his office. Valachi told him not to risk his life but Maranzano ignored his advice. The meeting was fixed for two o'clock. At 1.45 p.m. Valachi called him and was told all was well, so he took the day off and drove to Brooklyn with a friend to see two girls. In the early hours he returned to Manhattan and went home to Italian Harlem. Then he happened to open the newspaper only to see the headline, 'Park Avenue Murder'. Maranzano had been killed in his office that afternoon.

Valachi later discovered how Maranzano had died. Four Jews posing as policemen had gone to the office. A crowd of people were waiting there, each hoping to see Maranzano. The 'cops' flashed their badges. Two stayed with the crowd. The other two went with Maranzano into the other room. Suddenly he realized they had come to kill him. He went for his pistol but they shot him first and then stabbed him four times in the abdomen. According to Valachi one of the killers was 'Red' Levine who later told him what had happened. The Jews were acting under orders from Meyer Lansky, an ally of Luciano's in bootlegging and gambling rackets. Senator McClellan asked if Lansky was on the charts displayed at the hearings. No, said Valachi, he was not part of La Cosa Nostra. No senator gave Valachi the chance to talk about Lansky's organization.

Genovese told Valachi that the killers only 'made it by minutes'. Maranzano had lined up his own killer, Vincent 'Mad Dog' Coll, to slay Luciano and Genovese but they never came. As Maranzano's murderers left the building they met Coll coming in. As fellow-professionals they told him, 'Beat it, the cops are on the way.'

In the days that followed Valachi was asked first by his old boss, Tom Gagliano, and then by Vito Genovese to work for them. He chose to go with Genovese and stayed with him for thirty years. Had he chosen Gagliano and Lucchese, he would probably have been happier, risen higher and made more money.

Maranzano founded La Cosa Nostra in his Bronx speech. In six months Lucky Luciano had taken it over. As the apparent mastermind behind the murders of both Masseria and Maranzano, he faced few challengers. At only 33 years of age he had 'Americanized the mob'. He and his allies had dismissed the old bosses as 'Moustache Petes', peasants steeped in the quaint ways of the old country, incapable of seizing the opportunities that America's wide-open economy presented. One area of disagreement had been over relations with criminals of other races. Luciano did not believe in an exclusively Italian brethren, a view which came in handy when he used Lansky's hit men to murder Maranzano.

Luciano immediately reformed Maranzano's new structure for the American Mafia. He abolished the role of 'boss of bosses' substituting for it 'first among equals'. He also removed the power of Mafia capos to execute their soldiers. In future a capo must prove his case to the family's *consigliere* before he could order a killing. This greatly improved morale among the troops.

Luciano and Genovese had to go to Chicago to justify Maranzano's murder at a meeting of the bosses of all America's crime families. The excuse that he had been hijacking Lucky's trucks must have gone down well since all the bosses were bootleggers. They promptly sanctioned the killing and acclaimed Luciano as their leader.

Today the structure of the Mafia, or La Cosa Nostra,[2] is much as it was when Valachi testified. The FBI now says there are twenty-five families across America but some are really controlled by larger families. Rockford and Springfield, for example, two families in Illinois, come under the huge Chicago 'Outfit'. Madison, Wisconsin is under Milwaukee. San Francisco and San Jose probably form part of the Los Angeles family. Other cities, like Las Vegas and Miami, have no one family but are hotbeds of organized crime. The Mafia regards them as 'open cities'. As Americans have moved to the Sunshine Belt, the Mafia has moved too. Dade, Broward and Palm Beach counties in Florida now have the greatest concentration of organized-crime residents in America. Texas, Arizona and New Mexico have all reported increased La Cosa Nostra activity. And the Mafia knows no frontiers. There is a powerful family in Canada with large investments in Florida and Atlantic City. The Caribbean is riddled with Mafia-controlled casinos and banks. The families have interests in all the world's money centres, including London, and wherever heroin is big business.

Today the Mafia is a conglomerate as powerful as any of the world's major companies. Organized crime acts like a multinational corporation in the way it develops markets, exploits consumer demand, shuts out competition and eliminates opposition. As Herbie Gross, a former front man for the Mafia, puts it, 'There is the underworld and the overworld, which I call the legal underworld.' Where the Mafia uses guns, legitimate business uses lawyers. Today the Mafia is even more dangerous because it has gone 'legitimate' with huge business investments and smooth-talking, college-educated front men. It now has guns *and* lawyers.

Valachi died of cancer in jail in 1971. He never gave evidence in any trials but many former gangsters have since followed his example and testified against the Mafia in the courts. Since 1970 they have had a shield of sorts in the Witness Security Program. While they are testifying they have armed protection. They and their families are also given new identities to start life again, thousands of miles from their old haunts. They are meant to get help in finding a straight job. Many witnesses have endless complaints about 'Witsec' but their lives are safer now than they would have been not so long ago, when Mafia informers tended to be shot, blown up or thrown off skyscrapers before their fellow-mobsters even went on trial.

In making *Crime Inc.* we met many federal witnesses. Most refused to be filmed in case they were recognized by neighbours or workmates in the places where they now live. Eight agreed to appear, face-to-camera. Some grew beards or moustaches. One wanted heavy make-up to disguise his appearance. All these witnesses had taken part in organized crime for many years.

Aladena Fratianno, 'Jimmy the Weasel', was born near Naples in 1913. When he was four months old the family emigrated to Cleveland, living in Little Italy around Mayfield Road and Murray Hill. His father was an honest citizen but Jimmy became a street criminal. He won his nickname with a fleet-footed escape from a policeman who saw him stealing fruit. At 12 he was working as a waiter in a speakeasy. A few years later he was running crooked dice games and in his early twenties he was robbing customers at other crooks' gambling houses. At 23, married with a baby daughter, he and some buddies beat up a bookmaker and robbed him of $1600. They were caught and Jimmy was sent to the State Penitentiary. It was nearly eight years before he was released in 1945.

By then his wife had been forced by her family to divorce him. Jimmy went straight to Los Angeles and remarried her.

In California Fratianno returned to racketeering: selling black-market goods, hijacking trucks and bookmaking. He made friends with other Italian mobsters from Cleveland and met the leaders of the local Mafia crime family. He became especially friendly with Johnny Roselli, a prominent Chicago mobster who had just served a prison sentence for extorting huge sums from Hollywood movie studios in return for their freedom from industrial disruption.[2] With Roselli's backing Fratianno was initiated into the Los Angeles family. He is the only 'made' member of La Cosa Nostra since Valachi to have turned federal witness. Today he is a dapper senior citizen, wisecracking his way through boxes of fat cigars. Despite turning against the Mafia he is probably safer today as a relocated witness than he ever was inside the family.

Fratianno was 'made' in a winery in Los Angeles seventeen years after Valachi and 3000 miles from New York, yet their accounts of the ceremony differ only in minor details. Fratianno's finger was pricked by a sword, not a knife. After he had been initiated, he did not shake hands with the members of the family, he kissed them on the cheek. He was also told not to 'fool with narcotics'. But whatever the criminal activity the same code of Omerta applied: 'You can never reveal that you belong to anything or you get killed. They tell you that you come in alive and you go out dead'. Sceptics might say that he must have read Valachi's Senate testimony and learned it by heart. Defendants have claimed he learned it all from the FBI. But juries all over America have believed him. His evidence has helped convict many top mafiosi including the entire hierarchy of the Los Angeles family, Frank Tieri, the boss of the Genovese family in New York, and Russell Buffalino, the boss of north-east Pennsylvania. Fratianno is the most successful witness the Justice Department has ever had against organized crime.

In 1948 Fratianno soon found out what his main Mafia duty was to be: killing people. In five years he executed five gangsters and took part in the killing of four others. He was always acting on orders and was never paid.

In 1953, for example, Jimmy had orders to kill 'Russian Louis' Strauss who was blackmailing a Las Vegas casino owner. The Mafia's National Commission bans killings in Las Vegas because they scare off gamblers and could upset the cosy relationship which exists between organized crime and the local authorities.

Russian Louis was broke so Jimmy told him he had $12,000 a few hours' drive away at a house in California. Louis fell for the ploy. When they went in the house, 'One guy put his arm around Louis and Frank Bompensiero put the rope on him and we killed him. That was it. We choked him. There was about eight or nine people there, all members of our family. They heard I was coming in with Russian Louis so they stayed.'

In our interview I said that most people would prefer not to be around when someone was being strangled. Jimmy replied with a laugh, 'Oh, not people in the family. They're killers themselves so it didn't mean nothing.'

It was like a cabaret?

'Yeah, just like a little performance. See, like a magician: something disappears, then it comes back.'

But nobody comes back. Russian Louis' body was never found.

'No they don't come back again. They got to wait seven years before they can be pronounced dead.'

How did Jimmy feel about killing people?

'I didn't have much feeling because I never killed nobody that was innocent. They were all gangsters, they were killers themselves. It might bother me if I killed an innocent person, somebody that didn't deserve it. Guys that I fooled with, Mickey Cohen, they were out to kill us. I couldn't kill a woman, innocent people, kids. I couldn't do that.'

Even within the family there was work to be done. 'Frank Borgia was a member of our family. He had an argument with another member and they both went to the boss and the boss decided to kill Borgia.' Fratianno laughed. 'Borgia might have been right, I don't know, but they called me and told me to go to San Diego with Frank Bompensiero to clip Frank Borgia. So we had somebody bring him in the house and we choked him, buried him and that was it. He was a member of our family.'

Did it matter to Jimmy that Borgia was a member of the family?

'No. The boss said he had to go. I didn't know the reason. I knew you don't ask questions. When they tell you to do something you do it. You ain't gonna ask no questions.'

Killing was how Fratianno 'made his bones'. A killer is hard to find, even in the Mafia. 'Some people can kill and some can't. A lot of people in our family we'd never send to kill anybody because they couldn't do it. Either you got it or you haven't got it. Either you're capable or you're not. People that weren't capable, you use them for lookouts. We only had a few in our family that would kill.'

Fratianno was an even rarer creature in organized crime: a killer who could also make money. 'The purpose of La Cosa Nostra is to make money. Anybody gets in it for one reason, to make money.' He earned money for himself and his bosses from gambling, loan-sharking and other rackets. He made so much money that in 1952 he was promoted to the rank of caporegime. 'I was a good hustler, a good leader, I was an all-round man. I could kill, I could draw a man, I could get friendly. I could do things the way they wanted them done.'

Another federal witness was Joseph Cantalupo, arguably the most effective ever to betray the New York and New England families. A husky, well-built, good-looking man, he completed his military service in Germany in 1964 and went to work at his father's real estate office on 86th Street in the Bensonhurst section of Brooklyn. Soon he realized that his father Anthony was involved with Carlo Gambino, boss of the Gambino family. He also learned that one of Cantalupo Realty's other salesmen was Joe Colombo, who subsequently became boss of another New York family. Joey became close friends with Colombo and his sons, Anthony and Joe Jun. 'With the Colombo boys we could go any place in New York, anywhere in the United States and they would have a connection. Everything would be *carte blanche*, whatever we wanted.'

The Colombo boys were rapidly embraced in the family. In contrast, Joey had to work his way through the ranks of associate criminals before he might be offered membership. He was neither a killer nor a big moneymaker, however, and was never 'made'. None the less in his fourteen years on the streets of Brooklyn in the businesses and social clubs frequented by 'made' men, he became much more than a La Cosa Nostra 'associate' – the term used by the FBI to describe anyone working in organized crime who is not 'made'. He enjoyed friendships with members of four of the five New York families. This enabled him to help convict many Mafiosi, including Frank Tieri, after he voluntarily turned undercover informer and worked for the FBI in 1973, 'wired up' with tape-recorders and radio microphones on his body, in his shoes and in his Cadillac. He also won convictions against soldiers in the New England family. Today Cantalupo, like Fratianno, has to live under a new identity far away from his old Mafia haunts.

Joey had been sufficiently trusted by Colombo to be initiated into the Freemasons. The two secret societies had much in common, but Joey saw one difference: 'The Masons are a fraternal order of brothers. So is the Mafia. But if you disobey the Mafia's laws the possibilities are that you would wind up in a garbage pail, where in Masonry it does not happen that way.'

Joey recalled the huge power base that the Mafia has established: 'The organization is in business to make money, firstly from illegal businesses like vice and gambling. All that kind of stuff is essential to the United States because people need to have it. But the ultimate aim of these people is to legitimize as many businesses as they can because then they are bigger than the government. They have all the legitimate businesses but on the side they still have all the illegal businesses. And it's all making more and more money. It's just a vast, vast empire.'

Nowadays, according to Joey, the bosses want a different kind of member. ' "You, my friend, go out and kill Joe Schmoe, and you kill Bobo Bebee – they got all these crazy names – and after you do that we'll make you a member of our family." They don't do that any more. Today it's more sophisticated: "You go out and show me $1 million profit on a certain business deal and then we'll make you a "good fellow". We'll make you a member of our family."

'They're not interested in murderers any more because they can produce "Greaseballs" from the other side, from Sicily, for £100 and bring them into the USA just to kill somebody. Now they're interested in legitimate businesses and if you can produce for them – I don't have to say $1 million, let's say a $100,000 or $200,000 a year – you can be made a member of an organized-crime family.

'This makes it a much more dangerous organization today because they got their fingers into everything. There isn't anything that they do not have a part of in the United States. I don't care what it is, somebody somewhere has a piece of it.'

Gerry DeNono is another Mafia associate turned informer. Like Fratianno he killed for the mob but he did not make a habit of it. 'It was strictly business. This kid was on heroin. He went crazy and murdered a client of ours who we did not want anything to happen to. Business is business. He was my responsibility. He was in my crew. He broke our law. He got tried, convicted and executed. It was in a remote area. Nobody else was jeopardized. Very clean, neat. End of story. Goodbye, and that's it.'

DeNono's business has landed him in jail where he has to live in a special unit, out of reach of other prisoners who might try to kill him. He has informed on top mobsters in Chicago, Las Vegas, Florida and New Orleans. They would not now appreciate his impish sense of humour.

Gerry finished his military service and fell in with the Mafia on the golf courses of Florida. He was soon introduced to Caesar DiVarco, a caporegime in Chicago, his home town. He ran errands for Caesar in Chicago, like delivering bags of hot money to a crooked bank chairman who 'washed' it through the system. He also had to look after a heavy gambler who was an alcoholic and a diabetic. Gerry's job was to keep him alive to gamble away his fortune to the mob. Gerry then graduated to a crew of Mafia burglars robbing coin and stamp stores across seven states.

'In Chicago if I want to join a very sophisticated organization called the Mafia, La Cosa Nostra, the Outfit – whatever you want to call it – I must not only pay tribute to the family, I must also buy into it. Let's say I open up a restaurant, a nightclub, on Rush Street. I put 50 per cent of the business in the family's name. Now 50 per cent of my receipts go into the family's bundle. If I open a cigar factory, 50 per cent of those receipts go into the bundle. The money they get from whatever dealings – casinos, cocaine, heroin, prostitution, bookmaking – all goes into a pot.

'I am not privileged to the money I brought into the organization but this way I become a "made" member. They don't grab me off the street and say, "Because you shot John Doe in the head twice and did a great job, I now make you a "made" man which entitles you to a piece of all this action." That's baloney. The only ones who get "made" are those who have contributed $500,000, $200,000, whatever. Now you get a piece of the Mafia pie. *Now* you're "made" .

'Some guy working with the Outfit, he says, "I had a hell of a good year. Here's $500,000. I want to become 'made'." Now they go through the ritual and take him into the family because he bought his chair. Just like a stockbroker he bought his chair. Same thing.'

5

Tales of Bosses and 'Made' Men

'Carlo Gambino and Funzi Tieri were meek men,' says Joey Cantalupo recalling two mighty godfathers who led New York's biggest crime families until a few years ago. These absolute monarchs, with the power of life and death over hundreds of 'made' men and thousands of henchmen, both sponsored Cantalupo.

'You could run into Carlo Gambino in the street and you would never know this poor, meek, humble man was the boss of bosses and the boss of the biggest crime family in New York. He would fit in with anybody. The same with Funzi Tieri. . . . They demanded respect because of the tragic things they've done through all the years they were coming up in the families. People fear these bosses, even though today they don't go out and kill people (they would have somebody else do it!), but during the early years you can believe they've murdered people, cut 'em up and threw 'em to the fish.'

Born in Palermo in 1902, Carlo Gambino never became an American citizen. When he was arrested at Apalachin in 1957 he was in serious danger of deportation. He was in his sixties when Cantalupo first knew him and looked frail and weak. Appearances were deceptive; according to police records he had been a ruthless killer. In the early 1930s Gambino and his brother Paul had been at the heart of the victorious Castellamarese faction and Carlo became a boss when Albert Anastasia was murdered in 1957. He assumed the unofficial rank of boss of bosses when Vito Genovese died in jail in 1969. His immense power lay partly in his family's strength on the streets and its massive investments in legitimate businesses. All this had been insured over many years by corrupt cops, judges and politicians. As boss of bosses Gambino commanded respect from members of all the families. When it was not shown redress was swift.

'A typical for-instance,' recalls Cantalupo. 'There was a captain in the Colombo family named Mimi Sciala. He controlled Coney

Island which is a vast area with a large population. He had the numbers, the Shylocking and all the rackets. But Mimi had a terrible problem: he liked to drink. And when he drank he didn't care who you were. You could have been Carl Gambino and if he didn't like the way you looked he's say, "Hey, you look like a jerk, Carl." But he was drunk, the liquor was talking for him.

'And that really happened at a restaurant on Coney Island. Carl walked in and who's there falling on his face but Mimi. Now Mimi had his own crew of twenty or thirty men but because he insulted Carl it was decided this man has no respect – respect is a big thing – and eventually he had to die. So a wiseguy named Charlie, who was also a captain in the Colombo family, got the contract to kill Mimi and Mimi was killed.

'Now the people who worked for Mimi loved and cherished the guy. He supported them and everybody made money. So one night Tommy Barbusca and another member of the Colombo family, who were both in Mimi's crew, were sitting in a bar called the 1770 in Brooklyn. And they're talking: "Jeez, it wasn't right what they did to Mimi. We're going to have to get our guys together and take a stand or do something to Charlie."

'As they're talking the bartender overhears. He goes in the back, drops a dime, and tells whoever's on the other end of the phone what's going on. Tommy and his friend go out to the car across the street. They get in the car and the next thing you know, two blasts from a shotgun and they're dead. This shows the control they have over their own people. Nobody is going to step on anybody's feet. You're going to do what you're told.'

You had to show just as much respect to Funzi Tieri who was nearing 70 when he became boss of the mighty Genovese family. 'He was nothing to look at,' says Cantalupo, 'not more than 140 lb. A nothing man. I was partners with him in a flea market in Brooklyn. Another partner was a captain in the Genovese family named Louis La Rocca. Louis is a monster of a man. Six foot two, 280 lb. He also demands respect because of his fine position within the family. He answers only to the boss Funzi Tieri.

'We were behind in our rent. And I ran into Funzi and he asked me, "How are you doing in the flea market?"

'And I said, "Well, Funzi, we're behind on the rent."

'And this little meek man saying to me, "You tell that mother-fucking Louis to go and get the money or I'll cut his balls off."

'I go back to the flea market and Louis says, "Did you see the old man?"

'I says, "Yeah."

'He says, "What did he say? Did you tell him we're behind with the rent?" I was embarrassed to tell Louis.

'He says, "Tell me. What did he say?"

'So I say, "The old man says, go and get the money or he's gonna cut your balls off."

'The guy must have got diarrhoea in his pants. He was so scared that he ran out and got the $5000. That shows you the respect and the fear they had for this man. And it's not only Louis La Rocca. It's everybody in the family.'

Despite the danger, Cantalupo was exhilarated by his work for the Mafia: 'I was thrilled. I enjoyed being part of this tremendous organization that could open doors to you all over the world. Anything you wanted you could get.'

Joey soon became aware that another salesman working at Cantalupo Realty was Joe Colombo, at 40 the youngest family boss in New York and the youngest member of the National Commission. Cantalupo recalls how close Colombo was to Carlo Gambino. In about 1962 Colombo, then just a capo in the Profaci family, told Gambino that Joe Bonanno, boss of another crime family and a founder member of the Commission, was plotting to kill him. Gambino was naturally indebted to Colombo and showed his gratitude by ensuring that Colombo became boss of the Profaci family when Joe Magliocco died in 1963. Gambino then gave Colombo $1 million to put on the streets in Shylock loans. In this way the Colombo family became a subsidiary of the Gambinos.

Cantalupo felt that Colombo was too flash for a boss. Old-timers like Gambino and Tieri had chauffeur-bodyguards, but they drove modest Buicks or Chevrolets. Joe Colombo always had a Cadillac. He wore diamond rings, $400 suits and $200 shoes. It was as if at 5 ft 6 in he was not too sure people would respect him even though he was a boss.

Gambino, in contrast, was the Supreme Being. 'These people don't believe in God,' says Joey, 'but to them Carlo Gambino *was*

God.' Joey felt enthralled just to be in his presence and would willingly perform his most menial tasks. The pair were like grandfather and grandson. Once Joey wrecked his car on his way to visit Carlo. He was taken to hospital and awoke to find the boss of bosses at his bedside offering comfort and a new car. At Joey's wedding Gambino was an honoured guest.

Joey became a trusted mob underling, a role which invaded even his home. 'Early in 1960 Joe Colombo asked me if he could use my house for a meeting and I said yes.

'He says, "Fine. You have your wife make a pot of black coffee, set the table for six people, go out and get Italian cookies. About seven o'clock send your wife out, you be downstairs and we'll be coming in."

'So I would be sitting on the stoop and a car would pull up with a driver and a passenger. That's Joe Colombo with his bodyguard Rocky. Joe would go right upstairs. The next car would be Carl Gambino with his driver, Jimmy Brown. Carlo would come out of the car, we'd say hello, he'd go upstairs and the car would pull away. Then Funzi Tieri would come in. My job was to sit there until the meeting was over and keep my eyes open for cops or FBI.

'Then at a precise time a car would pull up, an individual would come down and he would be driven away. That meeting was very big. Three heads of families that I knew, so the other two had to be bosses. It was meeting of the five families. Since Apalachin this was the only way it could be held.'

There were countless meetings at different houses. On Sundays many crime family members used to gather at Colombo's home. Sometimes Joey would drive Colombo to Gambino's house, wait for an hour or two until Colombo came out and then drive him back to Cantalupo Realty.

The bosses have to meet to plan Mafia strategies, to co-ordinate tactics against the police and the FBI, to settle inter-family disputes and, most important of all, to talk business. New York's five families still dominate the fundamental rackets of gambling, loansharking, narcotics and extortion. They also handle goods stolen by freelance crooks in hijackings, burglaries and robberies. They have specialists who handle stolen stocks and bonds worth millions of dollars. They also organize arson for profit: a building is 'torched' so a fraudulent insurance claim may be made on both the structure and its non-existent contents.

The Mafia owns hundreds of outwardly straight businesses of all kinds: pizza parlours, pastry shops, catering halls, photographic and printing companies, car dealers, florists, funeral parlours, embalmers, liquor importers and wholesalers, furnishing stores, pinball arcades, vending-machine companies, entertainment agencies. They govern entire industries in New York: garments and garbage; fish, meat and poultry; trucking and construction.[1] These 'legal' businesses make a lot of money, not because they are well run but because they have the 'edge'. In garments or trucking so many companies are mob-owned that they face little genuine competition. Their brother mafiosi who control the labour unions corruptly depress the wages Mafia employers have to pay. Union troublemakers are easily fired and fired at. Genuine competitors are crippled by inflated wage bills or Mafia-inspired strikes and sabotage. This can go on until the straight operator goes out of business or, in desperation, pays off the mob and joins the club.[2]

Yet many of these businesses are never meant to make money. 'They are fronts,' says Joey. 'They gotta be covers because the families are making so much money. How do you maintain a style of life, spending say $5000 a week, if you're only bringing home $150 a week? Every legitimate business that you can draw a cheque from will help you tell the government, "Well, I'm making $500 a week here, $300 a week there." You won't have to worry about income tax evasion like Al Capone. This is how modern-day organized-crime families are living so lavishly because they are into so many businesses where they can show a legitimate income.'

Joe Colombo's job as a broker with Cantalupo Realty was just one of his business fronts: 'He had his own office in there with see-through mirrors to see who was coming in and out. Every day members of his crime family would come in to talk deals. Members of the Gambino and Genovese families would drop in too. If any of them were questioned by the cops or the FBI they would say they were coming in for a mortgage, to buy a house or rent an apartment.' Colombo had a house in Brooklyn, worth $150,000 in 1970. He had his Cadillacs, a home in upstate New York with 10 acres of land worth $250,000 and he belonged to the best country clubs.

This public display of wealth was essential when he moved into political prominence with the Italian American Civil Rights League.[3]

Colombo had a flamboyant way of showing affection for judges and politicians. 'He had an "in" with a tie maker. Every Christmas he gave expensive gift-wrapped ties to his friends and associates. Some people would get six ties, all custom-made. One top lawyer only wore bow-ties so he would get twenty bow-ties in a package to show Joe's gratitude for all he had done through the years.'

Cantalupo believes the New York bosses he knew were brilliant as underworld generals, businessmen and political strategists. The bosses of Los Angeles displayed no such talents, according to Jimmy 'the Weasel' Fratianno who was that family's under-boss while its hierarchy were in prison. If the New York bosses were men who, given a different start, might have headed legitimate corporations, the Los Angeles family was led by 'dead heads'.

'California was never organized like the East. The East goes back to the twenties. In California it was the forties before they got active. By then Mickey Cohen had everything. California was never successful because they never had a boss that was capable or had the "smarts" to move where everybody could make money. If they had made Johnny Roselli the boss we'd have been millionaires, richer than any family in the country. You just gotta have a capable boss that knows how to make money. They just didn't have the right people runnin' it.

'We even let Las Vegas slip out of our territory. I told Jack Dragna back in the forties to put a capo up there with a few soldiers. If we'd have done that then nobody would have come into that town. That was *our town*. He just didn't see it coming. In them days there was only three places on the Strip. Now? Forget about it!'

When a 'made' man goes to prison the crime family is meant to look after his wife and children. Jimmy Fratianno was jailed in 1964 for extortion. 'I left a lot of money and they squandered it away. Louis Dragna gave my wife a little money, $100 a week for two years. That was it. I stayed in six and a half years. The money I left just went down the drain. When I went in I had two bars, a dress shop and two offices. I had $100,000 in Shylock money on the street. They went through it all. Just ripped me off.'

Fratianno may have been treated badly by his own bosses when he was inside but in the wider community even the humble soldier has immense status. As Cantalupo puts it, 'When you are a "made" member of a family it demands respect from people under you and people on the street. They know you don't fool around with "made" men.'

Sometimes a soldier gets respect because he is mad as well as 'made'. Joey found one psychopath in the Colombo family was not good company for a night out.

'There was nothing nice about Shorty Spero. He lived by violence. I was in a sociable game of four-handed pinocle with him at the house of Michael Bolino who was also a "made" member of the Colombo family. Our wives were in the same area. I caught Shorty cheating and I said "Shorty, you can't do that."

'And he takes a .45 out of his pocket, he puts it to my head and he says, "Don't you ever call me a fuckin' cheat or I'll blow your brains out."

'At that time I got a little diarrhoea and . . . we left. But the man lived that way. And he died that way. His brother was shot to death. He tried to avenge his death and was killed himself. So there's no more Shorty Speros.'

Herbie Gross is another federal witness. In the 1960s he ran his own hotel in Lakewood, New Jersey and became a front man for organized crime. He ran gambling operations, sold stolen stocks and bonds and secured favourable land deals for the Mafia by corrupting local politicians. One man he worked with was Nicky Valvano, an associate of the Genovese family.

'Nicky Valvano had an extremely violent nature. I was present at a poker game where he became so annoyed and upset about comments being made by Jimmy 'the Brush' Fife that he grabbed his head, pulled him forward and bit off his earlobe. Bit it off and spat it out! And then he took the guy into his car and drove him down to the emergency hospital. About five minutes later they came rushing back to look for that piece of earlobe so they could sew it back on. That was Nicky Valvano.'

'He was the same guy who got a message once that his wife Dorothy wants to see him. He hadn't been home for several weeks – he had girlfriends all over the place – and so he asked me if I would drive him out to his house. He walked in and he says, "What's the matter, Dorothy?"

'She said, "You've got to do something about JoJo." (JoJo was his son, about 11 years old.)

' "What's the matter with JoJo?"

' "He's acting up. I was called to school. They want to throw him out. He's unmanageable. You've got to do something about him."

'He said, "Where is he now?"

' "He's out the back."

' "Hey, JoJo! Come here."

'And JoJo walks in and he says, "Yeah?"

' "Hey what's the matter with you? Why can't you be good in school? What are you acting up like that? Don't you like school?"

'He says, "No I don't."

' "What do you wanna be when you grow up?"

'The kid says, "I wanna be a thief, just like you."

'He says, "Then pay attention to me!"

'I witnessed this and I'm thinking of my pure kids back home: what am I in with here? I'm ordered to work with this paranoid bastard. If you knew him you didn't cross him. You didn't argue with him. I'm proud of my earlobes and I still have them!'

Herbie Gross knew an even more distasteful New Jersey organized-crime figure called Joe Celso. 'Early on in his mob career Celso was the official counter of foetuses aborted in an illegal abortion ring owned by 'Bayonne Joe' Zicarelli. He was there to make sure Bayonne Joe wasn't being short-changed on the number of abortions. You can imagine, just like people in prison look down on sexual offenders and child molesters, how mobsters would look down on Celso for doing that job.

'Some years ago the FBI got information that there were at least three bodies buried in a pit in a grave on Joe Celso's property where he lived and so they came down with warrants and dug it up. Sure enough, they found bones of three bodies. They had one positive identification of someone on the fringe of the mob but they couldn't bring any charges against Celso.

'Now about that time I sponsored a show in Lakewood where the headliner was Pat Henry. He was the warm-up comic for Frank Sinatra on all his shows. He got up on the stage and he said, "I know there's a guy here who's had quite a bit of trouble with all the authorities. Now I know he had nothing to do with the death of those people they've dug up on his property. His problem is that he was operating a cemetery in a residential zone."

'Everyone collapsed and laughed. Celso went as red as a beet, not so much embarrassed as discomforted by it, but he couldn't say a word. Most of the audience were mobsters and he was too low on the totem pole to have any comeback. He was an outcast, even among criminals.'

Even the sex life of a 'made' man, in and out of marriage, is a matter for respect. They place their wives on a pedestal, says Joey Cantalupo, but they keep them at home, 'pregnant and barefoot'. Ninety per cent of them also have girlfriends on whom they lavish money, 'but they go through girlfriends like they go through veal cutlets.

'One of the commandments in organized crime is that you do not fool with another member's wife or girlfriend. This is a law you do not break. If you do the penalty could be death. And a perfect example of this is that Joe Colombo's father was fooling around with a member of organized-crime's girlfriend or wife and they caught them in a car together. The next day when the cops found them they were both dead, shot in the head. But the unfortunate thing is that they cut off his prick and stuck it in his own mouth.'

In Chicago this rule was applied even to a mobster's extra-marital affairs. 'Milwaukee Phil' Alderisio was acting boss of the Chicago Outfit until he was jailed for bank fraud in 1970. Gerry DeNono, who later turned informer, was working with the Chicago family at that time under Joe 'Little Caesar' DiVarco. Once a week DeNono would drive DiVarco to a restaurant called Mio's where the bosses would meet. Mio's sister, Nancy, was Milwaukee Phil's girlfriend; he was married with children. DeNono recalls: 'She [Nancy] was dating this guy Blackie, a bookmaker in Cicero. Nan went to the jail to ask Milwaukee Phil for permission to get married to Blackie. You get this! Phil's married. He's in prison. He gives his permission to her to marry this other mustache, right? Then Milwaukee Phil dies in prison.

'Joe DiVarco tells me, "See Blackie over there? He's dead. He's gonna be killed."

'I said, "What for? Milwaukee Phil's dead. He died in prison and that was only his girlfriend, Joe, what's the difference?"

'He says, "From his grave he ordered the hit."

'Three weeks after they were married Blackie was shot right in front of Nan in a rockin' chair in the house. From the grave he ordered that hit. This told me, don't be foolin' around with nobody else's girlfriend. This man had so much power that out of respect they killed Blackie. It don't make any sense to me, but this is how their minds work.'[4]

6

The Politics of the Saloon

In the big cities of nineteenth-century America both politics and organized crime were run from the saloon. Saloon owners were among the few people who could afford the high cost of politics. They had the money to get the vote out on election days and with their bouncers and barmen they also had the muscle to beat up opponents and hijack ballot boxes. Most important of all, they had the incentive. They had to have political connections to protect their income. This came not so much from the legal sale of liquor but from what went on in back rooms and up the stairs: gambling and prostitution. Most illegal casinos and high-class brothels were connected with saloons, physically and financially, so their owners had to take out insurance against the raids and shutdowns demanded by law. This was best achieved by paying off the police and curbing their zeal. The perfect arrangement was a continuing alliance with the people who chose the police chief in any city: the machine politicians.

Ideally the saloon owner became a politician himself. If he was so inclined he could then direct an entire city's serious crime, from white slavery (coercive prostitution) to extortion, loansharking and the elimination of rival criminals. With a corrupt police force and the county sheriff in his pocket the saloon-owning politician could wipe out all opposition. If any employee or racket of his were brought to court he could get the charges thrown out by the judge, whose election he had secured or whom he had appointed in the time-honoured spoils system of American politics. If the worst happened and reformers won an election on an anti-corruption platform, the saloon syndicate usually had enough guile to outlast the reformers. After a few years the crooks would get re-elected, outwardly chastened perhaps but cannier than ever. As Richard Croker, the turn-of-the-century boss of New York's corrupt Democratic organization said after his candidate for mayor had been defeated, 'The people could not stand the rotten police corruption. We'll be back after the next election. They can't stand reform either.'

The pattern was the same in all America's big cities but it was most blatant in the boom town of Chicago. From its incorporation in 1837 Chicago had usually been run by saloon-owning, gambler-politicians. From the 1860s a gambler-gangster named Mike McDonald led an Irish immigrant bloc which financed the Democratic party machine on the profits of illegal gambling. McDonald returned mayor after mayor committed to a 'wide-open town' where gambling and prostitution could flourish. If his money and his newspaper did not deliver victory, McDonald made his man mayor through forged votes and stolen ballot boxes.

The most colourful in a long line of boodling city fathers were 'Bathhouse John' Coughlin and 'Hinky Dink' Kenna who presided over Chicago for forty years. Coughlin was a big, bluff, flamboyant man who ran a bathhouse in the heart of Chicago's business, entertainment and vice district. Most of his customers were gambling operators and sportsmen. In 1891 the city tried to shut down a racetrack. Coughlin's gentlemen patrons stood to lose a lot of business so they sought a political front man to represent their crooked interests. As they controlled the Democratic party organization in Chicago's First Ward their nominee for alderman was certain to be elected. The young Coughlin, a race-lover himself, was the ideal candidate and in the 1892 council elections he was victorious. The following year, however, in the race for mayor Coughlin was slow to support the man who won, the legendary Carter Harrison. Harrison showed his displeasure by ordering police raids on all First Ward gambling houses under Coughlin's protection. Since his sole duty as alderman was to protect illegal gambling, the 32-year-old's political career looked over before it had started.

One of his raided constituents was a glum little fellow called Michael 'Hinky Dink' Kenna. The Hink told the Bath that they should form an organization to protect the gambling operators and brothel-keepers in the ward from such political instability. All vice operators would pay into a fund nursed by Kenna and Coughlin. This would be used to retain some of Chicago's most able lawyers to defend any gambling house or whorehouse owner in trouble. The fund would also be tapped for the regular payoffs and gifts needed to soften the hearts of cops and judges. So effective was this scheme that the Bath was to remain the First Ward's alderman for forty-six years until his death in 1938 when the ancient Hink was wheeled out of retirement to replace him.

For a century Chicago's First Ward has included the city's downtown business district, with its banks and corporation headquarters, hotels, theatres, department stores and today some of the world's tallest skyscrapers. The First Ward also used to contain a wide-open vice district, twenty-two blocks south, known as the Levee. In the words of Kenna and Coughlin's biographies the ward was the habitat of

> . . . bums and thugs, thieves and gaudy prostitutes. . . . On these streets were the hop joints, concert saloons and brothels, from the 25 c. bagnios to the more expensive houses. . . . Off Dearborn Street in the heart of the city was Gamblers' Alley and nearby on Randolph was the infamous Hairtrigger Block lined with gambling houses of every description. . . . Throughout the ward were endless stretches of lesser saloons and dice and faro houses from which by night issued the pimps, piffers and pickpockets to prey upon citizens and visitors.[1]

The Levee was like a Wild West frontier boom town where there was no recognizable law and order.

By 1895 all this was the bailiwick of the Hink and the Bath. Kenna soon joined Coughlin at City Hall as the First Ward's second alderman. Coughlin had expanded from his bathhouse to his own saloon, the Silver Dollar, patronized by whores and gamblers alike. The pair had so mastered Chicago's corrupt politics that Carter Harrison Jun., the son of their one-time adversary, relied on them to get him re-elected as mayor four times. He was to call them his 'two Rocks of Gibraltar'. When he came back in 1911 to win his fifth election he was, however, forced to move against the men who once more had ensured his victory.

What was to sever Harrison from his 'two Rocks' was prostitution. His predecessor had appointed a commission to decide on whether there should be segregated vice districts and, if so, how they should be run. The Vice Commission was headed by churchmen, lawyers, academics and philanthropists and was staffed by tenacious investigators. Its report, published only two months after Harrison's re-election, did not condemn vice itself but it gave Chicago a basting. In a calm but horrified tone it talked of hundreds of seven-day-a-week gambling houses, 7000 licensed saloons and 5000 full-time prostitutes.

The report stated. 'Chicago's vice annually destroys the souls of 5000 young women', but asked, 'Is it any wonder that a tempted girl, who receives only $6 a week working with her hands, sells her body for $25 per week when she learns there is demand for it and men are willing to pay the price?' It claimed that the existing system of segregating vice away from residential areas under police supervision had failed. There was now more prostitution outside the red-light district than inside it. The police were either negligent or corrupt or both. The medical examination of prostitutes had failed. They plied their trade still infected, with the connivance of the supervising doctors.

The report named neither Kenna nor Coughlin but they were implicated throughout and condemned in a ferocious attack on their holiest institution. In 1896 they had hit upon the idea of a grand ball to raise money for the First Ward Democratic organization. It was first held at the Seventh Regiment Armory and patronized by high and low, especially the Levee's most decorous prostitutes, madams and pimps. The star was Coughlin himself, brilliantly attired in a green tail coat, lavender trousers, pink kid gloves and bright yellow shoes. Drunkenness and fornication broke out in front of the top politicians and policemen who were attending in obeisance to the aldermen. The romp outraged the clerics but it made the Hink and the Bath $25,000.

The First Ward ball became an outrageous tradition. In 1907 the *Chicago Tribune* asserted that, 'If a great disaster had befallen the Coliseum last night there would not have been a second-story worker, a dip or Plug Ugly, porch climber, dope fiend or scarlet woman remaining in Chicago.' Twenty thousand guests drank 10,000 quarts of champagne and 30,000 quarts of beer. Another $20,000 flowed into the aldermen's coffers. The 1908 ball went ahead despite a campaign to ban it. It was another drunken riot, notable for a large number of men dressed up as women, and greatly distressed an Episcopalian dean who infiltrated for the reformers. In 1909 the mayor refused a liquor licence. Only 3000 people came and the aldermen lost money. They never held another ball.

Harrison finally fell out with Coughlin and Kenna over a notorious brothel. In 1900 Minna and Ada Lester came to Chicago from Omaha where they had learned the brothel trade. The sisters took the surname Everleigh and opened a sumptuous resort in a fifty-room mansion at 2131–3 South Dearborn Street. The Everleigh Club became world renowned as the most splendid whorehouse on earth, with exotic fittings like its $15,000 gold piano, oriental rugs, oil paintings, golden silk curtains and gold-plated spittoons each costing $650. For rich patrons (only newspapermen received discounted favours) there were twelve soundproof parlours. To enter cost a staggering $10 and dinner was $50. A lady cost at least $50 but she would be a professional harlot of the highest class. By 1907 the Everleighs had piled up $250,000 in three Chicago banks alone as well as stockpiling millions elsewhere.

In 1911 they published a brochure illustrating the club's charms, including: 'steam heat throughout, with electric fans in summer: one never feels the winter's chill or summer's heat in this luxurious resort. Fortunate indeed, with all the comforts of life surrounding them, are the members of the Everleigh Club.' Harrison only learned the sisters had burst into print at a banquet in another city where his ogling host showed him the brochure. The mayor was outraged that the city he represented was best known elsewhere as the home of the Everleigh Club. Back in town he instantly ordered the police to shut it down. The sisters laid on a gala farewell and in the early hours of 25 October 1911 they were formally raided and shut down. They left on a six-month trip to Europe, reassured by Coughlin that everything would be sorted out by their return when it would be business as usual.

On the contrary, the clean-up gathered force. The mayor fired the police chief for failing to shut down brothels and replaced him with someone who would. The anti-vice crusade roared on, reaching a tragic climax in a battle in the Levee between two squads of police. A Morals Squad officer was accidentally killed by another detective but the aldermen were blamed because they had licensed the rampant vice which the cops were trying to shut down.

On their return the Everleighs decided to close down for good. They were not vindictive but felt twelve years of payoffs had been a waste of money. In 1911 they wrote a statement about First Ward corruption and entrusted it to a judge. In 1914 he released the statement, revealing that the sisters had paid Kenna and Coughlin over $100,000 to avoid raids, to get all charges dropped against their girls, to ensure rival whorehouses were shut down and to block new laws against vice. They said they had bribed detectives for years. They estimated that in little more than a decade the Levee had paid the Coughlin–Kenna syndicate $15 million in graft.

With this bombshell the anti-vice crusaders resolved to black out the red-light district. The Hink and the Bath looked beaten but they were master politicians. In 1915 Harrison ran again for mayor but the aldermen switched their support and ensured his slaughter. The new mayor was a Republican, William Hale Thompson. A charismatic former football star, he made the kind of promises the Hink and the Bath liked: a wide-open town and a flourishing Levee. He fulfilled those promises but no longer would Kenna and Coughlin rule the city's vice. Thompson delivered Chicago from saloon-owning politicians but he handed it over to the kind of mobsters who soon made the aldermen look benign.

The syndicate of vice-lords and crooks led by Kenna and Coughlin *was* organized crime. It is difficult to imagine any gang more damaging to society. Yet such a gang now emerged. Until the 1910s the Irish were the only large immigrant group with an identity distinct and separate from America's dominant Protestant culture. Now millions of Poles, Jews, Greeks and Italians flooded into the cities, all demanding their piece of the American pie. Most of that pie was legitimate but a large slice was criminal. Soon Chicago's first Italian crime boss emerged, the man from whom the city's organized-crime family of today is clearly descended.

'Big Jim' Colosimo was made a Democratic party precinct captain around 1900 by John Coughlin who saw him as the ideal man to whip in the Italian vote. The Irishman sponsored his rise from street sweeper to poolroom operator to saloon owner. Big Jim married a madam named Victoria Moresco who ran one of the First Ward's most successful brothels. Together they set up a chain of whorehouses and then moved into the restaurant business. Colosimo's Café at 2126 South Wabash became nationally famous for its food and its connections. Its host wore the wages of sin in diamond rings, tiepins and other jewellery. He also welded his Italian compatriots into a formidable political force with its own gang of enforcers. These were pressed into service whenever Coughlin and Kenna needed them but their violence soon became too much for the First Ward veterans. Now nearing 60, they had had enough of politics. Anyway Big Jim did not need them any more.

Their decline was hastened by Prohibition which, unlike the laws against vice and gambling, had to be outwardly enforced. Coughlin had shut down his Silver Dollar years before but now Kenna closed his fine old establishments too. In contrast Prohibition brought only riches to Colosimo. His Italian followers were soon producing home-brewed alcohol in their tenement homes and his young hoodlums were just developing the art of bootlegging. But Colosimo was not keeping his mind on business. He sought a companion to match his new wealth and left his wife Victoria to marry Dale Winter, a beautiful young singer. Just after returning from their honeymoon, on 11 May 1920, Big Jim went to his café to await the four o'clock delivery of two truckloads of whiskey. The delivery was never made. Instead he was shot dead in the café lobby.

Colosimo's wake and funeral were notable for the large numbers of aldermen, judges and congressmen who attended. Kenna was an honorary pallbearer. Coughlin knelt weeping at his casket. So many public figures turned out that Chicago was more or less telling the world that it was run by organized crime. If a pimp turned bootlegger could get this kind of send-off, the implications were not lost on rising Italian gangsters in Colosimo's cortège, especially his protégé, if failed protector, Johnny Torrio.

Torrio was Victoria Moresco's cousin. Visiting her in 1908, he was soon brought into her husband's business. Big Jim then had a problem. He was being 'shaken down' by some Black Handers.

Torrio, though small and reserved, had 'made his bones' as a killer in New York's notorious Five Points gang. He soon wiped out the Black Handers and then proceeded to mastermind Big Jim's rise, developing new gambling operations within Colosimo's pimping empire.

Torrio in turn recruited ferocious young gunmen as protectors and collectors. The toughest and most ambitious was Alphonse Caponi, alias Al Brown, 'Scarface', Al Capone. In 1919 Torrio brought Al to Chicago from New York. Capone became Colosimo's bodyguard for a while and was detained as a suspect when Big Jim was killed. With Colosimo gone Torrio became the biggest power in Chicago crime. He deputed Capone to oversee his gambling operations.

But Fate had bigger things in mind for Capone. It was his good luck that a law had just been passed in Washington creating a new criminal business which would ensure his immortality. The business was bootlegging. The law was Prohibition. The folly was America's.

7

The Nobbled Experiment

Al Capone was not only Prohibition's most notorious gangster – he was also its philosopher: 'I make my money by supplying a public demand. If I break the law my customers, who number hundreds of the best people in Chicago, are as guilty as I am. The only difference is that I sell and they buy. Everybody calls me a racketeer. I call myself a businessman. When I sell liquor it's bootlegging. When my patrons serve it on a silver tray it's hospitality.'

Prohibition was a disaster for America because it turned mobsters into public servants. Tony Berardi, a Chicago photographer who lived through Prohibition and frequently encountered Capone, says: 'At least 75 per cent of the people in this country didn't like Prohibition. That law made Capone a brewer. Hell, nobody would ever have known about this guy if it wasn't for Prohibition. He figured this was the way to make an easy buck. People enjoyed it, people wanted it and he was going to supply it.'

Scorning the new law, ordinary citizens viewed their illicit suppliers with some affection. As a 1931 editorial in *Collier*'s stated: 'So long as a vast public insists upon drinking alcoholic beverages somebody will supply the trade, whatever the cost in money, corruption or crime. Criminals under existing conditions do work which otherwise respectable citizens want done.'

How was so abused a law ever passed? Prohibition, in the words of a prominent temperance leader, was 'an honest effort to do away with a terrible evil'.[1] The Prohibition movement had grown steadily over many years. It exploited many fears: some were real, others were based on ignorance or prejudice. It symbolized rural America against the big city, native American against immigrant, Puritan against Catholic, put-upon woman against drunken man, white against black. Above all, it personified the church against the saloon. In time it became profit-minded capitalist against drink-sodden, absentee worker. During the First World War it triumphed as American patriot over German brewer.

America changed rapidly in the late nineteenth century. No longer a predominantly farming and frontier society, peopled by Protestants of English-speaking stock, it was becoming a nation of big cities filled with Catholics from countries like Ireland, Poland and Italy. Their attitude towards drink disturbed the long-standing temperance movements which were almost exclusively Protestant in membership.

Traditional forms of temperance did not rule out moderate drinking but pseudo-scientific evidence was now produced to show that Americans were degenerating through drunkenness. Prohibitionists claimed this was racial suicide and that drunkards must not be allowed to breed. In 1876 the *National Temperance Almanac* blamed 'King Alcohol' for most of America's poverty, crime, insanity and premature deaths. It had infused millions with the 'spirits of demons and degraded them below the level of brutes'. Worst of all it had 'introduced among us hereditary diseases, both physical and mental, thereby tending to deteriorate the human race'.

Alcohol, prohibitionists maintained, increased sexual desire. Propagandists demanded that all alcoholic drink be avoided: 'The control of sex impulses will then be easy and disease, dishonour, disgrace and degradation will be avoided.'[2] Venereal disease was branded as the inevitable consequence of a night out at the saloon. In the South prohibitionists allied with white Democrats who were easily convinced that alcohol unhinged the Negro's lust for white women.

The Prohibition party was founded in 1869, seeking the direct election of its own candidates. It failed and was overtaken in the 1890s by the Anti-Saloon League which endorsed candidates from either of the major parties provided they backed Prohibition. Up until then only three states had been consistently 'dry' but the league's policy of infiltration succeeded. Dry laws began to be passed in many states as the League's 50,000 field workers played Republican and Democrat candidates off against each other.

The 'wet' lobby, funded largely by brewers, wine-makers and distillers, failed partly because it was divided. Grape growers in

California tried to gain absolution from the league by supporting attacks on saloons and spirits. Brewers claimed beer was the temperance drink and tried to shift the blame on to hard liquor. The distillers claimed that the places themselves were the problem – the saloons owned by the brewers – not gin or whiskey.

What destroyed the Wets was that brewers of German origin funded pro-German organizations such as the German-American Alliance. This characterized Prohibition as a stand against 'German manners and customs and the joviality of the German people'. When America joined in the First World War against Germany the alliance was ordered to disband. The brewers tried to buy up newspapers to fight Prohibition but were exposed as plotting to stop America entering the war on the Allied side.

The historian Andrew Sinclair has aptly summed up the Prohibition movement:

> Pabst and Busch were German therefore beer was unpatriotic. Liquor stopped American soldiers from firing straight therefore liquor was a total evil. Brewing used up 11 million loaves of barley a day which could have fed the starving Allies, therefore the consumption of alcohol was treason. Pretzels were German in name therefore to defend Old Glory they were banned from the saloons of Cincinnati. Seven years after the war a Pennsylvania doctor was still suggesting the name of German measles be changed to victory or liberty measles.[3]

In 1917, overcome with war hysteria, Congress passed the 18th Amendment to the Constitution: the Senate by sixty-five votes to twenty and the House by 282 to 128. For Prohibition to be binding on the entire republic thirty-six state legislatures would now have to support the amendment. The wet, big-city states could have blocked it but they dried out and forty-five states voted for Prohibition in sixteen months. In 1919 Andrew Volstead, an obscure congressman from Minnesota, sponsored the law enforcing the amendment. Prohibition began on 16 January 1920. The Drys had won.

Or had they? The rich had already bought their way out by hoarding huge stocks of drink. The Yale Club laid down fourteen years' supply (thus outlasting Prohibition by forty days). In the weeks before the law came into forces Christmas and New Year revelries became wakes for liquor itself. Prohibition's tragic side-effects appeared before it began, as hundreds of carefree drinkers died from whiskey made from wood alcohol.

The 18th Amendment and the Volstead Act were both full of loopholes. The manufacture, sale and transportation of intoxicating liquors, their import and export, were all prohibited but buying and drinking the stuff were not. Liquor itself was not banned nor was the use of home-brewing or wine-making equipment. Making wine, beer and cider at home was still legal. The term 'intoxicating' proved indefinable in the courts. 'Alcoholic' might have been less ambiguous. Near beer remained legal but had to be made from real beer with the alcohol extracted. That extract was sure to find its way back into real but 'bootleg' beer.[4]

Also exempt was industrial alcohol which bootleggers easily acquired to make spirits. Prohibition agents retaliated by adding undrinkable, poisonous denaturants such as iodine and sulphuric acid to the alcohol. The bootleggers simply added more flavouring and sold the lethal mixture to a gullible public. Thousands died.

Medicinal alcohol was also exempt. Doctors made $40 million a year signing prescriptions for whiskey. The same went for sacramental wine. Sales boomed, giving the impression that Prohibition coincided with a miraculous upsurge in religious observance.

The law was also confounded by confused and corrupt application. Many states had laws in conflict with the Volstead Act. Michigan sentenced a mother of ten children to life imprisonment on her fourth conviction for possessing alcohol. According to federal law she had not even committed a crime. If all these laws had been strictly enforced the courts would have been overwhelmed. Most charges were thrown out on technicalities, some genuine but most conjured up by corrupt judges. If a federal Prohibition agent was zealous he would be fired or transferred for upsetting local politicians. If he was corrupt he might be fired by Washington.

The agent's hapless predicament must have made him profoundly cynical. His job was thankless and dangerous. Agents were often killed but they also had a habit of killing innocent mothers and children in shoot-outs with bootleggers. Anti-Prohibitionists ensured such deaths were widely reported, bringing hatred down on all agents. Working for low pay, they were more likely to become corrupt than risk their lives enforcing an unpopular law. President Hoover estimated that 250,000 agents would have been needed to enforce it properly. Even at its height the Prohibition Bureau employed only 2300 agents nationwide. Agent turnover was 100 per cent every three years. Meanwhile in each state the job of director of prohibition provided limitless opportunities for graft. Even top Washington officials were taking kickbacks from bootleggers who soon became so rich that they could buy anybody who had a price.

The business knew no frontiers as Americans soon tired of home-brewed beer and rotgut spirits. They wanted the real thing. 'Rum-runners' stepped in to supply Scotch whisky, London gin, Jamaican rum, French champagne and cognac. Ocean-going ships would anchor just outside America's 12-mile limit, on 'Rum Row', and home-grown gangsters would use speedboats to run the 'rum' ashore. The US coastguard was predominantly honest. It arrested thousands of smugglers and confiscated their ships but the task was overwhelming. America's immense coastline provided many 'rum points' where drink could be landed without fear of detection. Ports in Cuba and the Bahamas flourished on re-exporting spirits to Florida, only a day's sail away. At first most of the liquor was American rye and bourbon, shipped out of the USA before Prohibition. Supplies were soon exhausted and Nassau's huge warehouses were stocked up with millions of gallons of Scotch.

The Canadian border presented an even worse problem. Canada aped America with its own form of Prohibition but liquor exports remained legal. In Windsor, just across the river from Detroit, breweries and distilleries boomed. Most of their output was smuggled into the USA across the Great Lakes. Canada banned exports to America but instead the manufacturers filled in a form saying the beer or whiskey was bound for Cuba or the French islands of St Pierre and Miquelon. Canadian customs men asked no questions and wry headlines in local newspapers reported that barges had broken all records by sailing to Cuba and back twice in one day – a total of 10,000 miles! As everybody knew, they were simply ferrying the liquor over to Detroit. Americans were consuming a Niagara of Seagram's and a few coastguard patrols did little to stop them.

Within a decade the lobby for repealing Prohibition became impossible to ignore. It consisted partly of avenging American brewers and distillers, lusting for lost profits. They had never given up the fight, whereas the groups which had coerced and blackmailed politicians into passing Prohibition basked idly in victory, naively assuming the law alone would command obedience. The lobbyists were boosted by a largely emotional response to the mass unemployment which followed the Wall Street crash. Certainly repeal would bring back many legitimate jobs, but that argument would have counted for little if Prohibition had achieved its goal of extinguishing drinking and drunks.

In fact Prohibition worsened America's drinking habits. Many bibbers switched from beer, whose qualities home-brewers could not match, to hard liquor with the colour and flavour of genuine spirits. Such spirits only resembled the real thing because of poisonous additives. The deaths they caused argued eloquently for the return of legal distilling.

Even some temperance leaders had come to doubt the role of law in curbing private vices. Rufus Lusk of the Crusaders lamented the rise of neat gin, formerly known as a 'nigger drink', at society dinner tables. He attributed the cocktail craze to the scarcity of good wine. 'It is natural that the country should have turned to strong drink. It is easier to handle and gets quicker action.'

Bay rum was the worst evil. Thousands drank this 'canned heat'. Others extracted it through a handkerchief. So many people were crippled for life by drinking adulterated Jamaica ginger that they formed a pressure group to get damages from the government.

'Where do people drink today?' Lusk wailed. 'Practically everywhere. . . . In New York there is a beer saloon on 51st Street where anyone may walk in and buy potent and potable beer for 25 c. a stein. Ten waiters work at a furious pace to serve the thirsty customers. . . . The high-class speakeasies as represented by the New York nightclubs have provided more sumptuous bars than were ever known in the days of legalized liquor.'

Before Prohibition people rarely served hard liquor at home or in their office but now almost everyone had a liquor closet. Drinking in hotel rooms became so bad that hoteliers built in bottle-openers to protect their furniture. Lusk was horrified at the increase in drinking by young people: 'Hip flasks flourish at dances, picnics and excursions.' One morning a wealthy Cleveland businessman made a shocking discovery in his daughter's car: 'He opened the door and was amazed to find a bottle of liquor and a contraceptive device. He told her good mother what he had discovered and at the breakfast table they asked the girl bluntly if she was drinking liquor and she said, "Why, Daddy, don't be so old-fashioned." '

Summing up the impact of Prohibition Lusk wrote, 'People are drinking different stuff under different conditions but they are drinking as much alcohol as they ever did.'

On 5 December 1933 Utah became the thirty-sixth state to ratify the 21st Amendment. America was wet again, but in fourteen years Prohibition had wrought appalling social damage. It had criminalized a $2 billion business and handed it to gangsters. Organized crime's road to riches was paved with the good intentions of the temperance movement. That was bad enough. Far worse, this gift of boundless wealth would revolutionize organized crime, turning it into an indestructible feature of American life. Gangster syndicates would become the nation's Fifth Estate. Prohibition was the making of the mob.

8

Al Capone – Public Enemy, Public Servant

Immigrant Italian families across America supplemented their meagre income throughout Prohibition by making wine and selling it to bootleggers. The business could become nasty. Vincent Piersante, who later became a legendary anti-Mafia fighter in Detroit, had a frightening experience as a child.

'I was raised on a dairy farm just outside of Pittsburgh, Pennsylvania. One evening when I was about 6 years old I was sitting on the porch swing and I saw our barn, that housed sixteen dairy cows, was ablaze. I ran into the house and told my father but the whole thing was a loss. All the cows were destroyed. It was years later before I discovered that the barn had been burned down by some people who had attempted to get my father involved in the liquor business . . . they wanted to use his milk wagons – pulled by horses – to deliver moonshine whiskey. He resisted and this was a means of telling him they didn't appreciate his resistance.'

On Detroit's East Side, as in Little Italys all over America, alky-cooking was big business. Piersante was open-mouthed. 'There were bootleggers on almost every block. They made it in their own homes and garages and even built underground conduits under the street from one barn (as we called garages in those days) to another across the street. The trucks and wagons would regularly come to pick up the whiskey in 5-gallon cans. Occasionally there would be a police raid. They would go into the barns and throw the cans of moonshine out into the alley and break them open and let it spill on the ground. Then everybody in the neighbourhood would come running around with cups and pans and pick some of the moonshine up and run back home.'

In such communities the top bootlegger was a man of power who commanded respect, especially if he belonged to the Mafia. On Detroit's East Side the position was held by the notorious Santo Perrone: 'He was . . . our most prominent neighbour, the neighbour that everybody had most respect for, and awe and fear. He was also the neighbour who was best with the kids. . . . Occasionally he would use us to help him open the garage door so that the whiskey trucks could drive out quickly. Then we would close the doors and go back to his house and get our reward which was only appreciation, a pat on the head and something like, "That's a good boy!"

'You knew one thing when that happened to you: you had been touched by power. You were only 10, 11 or 12 years old but the reason you knew is because you noticed how your adults, your own father, mother, uncles, reacted to this individual when they saw him on the street. They would practically come to attention, bow slightly, and address him by his surname. It was always very formal. At the same time our parents would tell us to stay away from that end of the block: "Don't hang around there, those people are not the kind of people we want you to associate with," but you couldn't help it. They were there, just a block away.

'Years later, after I became a police officer, I found out that this same individual was a power in organized crime, in what we call the Mafia.'

All the ethnic communities contained such bootleggers; they were not all in the Mafia. Indeed, most of them were not even Italian. (The term itself was already 300 years old. America's first bootleggers were English colonists in the 1630s who smuggled bottles of spirits to Red Indians in the legs of their high boots.) Nevertheless, the one man who will forever epitomize both bootlegging and Prohibition was a twentieth-century Italian-American: Al Capone.

'All I've ever done is to supply a public demand. Laugh this off: when the United States went more or less dry there were 7000 saloons in Chicago, and the town and its suburbs spent something like $70 million a year for beer and liquor. And it votes wet 5 to 7. Well, you can't cure a thirst by law.'

Al Capone became a legend because he exploited an extraordinary series of coincidences. He was at the height of his physical and mental powers when America backed Prohibition, a law which many of his fellow-citizens found laughable, offensive and without moral foundation. Prohibition created an underground economy which Capone above all others was able to organize. He was the most ruthless of a horde of immigrant or second-generation American criminals whose race-memory of oppression in their homelands elevated law-breaking to a duty. Capone was lucky to move to Chicago, America's most corrupt city. He also seized power in the decade when three inventions revolutionized crime in America: the motor-car, the telephone and the Thompson sub-machine-gun.

In Chicago I talked with some of Al Capone's close relatives and friends old enough to recall his early days. He was not the gangster portrayed in the movies. He spoke without a trace of an Italian accent. He was born in Brooklyn in 1899, the fourth child of Gabriel and Teresa Caponi, immigrants who had come over from Naples six years before. As a teenager Alphonse fell under the influence of John Torrio, then a leader of the murderous Five Points street gang.[1] It was with the Five Pointers that Al gained his basic training, not with the Mafia or any other secret society. As a Neapolitan he could not then have joined the Mafia which was still wholly Sicilian, not did he belong to the Neapolitan Camorra. Indeed Capone never belonged to any secret criminal organization.

Capone hated Sicilians. He first encountered them when his father, a barber, was the victim of Black Hand extortion. Al found out the Black Handers were two Sicilians and shot them dead. Summoned to Chicago in 1919, Al was well able to staff Torrio's move into bootlegging. He soon called his brother Ralph and his cousins, the Fischetti brothers, to follow him from New York and increase the strength of Torrio's army. The relatively gentle era of gambler-gangsters was over. The Prohibition wars would be fought by violent men for whom committing murder was part of the job and being murdered was an occupational hazard.

As soon as America went 'dry' gangs sprang up all over Chicago and every other city to meet a bottomless demand for liquor. At first there was so much business that the gangs concentrated on the market rather than each other. Chicago drinkers were soon being supplied by a dozen big gangs, each with its own territory. Only two were Italian. Most were Irish and one was made up of all-American hoodlums. In time racial distinctions became unimportant as criminals with matching skills united and business sense dictated the merger of small independent operations.

From the start John Torrio was Chicago's most powerful bootlegger for he already led the strongest organized-crime syndicate in the city, the fruit of years working for Colosimo in the Levee. Torrio soon joined forces with the Irish Druggan–Lake gang who controlled part of the inner West Side but his smartest move was to go into partnership with Joseph Stenson, the black sheep of Chicago's leading brewing family. The Stensons were rich and respected. As Prohibition began Stenson outwardly converted his breweries to producing near beer; in fact they were brewing real beer for John Torrio. In 1924 the *Chicago Tribune* claimed Torrio and Stenson had piled up profits of $50 million in just four years. The *Daily News* branded them: 'joint rulers of the underworld, the two kings of crime'.

On Chicago's North Side the strongest operator was Dion O'Banion, known as Dean, the son of an Irish immigrant plasterer. He had started work as a newsboy, a job which bred some of America's leading gangsters. Around 1900 William Randolph Hearst resolved to establish newspapers in cities where competition was already stiff. Elmer Gertz, a Chicago criminal defence lawyer, remembers how hoodlums would kill each other to keep rival papers off the news-stands. 'There were pitched battles, newspapers destroyed, and newsboys hurt. The very same men who were active in the newspaper wars, people like Dean O'Banion, were the ideal recruits for the bootleg era. They had the training.' O'Banion had a brief career as a safe cracker, teaming up with two Polish Catholics deceptively named Hymie Weiss and George 'Bugs' Moran. All three proved more capable as bootleggers specializing in importing whiskey from Canada.

O'Banion combined his love of religion and flowers in a florist's shop opposite the Holy Name Cathedral on North State Street. Business merged with pleasure whenever floral tributes were required for a gangland funeral. He had been an altar boy at the cathedral, as had Jack McPhaul who later became a reporter for Hearst's *Herald Examiner*. 'The newsboy–Horatio Alger type and the good boy who faithfully goes to church are part of the American success story, the man who rises to wealth in business and industry. Dean had that start in life but he took a different path. You might call him the second most successful bootlegger in Chicago and that was a multi-million-dollar industry, so in terms of dollars this ex-altar boy and newsboy was an American success story.'

On Chicago's Sicilian West Side bootlegging was dominated by 'the terrible Gennas', six brothers from Marsala where wine has been made since Roman times. They brought the tradition to the New World in 1920 when they acquired a licence to sell industrial alcohol. Most of this went into making whiskey and other spirits. Demand was so great that they paid their impoverished countrymen to cook 'alky' in their homes. For $15 a day a denizen of Little Italy just had to keep a fire burning under a still and gently stir and skim. From time to time a still would explode, killing the operator or his family, but running that risk was better than working as a labourer or starving from no work at all.

In Sicilian neighbourhoods the law of the Gennas was enforced by John Scalise and Albert Anselmi. Also from Marsala this ferocious pair put the 'fluence' on victims by greasing their bullets with garlic. Anyone not killed outright was supposed to expire from garlic-induced gangrene. Few of their targets lived long enough to disprove the theory. In 1925 they shot two policemen dead at point-blank range. Tried for murder they seemed certain to hang but were cleared when the jury accepted that they were only defending themselves against unwarranted police aggression.

Like all other gang bosses the Gennas ruled their patch by owning politicians and police. A lawyer once argued their innocence on the grounds that they had been able to operate only with the connivance of local officials. 'For six years the Genna brothers maintained a barter house for moonshine alcohol, as openly and notoriously, as public as the greatest department store on State Street. And not a drop could have been sold unless it was done on the open permission of the law-enforcing agencies of Chicago. The Gennas became mighty men and influential. Three hundred policemen crossed the threshold of their Taylor Street shop every month. . . . They were not afraid of policemen. Why should they be?'

The Gennas sold spirits made of home-cooked mash blended with flavours and colouring, achieving instantly what took years in genuine whiskey. In went creosote, coal-tar dyes, fusel oil and wood alcohol which could kill the drinker in less than an hour.

Herman Bundesen, Chicago's commissioner of health in the early 1920s, branded the Gennas and their rivals, 'Distillers and Distributors of Death Unlimited'.

In 1923, with Chicago's liquor market overflowing, the Prohibition war started in earnest. From the South Side the Irish O'Donnell gang hijacked Torrio's beer trucks and smashed up six of his speakeasies. Torrio and his allies, the Saltis–McErlane gang, struck back by killing several O'Donnell drivers. In 1924 the war spread to the North Side where Dean O'Banion upset Torrio and Capone's empire by undercutting their prices. He also took on the Gennas by hijacking their trucks. 'To hell with them Sicilians,' he proclaimed to reporters.

He spoke too soon — he had made too many enemies. On 10 November 1924 three men came into his shop as he was clipping chrysanthemums. O'Banion thought they had come to order flowers for a prominent Italian's funeral. As he put out his arm to shake their hands they shot him dead. No one was ever charged with his murder, a routine procedure that has been upheld for a thousand Chicago gang killings since.

His obsequies befitted so pious and floral a gangster. In an Italian funeral parlour his cadaver was described in the press as 'lying in state'. The embalmer had worked wonders on the bullet holes in his throat and cheeks. After three days on view he was placed in a $10,000 casket brought all the way from Pennsylvania. Another $10,000 was spent on flowers, including one basket from Al Capone. Thousands of mourners lined the streets as the cortège travelled to Mount Carmel cemetery. The cardinal archbishop banned the dead man from consecrated ground but within five months Mrs O'Banion had him reinterred in holy ground.

One newspaper summed it up as the day when 'The elite of the gun world gave O'Banion a magnificent funeral, a testimony of the leadership he had attained in the realm where gunplay makes millionaires.' Hymie Weiss was said to have 'cried as a woman might'. O'Banion's most violent lieutenant, Weiss was already plotting revenge. He invented the method of death in which the victim sits in the front passenger seat of a car with his assassin directly behind him. He is then shot in the back of the head. After such a murder Weiss chuckled that his victim had been 'taken for a ride', coining a catch-phrase for generations of crime reporters and screenwriters.

Weiss knew Capone had ordered O'Banion's murder. On 12 January 1925 he tried to machine-gun him to death. (Capone's allies, Joe Saltis and Frank McErlane had introduced the Thompson sub-machine-gun to Chicago in 1923.) Al survived but twelve days later John Torrio was wounded in an attack by O'Banion's other henchman, Bugs Moran. A boy saw the shooting and identified Moran. Torrio also recognized his attacker but refused to name him. Moran was held for three days but never tried. The 'fix' had gone in. The incorruptible police captain, John Stege, lamented, 'You can figure out gangdom's murders with a pencil and paper but never with a judge and jury.'

Torrio recovered from his wounds but was jailed for operating an illegal brewery. On his release in October 1925 he announced that he was quitting Chicago because it was too violent. At 48 he had lost his nerve. He went to Italy for a while but returned to New York, surviving until 1957. He died in a Brooklyn barber's shop where he was hit not by the customary bullets but by a coronary.

The demise of the terrible Gennas also occurred in 1925. Three of the brothers were murdered in separate battles with Bugs Moran, the police and with other Sicilian hoodlums. The surviving Gennas left town. Capone, who had played no obvious part in their downfall, took over their territory. He now had no serious challengers as Chicago's leading Italian gangster.

His rise coincided with a savage increase in Chicago's gangland murders. In the 1910s underworld slayings numbered some twenty a year, mostly Black Hand killings. The number rose to thirty-seven in 1922, fifty two in 1923 and to an all-time peak of seventy-five in 1926. It stayed above forty until 1933, the year Prohibition ended. While it had lasted there had been more than 705 mob killings. Perpetrators were tried and convicted for only seven of these murders – less than 1 per cent. By 1926 such ruthless culling had reduced Chicago's once numerous gangs into two main armies. On one side were the remnants of O'Banion's mob, led by Hymie Weiss and Bugs Moran, allied with German, Polish and Jewish gangs. They dominated the North Side. On the other side was Capone who now controlled most of the Italian and Sicilian factions. His domain was even greater: the South Side and the western suburbs.

On 11 October 1926 Weiss was machine-gunned to death on the steps of Holy Name Cathedral. Only Moran was left to fight Capone. Al now felt invulnerable as Chicago's crime overlord so he decided to act the statesman. On 21 October he dominated a meeting of the city's gang bosses which agreed on the peaceful division of territory. Henceforth there would be no more slaughter. For two months gang murders almost ceased. There were some fraternal disputes – Capone could not stop Sicilians killing each other – but he showed he could impose a Pax Caponiana.

His power was based partly on his own surgical use of violence and partly on the machine he inherited from John Torrio. A master manipulator of politicians Torrio had kept up Colosimo's connection with the First Ward Democratic aldermen, Kenna and Coughlin. At the same time he also supported Big Bill Thompson, Chicago's Republican mayor from 1915 to 1923. Thompson derided Prohibition by proclaiming he was as 'wet as the Atlantic Ocean'. His big favour for the gangsters was to fulfil his promise of a wide-open town. He abolished the Morals Squad of the Chicago police and, in effect, licensed vice. This led to his defeat in 1923 by a reform Democrat, William Dever, who targeted Torrio and Capone. Torrio, anticipating such adversity well in advance, had taken over self-governing townships just outside Chicago like Burnham, a mile square, south of the city. Its 'boy mayor', John Patton, had been elected at the age of 19 when he had already run a saloon for five years. He gave Burnham to Torrio who set up dozens of brothels and gambling houses catering mainly for local steel workers.

Another Torrio village was Posen. Its claim to fame was the Roamer Inn, a brothel run by the brothers Harry and Alma Guzik. In 1921 they were convicted of selling a country girl into white slavery. She had been lured there with the offer of work as a hotel maid. In 1923 they were pardoned by Illinois govenor Len Small. In three years Small pardoned or paroled 1000 criminals, making him the most corrupt public official in the history of American organized crime. The *Chicago Tribune* estimated that 40 per cent of the freed men went to work for Torrio. By 1922 Torrio controlled six suburban townships. When Dever became mayor Torrio and Capone simply moved their most lucrative business out of his reach to the south-western suburb of Cicero.

Cicero looks small on the map next to Chicago, but in 1923 it was the fifth largest city in Illinois with 70,000 inhabitants, mostly immigrants from Bohemia. It had long been corrupt but in 1924, while Torrio was touring Europe, Capone transformed it into the vice capital of greater Chicago: 161 wide-open saloons mostly supplied by Torrio's breweries, dozens of gambling houses and a craven political hierarchy. Election day in Cicero in 1924 fell on 1 April. Capone made a deal with the incumbent town president and imported 200 thugs to beat up his Democratic opponents. Skulls were broken, throats slashed and one man was killed. More than 100 Chicago policemen were brought in to quell the riots. At dusk Al Capone, his brother Frank and cousin Charlie Fischetti had a gunfight with the law. Al escaped, Charlie was arrested but Frank was shot dead.

Frank Capone was given a statesman's funeral, attended by many of Chicago's most notable bootleggers. Al mourned his loss but at least his man had retained Cicero with an enormous victory. One month later Capone and Torrio launched a grand gambling house, the Hawthorne Smoke Shop, and in November Eddie Tancl, their only opponent in Cicero, was slain. Cicero now belonged to Capone.

State's Attorney Robert Crowe now vowed to crush vice in Cook County, which contained Chicago and all the townships controlled by Torrio and Capone: 'Cook County is going to be dry and moral for the next four years. . . . it is the end for liquor, beer and vice." But his vow fell flat when his chief assistant, William McSwiggin, was killed in a gangland shoot-out. Only 26 years old, McSwiggin had won the reputation of a hanging prosecutor, sending seven murderers to the gallows. None of them were gangsters. They always escaped his noose, notably Scalise and Anselmi, the hit men he had prosecuted for murdering two policemen. McSwiggin spent a lot of time with gangsters on the hoary excuse that he was gathering information. Even so it was strange that on 27 April 1926 he went out for a night's drinking in Cicero with two men he had just tried for Tancl's murder and had sworn to hang.

One was Myles O'Donnell, of the notorious West Side O'Donnell brothers. Once allies of Capone, they were now shipping beer into his Cicero territory and boasting about it. That night Capone's followers ambushed Myles, his brother Klondike and two other men as they staggered out of a speakeasy with McSwiggin. The brothers survived but their two cronies and McSwiggin were killed.

Public outrage led to five grand jury investigations, each inconclusive. Capone was a suspect but when interviewed by a newspaperman he upset the judicial applecart by talking about 'my friend, Bill McSwiggin. . . . Of course I didn't kill him. I liked the kid. Only the day before he was up to my place and I gave him a bottle of Scotch for his old man. . . . I paid McSwiggin. I paid him plenty and I got what I was paying for.'

By 1926 Al Capone was both feared and hailed as Chicago's gangland boss. His turnover was put at $100 million a year, $30 million of which went on graft to police, judges and politicians. He was the most powerful man in the city. In Capone the American gangster had come of age. As reporter Jack McPhaul says: 'Many of the gangsters started the Prohibition era as bullies for politicians but they made such tremendous sums of money that they were far richer than politicians and so became the bosses of men they once served as footpads.'

Capone now wanted to enjoy his wealth outside Chicago, especially with the uproar over McSwiggin's death and rumours that his own life was in more than usual danger. He soon found he was not particularly welcome elsewhere. In December 1927 he was thrown out of Los Angeles. He turned up in Miami where he bought a luxurious home on Palm Island. Straight citizens tried to oust him but he survived the controversy to become a regular visitor.

Back in Chicago he devoted some efforts to long-overdue good works. One of his friends was a rising young lawyer named Roland Libonati. Born in America, Libonati served as an army officer in the First World War. During Prohibition he became a defence lawyer. He was later elected US congressman for an area including the First Ward and served in Washington for sixteen years. He sternly denies the frequent accusation that he was a front man for organized crime.

Libonati found a compassionate side to Al Capone. In 1929 he saw him give $10,000 to Pennsylvania's striking miners. In 1930 Capone made his own contribution to fighting the Depression by opening seven soup kitchens in Chicago for down-and-outs. His personal donation was almost $2 million. One newsreel showed hundreds of derelicts enjoying Al's charity. Among those who spoke of their gratitude were two sharply dressed young men whose efforts to look needy were unconvincing. With the benefit of fifty years' hindsight they look more like members of Capone's youth guard destined for a great career in the Chicago mob.

Libonati recalls a donation by Capone of $7500 to repair a church roof, damaged by fire. He also claims that Capone even had a streak of morality when it came to vice. 'In his first job in Chicago he was assigned to 2222 South Dearborn Street. The Four Deuces it was called; it was a house of assignation. There was a complaint made by the pimps who had girls in this place that they were running away. Mr Capone, they said, was putting $100 bills under their plates, either at breakfast, lunch or dinner, and they were running away. He was very much against prostitution. He had married Mae, a wonderful person, and loved her and was a one-man person with womanhood was noted for that.' According to Libonati Capone's greatest service for the Italian people of Chicago was to end extortion by Black Handers. He told them that they weren't going to shake people down any more and he got his way. Capone sent for them and he laid down the law that they were all through, that they would have to go to work. One person said to him, "You have your racket, I have mine."

'Capone said, "Is that the way you feel about it?"

'He said "Yes."

'Nobody knows what happened to this fellow. Some claim he went to Utica, New York. Some claim he left for Italy. Nobody knew. But everybody knows that Capone's statements were always treated with great respect.'

In the 1920s Libonati was told how Capone had risen above every other gangster in Chicago. 'I asked one of his right-hand men how they happened to pick Capone as a leader and he said to me, "He doesn't love money; a man who doesn't love money you can trust." And he was right. . . . Any violence in the underworld only happens when you cheat somebody out of what is his, and then you have trouble.'

Capone ploughed most of the money back into the business, says Libonati. 'The cost of operation was tremendous. Just think of all the payoffs necessary to stay in an illegitimate business run in the open. Money to him was purely a method of staying in business, not a method of accumulating wealth.'

What of Capone's reputation as a murderer? I asked Libonati.

'Well, murder. Murder of who? Murder of those that transgressed in the bootleggers' policy of "You take this area, I take that area. You come over here and try to take my area and I have to prevent you from doing it." All of those murders were competitive murders between themselves. Not respectability. Not persons who were involved in legal pursuits. It was the bootleggers' competitive business arrangements which caused the murders.'

But what about bootlegging itself? Surely Capone was criminally involved?

'Most Americans did not consider a bootlegger as violating the law because he served the public what it desired . . . the average person even to this day doesn't consider violations of the Prohibition law violations at all. . . . Now Capone never robbed anybody on the streets, he never took advantage of anybody by selling them liquor that wasn't the real McCoy. He handled the best. He bought all his whiskies from England and Canada. People would go into the emporiums and ask for Al Capone's whiskey because no one dare refill those bottles. He had testers going round to see if anybody had refilled them. He said that if a man buys a drink, you ought to give him the right kind of a drink or get out of the business.'

Libonati's friendship with Capone brought him a lot of criticism. In 1931 at a Chicago baseball game Al Capone was photographed shaking hands with the Cubs' catcher, Gabby Harnett. That alone made the picture front-page news but also prominent in the shot, sitting with Al, was state congressman Roland Libonati.

Libonati claims: 'Capone called me down to talk to his son who wanted to become a lawyer. I went down there and he was surrounded by his friends; some were political.' When a photographer came up, 'All of his political friends left! I stayed there. It was the best thing I ever did for him and later on in life, when I ran out to him all the time, he had a great respect for me. And he had a lot of power too which he didn't use against me.'

The photographer was Tony Berardi. He saw Capone as far from benign. 'I felt that he and his mob hurt 500,000 Italian people who lived in the Chicago area. They were hard-working, honest people but folk with other ancestry thought we were all a bunch of gangsters. If I went somewhere and said, "My name is Tony Berardi," people thought I was a member of the Capone mob. I felt very bad about that and I still do.

'Quite a few people idolized the bum and I used to get so mad and say, "How could you idolize a bum like that? He hurt his father, he hurt you, he hurt your mother, he hurt every Italian that lived in Chicago and throughout the country. He was national. Hell! he corrupted congressmen, he corrupted every politician he could possibly corrupt."

'Later he became a sort of Robin Hood. Many kids loved him. I enjoyed photographing the guy. I enjoyed meeting him. But I didn't like him. I hated his guts.'

Capone was a kind of Italian-American success story. He may have shamed law-abiding Italians but his crimes were condoned, partly because he and his kind were major employers in an otherwise job-starved immigrant community. In Italian areas alky-cooking became a major source of employment and stimulated many offshoot industries. When there was a move to repeal Prohibition, Italians in Chicago protested with the slogan, 'No Vice, No Work'.

Bud Freeman, the jazz saxophonist, used to go round Chicago with Joe Marsala, another tenor player, who grew up in an Italian neighbourhood. 'In the Black Hand district poor Italian families competed with one another in the wine business. We used to go out and buy a jug of half a gallon of wine for 25c. That was their living and competition became very, very big. Of course when Capone took power he organized all that and out of a small impecunious business came big business.'

John Landesco, the pioneer sociologist who researched organized crime in Chicago during Prohibition, asked,

Why should bootleggers be outcasts in the opinion of the ignorant, humble, needy, hard-working people around them? They are the successes of the neighbourhood. The struggling, foreign-born peasant woman sees them in their expensive cars and their fur-trimmed overcoats. She hears that they are sending their children to private schools. She hears them called 'beer barons' and 'booze kings'. The word 'booze' has no criminal significance to her but the words 'king' and 'baron' have a most lofty significance. About all she knows is that these richly dressed young men are making or selling something that the Americans want to buy.

Incidentally she hears in gossip with another toil-worn neighbour that Johnny Torrio, 'king' of them all, gave his old mother back home in Italia a villa, with fifteen servants to run it.

Because gangsters always spread a lot of charity around the community, to churches, hospitals and children's homes, they can always count on popular support. 'Thus the whole issue between good and bad government, and good and bad men, is befuddled.'[2]

If Italian immigrants embraced bootlegging with enthusiasm, native Americans were not far behind them, as is clear from the relationship between Italian lawbreakers and the non-Italian ranks of Chicago's police force. Bootleggers were not the only corrupters. Gambling and vice rackets continued as openly as in earlier years. In June 1930 a North Side whoremonger named Jack Zuta was shot to death. Among his papers was a letter from William Freeman, police chief of the suburb of Evanston.

Dear Jack,

I am temporarily in need of four 'C's [$400] for a couple of months. Can you let me have it? The bearer does not know what it is, so put it in an envelope and seal it and address it to me.

Your old pal,

Bill Freeman

P.S. Will let you know the night of the party, so be sure and come.

When this letter was published in Chicago's newspapers Freeman resigned but suffered no other penalty.

Abner Bender joined the Chicago Police Department on 26 October 1922. After thirty days' training he soon saw how the system worked. 'I was first sent to a Polish neighbourhood and the saloon keepers would always welcome you. You couldn't pay for anything. The bottle was there and you were supposed to drink. I didn't drink so I'd take a hatful of cigars, not that I smoked either.'

Officer Bender soon found out he was not meant to shut down the saloons. 'We were just ordinary policemen and if you did anything in the way of enforcement they'd put you on a post where there was nothing but weeds. It was a conspiracy and the higher ups were being taken care of.

'In late 1923 I was put into the Italian neighbourhood of Maxwell Street and Taylor Street, around the stockyard. Every so often they'd clean up the local station and put in a new bunch of policemen. There were so many bootleggers down there. Every other house was a distillery.

'Almost my first night out in that district I was assigned to 12th Street and Halsted. I was going up and down and I backed into a doorway to observe what was going on. A fella dashed up to me and said. "This is for you." He handed me an envelope, I took it and he was gone. I opened it up and there were $75 in it. In those days that was a lot of money so that was probably a payoff intended for somebody else. I never found out who it was for.

'From then on it was nothing but moonshine. If you had a humid or a foggy day you'd just drive up and down the alleys and sniff around and you could smell the stills cooking. There were a few abandoned factories in the neighbourhood and they would put up stills that were two and three storeys high. The detectives would go in and chop them down, but they'd very seldom get any of the operators because as the agents knocked on the front door everybody would go out the back door. So it never stopped.

'In the police nobody took Saturday off because on Saturday, especially if you were assigned to the flivver, the old Ford patrol cars we had with high rubber tyres, you'd just pull up and somebody would come out and throw an envelope on the seat and you'd drive off. That's the way it went in those days.

'The payoff was such a common thing. Believe me, I never went out seeking it. It just came as a matter of course. I tried to do my job. We went out on several raids, made arrests and got convictions but the whole thing was rampant. It was laughable. We even had coloured preachers operating stills. They'd come and go. I guess the Italians got rid of them quick.'

After two years in the Maxwell Street district Bender was assigned to Chicago's mounted police. 'Being on a horse we had nothing to do with bootleggers. The only thing we had to do was if a truck drove up with a load of beer we could tell the guy on the beat. We ran into the high-class bootleggers who floated their whiskey over from Canada, or so they said. They even put watermarks on with Lake Michigan water to make it look really good. They'd ask me for my car keys and when I got in my car to go home there was a case of whiskey almost any time I wanted it. I had the biggest closet full of whiskey you ever saw.

'Sure, I felt I shouldn't be doing this but why be different? If you were different you ended up on some straight post at night. So you just went along with it and took the line of least resistance.'

Humble cops like Bender were, unknowingly and in a roundabout way, employed by Al Capone. Right at the top of Chicago public life Mayor Thompson was on the take. Capone gave him $260,000 when he ran again for mayor in 1927. He was re-elected and became rich far beyond his declared income. When he died a fortune in unaccounted cash was found among his property. There is little doubt who most of the money came from.

Al Capone was Chicago's real police chief in the late 1920s. This was acknowledged in 1928 by Frank Loesch, chairman of that impeccable group of concerned citizens, the Chicago Crime Commission. Loesch was alarmed that the murder and vote theft which had marred Chicago's recent elections should not besmirch the Cook County vote in November. He knew that the only person who could guarantee peace was Capone. He requested an audience which Capone granted at his headquarters in the Lexington Hotel. Loesch later recalled, 'I told Capone I wanted him to keep his damned hands off the election. He said he would not interfere. He kept his word. There was not one act of violence. It was the most orderly election Chicago had had in years.'

Coming from Loesch this was some tribute for he was the first man to brand Capone a 'Public Enemy'. This memorable phrase was invented by a Chicago judge, John Lyle, who realized that the old English common-law offence of vagrancy could be used against notorious gangsters. Lyle reasoned that if corruption in Chicago meant that these men could rarely be convicted of individual crimes, they could at least be held as vagrants who had no lawful explanation for their obvious wealth. In April 1930 the Crime Commission published its original list of public enemies. Public Enemy Number One was Alphonse Capone.

Public Enemy though he was, many people still saw him as a public servant and indeed public benefactor. For years he beguiled Chicago with his flair for publicity, his soup kitchens and acts of kindness. Behind this affable façade, however, Al Capone was the leader not just of a pack of hoodlum bootleggers but of a huge crime combination, the 'Outfit' as it is still known in Chicago.

Under Capone the Outfit took three evolutionary leaps to become the most sophisticated criminal organization in America. Through violence and corruption he achieved the first by eliminating all his major competitors, not just in liquor but in all criminal endeavours. In New York no single gang could establish complete control, so even today the city's rackets are divided among five, often conflicting, Mafia families. In America's second city the mob is monolithic.

The Outfit's second evolutionary leap was into 'legitimate' business. In 1928 Cook County investigators found that ninety-one business associations and labour unions were controlled by racketeers, most of them in the Capone syndicate. They included the Food and Fruit Dealers, the Junk Dealers and Peddlers, the Candy Jobbers, the Newspaper Wagon Drivers, the Building Trade Council, the City Hall Clerks, the Glaziers, the Bakers, the Window Shade Manufacturers, the Barbers, the Soda Pop Peddlers, the Ice Cream Dealers, the Garbage Haulers, the Street Sweepers, the Banquet Organizers, the Clothing Workers, the Musicians, the Safe Movers, the Florists, the Motion Picture Operators, the Undertakers and the Jewish Chicken Dealers!

Perhaps the best contemporary definition of a racketeer appeared in the *Chicago Journal of Commerce* in 1927:

A racketeer may be the boss of a supposedly legitimate business association; he may be a labor union organizer; he may pretend to be one or the other or both; or he may be just a journeyman thug.

Whether he is a gunman who has imposed himself upon some union as its leader or whether he is a business association organizer, his methods are the same; by throwing a few bricks into a few windows, an incidental and perhaps accidental murder, he succeeds in organizing a group of small businessmen into what he calls a protective association. He then proceeds to collect what fees and dues he likes, to impose what fines suit him, regulates prices and hours of work, and in various ways undertakes to boss the outfit to his own profit.

Any merchant who doesn't come in or who comes in and doesn't stay in and continue to pay tribute is bombed, slugged or otherwise intimidated.

The Employers' Association estimated that such extortion cost the city $136 million a year or $45 for each Chicagoan. Capone's syndicate extorted a clear profit of at least $10 million through such rackets in 1928, less than a tenth of its gross revenues but enough to weather the Depression and make the years after the repeal of Prohibition a good deal easier to survive.

Capone's third great contribution to organized crime was to make the mob multi-ethnic. Jews, Irishmen, Germans, Poles: he did not discriminate. In many respects he was an equal opportunity employer, although neither women nor blacks have ever figured on Chicago's 'board of directors'. Much of the Outfit's strength today is based on the strategic use of non-Italians.

Capone even suppressed his own hatred of Sicilians, recognizing that they were worth exploiting for their manpower alone. He made sure he had a say in Chicago's Unione Siciliana. The Unione was formed in New York in the late nineteenth century as a legitimate fraternal society of expatriate Sicilians. Soon it fell into the hands of mobsters such as Ignazio 'Lupo the Wolf' Saietta and Frankie Yale, who turned it into a Mafia front. In Chicago the Unione flourished. By the 1920s it had thirty-eight lodges and some 40,000 members. As a Neapolitan Capone himself could not be a member.

Presidency of the Unione was a much-prized office. With it went much of the profits from Little Italy's alky business. In the early 1920s the presidency was controlled by the Genna brothers but in 1925 two presidents (Angelo Genna and Samoots Amatuna) were murdered. Capone had ordered neither death but he was now free to take control through his nominee Tony Lombardo. In 1928 Lombardo was murdered as was his successor Pasquale Lolardo in 1929. Both were felled by Joey Aiello, an enemy of Capone's. His turn came in 1930, the sixth Unione president to be murdered in nine years. Al Capone replaced Aiello with Phil d'Andrea, a man who must have been surprised to die of natural causes.

Tony Berardi believes Capone 'sold himself to the Sicilians. Like a good salesman he said, "Hey, look we're Italians. Whether you're Sicilian and I'm a Neapolitan, we're all in the business so let's cooperate." ' If Capone used and exploited Sicilians, they also used and exploited him. The genius of a brilliant individual gangster would in time be overtaken by the less spectacular corporate skills of organization men. The Chicago Outfit would evolve in the same way as America's greatest business corporations. That is no coincidence.

9

Voices from Prohibition

Robert De Facci came to Chicago as a child of fair-skinned north Italian stock. He saw that Americans looked down on Italians 'as if they were the scum of the earth'. Even before he had left Italy young De Facci was advised how to deflect this racialism.

'I was told the first thing I should do when I can afford anything in America is to buy American-made clothes so as to take away that "greenhorn" look. Otherwise walking down the street you might attract attention and the other kids will throw rocks at you. So I did this as soon as I could and discarded all those European clothes I came with.'

De Facci became a bootlegger by chance. While he was working as a car salesman a customer asked him if he would like to make a buck in the liquor business. The man assured him it was not dangerous and told him how to rent a place, put in a still and buy the ingredients. Above all he had to get police 'protection'. De Facci established his police connection and made regular payoffs. A friendly lieutenant then handed him on to his connection: Ralph Capone, Al's older brother.

Ralph ordered 200 cans of alcohol at an agreed price and De Facci drove down to his barn south of Chicago to load up. He drove back to Chicago before turning west to meet Capone's people. It was two days before Christmas 1928 and in the bitter cold he jammed the gears, stopping traffic in all directions. A cop told him to move on. De Facci was terrified that the smell of alcohol would get him arrested but fortunately he started the truck just in time. When De Facci arrived at Ralph Capone's place his men said they did not have enough cash to pay the agreed price so he had to take a cheque signed by Ralph. It bounced. De Facci was outraged but, rather than claim the money, he thought it safer to bear the loss. He never did business with Capone again.

His profits as a small independent varied from $1000 to $4000 a week. Despite paying off the police he had to take the occasional raid. 'Of course I was raided. They had to keep up the pretence to save their faces and their jobs. I didn't complain. Once somebody fingered me, I was raided so I had to move the still. I didn't have a truck handy so I asked the police to let me use their patrol wagon to move the still into my next place. They agreed. I paid them, naturally, so everybody was satisfied.'

As a young reporter Jack McPhaul saw alcohol flowing down the throats of the judiciary. 'When the city police arrested a speakeasy operator they would bring him before the municipal judge with some whiskey as evidence. He would either fine the man or dismiss the case. The whiskey was then brought to his chambers, supposedly on its way to be destroyed. But it stayed there and the judge would take a sample bottle and send it to be analyzed. If it wasn't this terrible moonshine that destroyed your eyesight he would keep it, and then reporters and others would go to his chambers during recess at later trials and drink the evidence from previous cases.'

Chicago's chief Prohibition agent was Brice Armstrong. Armstrong used to raid the city's biggest bootleg operations but always had an eye for publicity. 'When he staged a big raid,' says McPhaul, 'he would tell the newspapers. We would go out and photograph him with an axe on the still and then he'd tell me this place made good booze. I used to pick up several cases and bring them back to the office to give to other members of the staff. Then we would write a story of Brice Armstrong, the mighty sleuth, destroying an evil bootleg plant.'

Only one Prohibition agent is remembered today: Eliot Ness. He, alas, has largely been made into a character of fiction. 'Ness was an honest man. That was his claim to fame,' says McPhaul. 'That's why they called him the "Untouchable". But he never fired a shot in anger and nobody ever shot at him. When he and his fellas went to raid a brewery the owners just went out the back door. They weren't going to shoot a federal man, it wasn't worth it. They could start another operation somewhere else. I knew Ness in Chicago and also years later when he was commissioner of public safety in Cleveland. He never lived to see his book published . . . but when the TV people purchased the rights all they kept was the title. In the series he was constantly shooting it out with Capone but in real life he had no dealings with him.'

George Peebles, another photographer, would also get tipped off. Once he learned a farm was to be raided, he got there first and innocently asked the moonshiner what was going on. At that moment the agents' cars kicked up a cloud of dust as they sped down the farmtrack. The moonshiner fled across the prairie, leaving a bemused Peebles to explain himself to the agents. 'Inside the barn were open vats and when the G-Men drained them there were all these rats on the bottom. Very careless beer-making but that's what they were selling.'

In the cities agents used their noses. 'In many raids they'd find nothing so they would go from manhole to manhole on the block and open them and smell the mash going through.' Some of the best alcohol was brewed in a glass factory. 'The building was four storeys high and they used the elevator shaft to take the fumes to the top so no one could smell them. But the mash had to be put into the sewers. It was so strong you could smell it in the basements of people's houses nearby.'

The biggest outlet for bootleg booze was, of course, the speakeasy. Chicago had thousands of speakeasies where crime and respectability were indistinguishable. All moral lines were blurred. It became almost a patriotic duty to drink yourself into oblivion. The city's reporters, never known to abstain, took to Prohibition like ducks to dry land.

Verne Waley was a newspaperman in Chicago in the late 1920s and a connoisseur of illegal saloons. 'We had one speakeasy in the basement of the Board of Education building, believe it or not, a real posh place owned by Mr Capone. You used to go down a dark hall and rap on a steel door. There was a certain signal . . . and a peephole would slide open and the guy would identify you. Inside was a beautiful Gay Nineties bar. The Bourbon was good, the Scotch was excellent and the prices were right, 75 c. a drink.

Elmer Gertz used to go to Nello's. 'You'd go in what seemed to be an ordinary restaurant that served fried chicken and spaghetti. The wine would be served in coffee cups so that if the police raided the place, which was very rare, you'd appear to be drinking coffee, not wine. There were many suburban clubs and restaurants serving fine liquor. They could operate only in cahoots with the police because you didn't have to go through subterranean channels to get there. They were open.'

There was no shame or stigma attached to drinking liquor or being a bootlegger. As Gertz puts it, 'Prohibition's great vice was that it taught America disrespect for the law. It taught many people that the pursuit of crime created very profitable careers, particularly in periods of economic stress. Deeply religious or moral people might have been offended but most people felt that there was nothing wrong, particularly when they knew the President was serving liquor in the White House.'

One group of people whose livelihoods depended on speakeasies were jazz musicians. For fourteen years popular music in America was sponsored and influenced by speakeasy operators who were usually gangsters. Bud Freeman was a high school student when he discovered the devil's music.

'You must understand that back in the twenties jazz was thought to be an immoral music and the only places you could play were run by underworld characters. I used to play in one place in Chicago where a fellow named George Bolton would be standing at the bar. He was the lookout man and whenever a federal agent came anywhere near he gave the sign and they dumped all the booze near a drain. One night he called me over to the bar and he said, "I've been watching you. You play very well but you're very frightened, aren't you?"

'I said, "Yes, I've always had a great fear of underworld people."

'He said, "Well, don't be afraid because they have more respect for you than your own people. They love music and that's the end of it."

'And what he said helped me since these were the places where you were allowed to play this esoteric music called jazz. The music was for dancing, and these people loved it.

'Once I was in East St Louis in a really tough place, a rendezvous for gunmen. They all wore black hats and black coats, collars turned up, all very sinister-looking, guns on either side. I went to audition and the boss said, "What do you think?"

'I said, "I'm not sure I want to work here, I'd like to finish my education and I want to live long enough to do so."

'Whereupon this very tough guy puts his arm around me and said, "Buddy, I don't want you to worry about anybody in this here joint because nobody will hurt you unless he gets paid for it."

'The boss of this club used to get very drunk and at four o'clock in the morning I would have to go with him, and his two guns, in his car at 80 miles an hour to a place where all the underworld characters and show people would hang out. Some "professional" women were there too. One night one of these girls came up and threw her arms around me. This guy was furious and he ran over and said, "Get away from my saxophone player, he's different than us." It broke me up.'

'I went to New York for the first time in 1928. I was playing with a group called the Mound City Blue Blowers at the Hotsy Totsy Club. It was a rendezvous for gunmen with a lot of money such as "Legs" Diamond who was very elegant. He wore a silk hat, a beautiful cloak, white tie and tails, a big white flower and a cane. He always positioned himself at a table so he could be facing the door and study who was going out and coming in. That's the way this man lived all those years. Sure enough one night a gunfight broke out. I dove under the piano. It wasn't the report of the gun that frightened me but the smell of gunpowder. That was the end of that. The club was closed, never to open again.

'One of my old friends was Jim Lanigan, a great bass player, who played in the Friars Society Orchestra at the Friars Inn in Chicago. One night a crazy guy by the name of Two Gun Louis came in and shot up the place. Luckily Jim and the band were upstairs having something to eat at the time but Two Gun Louis put five or six holes into this little tuba sitting on the bandstand. The next night he came back and gave Jim a tremendous amount of money to buy a new bass.

'Gangsters had a line, "Them musicians' noses is clean," meaning they could talk in the open and we would never say anything. We dared not. I used to be afraid that I knew so much. But in all the years I was in Chicago it was almost law and order because they ran the city. I used to walk home by myself at three or four in the morning with no fear. No one ever bothered you. Chicago was a peaceful place to be.'

Always Pay Your Income Tax

Capone welcomed the New Year of 1929 at his beautiful home on Palm Island, Miami. Not yet 30, he was the undisputed boss of the Chicago underworld – except that some people did dispute it. Bugs Moran and his North Siders, true to the tradition of their fallen leaders O'Banion and Weiss, kept on hijacking his liquor trucks. They made an alliance with Al's surviving Sicilian enemies and tried to kill off his henchmen. On 8 January his latest stooge president of the Unione Siciliana was murdered. Moran even dared to move into businesses dominated by Capone: dog racing and dry cleaning. In Florida Capone plotted Moran's end, conspiring daily on the phone with Jake Guzik, his trusted aide in Chicago. On the morning of 14 February he conspicuously kept an appointment with a Miami official who wanted to know how he had paid for his Palm Island home. The meeting gave Al the perfect alibi.

On that St Valentine's Day in Chicago, in the garage of the SMC Cartage Company at 2122 North Clark Street, six of Moran's men were waiting for a truckload of hijacked Canadian whiskey. By gangland standards they were an eminent crowd. Frank and Peter Gusenberg were Moran's top gunmen. In 1926 they had been in the team led by Moran and Weiss that shot up Capone's Hawthorne Inn when Capone himself was lucky to survive. Also at the garage was James Clark, a Sioux Indian who was Moran's brother-in-law; Adam Heyer, his business manager; Al Weinshank, another front man; and Johnny May, a safe cracker. One man who had no apparent business there that day was Dr Richard Schwimmer, an optometrist. He seems to have been a gangland 'groupie' who had happened to drop in. Moran and another gang member were expected but they were late.

At 10.30 Mrs Max Landesman of 2124 North Clark Street heard shots from the garage next door. She ran to a window and saw a man get into a large touring car. From the same house Josephine

Morin saw two men coming out of the garage with their hands up, followed by two armed policemen. They all climbed into a black Cadillac which was driven off by one of the men who, moments before, had appeared to be under arrest. Mrs Landesman ran to the garage but could not open it. She called a neighbour, Clair McAlister, who pushed open the door and saw seven men stretched out on the floor, some streaming with blood. One of them looked at him and said 'What is it?'

Mrs Landesman phoned the police and two carloads of officers soon arrived led by Sergeant Thomas Loftus.[1]

Frank Gusenberg was still conscious. Loftus tried to get him to explain the shooting. He refused. Gusenberg was taken to the Alexian Brothers' Hospital and a doctor came in and pronounced the other six men dead. On the floor were the survivor's fully loaded machine-gun shells and two shotgun shells. Some of the bullets had gone through the dead men and hit the wall.

Loftus followed Frank Gusenberg to the hospital and tried to get him to talk. Again he refused. At 1.30 p.m. he died. True to the underworld code he never revealed his killers.

The press soon arrived at the scene of the massacre. Photographer Tony Berardi captured the scene for posterity. 'The only eye-witness [to the shoot-out] was this poor shepherd dog, scared stiff because so many bullets went off. Then I learned there was a lookout place across the street where people had been watching for a week for Bugs Moran and his gang to enter the building. The lookouts thought Moran was in the place when the massacre occurred, otherwise I'm sure they would have called it off.'

Two detectives were combing the rooming houses opposite. At 2119 Mrs Doody told them she had rented a front room in December to a man called Morrison. He said he was a cab-driver. He left at the end of January but she remembered him as 30 years old, 5 ft 10 in and looking 'like an Italian'. Two men visited him regularly. At the end of January at number 2139 Mrs Arvidson rented rooms to two men who also claimed they were taxi-drivers. One room was at the front on the first floor facing the garage. At midday on 14 February one of the men spoke to another lodger at 2139 as he was going out. 'Isn't it terrible, this murder across the street.' He never returned.

Arriving late Bugs Moran had seen the murderers' Cadillac parked outside the garage. He assumed it was a police patrol car on a raid and retreated to his office. When he was told what had happened he said, 'Only Capone kills like that.'

The police came to the same conclusion. They had to act quickly because two of the killers had worn police uniform and many people believed the first reports that they really were Chicago cops corruptly involved in a hijacking war with Moran. A few days later the Cadillac's sawn-up remains were found in a burnt-out garage, apparently rented by allies of Capone. 'Machine-Gun' Jack McGurn, Capone's most prized killer, was arrested on minimal evidence because the Gusenberg brothers had once machine-gunned him. McGurn had survived only after a long spell in hospital and vowed revenge. He claimed that he was with his girlfriend when the massacre occurred. He was indicted for perjury but married the girl so she could not be forced to testify. Other suspects were John Scalise and a young trigger man called Tony Accardo. The lookouts were said to have been brought in from Detroit. In the end no one was ever tried for the St Valentine's Day massacre and the case is still formally unsolved. Theories abound, but all maintain that Al Capone ordered the slaughter.

Down in Miami Al Capone concluded his interview with the Dade County solicitor and threw a party for a crowd of celebrities who were in town for a world title fight. Sports writers among them nervously asked their host about the massacre. Mischievously Capone blamed Bugs Moran.

Capone had all but wiped out opposition to his crime syndicate. Now he had to deal with problems within. Among his brigade of thugs were John Scalise and Albert Anselmi whom he had inherited from the Genna brothers. Berardi, who photographed them, recalls them as, 'well-dressed, like lawyers, but they were the toughest people. They would walk into a speakeasy which wasn't buying beer from Al, they would break up the barrels and then they would say, "From now on you're buying our booze or you don't stay in business." The speakeasy keeper would always give in.

'They were so tough they decided that Al Capone shouldn't be the boss, *they* should be. Now Al found out about this so on 8 May 1929 he took over a back room in a restaurant in Hammond,

Indiana and invited Scalise and Anselmi and many others. He made a speech praising his guests of honour. Then someone handed him a baseball bat and he said, "I understand you want my job. Well, here it is!" . . . and he clubbed the two of them to death with the baseball bat. There was a third man, Joey Giunta. I don't know how he was involved. But all three bodies were found in the bushes half a mile from the restaurant.'

Capone's brutality now spilled onto Chicagoans that gangsters usually left alone. For some years Capone had corrupted the more venal of Chicago's crime reporters. Some he wholly owned, although their colleagues knew nothing of it. Jake Lingle was the master of underworld information for the *Tribune*. He wasn't a writer but would phone in scoops for other reporters and sub-editors to rewrite. It dawned on them that he lived well above his meagre reporter's wage. After the last edition of the paper had been put to bed, Verne Waley, boxing editor of the *Chicago Evening Post*, would often play poker with Lingle. He noticed Lingle always had a thick roll of $100 and $1000 bills. Lingle claimed to have inherited the money from a rich uncle. He implied that his flash gambling habits helped win the confidence of Al Capone who once confessed to him he had gambled away $7,500,000 in eight years.

On 9 June 1930 Lingle was shot dead in the subway station of the Illinois Central Railroad. When *Tribune* publisher Colonel McCormick heard the news he proclaimed the death would be avenged. Lingle was instantly canonized as a national press martyr and given a spectacular funeral. Yet within days his true links with the underworld emerged. He had died wearing a diamond belt buckle which Capone had given him. He used to go to Florida and enjoy Capone's hospitality on Palm Island. His bank roll came not from his uncle but from Capone, as did the information which had made him Chicago's top crime reporter. Lingle died, it seems, because Capone believed he had double-crossed him.

Capone's reputation for ever more grotesque violence at last forced the federal government to act. In March 1929 Herbert Hoover was inaugurated President of the United States. He was obsessed with Capone. Hoover described Prohibition as the 'noble experiment' and if one man had nobbled that experiment it was

Capone. No sooner was Hoover in office than Capone was jailed, but apparently at his own instigation. By May 1929 he feared that either Moran or friends of Scalise and Anselmi would murder him in revenge. He forewarned a friendly policeman in Philadelphia that he would be passing through that city. He arrived, met the cop and instantly surrendered his revolver. Now he could be jailed for carrying a concealed weapon. So far the ploy had worked. Al looked forward to a few weeks' peace and quiet. To his horror he was imprisoned for a whole year. Soon the county jail recognized his status and he carried on business with little inconvenience. He was unable to buy his way out and, with only a good conduct discount of two months, he was not released until March 1930.

President Hoover, meantime, had ordered the Treasury to put Al in jail for good. The Justice Department's Bureau of Investigation had opted out. Its director, J. Edgar Hoover (who was not related to the President), shunned the task for fear of failure. The Prohibition Bureau was too inept or corrupt. The only agency willing and able was the Treasury's Special Intelligence Unit, led by Elmer Irey. He sent his crack investigator, Frank Wilson, to Chicago to get Capone for not paying his taxes.

Al had never filed tax returns. This was no crime provided he did not earn more than $5000 in any one year. Proving he did was not easy. He rarely put his name on anything that showed he had spent money or owned any assets.

Until 1927 all professional criminals believed they were immune from taxes. Bootlegger Manley Sullivan never filed any returns. His case went as far as the Supreme Court where he argued that income from illegal sources was not taxable because declaring it would be like confessing to a crime. He would thus sacrifice his constitutional rights under the 5th Amendment. The Supreme Court ruled against him, saying the 5th had not been passed so that criminals would have freedom from taxation.

Armed with the Sullivan decision, Wilson and his investigators jailed many Chicago bootleggers for non-payment of taxes. They jailed Capone's immediate deputy, Frank 'The Enforcer' Nitti, for eighteen months for not paying up on $700,000 earned over three years. 'Greasy Thumb' Jack Guzik, Capone's underworld accountant, went down for five years and his brother Sam 'Big Belly' for three. Even Al's brother Ralph was jailed for three years for banking $8 million in five years under false names. Al proved trickier than them all.

The 'T-Men' probed every piece of information about his personal spending. For the years 1926 to 1929 they proved he had ordered over $26,000 worth of furnishings for his homes in Chicago and Miami. He had spent more than $7000 on custom-made clothes, $20,000 on silverware and $39,000 on telephone calls. He had spent $1500 a week on hotels and thrown parties costing $3000 in one night. The investigators came up with evidence of at least $165,000 worth of taxable spending. This alone could have got Capone jailed but, if the American people were to be convinced he was truly a Public Enemy rather than a lovably extravagant Robin Hood, the agents had to go further and prove he had made hundreds of millions through crimes much more serious than tax evasion.

The investigators cracked the case by persuading some of Capone's Cicero gambling employees to talk. He was subsequently charged with non-payment of taxes on income totalling over $1 million from 1925 to 1929. His real gross income was probably more than £100 million each year so the charges were paltry, but they could still put him away for more than thirty years.

In July 1931 his prosecutors agreed that if he pleaded guilty he would go down for no more than two and a half years but the judge was outraged by the deal and rejected it. Capone withdrew his plea and in October a new trial began with Capone contesting the charges. His henchmen bribed the jury but at the last minute another jury was sworn in. Uncontaminated they heard of his extravagances: $135 on a custom-made shirt with a special pistol pocket, $50,000 on improvements to his Miami home, $8000 on thirty diamond belt buckles which Capone gave away to freeloaders like Jake Lingle. His dock foreman in Florida testified Capone had paid him $550 a month. This alone was more than Capone claimed he himself was earning.

Panicking at the last moment Capone's lawyers produced bookmakers who claimed he had lost $327,000 on horse betting in six years. They mistakenly believed that gambling losses could be deducted against income but in fact they could be weighed only against winnings. As Capone had claimed he never won anything the bookmakers' evidence only helped to convict him. On 24 October he was found guilty on all charges. Judge Wilkerson sentenced him to eleven years and fined him $50,000, the heaviest sentence ever imposed for tax evasion. The trial prosecutor thanked the judge and jury, predicting: 'This is the beginning of the end of gangs as Chicago has known them for the last ten years.'

Capone was lodged in Cook County jail until his appeal failed. In May 1932 he was moved to the Federal Penitentiary in Atlanta and in August 1933 he became a founder inmate of Alcatraz prison in San Francisco Bay. He was there for more than five years before being released from Lewisburg in November 1939. When reporters asked Jake Guzik if Capone would now return as boss of Chicago he said bluntly, 'Al is as nutty as a fruitcake.'

Capone's mental deterioration was caused by syphilis, diagnosed soon after his imprisonment in 1931. By 1939 it had reached advanced stage and as soon as he was released he was placed in the care of a leading specialist. Somewhat recovered, he was moved to his Florida home where he lingered on for seven years, surrounded by a loving and devoted family. His brain decayed irreversibly as his condition steadily worsened. Often delirious and abstracted, at last he suffered a brain haemorrhage followed by pneumonia. He died on 25 January 1947, only 48 years old. His body was taken to Chicago where he was buried in Mount Olivet cemetery.

Capone was the criminal anti-hero of his time. Through people like him millions of Americans got the illegal goods and services they wanted. Many admired him for that. Many others lusted for his destruction as proof that good does triumph eventually over evil. No one understood the hypocrisy of it all better than Capone himself: 'I've been made an issue and I'm not complaining. But why don't they go after these bankers who took the savings of thousands of poor people and lost them in bank failures? Isn't it lots worse to take the last few dollars some small family had saved – perhaps to live on while the head of a family is out of a job – than to sell a little beer, a little alky?'

His fall may have appeased President Hoover and some elements of public opinion but it did not halt the advance of organized crime. Indeed Capone's notoriety and love of publicity had only caused problems for the bootlegging and gambling syndicate which now stretched across America. His peers in other cities saw themselves as businessmen and preferred obscurity to headlines. With Al in jail, life became much easier. The heat came off. His ritual sacrifice left the field clear for everyone else as corrupt cops, judges and politicians continued to protect the mob in Chicago and everywhere else.

Unwittingly Capone decoyed the law enforcers into believing crime gangs were based on spectacular bosses rather than on a command structure like that of an army or a corporation. His giant personality also permanently distorted public perceptions about the racial background of America's leading bootleggers. As Mark Haller's study shows,[2] most were not Italians. Of over seventy bootleggers listed by Haller half were Jewish, 25 per cent were mainly Irish or Polish and only 25 per cent were Italian. Most bootleggers in Boston, New York, New Jersey, Philadelphia and Cleveland were Jewish. Only in Detroit, New Orleans and California did the Italians dominate. In Chicago most leading bootleggers were Irish.

Wrongly believing most bootleggers were aliens many WASPs felt Prohibition could have worked if only Mediterranean 'scum' had not overwhelmed the good sense of native Americans. The truth was that all Americans, native and immigrant, urban and rural, contributed to Prohibition's failure. If alky-cookers in the big cities were mainly Sicilians, most country moonshiners were Anglo-Saxons. If Cleveland's 'Jewish navy' imported boatloads of Canadian whiskey most of their consumers were American gentiles. If the spirits which haunted the speakeasies were whisky from Scotland, gin from London and rum from Jamaica, who was drinking them but citizens of the USA?

Prohibition died on 5 December 1933. Many who had clamoured for repeal believed it would put an end to gangsters like Capone. Deprived of bootlegging, criminal organizations would somehow fade away. Yet just as gangs and syndicates did not originate with Prohibition so repeal did not destroy them. Thirteen years spent running an industry worth $2 billion a year, centred on 300,000 speakeasies nationwide, was the making of the mob. Repeal made little difference. Organized crime was now so rich that it no longer needed the liquor business. With its stockpiled profits it could expand its traditional rackets of gambling, loansharking and prostitution and also buy up thousands of legitimate businesses. Legitimate, that is, until the mob took them over.

As for Al Capone, the mob didn't need him either. He was a meteor: only 26 years old when he became boss of Chicago's most powerful crime combine and only 32 when the taxmen destroyed him. The organization he inherited had existed for at least twenty years before he took it over. It would flourish without him.

11

The Outfit, the President and the CIA

On 11 August 1961 the 300-lb, near-nude hulk of 30-year-old William 'Action' Jackson was found stuffed in the boot of a Cadillac abandoned on Chicago's subterranean lower Wacker Drive. The autopsy showed no bullet or stab wounds. Jackson had been tortured and beaten to death. No one was ever charged with his murder.

Years later the FBI discovered that some Chicago mobsters would soon be gathering at a house in Florida to murder a union leader who lived nearby. Agents bugged the house and listened one night as the killers prepared to corner their prey. The mafiosi had a few drinks and began to talk about some of their greatest hits. The Outfit's future boss, Jackie 'the Lackey' Cerone, told his *compares* the do's and don'ts of killing people. He recalled how a black gambling boss he had hit at point-blank range had survived because he had used old ammunition. The conversation then turned to one victim whose attitude had always puzzled them: William 'Action' Jackson.

Jackson had been a 'juice' collector for the Outfit. His job was to stalk Chicago intimidating debtors into paying up. The bosses were sure he had turned informer. They decided he must die but before killing him they wanted him to admit that he had been working for the FBI. They abducted Action and took him to a meat plant where they hung his gross form on a meat hook. They proceeded to crank the hook off the ground and torture Jackson on the genitals with an electrified cattle prod. As he cried out in agony they interrogated him about his non-existent work for the FBI. After three days of horror Jackson died.

To the Mafia hit men Jackson's killing was a duty they had been proud to fulfil. Yet they could never get over the fact that, even as he neared death, he still would not admit he had ever been an informer. That earned their admiration. In their terms Jackson died a 'stand-up guy'.

The syndicate which rules organized crime in Chicago today is the most powerful mob in America. It is also the most violent. This monolithic, multi-ethnic Outfit which Capone welded together in the 1920s still flourishes. But it is not quite the same mob. In the 1940s and 1950s the Capone gang evolved one stage further: it was taken over by a Mafia crime family.

During Prohibition Chicago's Sicilian gangsters were either losers like the Gennas or foot soldiers for Capone. Yet from the time Al went to jail the Outfit has nearly always been led by Sicilians. Capone's successor was Frank 'the Enforcer' Nitti, who had been his front man in the Unione Siciliana. In 1943 Nitti committed suicide and was succeeded by Paul 'the Waiter' Ricca, a Neapolitan like Torrio and Capone. He was soon jailed for ten years for conspiring to extort money from the Hollywood movie industry. The 'fix' went in and after only three years Ricca was released.[1]

The man who arranged the fix was another man of Sicilian parentage, Antonio Accardo, also known as 'Joe Batters'. Accardo had the perfect pedigree. He was a henchman of Capone's and is thought to have carried a sub-machine-gun on the St Valentine's Day Massacre. At 5 ft 9 in and weighing 200 lb he had the build of a gorilla but he had brains too. For liberating Ricca and other top mobsters he was made boss of Chicago, a job he held until 1957 when he left to defend himself on income tax charges. At that time he lived in a grand mansion in one of the city's leafiest suburbs but still claimed he was a humble beer salesman.

His successor was another second-generation Sicilian, Sam 'Momo' Giancana. A womanizing widower aged 49, Giancana suddenly found himself leading America's most powerful mob, an army of 300 'made' mafiosi and many more associates. Overnight he had become 'president' of a huge conglomerate, controlling much of Chicago's 'legitimate' business as well as its conventional crime. He was in supreme charge of all the Mafia's activities west of the Mississippi, including the lion's share of Nevada's gambling rackets. Blessed with the political connections that belong automatically to the Outfit's chosen leader, Momo was now the most powerful man in America's second biggest city.

No one knows more about the Outfit than former FBI special agent William Roemer who spent twenty-three years fighting organized crime in Chicago. At 6 ft 2 in and weighing 220 lb he is a formidable man. Even in retirement he keeps in peak condition. Nothing less might be expected of a heavyweight boxing champion of Notre Dame University and the US Marine Corps, but 'Zip' Roemer adds up to far more than all-American muscle. As a lawyer he helped plan the FBI's strategy against criminals who had been protected for decades by local police and politicians. Not surprisingly they believed themselves to be indestructible – nobody had bothered them since the days of Al Capone.

Roemer began his work on organized crime in 1957. 'I had been in the FBI for seven years when the mob summit was discovered at Apalachin. J. Edgar Hoover was embarrassed because he couldn't explain what those individuals were doing there. He set up a Top Hoodlum Program which in Chicago meant developing background on the city's ten top hoodlums.

'We started by finding out where they lived, who they associated with, where they met. It's been publicly disclosed that the FBI was involved in electronic surveillance at that time. Microphones were installed in most of their meeting places so that by the end of 1959 we were getting to know a lot about the Chicago crime syndicate – the Outfit, the mob, the Mafia, La Cosa Nostra. All these terms mean the same thing.'

The FBI learned that the Outfit's headquarters were in a luxury custom tailorshop called Celano's at 620 North Michigan Avenue on Chicago's smartest shopping street known as the 'Magnificent Mile'. The bug in Celano's yielded staggering information from the day it was planted. 'We found out there was something nobody had ever known about before: the National Commission of organized crime. We knew they must have an Apalachin from time to time, conferences or seminars, but we didn't know it was formalized with individual families represented by their bosses.'

Conversations at Celano's soon revealed that Sam Giancana had just replaced Accardo as Chicago's man on the Commission. 'He was telling Accardo about his first meeting and which members had attended. There were guys like Joe Ida from Philadelphia. We told the Philadelphia FBI about the existence of the Commission and that Ida was their representative. They were flabbergasted. They thought he was a retired old man who was completely inactive.' Day after day Chicago's godfathers gathered at Celano's as if they were the board of directors of a giant corporation. Their main political fixer was Murray Humphreys, a Welsh American.

With listening devices in a dozen haunts the FBI quickly built up an intimate knowledge of life in the Outfit. The agents soon knew more about its activities than many of its 'made' men. 'I would rush into work,' recalls Roemer. 'I could hardly wait to learn what the mob was going to be involved in today. It was like watching a television soap opera. Yesterday that happened, now what's going to happen today? What's the sequel? How are they going to resolve the problem? What are they going to do about it and what can we do to cope with it?'

Most of the talk was about gambling, the life-blood of organized crime. Every bookmaker in Chicago had to split his profits with the mob. 'They worked like accountants . . . making sure they got their 50 per cent. Anyone who didn't pay up or was skimming the cream would get their legs broken. One day every month Humphreys and the others would have a heck of a time going over the sums. They couldn't even work the adding machine but, as crude and rudimentary as their accounting principles might be, they really were the bosses of a big corporation with profits ranking alongside those of IBM and General Motors.'

Occasionally shades of Capone would disturb his successors. They took care of his wife and son with a regular pension. 'This wasn't humanitarian,' says Roemer, 'they did it for all the widows. They even had a fellow whose job was to go around taking care of all dead mobsters' families, making sure they never got the idea that if they needed money they should go to the FBI to get some.' A plea came in from Sonny Capone, Al's son, who was running a restaurant in Florida. It was not doing well so he asked for an advance. Chicago's leaders met to vote on his request. Everyone was in favour except Giancana who said, 'We're not going to send him any money. He's got to live under control.' Because Giancana was boss his vote overruled everyone else's so Humphreys dictated a corporate refusal. The letter was typed up by a tailorshop employee and sent off to the hapless Sonny.

Giancana's dictatorial style convinced the FBI that he was the boss not just in rank but in reality. They researched his past and found that in 1925, when he was only 18, he had been a leader of the 42 Gang. This fraternity of violent young thugs was based in the 'Patch', a largely Italian neighbourhood on Chicago's Near West Side. Giancana's first conviction was for stealing cars and stripping them down. After thirty days in jail he was back on the streets burgling dress shops. In 1926 he took part in a robbery in which a cigar-store assistant was killed. He faced trial for murder but all charges were dropped when the key witness was himself murdered, set up by Giancana.

From then on he sold his skills as an election-day bomber and union goon until 1929 when he was jailed for robbing a clothing store. He spent nearly four years inside and in 1939 he began another three for post-Prohibition bootlegging. When he came out he murdered and bombed his way into controlling Chicago's huge black 'policy' racket.[2] By the late 1940s he was making so much money for the Outfit from all kinds of gambling (policy, bookmaking and illegal casinos) that he was able to buy his way into its upper ranks. His arrival at the top a few years later coincided with the unsolved murders of several old-timers who had stood in his way.

Roemer made Giancana a personal target. 'I knew that he was an animal. . . . He had raped, killed, murdered and tortured. That was the way he became the number one guy. He had "made his bones" by getting involved in what they call the "heavy work" and he was a *master* at the heavy work.'

When Roemer first encountered Giancana they declared war. In 1961 Sam flew into Chicago's O'Hare airport with his latest mistress, Phyllis McGuire. She was one of America's singing sweethearts, the McGuire Sisters. When the lovebirds landed they had no idea that four FBI men were poised to bring Phyllis before a grand jury to testify about her Mafia lover. The agents accosted her and took her away to a room where they served the subpoena. As the Mafia boss burned with outrage he had the unwelcome company of Bill Roemer.

'Giancana was just livid. He became the animal he really was. We were in the public waiting area of the terminal, with a hundred people around, and he tore into me. He called me every obscene name you can think of.

'Now nobody ever called me those kind of names and got away with it . . . but he was a runty little fellow and he wouldn't have been much of a match so I didn't physically assault him, but a big crowd had gathered . . . so I called everybody over.

' "All you people! Come over here! You may just be passing through Chicago. You don't have to live with this scum, this slime right here!" and I pointed to Giancana. . . . "This is the boss of the underworld here in Chicago. You are so lucky you're just passing through. Those of us who live here have to put up with this runty little slime, this piece of garbage."

'And, oh my Lord! nobody ever talked to Giancana like that. . . . He lost his mind. He became hysterical and he told me, "Roemer, this you will never forget. You will rue the day you ever did this . . . You've lit a fire tonight that will never go out." '

Giancana's personal headquarters were in the suburb of Forest Park in the Armory Lounge restaurant. There in the quiet of his private office, secure behind a peephole and a barred door, Sam was at his ease so the place yielded the FBI excellent information when they inevitably bugged it. Alas, in 1962 it was remodelled and Sam moved out to a table near the bar where background noise strained the G-Men's ears.

Judith Exner, another of Sam's beautiful girlfriends, would sit with Sam at that table for hours when the restaurant was closed. 'People were always coming in to see him. They wouldn't speak English – it was always Sicilian – and I would tease him about it. Several times he would say, "You don't want to *know* what we're talking about." I realize now he went to great pains to protect me, by making sure I did not know what was going on.'

If Judith Exner did not understand Sicilian the FBI had agents who did. They had plenty of practice, listening in to live bugs strategically planted all over Chicago. Their legality is a vexed issue. They were authorized by J. Edgar Hoover but not by the courts. In 1961 they were authorized by the new attorney-general, Robert Kennedy, although he later tried to deny it.[3] At the time the FBI could claim reasons of state. Giancana was trying to set up gambling in the Dominican Republic. Had he succeeded he would have had a large income outside the USA, making him even more dangerous at home. To ruin his plans the FBI applied 'lockstep' surveillance. 'No matter where he went, we were going to stay right by his side,' says Roemer. 'If he went to the toilet in a restaurant we would go with him . . . .

'He used to play golf with three bodyguards so we would have a foursome right behind. I hit a very erratic golf ball but it's long. I delighted in bouncing the ball through his legs. I never hit him in the head but I harassed his game. In 1963 he got so mad he decided to film us on the course. I ended up on a movie in federal court. He won an injunction to stop the lockstep. We were ordered to keep at least one foursome between ourselves and Sam but that was later overturned.'

Giancana's Dominican plans collapsed because the corrupt politicians he was dealing with lost power, but Sam, as usual, blamed the FBI. He was outraged but not only because they were messing up his Outfit business, his love life and his golf. He felt double-crossed for reasons which neither Roemer nor even J. Edgar Hoover knew anything about at the time.

Giancana had long been a friend of the singer, Frank Sinatra.[+] It was through Sinatra that Giancana met Judith Exner in the early 1960s. Her name was then Judy Campbell and she was a painter from Hollywood. She had money of her own and was certainly not a hooker or prostitute, as some writers have alleged. She and Sinatra had had an affair. They broke up but remained friends and Frank would still invite her to spend time with him and his 'Rat Pack'. On one occasion she went to Miami when they were putting on a stage show. At a party after the closing night Frank introduced her to a man called Sam Flood. To the FBI he was Sam Giancana.

At first Judy and Sam did not become close friends. She was then deeply in love with another man whom she had also met through Sinatra: John F. Kennedy. In 1960 the then Senator Kennedy was in Las Vegas campaigning for the presidency. At a gathering of the Rat Pack Sinatra introduced Judy to the senator. They soon became lovers and the affair continued into Kennedy's White House years.

In the months before the November 1960 presidential election Giancana came to know a lot about Jack Kennedy. Their social circles overlapped. Not only was Kennedy then a friend of Sinatra's but Kennedy's sister, Pat, was married to Peter Lawford, the British-born actor who belonged to Sinatra's Rat Pack. It is unclear whether Giancana met Kennedy at this time, although Judith Exner is sure they knew each other personally. What is clear is that Giancana worked very hard for Kennedy's election. It turned out to be a close-run thing. In terms of the popular vote Kennedy won the narrowest victory since 1888. Crucial to that victory was the state of Illinois which is dominated by Chicago. In a poll of nearly 5 million voters Kennedy defeated Richard Nixon by only 9000 votes, yet this was enough to give him all Illinois' votes in the electoral college. Kennedy could just have won without Illinois but any news, or even a prediction, of a Kennedy defeat in that state could have lost him states further west where polling was still going on. A Nixon victory in Illinois could have given him the presidency.

Bill Roemer recalls Giancana's crucial role: 'With his control of the West Side bloc and the politicians under his influence and control Giancana materially assisted in the election of John Kennedy. He made sure those politicians worked their tails off so the electorate turned out for Kennedy.' It was also alleged but not proved that election fraud had occurred on a massive scale, some casting their vote many times for Kennedy – the dead at least once – while votes for Nixon were thrown into the Chicago River.

Conversations overheard on FBI bugs some time after the election revealed why Giancana had campaigned so enthusiastically for Kennedy. A Mafia lieutenant named Johnny Formosa came into the Armory Lounge and lamented to him that, although they had done everything to get Kennedy into the White House, the war on organized crime in Chicago was hotter than ever. The words led the FBI to believe Giancana was claiming an understanding from Sinatra that if Kennedy were elected president he would go easy on Giancana. In fact the opposite happened.

To Giancana the President's worst enormity was appointing his brother Bobby attorney-general. He was upset not by the nepotism but because Bobby had been counsel to the Senate Rackets Committee and interrogated many top mobsters, including Chicagoans like Tony Accardo. Bill Roemer, who worked with Robert Kennedy, remembers him as a most dedicated crime-fighter who recognized that in Chicago organized crime was at the height of its power. He also knew that Giancana was a very aggressive leader and decided he should be the 'number one target of organized crime investigations in the United States'. Robert Kennedy appointed a young lawyer named David Schippers as head of the city's first federal strike force. Schippers recalls the attorney-general saying: 'Chicago is the most corrupt city in the United States. It needs the most work and we intend to give it the most work.'

There is no evidence that Sinatra ever told Giancana to work for Kennedy's election, or that he ever claimed he could influence him to get the FBI off Giancana's back. Yet in that bugged conversation at the Armory Lounge Johnny Formosa offered to kill Sinatra to avenge Giancana's honour. Sam rejected the offer, saying he had other plans. Undeterred Formosa pleaded, 'At least let me put the other eye of that little nigger out' (meaning Sinatra's buddy, Sammy Davis Jun.) When Giancana turned down even this scheme, the hoodlum begged to pay back the Kennedys by reshaping the physique of Peter Lawford.

Later Sinatra, Sammy Davis Jun. and other Rat Pack members turned up to perform at the Villa Venice, a supper-club rendezvous run by Giancana in the suburbs of Chicago. It was not the kind of place one would expect Sinatra and his friends to play very often once they were superstars, but the fee on Sinatra's contract matched his usual rates. What made the show worth Giancana's while was that, alongside the Villa Venice, he was running an illegal casino throughout Sinatra's engagement. The Mafia boss took hundreds of thousands of dollars from gullible high-rollers attracted there by the name of their favourite entertainer.[5]

Judith Exner saw Sinatra and Sammy Davis Jun. perform at the Villa Venice. She often saw Sinatra with Giancana and with Joe Fischetti (Al Capone's cousin). She even saw him with Johnny Formosa, his would-be assassin, in Sinatra's own home in Palm Springs. Giancana told Judith how much he had helped Kennedy's victory. The subject came up when Sam wanted her to stop seeing the President. 'He didn't force it but he wanted a relationship. He didn't like Jack and at one point he said, "Your boyfriend wouldn't even be president if it wasn't for me." He didn't explain anything. The only thing it meant to me in later years was that a great many votes had been stolen and Sam claimed responsibility.'

No wonder Giancana was bitter. The President had captivated a beautiful woman to whom he himself was deeply attracted and had licensed his brother to unleash even more FBI dogs like Roemer on him. But he had another reason to be more bitter still.

In Las Vegas the Outfit has so big a share of the rackets that a Chicago capo is always resident in the city to oversee its interests.[6] Giancana's man in Las Vegas was Johnny Roselli, a suave and handsome racketeer who had been jailed in 1944 with Paul Ricca for extorting money from Hollywood's movie-makers.[7]

By 1960 Roselli knew a man named Robert Maheu, a former FBI agent and CIA operative turned private investigator who was working for Howard Hughes when that billionaire recluse was buying up as many Las Vegas casinos as he could get hold of. In 1960 top CIA men asked Maheu to contract the Mafia, through Roselli, to carry out a political assassination. The target was Cuba's new leader, Fidel Castro. In 1959 the revolutionary Castro had overthrown Cuba's corrupt dictatorship and rapidly turned the island from an American fiefdom into an anti-American, communist state. America's Castro Complex had only just begun. It peaked in 1962 with the Cuban missile crisis.

The CIA reasoned that organized crime must surely share Washington's displeasure with Castro. Revolutionary Cuba was not well disposed to the Mafia and had initially shut down all its casinos. The revolution had cost Meyer Lansky, the mob's legendary financial genius, millions of dollars which he had stockpiled in Havana.[8] Giancana and the Chicago mob had interests there too. So had the Cleveland syndicate. So had Santo Trafficante, the Mafia boss of Tampa. Indeed, when Trafficante was caught at Apalachin in 1957 he gave a Hispanic name, 'Louis Santos', and a Havana address.

In September 1960 Roselli met Maheu and a full-time CIA agent to discuss the plot. Roselli, facing deportation proceedings and tempted by the offer of $150,000 for a successful hit, displayed rare patriotic endeavour and went off to enlist his boss, Sam Giancana. The pair then approached Santo Trafficante, the mafioso best placed to carry out the assassination. Roselli later explained their thinking to the California-based mafioso, Jimmy Fratianno. 'Giancana and Roselli said Santo would be the logical guy because he was in Cuba all the time. They went to Santo and told him: 'Kill him some way and, if you do, we get all the favours we want from the government." So he says he would do it.

'Roselli told me that if Santo had went through with it, we'd have had the government right by the throat. Santo could have killed him in a minute. Castro was running around there loose as a goose when he first took over. That would have been no problem. But Santo just didn't want to do it. He *didn't* do it.'

It is unclear why Santo did nothing. He had been jailed in Cuba when Castro first seized power but perhaps he was appeased when Castro allowed the casinos to re-open in February 1959 (they were only finally closed in September 1961). Because Trafficante did nothing the plot came to nothing, like all the CIA's other fantastical plans to kill Castro. After the fiasco of the Bay of Pigs' invasion in April 1961 President Kennedy forbade further such escapades.

Sam Giancana nevertheless believed he had done some service for America. For a gangster who had spent the Second World War either in jail or blowing up rival gambling bosses, he must have felt a belated surge of patriotic self-esteem. Bill Roemer recalls that during their shouting match at O'Hare airport in 1961 Giancana told him, 'Hey, we're supposed to be on the same side, aren't we?' The FBI man had no idea what he meant until 1975 when the plot was related in Senate hearings by none other than Johnny Roselli.

Those same hearings were called with the intention of finding out if President Kennedy had ever sanctioned the plots to kill Castro. One of the people who might have known was Judith Exner, suspected by some as having relayed information between Giancana and Kennedy. She denies passing information in either direction, about plots to kill Castro or anything else. The mobster wanted her to stop seeing the President and the President wanted her to stop seeing the mobster. They each spent their spare moments with Judith trying to run the other man out of her life. Besides, if Kennedy and Giancana had wanted to talk to each other through mutual friends there were others better placed than Judith.

This welter of interplay between the mob, the presidency and the CIA is perhaps still puzzling, however, to the public. Bill Roemer is phlegmatic: 'The job the CIA does is so important they should use every tool they can find. If they were going to use Giancana or Roselli to attempt to further what they consider to be their best interest, then I have no quarrel with that whatsoever.'

Judith Exner draws a different lesson: 'The one thing I recognized was: there are no black hats and there are no white hats. They all conduct themselves the exact same way. And very good evidence of that is that the CIA would hire two, so-called Mafia hit men, Sam Giancana and Johnny Roselli, to assassinate Fidel Castro. They're not supposed to have anything to do with each other but in essence the remark is, they are all in bed together. They all do business together, and the same way, unfortunately.'

Giancana's work for the government earned him no favours from the FBI. In 1965 he was brought before a grand jury and given immunity provided he told the truth. This meant he could not shelter behind the 5th Amendment (for nothing he said could now legally incriminate him), but he could not answer the hundreds of questions awaiting him without breaking the Mafia code of Omerta and thus signing his own death warrant. Yet if he told a provable lie (as was inevitable) he would be found guilty of perjury and jailed. He decided to refuse immunity, thus committing contempt for which he was jailed for more than a year. When he came out he feared a repeat performance and fled the country. He travelled to London, Beirut and many other cities before settling in Mexico where he stayed for eight years until the country threw him out. When he came home in 1974 he was no longer a force in Chicago organized crime.

The news of his return brought no joy to his Mafia *compares*. As far as the publicity-shunning Tony Accardo and Joey 'Doves' Aiuppa, who were now the Outfit's joint-bosses, were concerned Giancana was a liability. Wherever he went bad news hit the papers. Because of his years of misrule and his selfish scuttle abroad all Chicago's other organized-crime bosses had been subjected to even fiercer FBI scrutiny. Many had been jailed and two had died in prison.

Giancana acted as if he could resume his place at the pinnacle of the Outfit pyramid. Batters and Doves would have none of it. By May 1975 he was seriously ill from an acute gall-bladder condition and would probably have died soon enough of natural causes but the Outfit decreed he had to go. On 19 June 1975 in the basement den of his Chicago home he was shot dead with a sawn-off .22 pistol. It was a perfect hit. His housekeepers heard nothing for the gun's silencer had been modified to make its shots almost inaudible. Giancana must have known and trusted his killer. The gunman met no resistance and finished off his one-time boss with seven bullets around the mouth.

Giancana was murdered only a few days before he was due to testify before the Church Committee investigating the Mafia–CIA plot against Castro. That may have been why he died but his peers were also angry over some gambling ships he had sailing around the Caribbean. Giancana would not split his large profits from this venture which he regarded as his personal racket. He forgot that in the Outfit there are no private shareholdings.

After Momo's death anyone associated with him faced execution. In 1975 Johnny Roselli testified before the Church Committee in Washington. A year later he met Santo Trafficante in Florida. Two weeks afterwards he went missing. Before long he reappeared – in Miami's Biscayne Bay in an oil drum. He had been stabbed and garrotted. Then his legs were sawn off and neatly tucked inside.

The Outfit became obsessed with wiping out anyone who might want to avenge these murders. An obvious suspect was Jimmy Fratianno, Roselli's ally in California who was known to be his friend. He soon found himself alone with Aiuppa, in circumstances which reminded him of the times when he himself had tested gangsters before killing them off.

'Aiuppa said, "Jimmy, remember that guy . . . ?" – he's going like this with his finger [shaking it as if trying to remember] – ". . . the guy they found in a barrel? What's his name?" He's lookin' at me in the eye. I'm lookin' at him, right?

'I says, "Who you talking about? Roselli?"

' "Oh yeah, yeah. . . . What do you think of that?" he said and he's still lookin' at me, right?

'So I says, "It's one of them things." You know, what are you gonna do? He was waiting for my reaction, so if I would have said, "Hey! I'd like to find out who . . ." I'd have never left that room alive.'

Today the Outfit is led by Aiuppa and Tony Accardo, the latter still in Roemer's estimate, 'the most respected leader of organized crime Chicago has ever had, a force in organized crime over seven decades'. Accardo eventually beat the tax case which had forced him to hand over to Giancana in 1957. Today he would prefer to stay at his home near Palm Springs but the Outfit demands his return for every major policy decision.

Despite an affable, avuncular manner Accardo can still summon up the qualities that first recommended him to Capone in the 1920s. In December 1977 five burglars carried out a $1 million robbery on a jeweller who was a friend of Accardo's. He found out who they were and ordered them to return the jewels. They obeyed but vowed revenge. They thought he was keeping the jewels for himself or at best only returning them to the jeweller for a fat fee. In revenge they dared to burgle Accardo's own home. Early in 1978 all five were discovered dead in cars dumped all over Chicago, four of them with their throats slashed from ear to ear. The massacre proved how tightly the Outfit still controls even the toughest of Chicago's 'independent' criminals.

Accardo and Aiuppa leave the day-to-day running of the Outfit to Jackie 'the Lackey' Cerone, its 'operating director'. Also known as 'Tarbaby', Cerone is now 70 years old but looks little more than 50. His innocent-looking, cherubic face makes it difficult to believe that he too 'made his bones' through years of 'the heavy work'. Today Cerone keeps in perfect trim with daily workouts at the gym. This wins him some respect from the equally health-conscious Roemer but the former FBI man also acknowledges Cerone's high-powered intellect.

Not every Chicago gangster has earned Roemer's respect. One who did not was Sam De Stefano, 'the worst torturer and murderer in the history of Chicago'. He ran a moneylending business with a restaurateur called Arty Adler until Adler's nude body turned up in a sewer. Roemer first met De Stefano when he went to see him about Adler's killing and bluntly accused him of the evil deed. De Stefano feigned outrage. He summoned his wife, son and twin daughters, and some young friends of theirs who happened to be in the house. He then declaimed: 'May the good Lord up above come down and put cancer in the eyeballs of my wife and my daughters and my son and their friends if I had anything to do with the murder of Arthur Adler.' Roemer noted that De Stefano left himself out of the curse.

One winter another lieutenant ran off with some of his 'juice' money. Sam captured him and took him to a restaurant he controlled. There he was stripped and handcuffed to a hot radiator and left for three days so his wrists were badly burned. According to Roemer, De Stefano now telephoned the victim's family and invited them to dinner. The man's wife, mother, father and children all sat down to a beautiful Italian meal. When it was over De Stefano said, 'All right, let's bring your man down. He has returned to us.'

'They brought him in naked and laid him down in the middle of the tables which were arranged like a horseshoe. Sam then forced the man's mother, father, wife and children to urinate on him. That's how he disciplined him. The man went back to work for Sam, a completely subordinate, obedient underling.'

Roemer would often call on De Stefano. If Sam was out his charming wife always gave the FBI agent a good meal. 'If I came at breakfast I got a very nice breakfast, if I came at lunch I got a very nice lunch.

'Now one time I got a call from Bill Duffy who then commanded the intelligence unit of the Chicago Police. He said, "Have you been out to see Sam De Stefano?" Now I was seeing Sam mostly to develop him as an informant so I was non-committal to Bill about whether I had or had not been seeing him.

'I said, "Well, if I have, why are you asking?"

'He said, "Because he's been urinating in your coffee, you dumb ass!"

"And then I realized why the coffee I had been drinking at De Stefano's house tasted unlike any other coffee I had ever drunk.'

De Stefano was not a 'made' member of the Outfit. He had belonged to the 42 gang with Giancana but he would not take orders and he was so sadistic a killer that even the Mafia would not let him join. In 1973 he was murdered in his garage by persons unknown. Roemer believes he was probably killed because he had gone wholly out of control and off his head. 'Even though he wasn't one of theirs, the mob felt they just had to get rid of him.'

The outsider might think that with its incessant, ritual culling the Outfit might be on the verge of running out of members. On the contrary, the heavier the culling the fitter the herd. There never seems to be any shortage of men wanting to join this fraternity. In 1978 a remarkable photo was taken at a restaurant called the Sicilian Manor on Chicago's North Harlem Avenue. Ten men are sitting and standing around a table, decked with glasses and a bottle of wine. They are the leaders of Chicago's Mafia crime family gathered in secret session. Benign smiles adorn them all: the bosses Accardo and Aiuppa, the operating director Cerone and seven other mob moguls including Joey 'the Clown' Lombardo, who oversees the Outfit's labour rackets and pension fund scams.[9] Each of the men has distinguished himself in the Mafia, either as an enforcer or as a moneymaker or as both. Together they command a crime army of some 200 'made' men and many more associate full-time racketeers.

Someone near enough their equal must have taken the photograph. The identity of only one participant is in doubt. The FBI say the sick-looking man is Martin Accardo, Tony's brother. Bill Roemer believes it was a 'last supper' for Dominic DiBella who was dying of cancer. 'He'd lost 100 lb and he's very difficult to recognize but in any event the picture is so significant because it is the only time in the history of any mob where they all sat down to be counted for a colour photograph.'

12

The Unholy Alliance

Although the Outfit is governed by the Mafia, organized crime in Chicago is unique because there so many top positions are filled by non-Italians. The Mafia has always worked closely with non-Italians, above all Meyer Lansky who was more influential than almost any Mafia boss for more than fifty years. Chicago has had a long line of Lanskys. From the 1920s to the 1950s its master political fixer was a Jew, 'Greasy Thumb' Jake Guzik. His successor was the Welshman, Murray Humphreys, who in turn was succeeded by a Greek, Gus Alex. In 1963 the US Senate Subcommittee on Investigations identified twenty-nine top 'non-member associates' of the Chicago family. Fourteen were Jews, five were Greek and five were German. The rest were Anglo-Saxons, Celts and Poles.

The Outfit has always used non-Italians, in particular to grease the alliance between crime and politics which is the basis of its power. The bosses know that the politicians they own or wish to embrace might be ruined if their names were linked in public to mafiosi. Their stooge politicians must appear 'clean' if they are to remain effective as fronts. For decades men like Murray Humphreys have mingled with top politicians, labour leaders, judges and businessmen without soiling their public image or making them feel bad about being bad.

Murray Llewellyn Humphreys was Welsh through his mother who was born in north Wales. He became known as the Camel either because he used to wear camelhair coats or because reporters shortened his name to Hump and thence to Camel. His Outfit cronies called him Curly. When Guzik died in 1956 Hump took over the 'corruption squad'. He was the master fixer. Whenever a mobster went on trial he schemed the defence. Despite the fact that he had no legal training he was a better lawyer than all the mob's highly paid attorneys. He would not only plan the presentation of the defence, he would also ensure the jury was bribed and bullied into acquitting.

'Humphreys made and broke judges through the political patronage system,' says Roemer. 'It was his strategy to have what he called "hanging judges". He would tell them. "You're one of us, OK! Whenever you have a case that doesn't involve us, be sure you do everything to convict. Build yourself a reputation so that when you do something for us you can't be criticized. You can always point to your 99 per cent conviction record if anyone attacks you when our guy is cleared." '

Humphreys put top people at their ease, talking with an informed air about politics and foreign affairs. Yet on his trips to Washington it was his cash not his conversation which persuaded politicians of the justice of his cause. FBI agents followed him to the Capitol and saw him deliver packets to two congressmen in one day. The Camel died in 1966 from a heart attack, a few hours after resisting FBI men with their own form of mail: a warrant to search his home.

Organized crime's alliance with politicians has reinforced its chokehold on Chicago for more than 100 years. Its grip is as tight today as it was in the days when Bathhouse John and Hinky Dink were the 'Lords of the Levee'. Bill Roemer says of the First Ward: 'It's the most strategic area of Chicago. Some First Ward politicians are nothing but conduits through which the orders of organized crime pass to those officials who are under its influence and control.'

In 1983 the heart of the problem still lay in the First Ward Democratic party organization. In that year its secretary, Pat Marcy, was named in a Senate hearing as a 'made' member of organized crime. His real name is Pasqualino Marchone. Next to him in importance is another politician close to the underworld: John D'Arco.

Back in the early 1960s the FBI placed a bug in the offices of the First Ward organization. Roemer recalls a horrifying conversation. 'On South State Street there was a bunch of pornography and strip joints under mob control. Most police officers in the vice squad covering that area were influenced through bribes and promotions by First Ward politicians to whose demands they always esponded. But one officer did not respond. I can remember one First Ward official called in a policeman and together they plotted the killing of this man. We communicated this to Attorney-General Bobby Kennedy who was appalled that an official of a Democratic party organization could plot the killing of a police officer. The intended victim was eventually assigned to other tasks. He was never killed but they sure as heck plotted it that day. I'll never forget that.'

In the 1950s and early 1960s John D'Arco was the alderman for the First Ward. He was also a friend of Giancana's. In 1959 Giancana returned from a trip to Mexico. Customs officials searched him and found a list of Chicago's top mobsters, identifiable by their nicknames. After each name was a figure. The FBI learned that Giancana had gone to Mexico to buy a racetrack and the figures represented each boss's percentage share of the expected profits. At the bottom of the list was John D'Arco with one point.

Roemer visited D'Arco to ask him about the list. He suggested to D'Arco that he was a public-minded public official who would like to help the FBI unravel the mystery. D'Arco asked, 'Why would you come and ask me such a question?'

Roemer replied, 'Because I prefer not to embarrass you by first going to anyone else. I've come to you instead of asking your associates.'

'Roemer,' D'Arco replied, 'you cannot embarrass me. The FBI cannot embarrass me. You go ahead and throw your best shot. You'll find I'm too big a man in this town.'

Roemer simmered for years over D'Arco's remarks until 1962 when the FBI learned Giancana had decided to replace D'Arco as First Ward alderman. Accardo and Humphreys were trying to convince him to keep D'Arco in place. The FBI decided it would be in the best interests of Chicago and the United States for D'Arco to be deposed. One day Roemer learned that D'Arco was going to lunch with Giancana at a West Side restaurant called the Czech Lodge. Three agents arrived to find it had private dining rooms. Roemer spotted one of D'Arco's political aides standing lookout outside a door. Roemer breezed past him into the private room. Hunched over a table all by themselves, were 'Momo' Giancana and John D'Arco. The alderman was pleading for his political career.

Roemer recalls the incident: 'I went up to Giancana and I yelled, "Ho, Ho, Ho! It's Mo!" he glared and recognized me right away. I turned to D'Arco and I said, "Hello John." With the reflex action of a politician D'Arco jumped up, smiled as if he was at a political meeting and shook my hand.

'Giancana kicked him under the table right in the shins and said, "This is Roemer, you idiot!" And with that D'Arco looked at both of us and he realized for the first time that he *could* be embarrassed by the FBI.

'The next day he announced he'd had a heart attack and went into hospital. The mob later compromised with him. They told him not to run again as alderman but he continues till this day as ward committee man in charge of all First Ward patronage.'

In the 1960s Roemer investigated a racket which exposed how the nexus between Chicago politicians and organized crime works to their mutual benefit. In the Loop (the downtown business area of the First Ward) any building work, from major construction to erecting a restaurant canopy, requires a zoning variation. The FBI learned that people needing downtown variation usually insured their premises with Anco Insurance, then owned by, among others, Alderman D'Arco.

The FBI decided to find out if Anco ever got business through extortion. Its agents talked to a hotel owner from out of town who had naively embarked on building a motel in the First Ward. One day he arrived to find his workers idle. They had been told to stop work because they had no variation permit. Days went by and still the permit did not come through. In despair the builder saw a First Ward party official who told him his problems might disappear if he took out an Anco policy. The builder did as he was advised, his problems vanished and the motel soon opened for business.

The extent of corruption in Chicago is impossible to prove because it suffocates all investigations. Something of what goes on was revealed in 1960 in the suburb of Northlake. The International Paper Company was about to build a plant there when it was approached by a hoodlum named Rocco Pranno. He announced that unless he was paid $20,000 there would be no plant. The company ignored the extortion demand and went ahead with its plans. The city fathers soon told the company that unless Pranno got his money they would not issue a building permit. In the end the company paid $16,000 by certified cheque. Later Pranno was convicted and jailed. It then emerged that Sam Giancana had settled the dispute and named the price.

The biggest enemy of both organized crime and grafting politicians in Chicago today is still the Crime Commission, for three-quarters of a century the voice of Chicago's concerned citizens. Its current director is Pat Healy, a tireless campaigner for integrity in public life. 'The problem in Chicago is that for at least sixty years organized crime has not been attacked as it should have been. Its ties with business and politics are so entrenched that they are almost impossible to eliminate. The mob determines who runs for office, who become aldermen, top policemen, judges. It decides whether a piece of city legislation should be supported or killed. All these things are crucial for the benefit of the community.'

This power is reflected in official inertia. 'I'm hard pressed to think of anybody important who has been jailed by local law enforcement. It's disgraceful. We look at the bottom line. We say, "No one's going to jail. You people are not doing your job."

'Half the politicians are in bed with organized crime. The mob benefits by getting preferential treatment for its businesses and inside contracts for public works. They have a head start over legitimate businessmen who must go the legitimate route. The politician is worse than the mobster. He's a self-confessed thief but the politician is supposed to represent the people. He takes an oath to discharge his duties as best he can. Then he gets in office and "Zappo!" he sells the people down the river for a dollar. He may not have the stench that organized-crime people have but he has violated a sacred trust.'

Patronage in Chicago is still immense. There are 30,000 jobs in the gift of City Hall, from lucrative legal sinecures down to dustmen and car mechanics. Many of these are handed out to party faithfuls. 'We've had a patronage system from time immemorial,' says Pat Healy. 'I don't think we'll ever shake it. It perpetuates its own constituency: people with jobs at City Hall or with Cook County have husbands, wives, aunts and uncles. They all do what they can to keep that job in the family.' When the officials who give out the jobs are controlled by organized crime the consequences are disastrous.

The Outfit's power lies not in the number but in the kind of jobs it controls. 'Take the police department,' says Healy. 'A traffic cop isn't going to do you any good. You want someone in a central point where all reports cross his desk. He may be in intelligence or in the narcotics bureau. That one person is much more use than a hundred cops in other jobs.'

The Chicago police have occasionally mounted an intelligence effort against the Outfit. 'We had a unit called the Red Squad,' says Healy, 'building raw intelligence on organized crime. They started to look at neighbourhood, civic, religious and political groups. That's when the hue and cry forced the police to abandon the unit and purge its records. Now they don't know what organized-crime figures are doing. Every time I speak to them they recite glowing reports, numerous convictions and accelerated efforts but I'm not talking about two people gambling on the street corner for a few dollars. That's not organized crime. We did a survey on gambling and we found out of 117 raids brought to court the judge threw out every case. I asked him why and he said, "What's wrong with a little gambling?" If that's what the judge thinks, what do you expect the cop to do? Go out and do a useless act? He'd rather stay and have another cup of coffee.'

Today gangland murders are rather fewer than in the 1920s but just as few are solved. Chicago seems untroubled. In Healy's words: 'Society here is blasé about mob homicides: another body in a trunk, another body in the river with chains on it, shotgun to the face, hanging on a meat hook. If a woman coming out of a shop were killed that way or children crossing the street, citizens would be in uproar. Why don't we think that way about organized crime? People say, "As long as they only kill each other let's not worry about it". You can't think that way because it may be you tomorrow.'

It is more than twenty years since Attorney-General Robert Kennedy appointed Dave Schippers head of Chicago's first strike force. With the FBI Schippers led the war on the Outfit and put most of its bosses in jail. 'I loved the city and I hated what was happening to it. I was vitally interested in stamping out organized crime.' Today Schippers is in private practice and he paints a gloomy picture. 'The problem today is exactly the problem we faced with Al Capone. It's the unholy alliance of politicians, hoodlums and the police. It hasn't changed. It's just gone a little deeper under cover.'

'Organized crime cannot function in a major city without the direct, specific, intentional co-operation of police and politicians. This city's budget is massive. If organized crime can control the handing-out of city business they can control the business life of the entire city. That is what happens in Chicago today and it has ever been thus. You can get an awful lot more done by going to your local hoodlums than by going to your politicians.'

In 1983 Chicago elected its first black mayor. Will that mean the overthrow of the corrupt white axis? No, says Schippers. 'The race, the colour, the party of the mayor is irrelevant. The city is divided into fifty separate wards. Each ward is its own little fiefdom. The hoodlums don't go to the mayor and hope it will filter down. They corrupt at the bottom and at every level, so a change at the top has very little effect.'

In 1983 a series of events occurred which justifies Schippers' pessimism. A 63-year-old oriental called Ken Eto faced a long jail term for his part in an illegal gambling racket controlled by the Outfit. The bosses feared that Eto was going to get a light sentence in return for exposing the many mobsters he had worked with in his thirty-five years with the Outfit. In February 1983 he was shot three times in the back of the head and left for dead, but Eto survived and named the men who had tried to kill him. They were Jasper Campise, an old-time Mafia loanshark, and John Gattuso, a 47-year-old deputy sheriff of Cook County.

The sheriff of Cook County is one of the most important law enforcement officials in greater Chicago. Although the sheriff had nothing to do with the shooting, the news that one of his deputies was a Mafia hit man dismayed many Chicagoans who thought this kind of moonlighting had ended with Prohibition. Other deputies had recently been convicted of theft and extortion, more faced trial for thieving car parts and another was involved in child pornography. This shabby record was partly explained when a Chicago alderman was convicted of 'selling' a dozen deputies' jobs for $2000 a badge.

Campise and Gattuso were charged with attempted murder but they never went on trial. In July 1983 they disappeared. A few days later a car in a suburban parking space was reported for stinking out the neighbourhood. It was Campise's Volvo. Local police were called in and prized open the boot. Inside were the bloated, decomposing bodies of Campise and Gattuso. They had both been tortured and stabbed repeatedly. John Gattuso had been strangled. The two men had screwed up a Mafia hit and had thus endangered mobsters right at the top of the Chicago family. They had to die and in such an appalling way that every other Mafia underling would be sure to try harder.

This double murder was grotesque evidence of the continuing power of organized crime in the city. The cop and the mobster were united in death as they had been in life, symbols of that unholy alliance which still rules much of Chicago. Does Dave Schippers think the hoodlum influence over Chicago is any less today than it was during the days of Al Capone? 'No. It's just a little better hidden. You don't have an Al Capone out at the ball park, eating hot dogs with the mayor. Now it's all going on in back rooms. But it's there. It's there as it has *never* been there and one wonders if it will ever change.'

13

Racketeers, Racketbusters and Tammany Hall

In America's big cities politics in the nineteenth century was more than bound up with organized crime: it *was* organized crime. In New York this corrupt nexus was personified by John Morrissey, an Irish immigrant born in Tipperary in 1831, who rose to become a United States congressman and a state senator. When he died at the age of 46 his pallbearers were the governor of New York and eight senators.

Morrissey died an American success story not least because he was a thug, gang leader and illegal gambling-house owner. In 1848 in his adopted town of Troy he was indicted for assault with intent to kill. In 1849 he was jailed for sixty days for burglary. He moved to New York City where he endeared himself to Democratic party bosses by raising armies of goons on election days to guard polling stations and beat up gangs working for other parties.

Over 6 feet tall and a brave fighter, Morrissey won the heavyweight championship of America in 1858. He promptly retired and moved into the twin professions of saloon keeper and gambling-house owner. Protected by the police, who were appointed by politicians including himself, Morrissey made so much money that he built a racetrack at Saratoga Springs in 1863. Inevitably he attached to it a luxurious gambling house which was patronized by leaders of high society such as the Vanderbilts and the Belmonts whose friend he became. One visitor wrote, 'His table, attendants, cooking and company are exceeded by nothing on this side of the Atlantic.' Morrissey's prizefighter mentality helped his rise to become one of Tammany Hall's joint leaders, founding a century of incest between New York's mobsters and its politicians.

The Society of St Tammany was born in 1789 and dedicated to the ideals of the American Revolution. It was named after a legendary Indian chief whose statue adorned Tammany Hall, the society's headquarters on 14th Street. Its original ideals were soon lost as Tammany became a byword for corruption. Except for spasms of reform Tammany Hall ruled City Hall and took the 'spoils'. Its leaders became rich on crooked land deals, kickbacks on public works' contracts and the sale of thousands of city jobs. One Tammany boss was alleged to have pocketed $75 million in the 1860s. Up until the 1950s the story of organized crime in New York is largely the story of Tammany Hall, ethnic politics and the rise of the gangs from street bullies to crime corporations.

The gangs of New York had a long and dishonourable history. They emerged as early as the 1830s in the once-prosperous but crumbling Five Points area. Built on a swamp it had become so unhealthy that the only people living there were poor Irish immigrants and freed slaves. By the 1860s its only industries were vice and crime. It was a Dickensian world of slums and rookeries described by Dickens himself in his *American Notes*.

> Let us go again and plunge into the Five Points. . . . Debauchery has made the very houses prematurely old. See how the rotten beams are tumbling down and how the patched and broken windows seem to scowl dimly, like eyes that have been hurt in drunken frays . . . From every corner . . . some figure crawls half-awakened, as if the judgement hour were near at hand, and every obscure grave were giving up its dead . . . ruined houses, open to the street, whence through wide gaps in the walls other ruins loom upon the eye, as though the world of vice and misery had nothing else to show; hideous tenements which take their name from robbery and murder; all that is loathsome, drooping and decayed is here.

Even if one discounts Dicken's imagination, the Five Points was fertile ground for crime. With its abundance of saloons and speakeasies, dance halls and whorehouses, many gangs started there each with their own territory: the Forty Thieves, Kerryonians, Chichesters, Roach Guards, Plug Uglies and the Dead Rabbits. The Plug Uglies were large Irishmen who took their name from plug hats stuffed with wool and leather which they wore as helmets in street battles. Nearby in the equally licentious Bowery other gangs grew up: the Bowery Boys, True Blue Americans and the O'Connell Guards. Again mostly Irish, they often fought each other but united to denounce the British Empire. They exploited civil disorder, particularly the 1863 Draft riots (against compulsory service in the Civil War) which turned into a week-long insurrection of murder, looting and destruction.

Herbert Asbury, the popular chronicler of American vice and depravity has described how Tammany leaders exploited these gangs as early as the 1830s. They

> . . . were quick to see the practical value of the gangsters and to realize the advisability of providing them with meeting and hiding places, that their favor might be curried and their peculiar talents employed on election day to assure government by and for Tammany. Many ward and district leaders acquired title to the green-grocery speakeasies in which the first of the Five Points gangs had been organized while others operated saloons and dance-houses along the Bowery or took gambling houses and places of prostitution under their protection. The underworld thus became an important factor in politics.[1]

In the 1880s the Whyos were born. They were more than street thugs. They were full-time criminals: thieves, burglars, protection racketeers and contract killers. They sold violence on a sliding scale. One Whyo was arrested with a printed price-list in his pocket:

Punching	$2
Both eyes blacked	$4
Nose and Jaw broke	$10
Jacked out [knocked out with a blackjack]	$15
Ear chawed off	$15
Leg or arm broke	$19
Shot in leg	$25
Stab	$25
Doing the big job	$100 and up

By the late 1890s the Whyos had become the Five Pointers, 1500 strong. Their bitter rivals across the Bowery were the Eastmans with 1200 members. In territorial wars thirty men were killed. Further north the streets belonged to the Gas House Gang and the Gophers.

All these gangs were hired and protected by politicians but whereas the earlier gangs were mainly Irish, the Eastmans were led by a Jew, Monk Eastman, and the Five Pointers by an Italian, Paulo Vaccarelli. He preferred to use the alias Paul Kelly, probably because New York's mostly Irish policemen usually overlooked the crimes of their fellow-countrymen. As has been mentioned Al Capone began his criminal career with the Five Points gang before scuttling to Chicago in 1919.

The rise of Jewish and Italian gangs in New York was a reflection of the rapid changes in the city's racial balance. In 1880 there were only 250,000 Jews in America, mostly of German origin. Of those 80,000 lived in New York. By 1910 there were 1,250,000 Jews in New York alone, nearly all from eastern Europe. Mass Italian immigration came a little later, reaching 100,000 a year in 1900 and totalling more than 3 million in the next fifteen years. In New York both peoples settled heavily on the Lower East Side: 12 square miles from Brooklyn Bridge to 14th Street and from the East River to Broadway.

The newcomers soon showed up in New York's crime statistics. In 1908 Police Commissioner Theodore Bingham claimed that half the city's criminals were Jews. This started a row between assimilated, 'uptown Jews' who believed Bingham was right and Yiddish-speaking immigrants who claimed that he and his force were anti-Semites.

As commissioner of a politically controlled police force Bingham knew that the time-honoured bonds of corruption between Irish gangs and Tammany Hall were now matched by a Jewish connection. Some Jewish criminals were buying protection through payoffs to police and politicians. They returned the favour by delivering the Jewish vote on election day.

In 1912 a Jewish gambling-house operator called Herman Rosenthal found that he could not buy protection unless he made a policeman his partner. The policeman was no mere cop – he was Lieutenant Charles Becker, head of the Gambling Squad. The arrangement collapsed because Rosenthal refused to contribute $500 when Becker's press agent went on trial for murder. Becker retaliated by raiding Rosenthal's gambling house, whereupon Rosenthal revealed all to the press. On 13 July *The World* published an affidavit from Rosenthal in which he swore Becker had taken 20 per cent of his gambling profits. The district attorney summoned him to prove his charges but as Rosenthal left the DA's office at midnight on 15 July he was gunned to death. Four men were later arrested and charged when a witness revealed they had been hired by none other than Lieutenant Becker. All four were convicted of first-degree murder and were put to death in Sing Sing's electric chair. Becker was also found guilty and died in the same chair in July 1915.

Although Becker was not Jewish Rosenthal and three of his assassins were. So was the man who had put the killers at Becker's disposal. The scandal convinced uptown Jews that they had to act against crime among their downtown brethren. A communal body called the Kehillah set up a Bureau of Social Morals to 'stir the conscience' of Jews to the 'political and moral corruption of which the Rosenthal case is but a symptom'. It employed undercover investigators to identify Jewish criminals and the places they frequented. The Kehillah's chairman, Judah L. Magnes, then told the mayor and the commissioner which premises the police should raid and shut down.

From August 1912 the bureau's leading investigator, Abe Shoenfeld, probed every area of crime in which Jews were active: theft, receiving, gambling, prostitution, pimping, drugs, labour racketeering, extortion, horse poisoning, diamond smuggling and corruption of public officials. He soon discovered that payoffs by gamblers like Rosenthal to policemen like Becker were commonplace. Inspector Titus and Captain Corcoran had made a fortune out of gambling houses. 'When these men were in the district of 2nd Avenue and 114th Street they cleaned up and made loads of money, and the proof of it is that they are wealthy men today. . . . Imagine, there were one dozen houses running in this district four years ago and each paying over $1200 a month. This meant $14,400 for cops, of which about $8000 went to the above two mentioned men.'

Shoenfeld's most painful testimony concerned Jewish prostitutes, some as young as 17. They began their careers self-employed but soon fell among pimps. If they lived till their twenties they would be eaten away by disease. The grotesque fate awaiting them could be seen in Jennie Morris, 'Jennie the Factory'. 'She was given this name because she is so big and once stated she would not "take a bluff" from the 71st if the 69th Regiment had just finished with her".' In 1912 she was 'about 38 years old – a horse – walks like a general – well-shaped – pale face – full of syphilis'.

Crazy Dora, Cock Eye Rosie, and Mary the Bum were all prostitutes, as were the 'three Muskateers'. Each muskateer had her own Italian pimp. One bragged that 'no Jew pimp can get her money, he must be a wop and a good one'. The investigators were appalled at the fall of Jewish womanhood, especially Rosie Hertz. Her family came from Hungary. They ran 7 East 1st Street, known as the Colombian Hotel, 'One of the most notorious breeders and incubators of prostitution this city has ever had.' Rosie, known to all as Mother Hertz, was over 50 and had been whoring in New York for thirty years. She had made $1 million from prostitution and shrewd investments. Rosie knew many friendly police captains who protected her from raids by reform mayors or district attorneys. She gave $1000 a year to both Democratic and Republican parties. In return she was not troubled by detectives or uniformed police. Any cop who dared raid her would be transferred as soon as she complained.

Because of the Hertz family, 'Firesides have crumbled, hearts have been broken, virginity has been polluted, virtue has been contaminated and the very East Side leprously disgraced.' The Kehillah's protests forced a police raid in October 1912. For two months Rosie sold no flesh. She was jailed but soon returned to her profession, operating her brothel with impunity. Suddenly in 1912 she fled New York. When last heard of she was running a disorderly house in Norfolk, Virginia.

Another bureau target was Abe Rabbells, alias the Rabbi. Born in Russia, he had 'the notorious reputation of causing the downfall of many respectable East Side girls'. On 2nd Avenue he ran a restaurant where gamblers, gunmen, thieves and pimps consorted. Rabbells was president of the New York Independent Benevolent Association. No more than a brotherhood of pimps, it ran a mutual defence fund and owned its own burial ground.

Some gangs like the Yiddisha Gophers took on 'guerilla' work for employers to break strikes. They were just as willing to work for unions against employers. Frequently union leaders hired them to break the heads of their own members. After a strike workers often found their union leader had agreed a poor wage settlement and would accuse him of taking a payoff. At that point the Gophers would beat up anyone who dared protest.

Before motorized trucks became commonplace horses were used to move goods around the city. One gang called the Yiddish Blackhand or Commorra extorted hundreds of dollars a week from Jewish trucking companies and punished the recalcitrant by poisoning horses with strychnine or chloroform. The Jackson Brothers, 'the biggest trucking firm in the city', refused to submit. After six of their horses were poisoned they paid. 'Can you imagine a firm of this size and nature submitting to this Commorra! And never a word of protest from them.' The Kehillah's investigator vowed to fight poison with poison and shot with shot, 'The East Side has suffered long enough.'

To some extent the Kehillah did clean up the Lower East Side, yet its investigators knew they were fighting a deeply corrupt system. In 1913 they assailed the wide-open doors of the German Hotel, a notorious whorehouse: 'We have 10,000 police in New York and it appears that, with all these, we have no detectives who can go around and get the goods on a dump of this sort.'

They noted the rise of Tammany's Italian connection. In January 1914: 'CHICK TRICKER will run a ball at TAMMANY HALL under the name of the SARANAC Club. . . . There will be any number of Italian gunmen at the ball and on the show card the names of such celebrities as TOM FOLEY [sheriff of New York] appear very promiscuously. . . . They should be dealt with as if they were so many brutes and convicts as they are. . . . The police . . . should see to it that there shall be no congregation on this night of THIEVES, GANGSTERS, PIMPS, DISORDERLY HOUSE-KEEPERS and INMATES, both men and women.'

By September 1913 the investigators felt they had broken Jewish organized crime. They claimed they had almost wiped out horse betting and shut down fifty-five pool parlors. There was now not a single whorehouse in the East Side. Extortioners no longer preyed on Jewish traders for fear of exposure by the Kehillah. Perhaps the Kehillah's very success caused its investigations to peter out in 1914, but any self-congratulations were premature.

In 1917 the Kehillah was revived for its final onslaught on Jewish crime. The city was now full of opium, cocaine and 'hop-joints' where narcotics were consumed. 'These men are creeping into the homes of the East Side, Bronx, Harlem and Brooklyn with their poisonous drugs,' the investigators lamented in biblical despair, 'and if this thing is not curbed . . . tens of thousands of our men and women will be hopelessly addicted to the use of cocaine and opium. The mind and body of Jewry is being attacked and poisoned. The rats are carrying the plague into the homes of the Jews. Our own kind are accomplishing what a once fanatic, religion-crazed world could not bring about; what anti-Semites cannot do today.' In a 102-page report the Kehillah exposed Italian, black, Greek and Irish drug-dealers, as well as Jews, but the name which cropped up most often was 'Waxey Gordon', Irving Wexler, a gangster whose career would take him to the heights and depths of organized crime.

Gordon was first named in Kehillah files in 1913 as a strike-breaker, silencing Painters Union members who objected to the corruptly negotiated terms of a strike settlement. By 1914 he was 'leading a mob of gorillas in a dress strike', but his old friends in Dopey Bennie's mob were 'very sore because he is hiring all the fellows from Houston St and E 4th St. Silent war has been declared and they may kill Waxey Gordon in a short while since he is depriving them of their bread and butter.'

Unfortunately Waxey survived. In 1917 he was described as a stocky 30-year-old, 5 ft 6 in, clean-shaven gangster. 'He broke many a poor Jew's head and was always a bully in the mob.' Now Waxey was plying 14th Street with opium and cocaine. He recruited more Jews so that by June 1917 he was a 'big man in the poison game', even running dope into Philadelphia. When the Kehillah filed its last reports in September 1917 the 'Waxey Gordon Combination' was one of New York's biggest dope syndicates.

Gordon became one of America's richest criminals but not through narcotics. In 1920 Prohibition made liquor much more profitable and very soon Waxey moved into bootlegging. His sponsor was Arnold Rothstein, arguably the founder of modern American organized crime. Rothstein's grandfather had fled to the Lower East Side from the pogroms of Bessarabia. His father built up a cotton-converting business in the garment district where he was highly respected. The family was living on the desirable East 79th Street when young Arnold opted for the twilight world of pool rooms and gambling houses. In the gangster kingdoms of the Lower East Side he soon became a successful moneylender but his obsession was gambling. He would bet on dice games, cards, horse races, even his own skill at pool. He became a multi-millionaire, winning $800,000 on one race by placing his bets with a multitude of unsuspecting bookmakers across the nation so as not to bring down the odds. He became a layoff banker for other bookmakers and like John Morrissey operated a luxurious gambling house at Saratoga during the August races.

Rothstein masterminded many of the greatest criminal coups of his day. He was said to have been the man who fixed the 1919 World Series – baseball's Cup Final. At least eight members of the Chicago White Sox team took bribes of $10,000 to lose to Cincinnati. The Sox lost, the scandal broke and the players were charged but all the evidence disappeared before they were tried and the case was dismissed. Rothstein was not charged. He told the grand jury he had turned down other gamblers when they asked him for $100,000 to bribe the players. Their approach forewarned him the series was fixed and he won $350,000. In *The Great Gatsby* Scott Fitzgerald immortalized Rothstein as Meyer Wolfsheim. When Gatsby tells the narrator, Nick Carraway, that Wolfsheim fixed the World Series Carraway laments, 'It never occurred to me that one man could start to play with the faith of fifty million people – with the single-mindedness of a burglar blowing a safe.'

Rothstein also had a part in the Liberty Bonds scam involving Nicky Arnstein, husband of the actress Fanny Brice. Arnstein was jailed for the theft of $5 million worth of bonds from Wall Street, although the bonds were never found. Rothstein probably fenced them abroad but again he was never indicted. Indeed he never spent a day in jail. Throughout his life of crime he was protected by the top bosses of Tammany Hall who had, of course, benefited from his generosity.

Rothstein was a labour fixer in the garment district, renting gangs of goons to both unions and employers. In 1926 he was called in to end the district's longest strike. For six months 50,000 men and women had withdrawn their labour, paralyzing New York's biggest industry. Rothstein persuaded the gangs hired by both sides to leave the streets. His underworld authority must have been immense for the gangs were led by the notorious thugs, 'Little Augie' Orgen and 'Legs' Diamond. He then persuaded the unions and employers' sides to negotiate a settlement, proof of his equally high standing in the 'overworld'.

When someone needed money to set up a crime Rothstein would supply it. In return he did not simply demand a fat slice of the profit. He would also mortgage the criminal's property and make him take out a large life policy with his assurance firm. He owned property all over New York: houses, offices, tenement blocks, an import-export business, art and antique shops and a hotel. He was a partner in restaurants, clothing stores and real estate projects on Long Island. He laundered huge criminal earnings into an even greater 'respectable' fortune, a system copied by all the most successful organized-crime figures ever since.

When Prohibition began Rothstein backed Waxey Gordon's first rum-running enterprises by putting up $175,000 to smuggle boatloads of Scotch whisky into New York. The money paid for the Scotch, the ocean crossing, speedboats, trucks and bribes to the coastguard and local police. Rothstein financed ten transatlantic shipments and made fortunes for himself and Gordon. He started off 'Legs' Diamond in the bootlegging business, supplying funds for the Irishman to buy trucks, warehouses and protection. Rothstein himself soon tired of rum-running – scarcely the business to stimulate 'the Brain' as he was called – but the men he backed, Gordon and Diamond, became two of Prohibition's biggest bootleggers. He also helped launch Lucky Luciano.

By the late 1920s in each major city bootleggers like Gordon, Diamond and Luciano had killed off the competition and built a criminal cartel. Most of the victors were in their twenties or thirties and were either immigrants or the sons of immigrants. In December 1928 the first known gathering of Sicilian–American crime bosses took place in Cleveland, Ohio.[2] It was broken up by the police but the fact that it had even occurred shows there was already a Mafia organization covering much of urban America. Five months later in May 1929 at the President Hotel in Atlantic City another organized-crime conclave took place, attended by Italians from Sicily and the mainland, Poles, Irishmen and Jews.

This was an assembly of the mob's biggest brains. For three days some thirty gangsters, including Al Capone and Jake Guzik from Chicago, Dutch Schultz, Lucky Luciano and Frank Costello from New York and Max 'Boo Boo' Hoff from Philadelphia, thrashed out a bootleggers' cartel. They agreed not to hijack each other's booze or gun each other down. They would co-operate against informers and honest police. America would be divided into territories where those represented at Atlantic City would control not just liquor but all kinds of gambling, vice and racketeering. Organized crime was now formally multi-ethnic. Italians might come to dominate it because of their numbers and their violence but they would never have it all.

Law enforcement's collective failure to fight gangsters and racketeers in the 1920s was a scandal. Local police forces either knew nothing of organized crime or were owned by it. Federal agencies like the Bureau of Prohibition were undermanned, demoralized or similarly eaten away by corruption. The US Bureau of Investigation, headed from 1924 by director J. Edgar Hoover, ignored gangsters.[3] Only by the late 1920s did the investigators of the Internal Revenue Service feel empowered to investigate tax evasion by the nation's top hoodlums such as Al Capone.[4]

In November 1928 the slumbers of New York law enforcement were at last disturbed by an underworld murder. Arnold Rothstein died in hospital after being shot in the stomach in Room 349 of the Park Central Hotel. He was killed for not settling losses of $300,000 incurred in a poker game three weeks before. A gambler named George McManus had booked the room where the shooting occurred. He had also hosted the game at which Rothstein had lost the money and was thus responsible for its payment. A year later he was tried for Rothstein's murder but acquitted for lack of evidence.

Among papers found at Rothstein's offices was an IOU from Albert Vitale, a magistrate. He had been appointed through his Tammany Hall connections, which made the IOU of great interest to Fiorello LaGuardia, Tammany's main adversary. In 1929 LaGuardia was running for mayor against the incumbent, Tammany's Jimmy Walker. LaGuardia was defeated but in the course of the campaign he acquired Vitale's IOU. He revealed that this custodian of public morality owed $19,400 to one of America's most notorious criminals. Vitale had taken the money to dismiss robbery charges against one of Rothstein's associates but he blustered that he had borrowed it for 'speculative purposes'.

Vitale was a buffoon but with Walker re-elected mayor and the Tammany machine ruling City Hall he survived LaGuardia's onslaught. A month after the election he was guest of honour at a dinner in a Democratic club in the Bronx. Also present were city detectives and notorious mafiosi such as Ciro Terranova the 'Artichoke King'. Their revelries were shattered by six masked gunmen who lined them all up against a wall and stole their jewellery and cash. Vitale was humiliated and outraged. He promptly reached out to his underworld friends. In a few hours everything that had been stolen was recovered, including a detective's gun. He may have thought that he would now be hailed as a hero but all he did was prove that he had the wrong connections for someone of his calling.

In 1930 New York State's highest judges (the Appellate Division of the Supreme Court) deemed Vitale unfit to be a magistrate and dismissed him. They also set up an investigation into the magistrates' courts. It would be led by Judge Samuel Seabury.

Seabury had been the judge in the trial which sent Lieutenant Becker to the electric chair in 1914. His investigation of the magistrates revealed corruption just as evil as Becker's. Some of the worst crookery surrounded prostitution. *Agents provocateurs* were framing women in vice raids. Some of the women were indeed prostitutes, who preferred to pay graft rather than go to jail, but most were not. Sometimes the *agent provocateur* would enter a doctor's surgery while the doctor was out. He would demand treatment from a bemused nurse, lay marked money down on a table and start to undress. Suddenly in would burst the vice squad and arrest the nurse for prostitution. The 'client' would then give a false address, he would be released and would never show up if the case reached court. The hapless nurse would now either pay a large bribe to save her reputation or she would be convicted by the magistrate for prostitution with an 'unknown man'. The magistrate, of course, completed the ring of corruption.

Seabury won pardons from New York Governor Franklin D. Roosevelt for six wholly innocent women who had been jailed by the magistrates. Their persecutors had made fortunes. One policeman had banked $90,000 in five years, another nearly $200,000. As the money could not have come from their meagre salaries the officers claimed a run of luck at the racetrack or rich but sadly dead uncles. One policeman swore he had kept his cash in a tin box in a bank and a long line of his colleagues spun Seabury similar unlikely tales.

The worst persecutor of the innocent had been Jean Norris, New York City's first and only woman magistrate, herself a Tammany politician. Many others had bought their jobs from Tammany Hall. Some held fortunes in oil stocks or shares in Havana casinos. Two magistrates were dismissed, three resigned and another left town. Their entire careers on the bench had been dedicated to fixing cases for the politicians who had got them the jobs.

In 1931 Seabury investigated the elected district attorney of New York County (the island of Manhattan). DA Thomas Crain, another Tammany nominee, was accused of failing to investigate corrupt officials and racketeers. Every kind of business was being extorted, including the Fulton Fish Market, from which fresh fish was sold to a fifth of America's population. Joe 'Socks' Lanza of the Sea Food Workers Union dictated to employers how much they had to pay for labour peace. He would sell out his own members for a cash payment of several thousand dollars and extract a few thousand more to keep a firm wholly non-union. Seabury discovered that the district attorney's inaction convinced employers that no one would bring their extortioners to justice. The garment district felt equally defenceless.[5]

Seabury next counselled a state committee to investigate the city's entire government. In 1930 the spoils were far greater than when Tammany had first raped Manhattan. New York now had 7 million citizens and an annual budget of $600 million. The sum of $300 million was paid to 148,000 city employees. Many held their jobs only on the say-so of Mayor Walker and Tammany Hall.

Seabury's team probed hundreds of officials paid by businessmen to help them override health, fire and building regulations. Millions of dollars had been misappropriated from the city's unemployment funds, nearly all of which went to Democratic voters. Bus contracts were sold to the highest bidders rather than the lowest. Corrupt officials piled up fortunes in tin boxes. Several had become millionaires on salaries of less than $20,000 a year.

Seabury revealed that both Democratic and Republican clubhouses were devoted as much to gambling as to politics. The sheriff of New York, Tom Farley, ran a clubhouse modestly named the Thomas M. Farley Association. It was raided one morning by some incorruptible police who found gambling in progress. The players included many gangsters. When Farley was found to have saved $400,000 in six years on a salary of $8,500 he too told Seabury he kept the money in a tin box but he could not say where it came from. Governor Roosevelt dismissed Farley as sheriff for not disclosing the source of his wealth.

Other greedy office-holders shuffled before Seabury and the senators. James McCormick, known as the 'Tammany Cupid', ran the city's marriage licence bureau. He had a total of thirty bank accounts containing nearly $400,000, all the proceeds of tips extorted from nervous bridegrooms. Over at the docks a steamship company had waited nine years to get its own pier. The company eventually paid $50,000 to a law firm with Tammany Hall connections. The message was clear: to do public business in New York you had to use a Tammany middle man.

At the top of this corrupt pyramid was Mayor Jimmy Walker, the 'night mayor of New York'. An exhibitionist of superabundant charm, he had built up a huge public following years before as a writer of popular songs. His great hit was 'Will You Love Me in December as You Do in May?' and also did well with 'There's Music in the Rustle of a Skirt' and 'In the Valley Where My Sally Said Goodbye'. He derided Prohibition by leading beer parades along Broadway. This was only fitting since the city he claimed to be the 'most moral, best-regulated and best-policed city in the civilized world' contained 30,000 speakeasies and nightclubs all of which made fortunes for organized crime.

At public hearings in May 1932 Seabury showed that Walker had benefited from a slush fund put together by businessmen seeking a monopoly of city bus contracts. A newspaper mogul had given him a $250,000 – out of nothing more than friendship, claimed Walker. Seabury then proved that even the mayor had a tin box: a safe-deposit box he shared with his financial adviser, Russell Sherwood. From January 1926 until August 1931 Sherwood put $7 million in the box on Walker's behalf, $750,000 of it in cash. Walker lamely denied all knowledge of the money but since Sherwood had fled to Mexico to avoid a subpoena Walker had no way of proving the money was not his.

Walker performed so badly in the hearings that he had to face proceedings in Albany to remove him as mayor. His accuser was Seabury, his judge Roosevelt. Again Sherwood did not appear. Walker had not even tried to bring him back. Roosevelt forced him to resign. Without Walker as its front Tammany Hall was doomed. When Seabury publicly derided Tammany as 'the Amalgamated Order of Grafters and Crooks' it was effectively destroyed.

Tammany's reign was finally ended by Fiorello LaGuardia. In 1933 he ran again for mayor, backed by Samuel Seabury who helped him win the support of thousands of voters sick of corruption. LaGuardia was victorious and in the next twelve years he proved that 'non-partisan, non-political local government' was possible in New York.

Throwing Tammany out of City Hall did not, however, destroy organized crime. Certainly without its protection top hoodlums could no longer be sure that corrupt judges would shield them. Yet there were still no prosecutors with either the will or the ability to put the mob on trial, even in front of straight judges. Seabury had proved District Attorney Crain, the top prosecutor in America's biggest city, was incompetent. In 1935 his successor, William Dodge, was clearly disabling a grand jury investigation into Harlem gambling to protect his political masters. The jurors realized what was going on and demanded a new prosecutor. Governor Lehman gave the job to an ambitious young lawyer named Thomas Dewey.

Dewey was the first of the racketbusters. He did not just pursue known gangsters; he dug up every detail on the rackets they controlled. The son of a small-town newspaper owner from Michigan, he had been appointed chief assistant US attorney for the southern district of New York State in 1931. This boggling title meant that he had to apply the criminal law of the USA to New York City. At 29 Dewey was the youngest man ever to hold the post.

Much of his early work related to the fraudsters of the 'overworld', like stockbrokers who artificially boosted share prices. But Dewey's main task was to hunt down the racketeers of the underworld. In August 1931 he tried the bootlegger, John Nolan, alias 'Legs' Diamond, for operating an illegal still. Diamond was convicted, fined $10,000 and jailed for four years. Four months later on bail awaiting appeal Diamond was murdered.

Dewey indicted another notorious bootlegger, Arthur Flegenheimer, alias 'Dutch' Schultz. He was charged for evading taxes on a token $481,000 but the prospect of jail so vexed him that he vowed to kill Dewey. Foolishly he trumpeted his intentions to his underworld peers. They thought Dewey dead would be even worse than Dewey alive. His murder would bring too much 'heat' on them. They decided to kill Schultz before he could kill Dewey and in October 1935 in a restaurant in Newark, New Jersey, he was gunned down with three of his gang.

One man who did live long enough for Dewey to put him in jail was 'Waxey' Gordon. The one-time sneakthief, turned dope-pedlar and labour racketeer, was now one of America's biggest bootleggers. Dewey's men proved he had made $4,500,000 in two years and paid only $2010 in tax. He had sorted the money away in 200 banks. He owned breweries, nightclubs and hotels. He backed Broadway shows. He sent his children to the most expensive schools and spent $4000 on books with leather binding for his private library. None of them had ever been opened. Dewey's evidence sent Gordon to jail for ten years. He was convicted only five days before Prohibition was repealed.

Dewey jailed labour thugs, gambling bosses, loansharks and racketeers extorting the garment, fresh food and restaurant industries. In 1937 he was elected district attorney and did his bit to bury Tammany Hall. Back in 1932 he had convicted the black bosses of Harlem's numbers (or policy) rackets for tax evasion. At that time

Dutch Schultz forced these racketeers into his combination. They were no longer independent but profited from Schultz's financial backing and his connections. His most powerful friend was the Tammany leader James J. Hines.

Now as district attorney, Dewey persuaded some of Schultz's minions to reveal the true role of Jimmy Hines. George Weinberg swore he gave Hines $30,000 for the election campaign of William Dodge, Dewey's predecessor as DA. It was Dodge who in 1935 had sabotaged the grand jury investigating Schultz's Harlem gambling rackets. Weinberg paid Hines $500 a week to sweeten the police and the magistrates. Hines ensured that any police who raided Schultz's operations were transferred out of Harlem. Dewey claimed Hines was a salaried member of Schultz's gang. At the age of 63 this top New York politician was jailed for four to eight years.

Summing up Dewey told the jury, 'It is not a pleasant task for a district attorney to go through a case like this. . . . The important thing is that you declare to the people of New York, the police of New York, that they are free; that they will no longer be betrayed by a corrupt alliance between crime and politics. . . . We don't want protection of gangsters by political leaders.' Throughout the 1930s Dewey destroyed many of New York's top hoodlums and their political friends. In 1936 he took on the biggest criminal conspiracy of all – without even realizing it.

14

The Fall and Rise of Lucky Luciano

In his introduction to *The Gangs of New York*, published in 1927, Herbert Asbury wrote that the age of the gangster was over. For nearly fifty years the gangster had, he maintained, existed mainly in the imagination of newspapermen who:

> . . . resurrect him every time there is a mysterious killing in the slum districts or among the white lights of Broadway. No matter how obviously the crime be rooted in bootlegging, dope-peddling or what not, it is hailed as a new gang murder; words and phrases which have grown hoary and infirm in the service are trundled out and dusted off, and next morning shriek to a delighted populace that there is blood on the face of the moon and a new gang war impends.
>
> But the conflict never materializes and it is quite unlikely that it ever will again, for there are now no gangs in New York, and no gangsters in the sense that the word has come into common use. In his day the gangster flourished under the protection and manipulation of the crooked politician to whom he was an invaluable ally at election time, but his day has simply passed. Improved social, economic and educational conditions have lessened the number of recruits and the organized gangs have been clubbed out of existence by the police.'

So excellent a popular historian as Asbury must be forgiven for wholly misreading the evolution of crime in the 1920s. He saw bootlegging and drugs as signifying the end of gangsterism whereas today Prohibition is regarded as having made the mob and drugs are its most lucrative activity. If for Asbury 'gangs' were synonymous with street thugs who doubled as political bully-boys he might have been right, but he clearly meant huge organizations corruptly involved with top politicians which controlled city-wide rackets. While Asbury was writing the obituary of such gangs they were only just coming of age.

The Gangs of New York was published before Seabury ripped open the guts of the Tammany tiger and Dewey proved that bootleggers were making fortunes beyond the dreams of earlier gangsters. Until Dewey no prosecutor seemed to know where to start. There was little hard evidence of the growth in organized crime because no one knew how to look for it. Dewey sought out incorruptible detectives to lead his investigations. For assistants he hired the brightest young lawyers, some only just out of law school and untainted by machine politics. Most important of all he hired fully qualified accountants with a nose for investigation to go through the books and papers of every business which the gangsters controlled. As the main aim of organized crime is to make money it is astonishing that no one before Dewey had realized that financial investigators were fundamental to successful racketbusting.

In 1935 police raided the apartment of Polly Adler, New York's most notorious madam. Her customers at the time were two prominent businessmen whose names were tastefully left out of the newspapers. Miss Adler received no such favours, nor did her bookers, the pimps who supplied girls for her brothels and took 10 per cent of their earnings. They were jailed and branded 'vice tsars' by the press although in fact they were just low-level pimps as Eunice Carter discovered. She was a black lawyer and the only woman on Dewey's legal staff. At the Women's Court where prostitutes were arraigned she noticed that dozens of girls represented by the same lawyer were always acquitted. She realized that prostitution was organized and voiced her suspicions to Dewey. He was reluctant to waste resources on low-level vice but she convinced him that top mobsters were involved. Phones were tapped and conversations overheard which proved there was a legal hotline to get girls out of jail, off charges and back to the brothels earning money.

Each prostitute was forced to make weekly payments into a bail-bonding fund. The ring included madams, bookers, bondsmen and enforcers. Mrs Carter and her team identified most of the people running the racket. On Saturday, 1 February 1936 pimps were arrested all over New York and in Philadelphia. One hundred and fifty plain-clothes police raided more than seventy whorehouses and brought vanloads of vice vendors to Dewey's offices in the Woolworth Building. A hundred hookers assumed this was the usual charade and that in a few minutes they would be free to return to their customers.

Victor Herwitz, one of Tom Dewey's assistants, saw it all happen. 'Starting at nine o'clock that night into the office came hordes of prostitutes, pimps, telephone operators at whorehouses, dope addicts, all kinds of people, venereal and otherwise. We worked throughout the night and the weekend. There were witnesses sprawled all over the floor, having withdrawal symptoms because they weren't getting their drugs – a disgusting scene with disgusting people. In those days we weren't confined to constitutional rights. We were pretty rough. We broke people, we got them to talk. We didn't use violence but in those days they expected to be beaten up. One telephone operator was not co-operating so I got out of the chair to pull the blind down. He recognised this as a sign he was now going to get his beating so he pulled back cowering and said, "OK, OK, I'll tell you what you want to know".'

One by one witnesses broke and named the men who ran the racket. A booker asked that his wife, who had also been arrested, be released to take care of their children. Then he told his interrogators the name of the top man 'Charlie Luciano', alias Charlie Lucky. At about the same time a madam called Mildred Harris also named 'Charlie Lucky' as the boss. Dewey's secretary, Lillian Ross, recalls that: 'Nobody had suspected Luciano. They knew he was in narcotics and every other rotten business but they didn't know he was in prostitution. They didn't even suspect it.'

After questioning hundreds of witnesses Dewey's team were sure that the man ruling much of New York prostitution was its most prominent Italian gangster: Charlie Lucky to the underworld but to the 'overworld' Mr Charles Ross of the Waldorf-Astoria Hotel where he lived in style. Through his minions Luciano was said to control 200 madams and 1000 prostitutes who paid his men some $10 million a year for 'protection'. Those who did not pay were beaten or slashed by Luciano's enforcer, Little Davie Betillo who would also wreck their whorehouses. On a tapped phone Lucky told one henchman, 'Whores is whores. They can always be handled. They ain't got no guts.' Several embittered madams proved him wrong by testifying that Luciano knew all about the prostitution racket and was directly involved. It was Lucky, said Cokey Flo Brown, who told Betillo when to 'put the screws' on madams who were not paying their dues.

Dewey and his detectives were well aware that Luciano was a top gangster, perhaps *the* top gangster, in New York, but they had no idea he was the American Mafia's boss of bosses. Indeed they knew little if anything about the Mafia. They could recall the grotesque 'barrel murders' perpetrated by the Black Hand. They knew that Sicilian crooks extorted from their fellow-countrymen in ghettoes like Mulberry Street. They also knew something about the Unione Siciliana led by Joe 'the Boss' Masseria until his murder in 1931. That, however, was all.

Police records showed Luciano was born Salvatore Lucania in Sicily in 1897. Brought to New York in 1907, he grew up on 14th Street, on the fringe of the Lower East Side. He became a street gambler and made friends with two young Jews, Meyer Lansky and Ben 'Bugsy' Siegel who were to climb with him through the ranks of organized crime. At 18 he gained a minor conviction for selling drugs. During Prohibition he became a bootlegger. Homicide files showed that among those who visited Arnold Rothstein's offices the morning after he was shot in 1928 was Charles Lucania, alias Luciano, 'a waiter'. He had come to pillage the dying man's papers for IOUs and information on narcotics deals in progress.

Police records also noted that by 1929 Luciano had become Joe Masseria's right-hand man. Despite this one night he was found unconscious in Staten Island with his head beaten, his face slashed and his mouth taped over. His survival was deemed miraculous and earned him the the soubriquet Lucky. Whatever the reason for the attack (and many reasons have been dreamed up since) Luciano refused to talk.

On 15 April 1931 Masseria was murdered at a Coney Island restaurant. Detectives observed his spectacular funeral: a $15,000 coffin, forty Cadillacs, huge clocks of lilies with the hands pointing at 3.20 – the hour he died. But twenty of the Cadillacs were empty: the underworld had stayed away. The detectives knew Luciano had something to do with the murder and thought he had now replaced Joe as boss of the Unione Siciliana. But in February 1936, when the madams started to squeal, the police knew very little about him, except that he was suave, charming and had an expensive taste for show girls.

Dewey soon had enough evidence to indict Luciano who was now 1200 miles away in Hot Springs, Arkansas. This gambling spa was a resort and refuge for gangsters, controlled by Owney Madden, the English-born bootlegger and killer who was an old friend of Lucky's. Luciano was not far away enough, however. He was extradited to New York, proclaiming: 'I may not be the most moral and upright man who lives but I have never stooped so low as to become involved in prostitution.' On 11 May 1936 he went on trial with nine underlings at New York's County Courthouse.

The madams giving evidence – Nancy Presser, Mildred Harris and Cokey Flo Brown – may not have had the best of characters but they were supported by a string of hotel employees who recognized Luciano's co-defendants as frequent visitors to his Waldorf-Astoria apartment. These man ran the racket, collected from the madams, bailed out the prostitutes and supplied them with lawyers.

Luciano claimed he was just a gambler and called police officers to discredit the pimps testifying for Dewey. When Dewey brought up his 1926 arrest for carrying pistols and shotguns he claimed he had been hunting. Dewey asked him what kind of birds he had shot. 'Peasants,' said Lucky, reducing the courtroom to laughter. Dewey was prepared to overlook the mispronunciation but found it hard to believe the story.

Luciano admitted his convictions, for running a gambling house in 1930 and for narcotics in 1916. He claimed he had never touched dope again but Dewey proved he had been caught selling drugs in 1923 when police had found morphine and heroin at his home. Luciano told them that at 163 Mulberry Street there was a trunk full of narcotics. When they found the trunk he was released uncharged. Thirteen years later Dewey revealed his treachery, showing that even the great Luciano would turn stool pigeon when it suited him. Students of Omerta may be as interested in his conduct as the folk who owned the trunk must have been when they belatedly realized who had betrayed them.

The jury found Dewey's case overwhelming and convicted all the defendants. Luciano was found guilty on sixty-two counts of compulsory prostitution. He was sentenced to thirty to fifty years. In effect he was jailed for life. His criminal career should have been over. Nailing Luciano was Dewey's greatest racketbusting achievement. Yet there was another code of law in New York – that of the underworld itself. In time it would rehabilitate even Luciano.

Organized crime in America was still evolving. As Jewish gangs had taken over from the Irish by the 1900s, so thirty years later Italian gangs were taking over from the Jews. In a few years the Jews who had dominated bootlegging in America's biggest cities apart from Chicago had either been murdered, jailed or incorporated into a combination dominated by the Mafia. The ethnic balance of the national crime syndicate whose leaders had gathered at Atlantic City in 1929 had shifted decisively to the Italians.

Dewey and his team did not realize that Italians now ruled organized crime. After Dutch Schultz was murdered in 1935 the New York police listed its underworld Big Six. Five were Jewish, the exception being Luciano. The police were unaware that the Jews were all working with Lucky and the Mafia. They knew nothing of the Mafia's structure and did not understand that putting Luciano in jail would neither destroy him nor halt the advance of his criminal organization.

Joe Valachi, the gangster turned informer, only revealed the Mafia's family structure in 1963. Back in the 1930s Dewey had no Valachi so he knew nothing of the Mafia's extraordinary capacity for regeneration. Rothstein, Gordon and Schultz left no heirs. Childless bachelor though he was, Luciano founded a dynasty.

Luciano's liberation occurred in extraordinary circumstances. On 11 December 1941 Germany and Italy declared war on the USA. By the end of February 1942 America had lost seventy-one merchant ships to German submarines. The Atlantic sea-lanes had to be made safe. US naval intelligence suspected that the U-boats were being refuelled and resupplied off the coast by Italian- or German-born criminals with waterfront connections who might also be informing on Allied shipping movements in and out of eastern ports. On 9 February the SS *Normandie*, the former French liner and once the fastest passenger ship across the Atlantic, was burnt out at her Manhattan berth while undergoing conversion to a troop carrier. The fire may have been an accident but may equally well have been sabotage.

One intelligence officer saw a way to end the sabotage. Lieutenant Commander Charles Haffenden told his chiefs to recruit the underworld. Haffenden knew that gangsters controlled New York's piers and docks through the ILA – the International Longshoremen's Association – and the Fulton Fish Market. In the fish market the rackets' boss was Joe 'Socks' Lanza, business agent of the United Seafood Workers Union. His patriotism was difficult to gauge and, besides, patriotism for which nation, America or Italy? There was another problem: he faced trial for extortion. The district attorney refused to give him a deal but at a meeting in a Manhattan park Lanza enthusiastically agreed to exert his influence over fishing fleets and tramp steamers from Maine to Florida. He would instruct them to watch out for enemy shipping, expose collaborators and work with naval intelligence. Lanza would give navy agents union cards so they could work under cover on board vessels sailing all along the coast. The racketeer was as good as his word. If there had ever been any offshore aid to the U-boats, it now ceased.

Naval intelligence wanted to extend the arrangement to New York's biggest piers and docks: in Brooklyn, west Manhattan and New Jersey. Lanza could only deliver the small downtown fishing piers. He had no power where transatlantic ships tied up. Only one man had that power he told them: Lucky Luciano. Not only was he the Mafia overlord of the Italian-American waterfront bosses. He also had immense prestige among recent Italian immigrants, especially Sicilian mafiosi who had been jailed and tortured by Mussolini. He could even deliver the Manhattan ILA locals controlled by Irish racketeers. There was another factor: the waterfront mafiosi. They suspected that Lanza was using naval intelligence to keep out of prison and if they were going to help anyone out of his problems it would be their boss of bosses, Lucky Luciano, not a malodorous fish-pedlar.

To naval intelligence a fish-pedlar at liberty seemed a better bet than a pimp in the slammer. By April 1942 Luciano had been in jail for nearly six years. At Sing Sing he had been diagnosed as a drug addict suffering from syphilis. He was soon transferred to Dannemora, the 'Siberia' of prisons in New York State's frozen north. How such a man could help America's war effort bemused the navy men but Haffenden persuaded them to follow Lanza's advice.

Luciano was contacted through Moses Polakoff, his lawyer. Polakoff brought the Jewish racketeer, Meyer Lansky, into the scheme because he felt Lansky, who had been Luciano's friend since they were boys, would have more influence. Polakoff himself had enough influence to get Luciano moved immediately to Great Meadows Penitentiary near Albany, cured of syphilis but suffering from a weak heart. In May 1942 he was visited by Lansky and Polakoff. He was reluctant to help, partly because he knew he would be deported on his release. He did not want to be sent back to Italy and branded a traitor for helping America. Yet when 'Socks' Lanza visited him in June Luciano told him to use his name in approaching both Italian and Irish ILA bosses, including Albert Anastasia. He also instructed Lanza to enroll the men who were running his Mafia family while he was in jail: Joe Adonis and Frank Costello. New York Harbor thus became a safe place for America's shipping on the order of the Mafia's boss of bosses. Only Luciano could have drafted the entire American Mafia into the war against Mussolini!

Orchestrating the entire operation was Meyer Lansky to whom Luciano gave overall authority. In the meantime Lucky revived his own underworld activities. The prison visits he was allowed for the war effort became organized-crime summits. His under-boss, Frank Costello, would show up with another top racketeer, Mike Miranda. But whatever nefarious business they discussed there is no doubt that New York's waterfront had been secured by the end of 1942. For the rest of the war there was no sabotage, union disputes or delay to shipping.

Soon there was another job for Lucky's friends. In January 1943 at Casablanca President Franklin D. Roosevelt, Prime Minister Winston Churchill and their chiefs of staff decided on the invasion of Italy. The first landings were to be made on Sicily. In America recent immigrants or visitors to the island were called on to supply any photographs of its coastline and terrain.

In New York there were hundreds of mafiosi who hated Mussolini because his prefect, Cesare Mori, had executed dozens of their Sicilian cousins without trial. They hoped Italy would lose the war and overthrow Mussolini who had dared to treat the Mafia as the Mafia treated everyone else. Would the Mafia in Sicily now work as an underground movement for the Allies?

Again Haffenden asked the New York Mafia to organize the city's Italian immigrants. Joe Adonis, Luciano's gambling boss, took charge as Lansky later recalled. 'Haffenden was looking for Italians that he thought had a knowledge of Sicily and all the surrounding islands there, and had relatives. I went to Adonis to find me such Italians. . . . I didn't know the people. . . . The American-Italians were the ones that got me the foreign Italians to bring up to the navy through Charlie Luciano.'

Haffenden was getting carried away. He proposed that Luciano himself be freed and infiltrated into Sicily before the invasion. He dreamed up a plan in which Luciano would be taken to a neutral country like Portugal and then make his way to Sicily to win over the islanders and supply military intelligence. He claimed he could arrange Luciano's release for this task of national importance. His colleagues now felt Haffenden had become too close to the underworld. Contrary to fictional accounts Luciano did not win such a deal. For the duration of the war he never left jail, let alone America. 'Socks' Lanza did no better. In January 1943 he pleaded guilty to charges of extorting the fishing industry and was jailed for up to fifteen years.

At 2.30 a.m. on 10 July 1943 the US 7th Army landed at Gela and Licata on the south Sicilian coast. In the vanguard were four naval intelligence officers armed with the Mafia-inspired information gathered in New York. They swiftly seized the Italian naval command HQ and captured documents showing the disposition of the enemy's entire Mediterranean fleet. They also found maps of minefields and routes of safe passage through them. This brilliant operation won honours for the intelligence men and fully justified the navy's handshake with the Mafia.

The conquest of Sicily took thirty-seven days, resistance coming mainly from 60,000 German troops. Local civilians gave their wholehearted aid to the quartet from naval intelligence, particularly in the ports of Palermo and western Sicily. One of them later said that the Mafia had been invaluable in organizing the Sicilian fishing fleet. Soon Mafia prisoners were released from Mussolini's jails. At the time this may have seemed wise because they were virulently anti-Fascist, but it was like unlocking Pandora's box. The decision was taken by the Office of Strategic Services (OSS), the forerunner of the CIA. Naval intelligence had nothing to do with it.

When the war in Europe ended on 8 May 1945 Lucky Luciano was still in jail. Commander Haffenden had won the Purple Heart at Iwo Jima and almost died from stomach wounds. From hospital he wrote to Polakoff, at the lawyer's request, confirming Luciano's great assistance during the war. On 23 May a New York newspaper stated that Luciano was seeking early release because of his help in the invasion of Sicily. But when the State Parole Board asked Haffenden to give evidence about Luciano's role he replied that henceforth he could be questioned only with the navy's prior permission. Embarrassed by its handshake with the Devil, the navy was now trying to pretend the whole affair had never happened.

Despite the navy's wall of silence, fortified by some outright lies, the Parole Board unanimously recommended clemency to the governor, on whose decision Luciano's fate now depended. Ironically the governor was Thomas Dewey who had put Luciano in jail nearly ten years previously. On 3 January 1946 Dewey accepted the judgment of the board which granted Luciano parole on condition that he was deported. Dewey added a sphinx-like paragraph to his explanation:

> Upon the entry of the United States into the war, Luciano's aid was sought by the armed services in inducing others to provide information concerning possible enemy attack. It appears that he co-operated in such effort, although the actual value of the information procured is not clear.

With that enigmatic testimonial Luciano was put on board the SS *Laura Keene* in New York Harbor on 8 February 1946. Next morning reporters beseiged the ship to interview him. Hulking longshoremen, armed with baling hooks, barred their way but underworld figures boarded the ship without trouble. One was

Frank Costello. They dined with Lucky off lobster, spaghetti and wine. In the early hours of 10 February they said farewell and left the ship. By 9 a.m. the *Laura Keene* was on her way to Italy.

In the post-war years the ramifications of Luciano's release damaged many people. The navy continued to deny any involvement with Luciano, destroying all the documentary evidence and discrediting Haffenden. He never recovered from his war wounds or the navy's character assassination. After a succession of lowly jobs he died in 1952.

Governor Dewey suffered too. Believing the navy's denials some observers were convinced that Luciano had bought his freedom from Dewey. One author claimed Luciano told him he had paid $75,000 into Republican party funds. A Democratic congressman claimed the bribe was $300,000. In 1954 Governor Dewey commissioned an official investigation which confirmed that there had been substantial collaboration between the navy, Luciano and the underworld. Commissioner William Herlands also found that naval intelligence had instigated the affair, not Luciano. No evidence emerged against Dewey but he was not permitted to use the investigation to clear his name. In November 1954 the director of naval intelligence wrote to him claiming that publication of Herlands's report might harm the navy: 'That there is potential for embarrassment to the navy public-relations-wise is apparent.' Tom Dewey agreed not to publish the report and it was only released with its evidence to the author Rodney Campbell in 1976.[1]

In the late 1940s many people were astonished at Luciano's release. One of the grand jurors who had indicted him in 1936 wrote to Dewey saying that he viewed Luciano as the 'type of man who would return to his profitable and nefarious practice when given the opportunity. The People must be protected from the diabolical schemes of this man, contrite as he now appears.'

In Washington at the Federal Bureau of Narcotics, they were even angrier. Since its formation in 1930 the bureau's chief had been Harry Anslinger. He and his agents had quickly realized there was a Mafia and that it was the most powerful criminal conspiracy in America. Anslinger developed networks of Mafia informers and techniques of undercover penetration. He hired men of Italian extraction who spoke the dialects of the bureau's main adversaries, including Charles Siragusa who hailed Anslinger as the first man to see the 'evil of organized crime in the United States. I recall back in the 1930s we started to assemble files on Lucky Luciano and Frank Costello and all the big hoods. At that time they were considered to be temporary nuisances but he foresaw they would become as powerful as they have become.'

Anslinger was appalled at Luciano's release. His worst fears were confirmed when within a year Luciano returned, flew into Cuba and promptly started to run the American Mafia from this offshore haven. Cuba's politicians were already in the pocket of the mob through Meyer Lansky who had first bought their affections in the 1930s and masterminded organized-crime's development of gambling casinos in Havana. When Lucky checked into the Hotel Nacional Lansky and dozens of mafiosi like Joe Adonis soon joined him. Even the singer Frank Sinatra ran into him.

Also in Havana were two Bureau of Narcotics agents who discovered that he had brought shipments of heroin into Cuba to be smuggled into the United States. Anslinger demanded that Luciano be deported straight back to Italy or America would ban the export of all medical drugs to Cuba. After just six weeks in Havana Lucky was dumped on a freighter bound for Genoa.

Back in Naples Luciano was fined for illegally importing $57,000 and a new American car. His main adversary was his fellow-Sicilian, narcotics agent Charlie Siragusa. 'Mr Anslinger, with his usual keen foresight, saw an influx of heroin coming into the United States when World War Two ended. I was sent to Europe to corroborate our worst fear, that Luciano was responsible for the flow of heroin coming through the port of New York.' Siragusa went under cover and soon purchased some heroin. It was packed in bags stamped 'Schiaparelli', the name of the drug manufacturers in Turin. He proved that mafiosi in four American cities were getting heroin under this legitimate cover. He also proved that the men running the Italian end were American-reared mafiosi, all under Luciano's command. They had corrupted a Schiaparelli executive who diverted 350-kg of medicinal heroin, worth more than $2 million to the streets on New York.

The Italian authorities charged Luciano's couriers and said he was the ultimate source of supply to the USA. There was not enough evidence to charge Luciano but Siragusa had him declared a social menace under a law of Mussolini's. He now had to live a decent life, could not stay out after dark or go to places like racetracks. Caught at a racetrack Luciano was jailed for sixty days.

To Siragusa Luciano was 'nothing but a pimp and a dope-pedlar which, ironically, are the two things no gangster wants to be considered. It was my duty to do everything legal to neutralize this man. He should never have been paroled from his American jail. We got him out of the country but we didn't neutralize his activities. In Italy he made transatlantic telephone calls. He entertained gangster visitors from the United States like Meyer Lansky. We know Lansky brought him a satchel of money as his share of the proceeds of American racketeering. His power in the American underworld was not diminished. It was increased.'

Luciano survived Siragusa's onslaught but was never allowed back to live in America. On 26 January 1962 he collapsed of a heart attack at Naples airport and died. At last America relented. His relatives were allowed to bring his body back to New York, for burial in St John's Cemetery, Queens. He was 64 years old.

If Luciano's release had been a disaster for America so too was the grotesque way in which his *compare*, Vito Genovese, escaped justice for nearly thirty years. In 1937 Genovese was wanted for murder in New York. He fled to Italy where he became a close friend of Mussolini's son and of Mussolini himself. He gave huge sums to the dictator's party and was awarded the title of Commendatore, one of Italy's highest honours. When southern Italy fell the Allies set up military government headquarters in Nola near Naples, Genovese's home town. The mafioso became a trusted interpreter to the conquerors, insinuating himself into the affections of high-ranking officers. He donated a luxurious Packard car for the use of Governor Charles Poletti. Brigadier Poletti was appointed governor largely because of his experience as interim governor of New York State, a job he had held for only seventeen days.

The wily Genovese exploited his privileged position with the Allied military government by running the black market in stolen American food, trucks, petrol and anything the liberators brought in. A young military detective named Orange Dickey realized what was going on and arrested him. He then learned that Genovese was wanted in America for murder. For months he tried to get the AMG to help him ship Genovese back to New York for trial but was met only with obstruction. He even had to hide his prisoner from the AMG lest his friends attempted to free him. Dickey eventually took Genovese back himself, sleeping in the same cabin all the way back to New Jersey.

Just before Genovese went on trial a witness to the murder was himself murdered. The evidence of the only other witness could no longer be corroborated and Genovese was freed, resuming his criminal career. Dickey was furious. He recalled how Genovese would thank him for his free trip back to America. Over the next twelve years Genovese eliminated all his rivals to become the Mafia's boss of bosses in America.

In the post-war years Anslinger tried to find a politician who would lead a nationwide war on organized crime and the Mafia in particular. His search coincided with a campaign led by Virgil Peterson of the Chicago Crime Commission who was appalled at the impact of corruption on local government. Both Peterson and Anslinger found their man in Senator Estes Kefauver, a lawyer from Tennessee with presidential aspirations. In 1950 Kefauver established a Senate committee 'to investigate organized crime in interstate commerce'.

In the next year Kefauver's committee visited fourteen cities and heard more than 600 witnesses. Its New York hearings were televized and more than 30 million people sat mesmerized as notorious hoodlums treated America's highest elected body with disdain. Most of them refused to answer questions, taking the 5th Amendment on the grounds that their answers might tend to incriminate them.

A spectacular exception was Frank Costello, the man running Lucky Luciano's empire while the boss had been in exile. Born in Calabria, Costello was known as the 'prime minister of crime' for his charm, diplomacy and political connections. Suffering from a sore throat he croaked denials of criminal activity until he was upset by the bombastic questions of Senator Charles Tobey. He staged a walk-out but meekly returned when threatened with an instant jail sentence. Tobey castigated him for his lack of military service and his unpatriotic acts in the land which had given him citizenship.

'What have you ever done for your country?' asked Tobey.

Costello thought long and hard and then replied, 'I've paid my taxes.' There were roars of laughter but Costello could not see the joke.

The committee concluded that crime was organized in many American cities. The two major groups were 'the Accardo–Guzik–Fischetti syndicate, whose headquarters are in Chicago, and the Costello–Adonis–Lansky syndicate based in New York'. In a paragraph which could have been written by Anslinger the committee stated:

> There is a sinister criminal organization known as the Mafia operating throughout the country. . . . The Mafia is a loose-knit organization specializing in the sale and distribution of narcotics, the conduct of various gambling enterprises, prostitution and other rackets based on extortion and violence. The Mafia is the binder which ties together the two major criminal syndicates as well as numerous other criminal groups throughout the country. The power of the Mafia is based on a ruthless enforcement of its edicts and its own law of vengeance.

Kefauver's evidence did not quite prove the Mafia's imperial power over American crime but the huge public interest generated by the committee should at least have provoked some response by law enforcement. Astonishingly nothing much happened. In 1952 the committee was forgotten as Senator Joe McCarthy's Un-American Activities Committee grabbed the headlines. Kefauver had proved so many public officials were on the take that, whatever the role of the Mafia, no one could say organized crime was un-American. The unpatriotic implications were hard to swallow. McCarthy's war on Reds had more comfortable appeal.

For the next few years the Mafia was given few problems, except by Anslinger and the FBN. Only the discovery of the Apalachin summit in 1957 forced the Mafia into the consciousness of the Justice Department. That same year the McClellan Committee unearthed a wealth of evidence proving organized crime's power over organized labour. It was in front of this committee in 1963 that Joe Valachi told his story. The public interest aroused by the hearings and by Attorney-General Robert Kennedy's commitment to the war on organized crime survived both his brother's assassination and his own resignation in 1964.

As part of his 'Great Society' programme President Lyndon Johnson set up a crime commission which included an Organized Crime Task Force which gathered and re-evaluated all the evidence on organized crime. It queried terms, attempted definitions and wrote a blueprint for action. It called for legislation authorizing wiretaps and bugs. It sought heavier punishments when crimes were committed as part of a continuing criminal conspiracy (such as the Mafia although no such ethnic term was used). It demanded protection for witnesses, before, during and after they testified against organized-crime figures. They should be given new jobs and identities far away from the mobsters they helped to prosecute. The task force also recommended greater co-operation between all levels of law enforcement and specialized training for prosecutors and investigators. In the next few years almost all the commission's recommendations were carried out. Strike forces were set up in cities where organized crime was at its strongest. At last the racketbusters were getting organized.

But what was the attitude of the FBI and of that brooding enigma J. Edgar Hoover who had been its director for almost forty years? The history of organized crime and of those who have fought it can be written without any reference to the FBI before the late 1950s. In the ranks of the racketbusters – Seabury, Dewey and Anslinger – Hoover has no place. It was his choice. It is widely asserted that he used to say organized crime and/or the Mafia did not exist; biographies of Hoover and histories of the FBI cite no public occasion when he said this, however. In researching *Crime Inc.* we spoke to many FBI men who served under Hoover from 1930 until his death. None could recall any such statement. Yet it is clear from Hoover's actions and omissions that if organized crime or the Mafia did exist he was not going to let his agents dirty their hands with them.

Hoover, the son of a Washington civil servant, became a clerk in the Justice Department in 1917. Two years later he was in charge of the General Intelligence Division, keeping track of bolsheviks, subversives and radicals during America's first 'Red Scare'. Hoover did the job so well that when the Bureau of Investigation needed a new director in 1924 he was the obvious choice. Aged only 29 he became America's top policeman without ever having policed crime. Hoover was not a cop. He was a secret policeman. His preference for chasing Reds stayed with him to the end. He was prominent in every anti-communist scare and was one of Joe McCarthy's staunchest allies.

Hoover's kind of gang-busting did not take place in the murky world of big city vice and corruption. It was about bank robbers and kidnappers: country-boy killers with a machine-gun and a stolen motor-car. A master of publicity (in contrast to Anslinger), Hoover manipulated the press, radio and cinema newsreels with a continuous stream of stories about his agents getting their man. He hijacked the Chicago Crime Commission's 'Public Enemy' stamp and applied it to gangs of bandits. In the early 1930s the instant legends of America's criminal folklore fell in rapid succession before the guns of the G-Men: 'Pretty Boy' Floyd, 'Baby-Face' Nelson, John Dillinger, Ma Barker and her Boys. Their corpses were usually filmed for the newsreels. The few who weren't killed were captured in spectacular fashion, like Alvin Karpis and 'Machine-Gun' Kelly.

Behind this carefully nurtured myth there are a few flaws in the FBI story. 'Machine-Gun' Kelly, a numbskull dominated by his bully of a wife, had kidnapped an Oklahoma oil millionaire and ransomed him for $200,000. The Kellys got the money but were later arrested. Just before he surrendered, Kelly (who never killed anybody despite his nickname) is alleged to have cried out, 'Don't shoot G-Man,' coining the FBI's honoured nickname. Yet Kelly did not surrender to the FBI but to the Memphis police. Often the bandits killed G-Men before G-Men killed them. John Dillinger's getaway at Little Bohemia was a fiasco which made his killing at the Biograph Cinema in Chicago an act of public cleansing for the FBI. There is no doubt that most FBI agents were brave men who risked their lives against the relentless killers terrorizing much of rural America. But Hoover was clinging to an outdated notion of crime straight out of the Old West, of bloodletters and bandits like Butch Cassidy and Jesse James.

He could not grasp that crime had undergone a revolution in the big cities where most Americans now lived. In the shadow of the skyscrapers immigrants and their children were trying to make a living in what they had been told was the land of opportunity. For many it proved to be a land of poverty, violence and oppression. Among these people parasitic gangs had developed criminal organizations far beyond Hoover's understanding.

For decades Hoover sheltered behind the fact that in Washington there were other agencies responsible for some of the main areas of organized crime: the Bureau of Prohibition, the Internal Revenue Service and the Bureau of Narcotics. Crime in the big cities he left to district attorneys, especially when the FBI could not touch huge areas of crime such as gambling because there were no federal laws against them. Hoover made no attempt to demand such laws, despite his brilliant ability to get presidents and attorney-generals to do what he wanted.

At the root of it all Hoover was well aware that organized crime is not a black-and-white affair: goodies against baddies. It is largely about public demand. Millions of Americans seek the goods and services which organized crime provides. Where there is public demand there is public tolerance and huge profits to be made which mean that it is easy to buy up politicians and policemen wholesale. What Hoover feared above all else was the contamination of the lily-white image of his agents when almost every other police force in America was riddled with corruption.

When Sergeant Edgar Croswell discovered the Apalachin summit in 1957 Hoover was embarrassed because he knew nothing either about the men who were there or what they were doing. Only the Bureau of Narcotics had an explanation. But Hoover, the consummate politician, suddenly established his Top Hoodlum Program.[2] He was still not admitting there was a Mafia. How could he confess after twenty-five years that Anslinger was right and he had been wrong?

His chance came in 1963. When Joe Valachi testified at the Senate he referred not to the Mafia but to La Cosa Nostra. The adroit Hoover now made a brilliant, face-saving escape. Henceforth the FBI would harry La Cosa Nostra, or LCN as the FBI men soon called it. Any American who did not know much about organized crime might have thought Hoover had made a terrifying new discovery, an evil conspiracy which only the FBI could combat. It was of course the same organization against which Anslinger had incessantly campaigned since the 1930s. The Houdini of law enforcement had done it again.

15

The Cleveland Story

'This fuckin' Irishman,' moaned Jack White, the boss of the Cleveland family, about an upstart racketeer who had survived eight Mafia attempts on his life, 'he's gotta make a mistake. He's gotta goes. I hope he moves back to Texas. *They*'d kill him, the Texas green pins!'

By September 1977 when the FBI surreptitiously recorded these words the Cleveland Mafia was at its limited wits' end. For all its power and even bigger reputation the mob that ruled the underworld of America's tenth biggest city and its sixth most populous state had been 'psyched out' by a mock Irishman called Danny Greene. Even after his closest ally had been blown into pieces Danny would sit bare-chested on the street under a giant Irish tricolour and dare the Mafia to try again. 'If somebody wants to come after me, I'm over here by the Celtic Club. I'm not hard to find.'

Finding Greene was not the problem, however. Killing him was. As their attempts to destroy Greene became ever more desperate Cleveland's top mafiosi would destroy themselves.

Cleveland, Ohio stands on the shores of Lake Erie. From the 1870s thousands of immigrants came to work in its steel factories and heavy industries. The city first tasted organized crime in the 1910s when rival newspaper owners hired goons to knock each other out of business. They fought vicious battles, hijacking truckloads of newsprint, destroying entire editions and seizing street sales pitches. Mickey McBride and Tom McGinty, the circulation managers of the two main papers, operated exactly like gang bosses. McBride went on to monopolize Cleveland's taxicabs, own its football team and, in league with the Mafia, control the continental race-wire service which tyrannized bookmakers all over America until the 1950s. McGinty rose to nationwide notoriety in the casino gambling racket.

When Prohibition came into force in 1920 Cleveland scorned it. With Canada just across the lake the city promptly became the ideal centre for smuggling liquor into the USA. One combine which seized the opportunity was the 'Cleveland Syndicate', four men who would be partners in crime for forty years. The longest-lasting was Morris 'Moe' Dalitz, the son of a Russian immigrant who had built up a flourishing laundry business. Moe enjoyed a college education and became a professor of English but he used his respectable business image as a cover for rum-running. The syndicate ran Canadian whiskey across Lake Erie in a fleet of boats known as the 'Big Jewish Navy'. Occasionally they lost a vessel to Prohibition agents or the coastguard but they succeeded none the less in importing hundreds of thousands of cases. When repeal came in 1933 Dalitz and Co. moved effortlessly into illegal casino gambling and in 1949 slipped just as effortlessly into Las Vegas.[1]

By the 1920s Cleveland had its own Little Italy around Mayfield Road and Murray Hill on the East Side. Here criminals took to bootlegging with as much zeal as their cousins in New York and Chicago. The 'Mayfield Road Gang' hosted the first known Mafia summit in America at the Statler Hotel, Cleveland, in December 1928. The police broke up the gathering, humiliating Cleveland's boss, bootlegger Joseph Porello, who had to bail everyone out of the police station. At the time Porello and his brothers were involved in a mortal struggle with another blood family, the Lonardos. In the late 1920s they slaughtered each other to gain control of the Cleveland Mafia. The Lonardos triumphed but at such loss of life that leadership fell to their allies, the Milanos – Frank the boss, Anthony and Pete.

When Prohibition ended the Cleveland Mafia moved into legitimate business and muscled in on the 'numbers' or 'policy' games which were now enjoyed by the city's growing black population.[2] Gunning black gambling bosses into submission, they seized profits running into many millions of dollars a year. To avoid the tax man Frank Milano fled to Mexico and his successor, Big Al Polizzi, moved to Florida to build hotels. By 1943 John Scalish became boss, a job he held until he died of natural causes in 1975.

Scalish was succeeded by James Licavoli, who perversely adopted the alias Jack White because of his olive complexion. A gunman in Prohibition, by 1975 Licavoli was an ageing capo and he did not want the job. He was forced to take it because Scalish had not groomed any obvious successor or indeed 'made' any new members for many years. Some of Licavoli's relatives controlled the Mafia in Detroit and it was their influence with the National Commission which won him the Cleveland leadership. Perhaps they were reassured by the little old bachelor's modest lifestyle and his devotion to the Catholic Church. But he was in poor health and walked with a stick. Not only that, he was getting absent-minded and was later arrested for shoplifting a pair of trousers from a department store, a crime ill-befitting a Mafia godfather.

After years spent marking time under Scalish younger mafiosi wanted to boost the family's stagnating fortunes by moving into narcotics. Scalish had vetoed all drug-trafficking, which had allowed black organized crime in Cleveland to grow unchallenged to the point where blacks regained control over their own gambling. Bitter over Licavoli's appointment and despairing of his geriatric style, some young Turks broke away from the family. One rebel faction was led by a labour racketeer called John Nardi, who despite being 60 was young enough to be considered a young Turk by Cleveland's senile mob. Nardi went outside the Mafia to make an alliance with the brash Irish racketeer who had declared war on the Cleveland family: Danny Greene.

It is doubtful if Greene really had any Irish blood. He refused to talk about his childhood but some observers say he was part-Scots, part-Jewish and no parts Irish. Born in 1930 Danny was a handsome, well-built 'Irish type' of 5 ft 10 in, with thinning blond hair. Around a nucleus of young relatives and some genuine Irish-Americans he had developed an independent organized crime faction on Cleveland's West Side active in narcotics, gambling, loansharking and union racketeering. In alliance with Nardi he murdered several mafiosi in a campaign to take over all organized crime in northern Ohio and supersede the Mafia itself. Joe Griffin, now special agent in charge of Cleveland's FBI, says Greene was determined to achieve this under the Irish banner. 'He had a green Lincoln, he wrote in green ink, he had a green flag in front of his house. Everything about him was green. He would get on television and call the La Cosa Nostra figures maggots. He felt he was indestructible.'

In the mid-1970s Greene's war with the Mafia was costing so many lives that Cleveland seized the title of the 'bomb capital of America' from Youngstown 70 miles away, where Mafia factions have been blowing each other up for generations. It was probably Greene and Nardi who blew up Shondor Birns, a Jewish sidekick of the family, and disposed of Leo 'Lips' Moceri, for fifty years one of its most brutal enforcers. In August 1976 Moceri disappeared. Only his car was found, its boot drenched in blood.

Moceri had been Licavoli's right-hand man and the National Commission demanded to know what was going on. When a family like Cleveland cannot defend itself the entire Cosa Nostra is diminished. Its position as the most powerful force in American crime depends on its continuing ability to discipline its competitors and enforce its edicts. If the Cleveland Mafia was shown no 'respect' every other family would be threatened by rebellious non-Italian hoodlums. These days the Mafia's power over certain ethnic groups, particularly blacks and Hispanics, is declining.[3] This it has to accept but when another white faction is seen to be beating a family on its own territory La Cosa Nostra has lost its main weapon: fear.

According to one of his capos Jack White became quite distraught over Greene's insolent rise. The capo said of the situation: 'He's got control of the West Side. He's got the gambling. He's got the barbut,[4] the vending machines, the music, the prostitution, the dope. He's even into the union. Jack White is very upset. He's afraid of him and he wants him out of the way.'

What was particularly humiliating for the family was that Nardi was a disgruntled aspirant for the top job. By allying himself with Greene's West Side mob he threatened to seize the East Side and take by conquest what he had been deprived of by succession. He had already outflanked the family by moving into narcotics, which Licavoli still shunned. At last the boss decided Nardi had to die. The traitor survived a shooting and a bombing but in May 1977 he was killed when the family detonated a car bomb parked next to his Cadillac at his Teamster union headquarters.

Now it was time to finish Greene. As Joe Griffin recalls, 'They had made eight attempts to kill him. They blew up his house: he fell from the second floor to the basement, landed on the refrigerator and walked away. They tried to kill him when he was jogging: he took out a .38 revolver and killed one of the hit men. They failed so often to kill they felt they needed help from outside.'

Licavoli was in a dilemma. If he were to ask Mafia bosses in other cities to send him a hit team he would lose face. Cleveland was already known in Mafia circles as the 'gang that couldn't shoot straight'. Instead he found a face-saver in California where the family had a good friend in Jimmy 'the Weasel' Fratianno, a Cleveland boy who was a capo in the Los Angeles family and its acting boss while most of its leaders were in jail. He had always kept in touch with Tony 'Dope' Del Santer, a capo close to Licavoli. When Fratianno heard Cleveland wanted some help he introduced Del Santer to Raymond Ferritto, a professional burglar from Erie, Pennsylvania.

Ferritto, a handsome man in his late forties, had the right track record. In 1969 he had killed another expatriate Clevelander, Julius Petro, for the Los Angeles family. As Ferritto told the *Crime Inc.* team in the only interview he has ever given: 'A problem arose with a man who was bringing a lot of heat on other people from law enforcement agencies. He was a known bank robber and burglar and I took care of the problem by taking him out to the airport and shooting him in the head.'

Del Santer told Ferritto about Danny Greene. 'They wanted this man taken care of. For two years they had been trying to kill him and had failed each time so they decided to get somebody from outside who was capable of handling it.

'This was a family matter. If you have a problem and you have to call someone from Chicago to come in and take care of it you show weakness.' In hiring Ferritto Licavoli was not showing weakness because he was not a 'made' member of any family. Indeed the hit man was told that if he killed Greene he could join the Cleveland family, which made the assignment even more domestic. 'Not only was I going to be inducted, I was to share in the profits of the family. I would receive 25 per cent of all the gambling and loansharking that came out of several local towns. It ran into big money.'

In the following months Ferritto frequently met the Cleveland hierarchy including Licavoli, Del Santer and John Calandra, with whom he kept in almost daily touch. Calandra was a respected Cleveland businessman, a tool-and-die maker who was 'made' in the 1970s in the family's first induction session for decades. He rose instantly to near under-boss status.

Ferritto moved into Cleveland, living in motels. He soon understood why the family was unnerved by the Irishman. 'They were very disturbed. Every attempt they made was fouled up. Greene took precautions. He always carried a gun. Wherever he went there was someone with him. He seemed invincible, a man with nine lives.

'After a while it became clear that drastic measures would have to be taken to accomplish this thing. We decided to build a box and place it in the entrance of the building where Greene was living. We would put dynamite in it and set it off by remote control. I installed the box with the dynamite inside but a lot of old people living there used to sit in the entrance. If it went off a lot of them would be hurt so we discarded the plan.

'I moved into an apartment in the building. Shortly after we tapped Greene's telephone. We went down to the manager's office, found his line and hooked it up with the dead phone in my apartment. Whenever the phone rang it would activate a tape-recorder. If I happened to be away we could still listen to his calls. I especially remember he used to call the FBI using his alias "Mr Patrick". He was an FBI informant! When Licavoli and the others heard this tape they said, "We have to get him soon, it's embarrassing."

'During this time he made a dental appointment on the phone, which we taped. I met Licavoli, Calandra and three other family members. We took a boat out on a lake, played the tape and decided to give it one more shot. We would build a dynamite box on the inside of a car door. When Greene went to his dentist's we would park the car next to his and trigger it off at a distance.'

On 6 October 1977 Ferritto and his partner, Youngstown mafioso Ronald Carabbia, were joined by a team of Cleveland family members armed with a high-powered rifle. They drove to the dentist's where the back-up crew's behaviour showed Ferritto why the family had never managed to kill Greene. 'They were parked in the lot and were supposed to take a shot at him if there was an opening but they chickened out and drove off.

'When Greene came for his appointment we were there. After he parked his car and walked off I took the bomb car and parked it next to his. I left, got into another car and waited until he came out. As he was about to get into his car I ignited the dynamite with the remote-control device.'

The explosion was deafening. The bomb blew Greene apart. It tore off his clothing and severed his left arm, which landed 86 feet away across the car park. His gold ring, embossed with his initials DJPG, was still on his finger. Danny Greene had lost his war with the Cleveland Mafia. The Irishman was dead. That night in Little Italy grown men danced with joy.

Not everyone was so happy. One of the best witnesses would have been a woman with a small child. She saw Greene die but tissue from his body splattered all over her face. She became hysterical and was too shocked to testify.

How did Ferritto feel about finally killing Greene? Elated?

'Yes . . . not because I had killed someone. I was elated because the job was done and I was gonna become one of *them* and share in the profits. It was something that since I was a kid I had dreamed of, I had wanted, and this was my chance to do it.'

Did he have any compunction or remorse? What was it like to have a man as a target?

'To me it was like having a glass of wine. It didn't mean a thing. I killed him and there was no remorse that I killed a man because I was brought up all through my life believing in those . . . . You just have to put them out of your mind. Those were things or hurdles that you had to overcome. A man with a conscience doesn't last too long on the streets.

'I don't believe that anyone with a conscience, other than during a crime of passion or fear, could do that, you know, could just say: I'm gonna dump this guy for money . . . . All I know is that I went to bed that night and I slept.'

Greene's killing in broad daylight in a car park caused a public outcry. At the offices of the Cleveland Strike Force the racketbusters swung into action. One of sixteen strike forces across America under the US Department of Justice, it includes lawyers, accountants and detectives drawn from all arms of local and federal law enforcement. Its current chief is Steve Olah.

'It was clear we had a full-scale gangland war. If it continued innocent people would very likely die. The strike force made a concerted effort to solve these murders and stop the violence,' he explained. A taskforce was formed with FBI agents, bomb experts from the Alcohol, Tobacco and Firearms Bureau, the Cleveland Police homicide unit, police from Lyndhurst where Greene was murdered and county prosecutors. They worked together in a model of modern racketbusting with a degree of trust between agencies which would have been impossible before the strike forces were set up. The case also shows how the FBI can now co-operate with other agencies. Today 1500 of its agents investigate organized crime, over 20 per cent of the FBI's strength.

From the moment Greene died the investigators had luck on their side. A couple were driving by when the explosion took place and they saw a car leaving the scene. Catching up with it along the highway, they wrote down a description of the driver and the car and took its registration number. The car was soon traced to Ray Ferritto. When the couple were shown his photograph they recognized him instantly.

Ferritto was arrested. Held for murder, he felt neglected by the men who had hired him. After the killing but before his arrest Ferritto had met Licavoli who told him not to worry. If Ray were arrested Licavoli promised he would take care of him. In jail awaiting trial Ferritto found out the Mafia bosses intended to 'take care' of him by bailing him out and then killing him. He was appalled by their treachery.

'I decided maybe I did choose the wrong side. All my life I'd been one way and I always did what I was supposed to do and now, all of a sudden, I did them the biggest favour and they're talking about killing me! And here I am in jail, awaiting trial! I decided to flip, go to the authorities and tell 'em I wanted to talk, that I wanted a deal. It wasn't because I saw God or read a Bible. It was just that I thought at the time that I had to look out for me, Ray, and I thought this would be my best move.'

Ferritto betrayed the Mafia. His evidence would put almost every made man in Cleveland on trial for conspiring to murder Greene and Nardi and for belonging to a continuing criminal conspiracy of which those murders were part.[5] One defence lawyer told reporters that the defendants were 'gentle souls. They're not dangerous, they're just misunderstood.' Licavoli showed how gentle he could be by thwacking a woman photographer around the head with his walking stick.

Largely on Ferritto's evidence the strike force convicted James Licavoli, the reluctant boss who had brought the family to the verge of extinction. He was jailed for seventeen years for conspiracy to murder and for controlling the Mafia. John Calandra was sentenced to fourteen years. Also convicted was Tony Liberatore who had been jailed in 1938 for murdering two Cleveland policemen. On his release twenty years later he became a union boss and a power in city politics. For Greene's murder Liberatore had organized the cars and weapons. He was jailed for fourteen years.

As far as the FBI were concerned Liberatore's imprisonment had a special poignancy. In 1977 he had bought the loyalty of a bureau employee with access to its most secret files. Geraldine Linhart had worked loyally for the FBI for nine years but she was soon to be married and needed money to build a new home. Her fiancé knew Tony Liberatore who saw how he could exploit the couple. He asked Geraldine to find out the names of the FBI's informants in the Cleveland mob. She gave him an FBI report on Licavoli which identified fourteen informants but only by their code numbers. At Liberatore's urging she decoded the names and thus endangered the lives of the FBI's most trusted Mafia sources.

Liberatore gave her $1000 but by then the FBI had discovered that there was a leak. To limit the damage agents concocted a hoax informants' list, removing its real sources and inserting the names of staunch mafiosi who were telling the FBI nothing. Linhart duly handed this disinformation to Liberatore who 'loaned' the couple a further $15,000. The FBI still did not know who the leak was but in March 1978 some of the papers Linhart had copied were found by chance at a car showroom where her husband worked as a salesman. Linhart's handwritten notes gave her away. When

1. The massacre of Sicilians in the Parish Prison in New Orleans in 1891, as portrayed in a contemporary illustration

2a. 'Bathhouse' John Coughlin and (2b) 'Hinky Dink' Kenna, the saloon-owning politicians who ran Chicago's First Ward for the benefit of organized vice for more than thirty years

2c. Their power was already waning when Prohibition became law in 1920, outlawing the commercial manufacture, distribution and sale of alcoholic beverages

3a. 'Big' Jim Colosimo was the first Italian crime boss of Chicago. He ran brothels and a famous café where he was shot dead by persons unknown in 1920, a few weeks after the beginning of Prohibition.

3b. John Torrio (centre) was Colosimo's protégé and successor

3c. The power of organized crime over Chicago's politicians was celebrated in a *Chicago Tribune* cartoon of 1928, captioned: 'They are spoiling an otherwise engaging picture.'

4a. Alphonse Capone, alias Al Capone, Al Brown, 'Scarface'. The most notorious of all gangsters, although his reign lasted only six years and ended when he was thirty-two.

4b. Al Capone at the ball park with Chicago Cubs' catcher Gabby Harnett, his son Al Jr. and congressman Roland Libonati

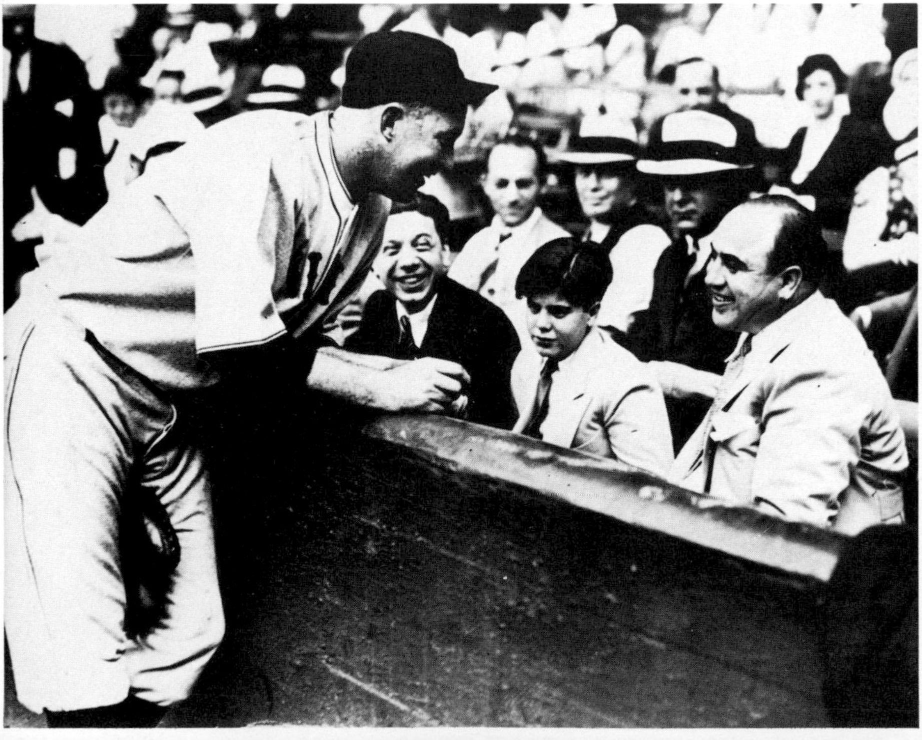

5. Capone's only enduring enemies in the bootlegging business were the Northside Gang, led first by Dean O'Bannion (5a) until his murder in 1924, and last by George 'Bugs' Moran (5b). In between, the gang was led by George 'Hymie' Weiss until he was murdered and received a classic gangland funeral (5c).

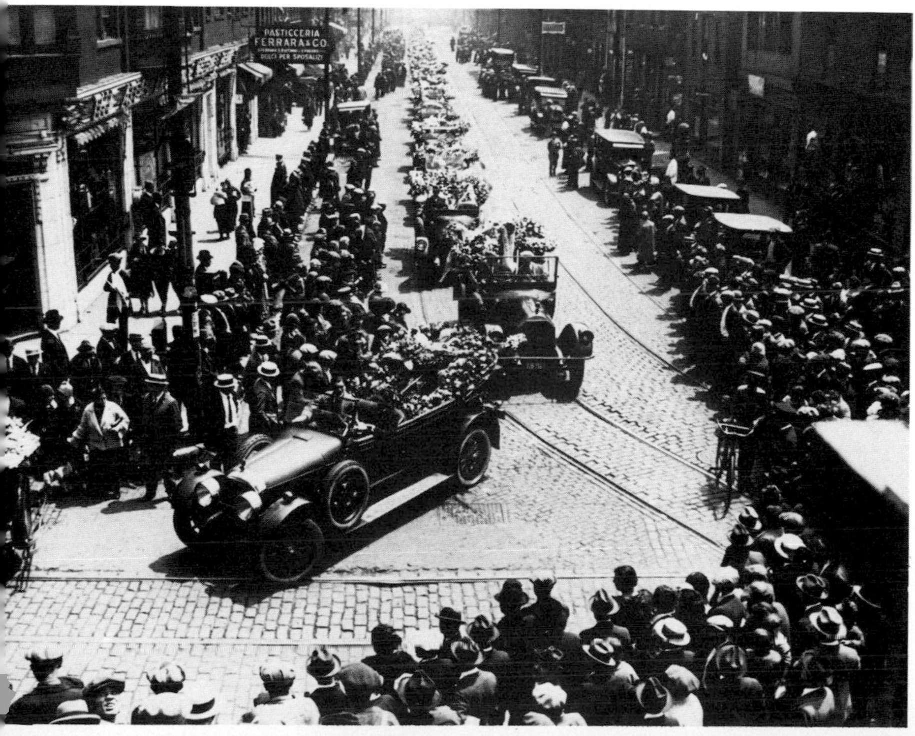

6. The St Valentine's Day Massacre of 1929. In all, seven of Moran's Northside Gang were murdered, but Moran himself turned up late and missed his own execution.

7a. Scalise and Anselmi, two of Capone's gunmen suspected of carrying out the St Valentine's Day Massacre

7b. Their bodies laid out at the morgue

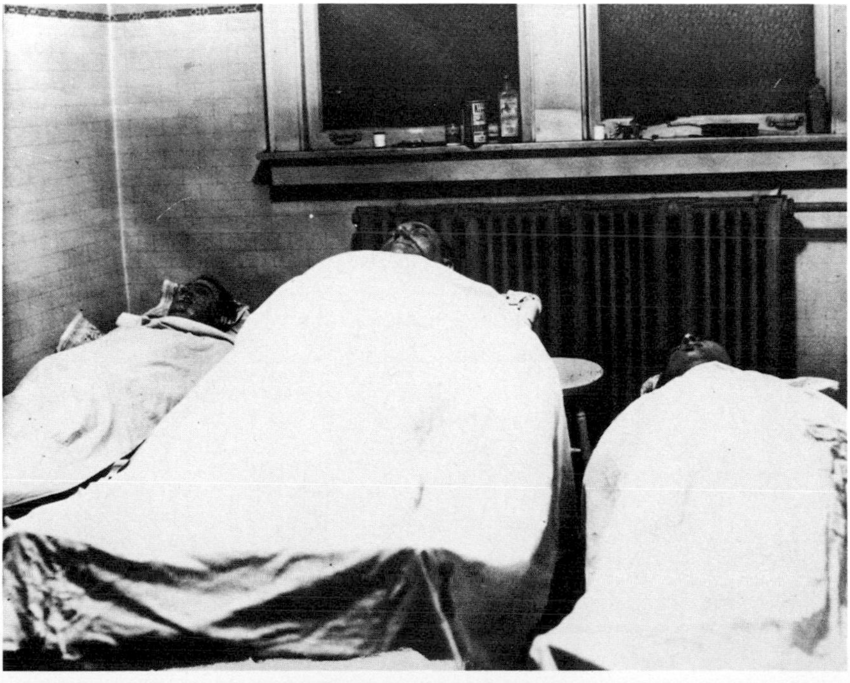

8a. Sam 'Momo' Giancana, the Prohibition hoodlum who became boss of the Chicago Outfit in the late 1950s. He was killed gangland-style in 1975.

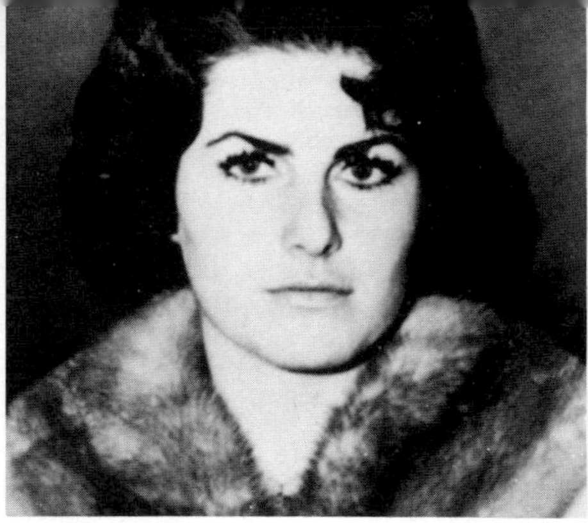

8b. Judith Exner in 1960. In the late 1950s she was the lover of Frank Sinatra, John F. Kennedy and Sam Giancana.

8c. The bosses of the Chicago Outfit in an extraordinary photograph taken at the Sicilian Manor Restaurant in 1978. Around the table (clockwise from the left) are: Joey Aiuppa, Domenic DiBella, Vincent Solano, Alfred Pilotto, Jackie Cerone, Joey 'the Clown' Lombardo, James 'Turk' Torello, Joe 'Caesar' DiVarco, Joe Amato and Tony Accardo.

9a. Lucky Luciano and Meyer Lansky (3rd and 4th from left) in a police line-up with leaders of the Chicago mob in 1932

9b. Lucky Luciano, mugshot taken about the time of his 1936 trial

9c. Meyer Lansky, the Mafia's financial mastermind

10a. Hundreds of gangland murders occurred throughout Prohibition all over America. In Cleveland in 1932 it was the turn of Raymond and Rosario Porello.

10b. The killings didn't stop with Prohibition. 'Dutch' Schultz was murdered in Newark, New Jersey in 1935.

10c. Thomas Dewey, the New York prosecutor who won convictions against Schultz, Luciano and many other racketeers. In 1938 Dewey convicted politican Jimmy Hines.

11. Lucky Luciano, jailed in 1936 for a minimum of thirty years, was freed after only ten years in recognition of his war efforts! Exiled to his native Italy Luciano, seen here in Rome in 1949, resumed his Mafia activities.

12a. Vito Genovese took over Luciano's crime family and became boss of bosses in 1957

12b. Sergeant Edgar Croswell, who caught most of the bosses of the American Mafia (including Genovese) in conclave at Apalachin

12c. The Apalachin property of Joe Barbara, in upstate New York, as it looked in 1957

13a. Harry J. Anslinger in 1930 when appointed US Commissioner of Narcotics

13b. Joe Valachi taking the oath before the Senate subcommittee on investigations in 1963

13c. President John F. Kennedy, FBI Director J. Edgar Hoover and Attorney-General Robert Kennedy in 1961

14a. A 1933 police line-up of nine men who later formed the nucleus of Murder Inc. Second from left: Ben 'Bugsy' Siegel, fourth: Louis 'Lepke' Buchalter, fifth: Harry Greenberg (later murdered by Siegel) and seventh: 'Gurrah' Jake Shapiro.

14b. Louis 'Lepke' Buchalter in 1937

14c. 'Gurrah' Jake Shapiro in 1936

15a. Benjamin 'Bugsy' Siegel with the actor George Raft, when the mobster was discovering Las Vegas and building the Flamingo Casino-Hotel

15b. Meyer Lansky who sponsored Siegel's casino ventures in Las Vegas and had to pick up the pieces

15c. Siegel shot dead in 1947 in the Beverly Hills home of his girlfriend Virginia Hill

16a. Morris 'Moe' Dalitz in the 1950s. Godfather or Grandfather of Las Vegas?

16b. Paul 'Red' Dorfman and his son Allen. 'Red' persuaded Jimmy Hoffa to let Allen handle Teamster Pension Fund loans which he handed out on the Mafia's orders for twenty years.

16c. Allen Glick, loaned nearly $100 million by the Fund, at the Stardust Hotel in Las Vegas. The casino's slot-machine takings were looted by organized crime.

17. Teamster President Jimmy Hoffa, centre left next to Tony Provenzano, the Mafioso who controlled the union in northern New Jersey, at an election rally in 1959

18a. Albert Anastasia, Mafia boss, 'Lord Executioner' of Murder Inc. and the overlord of the Brooklyn waterfront for more than twenty years

18b. Anastasia's murder in a Manhattan barbershop in 1957

19a. George Barone, one of the New York mobsters who muscled in on the Miami waterfront in the 1960s and 1970s

19b. Joey Teitelbaum, the Miami businessman who helped send Barone and many other mobsters to jail in the most successful case ever made against the Mafia in America

19c. Matthew Eason, the warehousemen's union leader with some of his members. Eason dared to fight the Mafia on its home territory, New York's garment centre.

20a. Frank Sinatra at the Westchester Premier Theatre in 1976, with a crowd of underworld admirers. From left: Paul Castellano, Gregory de Palma, Sinatra, Tommy Marson, Carlo Gambino, Jimmy Fratianno, Salvatore Spatola. Sitting, Joseph Gambino and Richard Fusco.

20b. Frank Sinatra with President Ronald Reagan in 1980

21a. Carlo Gambino, boss of bosses, flanked by FBI agents, in 1970

21b. Joe Colombo, pointing to a photograph of Columbus Circle, where a few days later Colombo himself would be shot

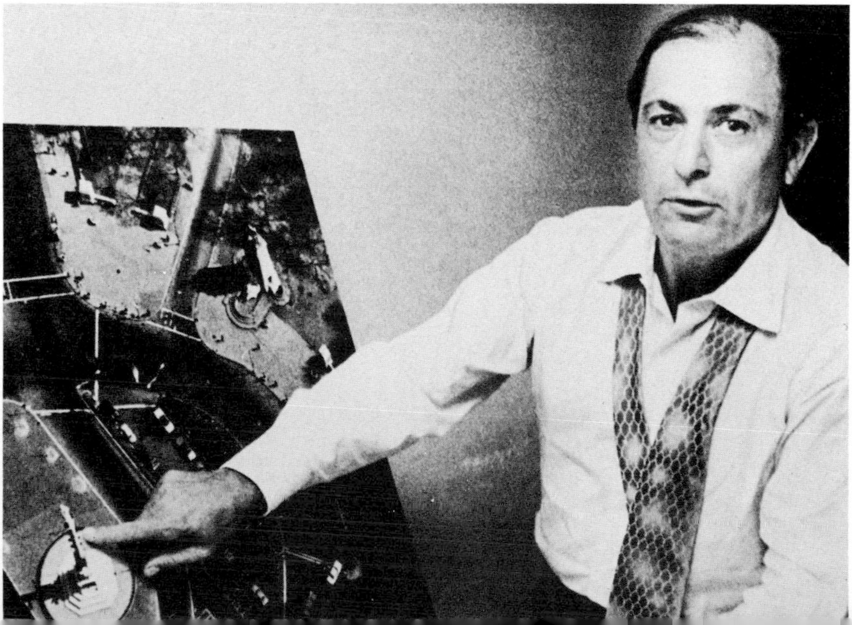

22a. Danny Greene, the Irishman who took on the might of the Cleveland Mafia, seen here in 1964

22b. Ray Ferritto, the hitman hired by Cleveland's Mafia bosses to kill Greene

22c. What Ferritto did to Greene in 1977

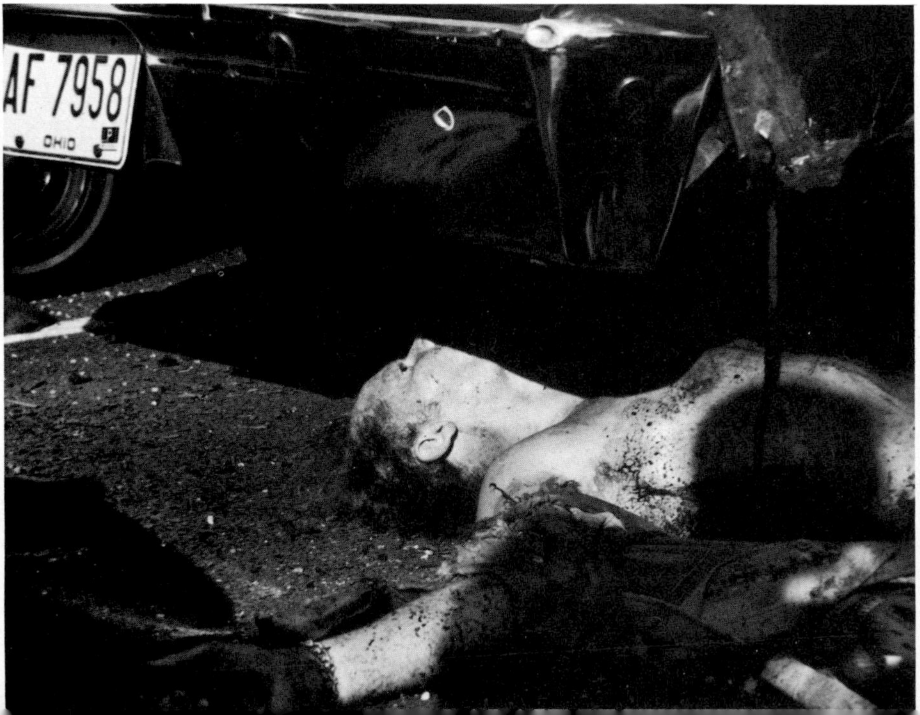

23a. Angelo Bruno, boss of the Philadelphia family, as portrayed in the FBN's Mafia book in the late 1950s

23b. Nicky Scarfo who took over the Philadelphia family in 1981

23c. Frank Tieri, boss of the Genovese family in the 1970s

23d. Jimmy Fratianno, former Los Angeles family boss, who turned federal witness in 1977. The highest-ranking mafioso ever to defect.

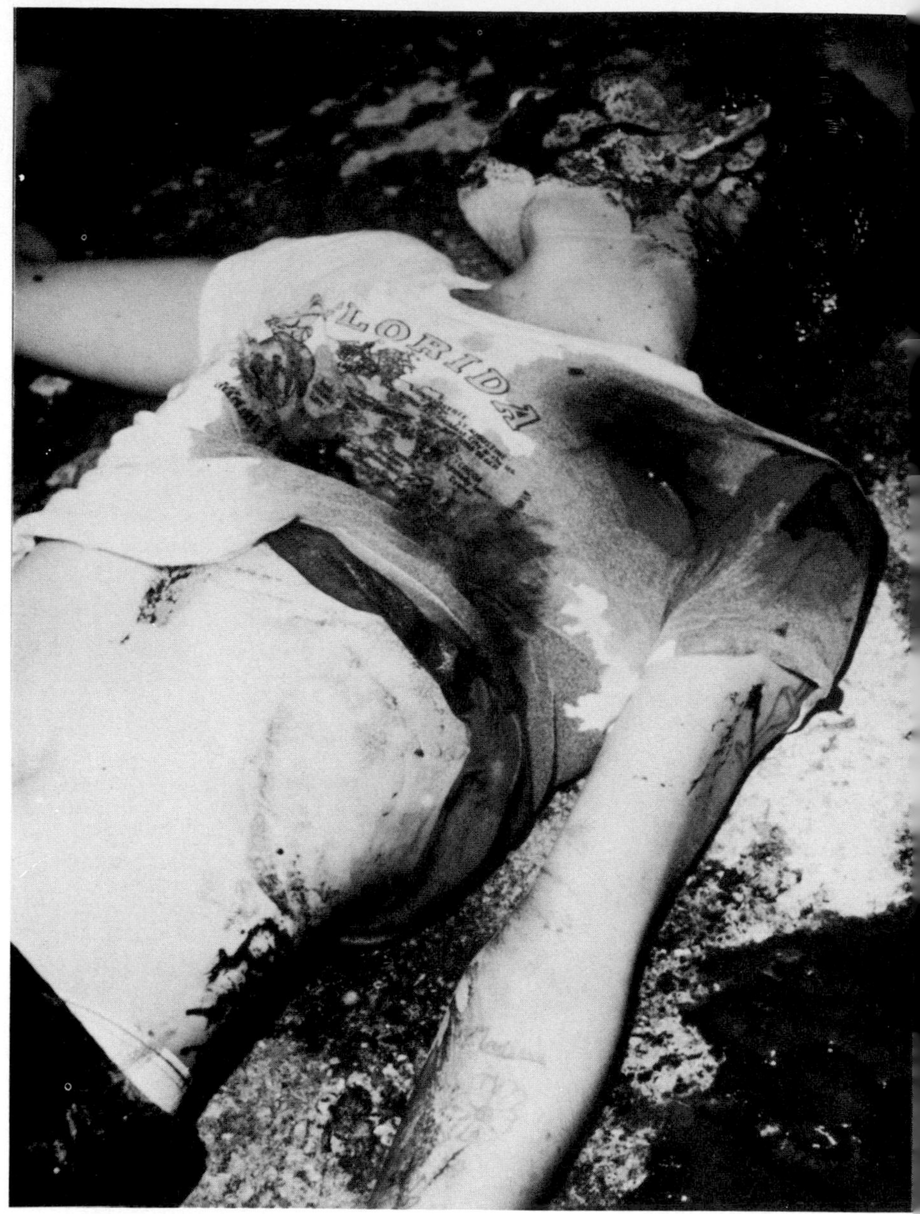

24. A drug dealer's view of Miami, one of hundreds of Hispanic victims of south Florida's murderous drug war

confronted she confessed her treachery. The FBI had plugged one of the worst security leaks in its history, but only just in time.

Ferritto's decision to turn informer had a domino effect on the Mafia from coast to coast. His evidence against Jimmy Fratianno meant that 'the Weasel' was also charged with Greene's murder. Fratianno says he does not know what Ferritto discussed with Del Santer when he introduced them to each other but rather than face a murder rap 'the Weasel' himself flipped. He had another good reason for turning. He knew from his friends in the Cleveland family that they had a source inside the FBI and he feared his name would soon show up as a government informant (he had been on the FBI payroll as a purveyor of low-level gossip since 1970). Rather than be killed for squealing Fratianno decided to tell the true story of his life in the Mafia over thirty years. He thus became the first 'made' member of La Cosa Nostra to turn public informer since Joe Valachi, but whereas Valachi never appeared in court against the Mafia, Fratianno has helped put dozens of mobsters in jail by testifying in trials from Los Angeles to New York.

In 1982 Cleveland's informer sickness struck a huge narcotics and murder conspiracy headed by the family's underboss, Angelo Lonardo. 'Big Ange' was a survivor of the clan who had fought the Porellos during Prohibition. They had murdered his father so in 1929 Big Ange carried out a revenge killing for which he was convicted but cleared on appeal. Fifty years later, with Licavoli in trouble over Greene's murder, Lonardo suddenly found himself Cleveland's acting boss.

Two Mafia underlings now talked Lonardo into sponsoring the drug-trafficking activities of a West Side gang led by Carmen Zagaria. Big Ange cast aside the family's drug ban because narcotics' profits were now so great and the family needed the money. Zagaria was not a 'made' man, indeed most of his gang were not Italians, yet Lonardo gave him the money to buy drugs and set up a distribution network. The deal also included police protection and muscle to kill off competition. In return the family would get the lion's share of Zagaria's profits which soon amounted to $15 million a year. Big Ange could still claim the family was not handling any drugs itself, simply making a huge profit on its loans.

The Cleveland Strike Force did not look at the conspiracy in the same way. Through several informers it gathered enough evidence to indict Lonardo, his few remaining soldiers and the Zagaria gang for murder and drug-trafficking. At first Zagaria went missing but later he turned up as yet another witness.

Steve Olah recalls how the strike force now uncovered 'the most grotesque and horrendous murders I have ever encountered. There were mutilations, there was beheading, victims bricked into walls, victims bludgeoned and thrown over boats in the middle of a lake, bodies wrapped with chains and thrown on to quarry ponds in the middle of winter so that when the ponds melted the bodies would fall to the bottom.'

The worst killer was Hans Graewe, so sadistic that even his fellow-executioners were scared of him. Graewe, who had kicked his wife to death in a bar, liked to be known as 'the Surgeon' because of his skill at cutting up bodies. He called his van his 'ambulance'. When he discussed what might happen if he was caught he would say gleefully, 'They can't get me for murder. All I did was commit malpractice!'

Graewe liked to tease Zagaria because, by his standards, Zagaria was squeamish. He once seized Zagaria's right arm and stuck it in a bucket containing the head and hands of a colleague whom Graewe had killed and cut up. Beaming, he urged Zagaria, 'Shake hands, say goodbye to your old buddy!' Graewe had cut off so many hands in his time that he wanted to display them as mascots in the rear window of his car, waving to people behind.

Zagaria's boys cut bodies up and destroyed them because they mistakenly believed that if none of their victims were ever found they could not be convicted of murder, but with Zagaria and other accomplices testifying against them Graewe and his fellow-murderers were jailed for life. So were Angelo Lonardo and his Mafia middlemen, on murder and drugs charges and also for controlling the conspiracy in which those crimes had been committed. Coming on top of the Greene convictions this left few 'made' members of the Cleveland family on the streets.

For the first time in the history of racketbusting the entire leadership of a Mafia family had been 'taken out'. Putting all Cleveland's bosses behind bars is the greatest success any strike force has ever had. It is also a unique achievement for the FBI but its local chief, Joe Griffin remains cautious: 'We haven't broken the back of the Cleveland LCN. All we've done is to take the leadership out but we still have a very active organization conducting loansharking, gambling, narcotics. We have to attack those operations for several years before we can say we have broken the family's back. If we stop now this problem would come back in six months.'

The Mafia in Cleveland isn't going to fade away. In time it will renew its leadership and re-assert its power. The local hierarchy may have been destroyed temporarily but Steve Olah guesses other mafiosi will move in from Chicago, Detroit, Buffalo or Pittsburgh. Perhaps emerging organized-crime groups such as the blacks or the motorcycle gangs will flourish if the Mafia does not recover.[6] He comments: 'There is too much money to be made in a city like Cleveland, which is a large industrial, blue-collar town with a ready and willing market for the goods and services that organized crime has to offer. It's not going to dry up as a source of wealth for organized crime. They're not going to allow their gambling to dry up, or their narcotics or their prostitution. They will re-instil their power into Cleveland.'

But what of the first mobster to turn on his Cleveland masters, whose evidence started the family's collapse? After three years in jail Ray Ferritto is back on the streets, bitter about what he regards as a series of broken promises by the authorities. He says they told him he would be released after twenty months but he actually had to serve thirty-eight. No one from the Justice Department spoke up for him at his parole hearing. He thought he was going to have some say over where he would be relocated under a new identity but this too turned out to be false. He feels that while he was in jail his own family was not cared for and did not get the funds he says they were promised. Whatever the truth Ferritto quit the government's witness protection programme. When he did get out of jail he went back to his home town to live with his family under his own name.

He now regrets ever having turned against the Mafia, maintaining: 'Death would have been better. I decided to go on my own, come on back home and take my chances. Whatever my chances are, they are better than being in the witness protection programme. I know that I'm as capable of taking care of myself as the guy that they send to take care of me. But it's just a matter of time for me and I'd be a fool to say that it isn't. Sooner or later they're going to get me.'

16

Gambling with the Mob

Illegal gambling is as American as apple pie. In the nineteenth century it was the main source of criminal wealth and corruption in New Orleans, Chicago and New York, cities in the thrall of gambler-gangster-politicians long before the Mafia crossed the Atlantic.[1] Gambling is still the fundamental racket of organized crime but the organization which has controlled it for most of the last fifty years is the Mafia. Charlie Siragusa, one of America's top narcotics and organized-crime investigators for many years, told *Crime Inc.*: 'In this country gambling is almost a birthright of gangsters. Since I was a kid in Little Italy the same gangsters who operate the big casinos today were operating crap games and poker games in Mulberry Street and Houston Street, New York City. They had the expertise. There's no one in this country that knows gambling better than organized crime.'

Gambling in America shows more clearly than any other criminal activity since the years of Prohibition how organized crime exploits the gap between public morality and personal conduct. The Protestant ethic on which the nation was founded condemned gambling. That view lives on in the majority of states, where most forms of gambling are still illegal. Yet most Americans gamble, wagering more than $20 billion a year on all kinds of legal gambling and another $50 billion on illegal gambling. As the chairman of the 1976 commission on gambling in America put it, 'How can *any* law which prohibits what 80 per cent of the people approve of be enforced?'

Those who run illegal gambling rackets are, by definition, criminals. When any criminal market yields a fat profit organized crime will take it over sooner or later through violence and corruption. Yet by giving people what they want in an area of vice widely regarded as harmless these same killers and corrupters have come to be respected as public benefactors, just as in Prohibition. Then the cry goes up: legalize gambling. In one stroke the mob will be cast out, corruption will end and the people will no longer respect the mobsters who once used to serve them.

Yet where gambling is legalized this has rarely happened. When the state sanctions its own lotteries and betting shops – primarily to raise revenue – illegal gambling seems to carry on at the same level as before. Indeed illegal-gambling operators find they have a far larger pool of potential customers because new gamblers are born: people who have never gambled before but who lose their moral qualms when the state absolves the activity as a vice. Even honest police officers become cynical about enforcing gambling laws, asking themselves how illegal gambling can be so wrong when the state is running its own games.

With the possible exception of puritan New England gambling seems to have been rampant all over colonized America for hundreds of years. One of the most popular games today among poor whites, blacks and Hispanics appears to have been brought to America from the lottery houses of eighteenth-century London. For years it was called 'policy' but today it is usually known as 'numbers'.

Explaining numbers to someone who does not play it is almost as difficult as explaining the rules of cricket to an American. The idea of the game is to pick a three-figure number, between 000 and 999, every day. The winning number is chosen by a different method in different cities. In the 1930s it used to be taken from the last three digits of the US Treasury's daily balance or the amount of money traded on the New York Stock Exchange or the amount bet at a local racetrack on a combination of races. Today the number is usually based on the last three digits of the total money bet on individual races, which is then added up in a bewildering variety of ways. How it is chosen does not greatly affect the game. If your number comes up you win 600 times your stake but the odds against you, even in a straight game, are 1000 to 1. The game's operator or 'banker' makes his profit in the gap between 600 and 1000. If the bets are spread evenly he should make $400 on every $1000 bet less running costs. Some days he makes more, some days less but over a long period he ought to clear this kind of profit regularly.

Most numbers gamblers live in poor neighbourhoods in America's big cities. They place their bets in little numbers shops or with a 'runner' who visits their home or workplace. Joey, a black citizen of Detroit, says that in the ghetto, 'Gambling is a way of life, a way of survival. When jobs are down and you just can't make a living – and a lot of people think welfare is not going to give them enough money to survive – the next best thing is numbers. If you don't want to go out and rob nobody, stick a gun in their face, then you play the numbers and you hope and pray that your number is going to come out one day that week.

'Some people bet the amount they spent at the grocery store: $6.97c would mean betting the number 697. Some people choose the number they have seen on a car licence plate, especially if they have seen the same three numbers on two plates. You meet someone who has a phone number similar to yours, or you buy a dream book which tells you what numbers to bet according to whatever you've dreamed about. You've dreamed about death, you look up death, the book will tell you what death plays for. Same with a person's name, you look it up and the book will tell you exactly what number to play.'

Nothing much has changed in the numbers game since the 1900s. The profits of the bankers have always been colossal, which is why notorious white gangsters muscled in on Harlem numbers in the 1930s. Victor Herwitz had just joined Tom Dewey's racket-busting team when he was given the job of investigating the policy or numbers racket. 'A complainant came in who was the son-in-law of one of the leading policy bankers of black Harlem. They were very respectable people, the top of society in Harlem where the numbers business was not regarded as illegal.

'Arthur Flegenheimer, also known as Dutch Schultz, had been a king pin in the liquor business. When Prohibition came to an end he had to seek other sources of income so he decided to take over the policy racket. He got hold of all the policy people in black Harlem, the five or six major bankers, and said, "We're now your partners. We're going to organize the racket. We're gonna get political connection for you. We're gonna get police connection for you." After all, Schultz had had that protection during Prohibition. So he took over the policy racket, the black bankers became his employees and Jimmy Hines, the most important political leader of the 11th District's Tammany Democratic organization was made a partner.'[2]

Whenever a Harlem numbers runner or banker was arrested Schultz's crooked lawyer Dixie Davis would provide bail. Then Jimmy Hines would tell the magistrate (whom he had helped appoint) to acquit them.[3] Hines also made sure that any cops honest enough to raid numbers banks and thus upset business were transferred. Dutch Schultz was soon netting $20 million a year from Harlem numbers which re-established him as one of the moguls of American organized crime. A Jewish convert to Catholicism, he had become an ally of the Mafia's during Prohibition. He was part of the multi-ethnic crime syndicate which had gathered in May 1929 in Atlantic City. Schultz represented New York with Lucky Luciano while Al Capone led the delegation from Chicago.

In 1935 this alliance, far from protecting him, would prove his undoing. Schultz, who was then on the run from an income tax conviction, bragged to his Mafia associates that he was going to murder the man who had prosecuted him, racketbuster Tom Dewey. This so alarmed Luciano that in October 1935 at the Palace Chop House in Newark, New Jersey, Schultz and three bodyguards were shot to death by Mafia-contracted hit men. 'This turned out to be one of the few organized-crime killings for which anyone was ever convicted. In 1941 Murder Inc. assassin Charlie 'the Bug' Workman was jailed for killing Schultz and his feeble protectors. The Bug was not released until 1964 but throughout his twenty-three years inside he was looked after by the Mafia, even though he was not Italian. Their gratitude was understandable. Schultz's murder gave them control of the numbers racket in Harlem and many other black districts for at least thirty years.

Today people gamble some $9 billion a year on illegal numbers, of which as much as $3.6 billion goes in untaxed profit to the operators and whoever is behind them. The Mafia does not control numbers by running its day-to-day operations, however. It never did. There have never been enough 'made' men to staff such a labour-intensive business. Most operators are people of the same race as the players: black, Hispanic or poor white. They run small, non-violent, 'mom-and-pop' businesses and, until recently at least, looked to the Mafia to resolve territorial disputes with other operators, to provide lay-off money and to buy police protection. All these services can be bought for a regular fee, rather like an insurance policy. In this sense the Mafia may still exercise overall control over big city numbers by protecting those operators who pay them and putting out of business those who don't.[4]

In Detroit Joey believes that black numbers are still controlled by the Mafia. 'I have always known high-echelon numbers men to be the Mafia. The white man has the big buck, the payoff. True enough, the blacks have got some big money but not quite enough to pay off. If ten people all hit the winning number each with a $10 bet you're talking about a $60,000 payout. How many blacks do you know with that kind of money to pay out? That's where the Mafia man comes in. Now when a black numbers boss claims he's independent, in reality he isn't. He takes his orders from the higher echelon which most blacks don't know anything about: white guys sitting up in rich, rich mansions somewhere. And in return for the layoff, the big payoff to protect the black numbers operator, the mafioso takes his share of the profit.'

The profits may be very big indeed. In one small Ohio town in 1982 a black-operated numbers bank was raided. Its books showed a turnover of $5000 a day which amounted to $1.5 million a year. If the bankers were taking the standard $400 out of every $1000 bet their revenue would be $600,000 a year, all from one small black neighbourhood. The local Mafia representative was providing the usual services and taking the usual cut.

This is not always the case though. In the 1960s Herbie Gross was a front man for New York's Lucchese family in New Jersey until he turned informer. While he was working with the family one mafioso persuaded him to take over a numbers bank. Gross had twenty-one runners collecting bets all over Ocean County. It was not as profitable as he had expected. 'Sometimes a weird coincidence happens and people bet a heck of a lot of money on one number because of some public event. For instance when Robert Kennedy was assassinated he was 42 years old. After John Kennedy and Martin Luther King he was the third prominent public figure to be assassinated. So you had a combination of 3+4+2 and they came in like crazy betting 342. Now some numbers bankers are greedy men and they will never lay off where they have a chance. In this case, at 1000 to 1, they decided to carry the bets on 342 themselves rather than lay it off to a mob clearing house. But on this occasion the number 342 came up, they got hit and numbers banks collapsed. Not even overnight. They just took off for parts unknown.'

Herbie Gross found that as a lowly banker he never made much money out of numbers. From the $400 'won' out of every $1000 gambled he had to pay the runners 25 per cent commission, the cops their protection money, the controller, who takes charge of all the bets and collates them, his wages and the lawyer a fat fee whenever the runners were 'pinched' (even when you buy police protection you still have to give up the occasional 'body' for form's sake!). The banker also has to pay the Mafia for the layoff facility, whether he uses it or not. So after paying out all round, says Gross, a numbers operator is lucky if he can put food on the table for his wife and kids.

The Mafia may lay on police protection but the operator still has to pay for it. 'That's the stone that drowns you,' says Gross. 'The cops become so greedy. They'll say, arbitrarily, it's gonna cost you an extra $50 from now on. You have no choice unless you want to walk away from it. But you can't walk away from a mob-controlled bank. You can complain, you can tell your boss, but you can't just say, "Hey, I've had it." '

Gross maintains no numbers bank can operate without police protection 'and the only ones the police trust, cooperate with and get their payoffs through is organized crime'. Once Gross had to tell the police to wipe out some rivals. 'I noticed business had been dropping. The runners complained there was an independent Puerto Rican bank operating on the streets. When the police lieutenant came in for his weekly payoff I said, "I'm not giving you a cent. Go out and do your job."

'He said, "What are you talking about?"

'I said, "There's an independent out there who's hurting me."

'He says, "Who?"

'I says, "Omerta – you don't squeal on anybody, no matter who! Just go out and do your job."

'It wasn't too much later when this Puerto Rican was busted. As an independent he had no protection. And the only reason he had been allowed to operate for so long was because the police thought he was working for me. He was operating courtesy of my protection money!'

All America's crime families are involved in illegal gambling. Card games are among their biggest money-earners. For eighteen hectic months in the 1970s John Vitale patronized Mafia games in New Jersey. A confessed cheque fraudster, he has since turned federal witness against the Mafia.

'I used to play poker in set games in Garfield, Jersey City and Newark five nights a week. At weekends they started on a Friday night and ran through Sunday morning. In each city the games are run by organized crime. Each game is under a local mob: in Newark it was the Campise mob, part of the Genovese family. We had good protection. The game was played in the house of a man whose brother was a Newark policeman. He lived right underneath so nobody would bother us. If anyone was gonna bust it I'm sure they would have known in advance. I never was in a game when it got busted.

'The house takes 5 per cent of each pot that's gambled. If the game runs eight to ten hours, the house takes in 2,500 bucks for itself. Some of the games have mechanics. A mechanic is somebody who fixes the cards. He can deal you a perfect hand or a garbage hand.

'Most of the players are Greeks. They are heavy gamblers. Quite a few players are women, regular housewives who have a thing for playing cards. They like to sit down with a bunch of men and try to beat them. Some are very successful.

'I would start out with maybe $500 or $600. I was good for the house because I started the game and I finished the game, whether it lasted two hours or two days. I was very welcome because they knew I was a "sitter". I was the first one in and the last one out. Playing cards to me was like getting laid – excuse my term but it was how I got off. I enjoyed it. I didn't mind losing the money because I never won. In eighteen months I must have lost a quarter of a million dollars. I used to play poker five nights a week and in that eighteen-month stretch I won on only two nights and the only reason why I won is because the games broke early.

'There's usually a girl at the house for the guys if they want to take a break and go upstairs and get their rocks off. They supply liquor, food, cigarettes, whatever's needed. If you want drugs they provide them too. Whatever it takes.

'The same people lay on floating games, with a different location every week. As corny as it sounds they do play cards in the back of a trailer truck while it's driving on the streets. I know people will say, "We've seen that on TV, it's only fiction," but it's the truth. They also have "cruises to nowhere". They leave on a Friday night and they come back on a Sunday night and all they do is cruise up and down the Hudson River. There is some heavy, heavy gambling done on those boats. Anybody can go on a cruise to nowhere but not anybody can get into them games.'

The 'Mr Big' of New York gambling today is James Napoli. 'Jimmy Nap' is still the boss despite being jailed in 1976 for controlling a $100 million numbers empire. A latecomer to the ranks of 'made' men in the Genovese family, Napoli made millions for years without belonging to any family. One detective who knows him is Pete Donohue, a New York state trooper who worked undercover for years against organized crime. 'Jimmy Napoli has been doing for all five families. He is their super banker, their main money guy. He takes care of the numbers, the sports betting and the service on the racing-line. He makes money and earns for all the crews.' Napoli has spread into all kinds of legitimate business but the heart of his empire remains gambling: slot machines, hidden shares in Las Vegas casinos and running 'barbut' games, beloved by dice-crazed Greeks. From gambling he finances other rackets, including a flourishing loanshark business. Any gambler who gets into debt – and most eventually do – needs money. Napoli will lend it to them.

Jimmy Nap is the lineal successor to the men who took over Harlem numbers from Dutch Schultz. 'Black Harlem?' says Donohue. 'You don't make a move unless Jimmy Nap gives the go-ahead. He uses black guys up-front as "beards" and they earn off him. How do I know? I know from being on the street, knowing guys that are close to him and moving in their circles. But I also know because I've listened to multiple wiretaps where they're saying, "Gotta get permission from Nap to do this", "Gotta go see Nap about this", "You've gotta have Jimmy Nap's OK on this." '

Recent research work has challenged the standard view that the Mafia controls illegal gambling in New York.[5] They argue that even police records show both numbers and illegal bookmaking are largely non-violent, *laissez-faire* and openly competitive businesses. Donohue, however, sticks to conventional wisdom. Wherever gambling yields big money organized crime is going to be in there making it, whatever the price in violence. To people who bet a dollar a day gambling may be a harmless pastime but to the men who run the mob's oldest racket it is a matter of life and death, says Donohue as he reels off a roll of dead mobsters.

'Paddy Macchiarole, partner with Napoli in his gambling operation, he went on trial with Napoli: found in the trunk of a car at the Brooklyn–Queens Expressway with some lead in his head that didn't belong there.

'Tom DiLio: trunk of a car at Kennedy Airport.

'Carmine Consalvo: he had his laundry in the washing machine at the Fort Lee Towers when he took a dive out the sixteenth-storey window in his shorts. His laundry was still in the machine. Two weeks later his brother took a dive. He fell out of a window on top of a firehouse out of an abandoned tenement building in New York.

'Jiggs Forlano and Ruby Stein were two more guys hooked up with Napoli in his activities. One ends up in the river, well, with his body in the river, head in a vacant lot. The other guy: he just dies, you know. Dies real strange.

'J. J. Frankel: he just took a dive out of a window – suicide they said – maybe he did take a dive, I don't know – maybe he had problems. Frankel was tied in with a guy named Arthur Milgram. He was involved with the lotteries and the vending machines: if he committed suicide with a shotgun the way he got it – it's very strange – in the back of the head.

'All you've got to do is look at some of the bodies around this gambling activity to know it's a violent business. It's not *laissez-faire*.'

By far the biggest form of illegal gambling in America is bookmaking or sports betting. Official sources estimate that Americans gamble as much as $40 billion this way every year, handing the bookmakers $6 billion in untaxed profits. No recent trials have shown the current national structure of illegal bookmaking or the role of organized crime but betting insiders say a syndicate of bookmakers in Las Vegas gives out the illegal 'line', the odds and prices on all sporting events. It is probable that most illegal sports betting is not mob-controlled but is handled by local independent operators serving the many millions of Americans who like a bet to go with televized sporting events such as Monday-night football. No one really knows what proportion of independents 'lay off' heavy bets with Mafia bookmakers but they might be wise to do so if they face losing a fortune on one result and being wiped out of business.

There is considerable evidence that organized crime continues to manipulate legal and illegal betting by rigging the outcome of big sporting events. Ever since baseball's World Series was fixed in 1919[6] mobsters have tried to carry off lucrative betting coups by bribing players. In America many people bet on the points spread between two sporting teams. In college basketball, one of the most heavily wagered sports, brilliant young players have been caught taking bribes from mob fixers to 'shave' points. They miss baskets and thus drop points to the margin of victory or defeat which will yield the greatest profit to the mob's bookmakers. In the same racket the mob's fixers may place bets with non-mob bookmakers on the result coming out at the points margin they have fixed with the corrupt players.

In the 1970s American horse-racing was disgraced by one of the worst fixing operations in the history of sport. Tony Sciulla was a young man from Boston who had been gambling on the horses since he was a boy. By the time he was 20 he was fixing races by bribing jockeys and trainers and by injecting horses with tranquillizers. Sciulla would bribe several jockeys in one race to hold back their mounts, then he and his associates would put all their bets on the only other horses with any hope of winning. Discreetly placing their bets across the country with many bookmakers, the gang could get long odds and win large sums. Sciulla would also make sure some horses ran poorly for much of the season until they had a reputation as no-hopers. When a horse had sunk to the odds of a rank outsider Sciulla would bribe other jockeys in a race to let it win. Many such coups 'won' him millions of dollars. Horseracing is legal in thirty-two states. Sciulla fixed races in thirty-one.

By the time he had fixed hundreds of races Sciulla was well known to many track operators who got him banned in several states. In 1975 a jockey cooperating with the New Jersey State Police wore a tape-recorder as Sciulla offered him $2000 to lose races. Sciulla was arrested and convicted of sports bribery. He did a deal, turned federal witness and testified in six states against some of the most successful and reputable jockeys and trainers in America to the pained surprise of the racing fraternity.

Sciulla had started as an independent but at 23 he learned that he could only carry on his career courtesy of the Mafia. By fixing several races he had unknowingly stung Boston's mob bookies for $28,000. They found out he was responsible, forced him to hand back his winnings and fined him $50,000. From then on he worked in consort with the Boston Mafia and their Irish sidekicks, the Howard Winter gang. As Sciulla became more and more notorious no legitimate bookmaker would knowingly take a bet from him. This forced him to place bets through mob bookmakers like 'Fat Tony' Salerno of New York's Genovese family and the Las Vegas line bookies, which meant the Mafia knew immediately which races he had fixed and how. However much money Sciulla made from race-fixing, the mob must have made far more.

Why did he pay that $50,000 fine? Why did he become partners with organized crime? Couldn't a 6 ft 3 in 320-pounder look after himself? As he told the *Horsemen's Journal*, 'My option was that I paid the fifty, with no questions asked, and I became partners with them. It was pay the fifty or be in a sleeping bag in a trunk.'

17

Las Vegas – the House that Bugsy Built

America's poorest housewife putting her dollar on the daily number has one thing in common with the tuxedoed millionaire losing $100,000 on a roulette wheel in a Las Vegas casino. They are both keeping organized crime in Cadillacs. The people who made Las Vegas the gambling capital of the world are the same people who took control of most of America's mob rackets sixty years ago.

Senator Estes Kefauver identified them back in 1951 when he reported that the Mafia was 'the cement' that helped to bind the two ruling syndicates of organized crime: the Costello–Adonis–Lansky syndicate of New York and the Accardo–Guzik–Fischetti syndicate of Chicago. The committee made it clear that the primary business of both syndicates was gambling. Prohibition had been a freak and fleeting opportunity seized by all these men to build their founding fortunes but gambling was always their staple racket.

Lucky Luciano was typical. He started as a small-time Lower East Side gambling hustler. He turned successively dope-pedlar, bootlegger and whoremonger, yet all along he kept up his gambling rackets. One of his caporegimes was Joe Adonis, who ran gambling clubs in New York and bookmaking at the racetracks. Luciano's under-boss was Frank Costello who ran the Luciano crime family after Lucky went to jail in 1936. In 1935 hundreds of Costello's slot machines had been pitched into the ocean by New York's Mayor La Guardia in a spectacular publicity stunt against illegal gambling. Sixteen years later Costello would be the star turn at the Kefauver hearings in New York. Luciano, Adonis and Costello were the super-smooth, manicured hierarchy of Italian organized crime in America, yet of all the syndicate bosses the most intriguing was not an Italian but a Jew.

Meyer Lansky lived the most extraordinary life of all the leaders of organized crime. Born in Russia in 1902 he grew up in the Hell's Kitchen section of New York's Lower East Side. As a boy Lansky made friends with Lucky Luciano. Working together as bootleggers during Prohibition they cut through the massed ranks of street hoodlums to take control of the New York underworld by their late twenties. Later Lansky would create a unique role for himself as the financial brains behind the Mafia but by 1930 he commanded a crew of killers known as the 'Bug and Meyer gang'.

Joe Valachi, testifying against the Mafia, told the senators in 1963 that the founding 'boss of bosses', Salvatore Maranzano, had been murdered in 1931 by a team acting on Lansky's orders. Luciano, the main beneficiary of the murder, so trusted Lansky that in 1932 he took him to Chicago for a summit meeting of the nation's Mafia bosses. The Chicago police arrested them both and immortalized the visit in a classic line-up photograph with Rocco Fischetti (Al Capone's cousin) and Paul Ricca, Chicago's future boss. One of the matters under discussion was what to do now that Prohibition was coming to an end. Illegal gambling had always made a lot of money but legal gambling could bring in even more. As usual Meyer knew what the national crime syndicate should do and where to do it.

Lansky now masterminded the mob's move into legal casinos. This he could not achieve in the USA where casinos were illegal except in the arid state of Nevada – inaccessible and inhospitable as far as most of America's 'high rolling' gamblers were concerned. Instead, as early as 1932 Lansky was cultivating the friendship of Fulgencio Batista, the strong man of Cuban politics who was later to become its dictator-president. By 1937 Lansky had cemented the friendship with huge bribes for the privilege of operating legal casinos on Cuba without American interference. At that time Havana was a resort much favoured by rich Americans. Lansky guaranteed Batista millions of dollars a year from the mob's casinos in return for a monopoly. Lansky's finest operation was in Havana's Hotel Nacional.

By the 1950s every major American syndicate boss had a piece of Cuban gambling, courtesy of Meyer Lansky. His brother Jake worked as pit boss at the Nacional, minding Meyer's interests. Improved air travel opened up the island to far more gamblers and organized crime's offshore profits soared. But at the beginning of 1959 Fidel Castro overthrew Batista. His guerillas smashed up the casinos and Castro closed what was left of them. He let them re-open for a while but soon closed them down for good. Lansky is said to have lost $17 million in cash he had left on the island to be transferred to Swiss banks. The Mafia never forgave Castro but Lansky had already laid the foundations of a mob gambling empire all over the Caribbean including the Bahamas. In the 1960s he even had a share in London's glamorous Colony Club casino, where his representative on the board was Dino Cellini, a brilliant casino 'mechanic' who, despite his well-known Mafia role, operated openly in London for nearly three years before the Home Office deported him.

From his first dablings in Cuba Lansky realized that the volatile politics of the Caribbean made it essential for the mob to build up legal casino gambling in America. Once again it was he who masterminded the mob's move west to Nevada.

Nevada had been wide-open for gambling ever since its first gold strike in 1859. Gambling was the miners' main recreation and they were going to gamble whatever the law of the land. Seventy-two years later the state decided to legalize the vice and raise revenue by taxing it. For decades Nevada officials had been taking bribes to allow illegal casinos to operate unhindered. The legislators reasoned optimistically that if those casinos were legalized all the graft would flow into the state treasury. The law of 1931 made no attempt to clean up or regulate the business, however. It did not prohibit convicted criminals from operating casinos, it gave customers no protection against crooked casinos and it established no authority to watch over the county sheriffs who were to collect the licence money. It was a crooks' charter.

In 1931 only 90,000 people lived in Nevada. Reno was the largest city with 18,000 inhabitants. Near to San Francisco and already the divorce capital of America, Reno was the first place in Nevada to thrive on legal casinos. In the south of the state, 270 miles from Los Angeles, was Las Vegas. In 1931 it was a sleepy railroad junction, an Indian town in the desert with only 5000 citizens. All that changed when 'Bugsy' Siegel came to town.

Benjamin Siegel was Lansky's other half in the Bug and Meyer gang. Of the two Siegel was more inclined towards enforcing and killing, talents he later used to good effect in Murder Incorporated, the underworld assassination squad of which he also became a leader. Lacking the discretion of the diminutive and taciturn Lansky, Siegel was a handsome, outgoing man with an eye for the ladies. In the late 1930s he moved from New York to California where he soon established gambling operations, including a racing-wire service and an ill-fated venture into offshore gambling ships with his old friend, movie star George Raft. Siegel slipped easily into Hollywood and became a mascot at movie industry parties where his underworld reputation added a touch of raw reality to Tinseltown.

In California Siegel carried on killing. Harry 'Big Greenie' Greenberg was one of his old New York buddies in Murder Inc., but he had turned informer. In November 1938 Greenberg was sitting in his car outside his Hollywood home when Siegel shot him. Two years later Siegel was indicted for the murder on the evidence of an accomplice, Allie Tannenbaum, but as his trial neared in 1941 a more important Murder Inc. killer named Abe Reles turned informer against Siegel. Reles was being kept in New York under round-the-clock police guard in the Half Moon Hotel in Coney Island. On 21 November at 7 a.m. he was found dead on a roof extension six floors below his open window.

Suicide was unlikely. So was the theory that he had fallen while trying to escape on the line of sheets found hanging from his window. Reles had been giving evidence on an alleged 1000 mob murders, so there must have been many who wanted him dead. He was probably thrown from the window but the policemen on duty said they had seen and heard nothing. Without Reles as a witness Tannenbaum's evidence against Siegel was unsupported and could not be heard. The case collapsed and Siegel walked free.

By this time Siegel had discovered Las Vegas. Instantly he knew that this town, so near to the large population of greater Los Angeles, was a better bet than Reno. Sooner or later it would boom. To begin with he took shares in some small downtown casinos but in 1945 he made an inspired investment. Through another mobster, Moe Sedway, he bought a piece of desert 7 miles out of town on what later became known as 'the Strip'. There Siegel started to build the Flamingo Hotel. At first he thought it would cost $1 million to build but the plumbing alone cost that. He paid inflated prices for top-quality materials at a time of post-war shortages but the materials were often stolen by the suppliers and resold to the unsuspecting Siegel at a higher price a few days later. He paid craftsmen top rates and huge overtime to finish the hotel but could do so only with mob money authorized by Lansky and Luciano. As the bills soared they suspected he was stealing. With his debts mounting Siegel decided he could not wait for the hotel to be completed. He announced that the Flamingo would hold its grand opening on 26 December 1946. He would pay his underworld creditors out of his casino winnings.

But the Flamingo turned out to be that rare bird: a casino which loses money. The first night was a disaster. Few of the Hollywood stars Siegel had invited showed up; only his loyal friend George Raft, George Sanders and Jimmy Durante, who was paid to be there as the Flamingo's first star entertainer. Throughout the opening week every gambler seemed to be a winner, everyone except George Raft who lost $65,000 at *chemin de fer*. Luck may have played a part but a lot of cheating went on as well. Some Flamingo croupiers were in league with Siegel's downtown casino rivals. His losses were so heavy that he was forced to close the Flamingo after only a few weeks. In March 1947 he re-opened the hotel which by then had cost $6 million to build and was still unfinished. The casino's fortunes did not improve and it kept on losing money.

Federal witness Jimmy 'the Weasel' Fratianno knew Ben Siegel. In 1945 Jimmy left jail in Ohio, went West and got involved with the Los Angeles Mafia family at a time when the family's boss, Jack Dragna, was working with Siegel in the race-wire racket. Fratianno recalls that even in the darkest days Benny never lost hope. 'I used to go to the Flamingo all the time when it was the only nice hotel on the Strip. Benny always said, "Why don't we move to Vegas? It's the coming country." He had a vision. He's the guy, he knew it! He says, "It's going to get bigger and bigger and bigger." '

Another man who knew Siegel was Hank Greenspun. He was running a 5c magazine called *Las Vegas Life* when Siegel came in one day and bought the back page for months ahead to advertise his casino. 'When the Flamingo opened it was like a morgue, nobody would go near it. First it was so far out on the Strip and secondly it was supposed to be a hoodlum place and people avoided it. When things got a little meagre at the magazine I started doing public relations for the Flamingo and that's when I met Siegel. If you didn't know his background you would think he was a character actor in the movies. He was a very handsome man and he wasn't too well spoken because he used a lot of epithets, but there wasn't anybody in the movie world that he didn't know.' But as the Flamingo plunged deeper into debt all the movie stars in Hollywood could not save Ben Siegel.

On the evening of 20 June 1947 Siegel was in Beverly Hills at the home of his tempestuous girlfriend, Virginia Hill, who was out. Siegel was sitting on a sofa with an old gambling buddy, Allen Smiley, when without any warning he was hit by six shots fired through the window. The first blew his eye 15 feet away on to the tile floor, the second smashed the rest of his face. The man George Raft called Baby Blue Eyes was dead. Smiley was unhurt.

No one was ever charged with Siegel's murder but there are two theories as to why he died. He may have been killed in the race-wire war. The wire was the instrument the mob used to control every bookmaker in America. It was the only way horserace entries, odds and results could be communicated fast enough to keep the punter in the betting shop wagering his life away. Siegel was running the California end of the Trans-America Service, one of only two coast-to-coast wire services. Both were controlled by mobsters. In 1946 the boss of the rival Continental Wire Service, James Ragen, was murdered in Chicago. Siegel's death may have been a reprisal.

The more likely explanation is that he was killed for stealing from the crime syndicate which had put so much money into the Flamingo. The execution may have been ordered when Luciano met Lansky at the Hotel Nacional in Havana early in 1947. Lansky may have won a stay for his old friend to give him time to pay his debts and turn the Flamingo into the money-factory he had promised. But by June that had still not happened. The mob thought Siegel and Virginia Hill were depositing huge sums in Swiss banks and no one can be seen to steal from the mob and get away with it.

Jimmy Fratianno heard the inside story. 'Johnny Roselli was mighty close to Siegel and he told me that Benny, who was a hot-tempered guy, was talking to Meyer on the phone. And he told him "To hell with them." He used four-letter words and hung up the phone on him. Five or six months later they killed him.' Would the old boyhood friendship have counted for nothing? 'Hell no!' says Fratianno. 'When they ordered him to be killed, what's that got to do with it? They just killed Meyer Lansky's stepson not so long ago. What the hell? What's that got to do with Meyer? You know, you've got to go regardless of who you are. You *go*, Jackson! That's it.'[1]

Ironically, it was partly because of Siegel's murder that Las Vegas caught America's imagination. 'That was really the start of Las Vegas,' recalls Hank Greenspun today, the city's elder statesman and owner-editor of the *Las Vegas Sun*. 'Even though Siegel was supposed to be such a sinister figure people were drawn to Las Vegas because of his macabre background. They came to see the house that Bugsy built.'

With Siegel gone Meyer Lansky put more reliable men into Las Vegas to watch over the mob's investments. His stalking horse Moe Sedway managed the Flamingo until he died in 1952 but Lansky's main front man was Gus Greenbaum, himself a degenerate gambler. Greenbaum was found at his Phoenix, Arizona home in 1958 with his head almost severed from his shoulders. His wife's throat was also slashed by a butcher's knife. Like Siegel he was killed for stealing, in Greenbaum's case to feed his own gambling habit. His murderers had flown in from Miami, Meyer Lansky's base of operations.

Lansky controlled other Las Vegas casinos. His brother Jake worked in the 'cage' or counting room at the Thunderbird casino until he was flushed out in the early 1950s. Meyer rarely visited the city to check on his investments and only once looked in danger of going to jail over them. In 1960 he was paid a 'finder's fee' of $500,000 by Sam Cohen and Morris Lansburgh when they bought the Flamingo. But Lansky was still in control as Lansburgh and Cohen 'skimmed' (stole from the counting room) some $30 million from the casino's profits in the 1960s. The money was carried by bagmen and one notorious bag-lady to cities like Miami where mob-run banks would send it on to banks in Switzerland under Lansky's influence. The whole chain of connections was a Lansky masterpiece.[2]

In an unguarded moment Lansburgh and Cohen admitted to a prospective buyer that they were skimming from the Flamingo and were soon investigated for evading income tax. One witness subpoenaed to appear before a grand jury in Miami in March 1971 was Meyer Lansky who was visiting Israel at the time. Given only eight days to turn up Lansky found a physician who told him he was too sick to travel. He did not leave Israel and was indicted in Miami for contempt.

In 1972 the USA forced Israel to deport Lansky and several Latin American states not to let him in. He was flown to Miami, tried for contempt and sentenced to a year in jail. However, the appeal court overturned the verdict because there was no evidence that Lansky had wilfully disregarded the subpoena. His Israeli doctor's advice may have been correct and had not been disproved by the government. Lansky was soon on trial again for a tax fraud involving London's Colony Club but he was acquitted. On the $30 million Flamingo skim Lansburgh and Cohen pleaded guilty and were given token jail sentences but charges against Lansky were dropped. Once again he had beaten the system.

With moneymaking activities all over the world Lansky rarely went to Las Vegas. He usually stayed in Miami, overseeing his local hotel interests and walking his dog. For fifty years he had masterminded the Mafia's gambling operations, helping mobsters invest their profits in outwardly 'legitimate' ways. By using overseas banks, especially in Switzerland, he perfected methods of laundering crooked earnings so they could be brought back into America without the tax man knowing. He was never convicted of a federal crime and only once went to jail: for two months in 1953 for running a gambling house in Saratoga Springs. When he died in January 1983 he was said to be worth hundreds of millions of dollars. No one in law enforcement can tell you where these millions are or who has them now.

With men like Lansky and Siegel driving the industry forward it is hardly surprising that fifty years of legal gambling has changed the face of Nevada. Today there are ninety casinos in greater Las Vegas, where between them gamblers lose nearly $2 billion a year. Gambling taxes produce more than 40 per cent of state revenues. Without them Nevada would be bankrupt. In recent years some 'high-tech' jobs have arrived but gambling is still the only game in town. If greater Detroit is run by the automobile industry, Dallas by oil, Hertford by insurance and Miami Beach by hotels, Las Vegas – indeed all of Nevada – is run by the casinos. What makes Las Vegas more bizarre than every other 'mono-economy' in America is that only gambling has a wholly criminal past. And only gambling, legal and illegal, is still manipulated by organized crime.

Most states believe that legalized gambling simply leads to more organized crime and that where there are casinos the Mafia is bound to follow. In contrast Nevada claims that, at least since 1955 when it introduced a licensing system, it has managed to clean up its casinos. Nevadans like to believe that behind the glitter and glamour of the Strip and downtown Las Vegas there lurks only more glitter and glamour.

The personification of gambling's alleged transformation from a crime to an honourable business is Morris Barney Dalitz. Fifty years ago 'Moe' Dalitz doubled as a legitimate laundry operator and as captain of the 'Big Jewish Navy' which smuggled Canadian whiskey across Lake Erie. He was also a member of the 'Cleveland Syndicate' described in Chapter 15. When Prohibition was repealed in 1933 the syndicate adjusted remarkably well by switching their main criminal activities to illegal casinos in Ohio and Kentucky.

At this point Dalitz shrewdly paid taxes on his illegal gambling earnings. American tax men are quite happy if criminals pay taxes and are not concerned about how the money is made. In 1949 Dalitz and his Cleveland friends used some of the millions they had laundered through the tax system to buy into Las Vegas. They chose the Desert Inn whose founder Wilbur Clark, like Siegel, had run out of money during construction and needed outside finance to complete. His fairy godmothers turned out to be godfathers. Soon Wilbur Clark quit, leaving Dalitz in control.

Dalitz claims he was acting for himself, but mafiosi like Jimmy Fratianno have their doubts. 'Italians never wanted to be in front and it's like that today. You never see 'em opening up a gambling house but they've always got a piece of it some way, somehow. Now that's how these Jews got big. Take the Cleveland family, for instance. They had Jews like Moe Dalitz, Sammy

Tucker, Maurice Kleinman – the ones that owned the Desert Inn. They had two or three gambling houses in Cleveland. Well, maybe they'd declare $1 million at the end of the year. Come the end of ten years, if you want to invest $5 or $10 million in something, you could show that you made that kind of money in the past. So *that*'s how they got successful. I think it was in 1940, 1941, they bought the Beverly Club in Kentucky. Well they *showed* money. They had money to show. The Italians couldn't do it. You give an Italian $1 million he puts it under the cellar! How could he invest a half a million? "Where did you get that money?" So that's how these Jews made money because they could show money. The more they made, the more they declared, the more they could invest. See, that's where the Italians made a mistake. They should have done it themselves. They're stupid. Didn't show no smarts.'

In 1951 the Kefauver Committee accused Dalitz of being a top member of organized crime, 'participating in the formation of the national crime syndicate'. Today in California, where he has substantial business interests, he is still officially regarded as a crime figure. In 1978 the state's Organized Crime Control Commission repeated Kefauver's condemnation and cited claims that Dalitz was 'one of the architects of the skimming process that developed in Las Vegas in the early 1960s'.

Yet in Las Vegas itself Dalitz is a most honoured citizen, showered with awards. In 1976 he was named Las Vegas's 'Man of the Year'. Top showbusiness entertainers came to pay him tribute, including an old friend, the comedian Bob Hope. Here was formal recognition that, at least in Nevada, Dalitz's criminal past had been forgiven. In 1983 the B'nai B'rith, a Jewish fraternal organization, held a dinner in his honour at which he was awarded the 'Torch of Liberty' and hailed as 'Mr Las Vegas'. Today top politicians value his financial backing, including President Reagan's closest adviser, Senator Paul Laxalt, another one-time casino owner.[3] Old Moe Dalitz has come a long way from bootleg booze.

Hank Greenspun respects Moe Dalitz today, although he has not always done so. 'The strange thing about this man, who's supposed to have been the head of the syndicate in Cleveland, Detroit, all over, is that every federal agency has been in here. They've put extra surveillance on him and he still has never been arrested and he's never been charged with a crime. He was an officer in the US army. So all you can judge a man by is his record. In his own community they put this man up on a pedestal, for his contributions to the university, to every worthwhile charity. He's built countless homes for retarded children. Now, you would think that if this man is supposed to be the Godfather, so to speak, of Las Vegas, they would have had him by now. So instead I would call him the Grandfather of Las Vegas because of all the contributions he has made here.'

Las Vegas has its own strange aristocracy. Many people in gambling here have criminal backgrounds elsewhere so no one casts any stones. Money is what matters, not how you made it. As Hank Greenspun puts it, 'Don't forget, in the early 1940s there were only about 8000 people here. Now there are close to 600,000, so they had to come from somewhere. People came here who were attracted to gambling and a lot of them had backgrounds in illegal gambling. That's not moral turpitude because 90 per cent of the nation gambles. They all flocked out here. Naturally they would be more tolerant of each other than, say, the FBI would be of them. Now when they have come here they've tried to elevate themselves, so from a subculture we've reached almost a superculture. It's like when Georgia was first colonized in the 1600s. It was a penal colony of England. All their felons were sent here. Then they sent over a boatload of prostitutes to keep the felons company. And from that group you've got presidents. You've got the top people in our country!'

Joe Yablonsky, head of the FBI's office in Las Vegas from 1980 to 1984, views the city with a less benevolent eye. 'When I first came here I had to ask whether this was really a part of the United States. It seems that Nevada sets itself apart from the rest of the USA because of legalized gambling. There's a climate almost of paranoia here about the federal government. They get very upset about negative publicity getting out to the rest of the nation indicating organized crime is here and there's an attempt, cosmetically, to cover it up. They tolerate, even accommodate, this cancer of America right here in Las Vegas.

'Nevada is still the place Mark Twain described back in the 1870s when he said that the "saloon keeper, the chief desperado, the lawyer and the publisher all occupy the same level of society and it is the highest". This is what I see today in Las Vegas. In most American cities wealth counts for a lot but you will not see people who are associated with organized crime mingling with other people of high status in the community. You go to a function in Las Vegas and somehow it all mixes together. It's a very interesting phenomenon that I have observed no place else in the country.'

For the Mafia Las Vegas is an open city. Members of all America's crime families operate here. It is a safe place to run to from your home-town police. When a Mafia burglary in Chicago ended in murder Gerry DeNono went to Las Vegas until things cooled down. 'I just split and went there. I played golf, met up with another crew there and then I met a girl who was a cocktail waitress. I went crazy over her like a fool and ended up marrying her. One of the boys came down from Chicago and he said to me, "You have to come back, Joe," – that's my boss Caesar DiVarco – "Joe wants you to come back."

'I says, "I'd rather stay here. I've found somebody I really care for." I was pussy-whipped. I'm going to say it the way it was: my nose was open, I was in love with the illusion of the cocktail waitress and the long legs and the long blonde hair and it was just a fantasy, the lights and the whole bit. No realism attached to it all. So I stayed.

'Now, coming from Chicago to Las Vegas, because of the people that I was around and associated with and being seen with, the same people that saw me later by myself treated me with a different kind of respect. I was getting "comped" at the casinos connected with Chicago: free rooms, free food and drink, free shows, all the favours they lay on for "high rollers" to keep them losing fortunes at the tables. I'm getting these favours even though I don't gamble. Because of the association with the Chicago mob your reputation runs in front of you and you haven't said a word. And cocktail waitresses, bartenders, captains in the restaurants treated you as if you were the closest thing to Al Capone's cousin. Now this, of course, isn't really too good for your mind because you start to believe your own headlines. You start to read things into relationships that are not there. And that's how I met the cocktail waitress because, seeing me with these people she's figured I'm some "mustache" from Chicago, loaded with money and just throwing it around.'

It is not surprising that even a low-level mobster like Gerry DeNono benefited from the fearsome reputation of the Chicago mob. Chicago has the strongest presence of any Mafia crime family in Las Vegas but all the families take their piece of the action.

Almost all the big Las Vegas casinos have been proved at one time or another to be under organized crime's control: the Flamingo under New York, the Frontier and the Aladdin under Detroit, and from 1975 to 1979 the Tropicana under Kansas City. Reputable corporations have now bought all these casinos but time and again it has been proved that the Mafia families will find some way of stealing millions from under the noses of casino owners. In this way they also rob the state of Nevada whose taxes are based on the casinos' declared profits. They use employees to skim huge sums from the counting room. They own blocks of shares in the names of respectable front men. They then take a percentage of the profits, known as 'points'.

Gerry DeNono knows exactly how the men from Chicago operate in Las Vegas. First they invest money in a casino in someone else's name. 'They take percentage points of ownership in the casino: 5 points, 3 points, whether that point is worth $1 or $10 million. The other shareholders don't see any of this. It's not visible. These points may be in a ghost name, some square, maybe a grave, but that money is taken right off the top. And this is the money that the bagmen, the couriers, carry to the cities. Now when the money gets to Chicago they whack it up to the families in different parts. The North Side, the Near North Side, the West Side, Melrose Park and all those areas of Chicago each get their share.'

Chicago's power in Las Vegas comes from its preeminent muscle west of the Mississippi. As the biggest mob in America it has the men and the guns to defeat all-comers. Since 1955 its greatest asset has been the pension fund for the central states area of America's largest union, the Teamsters. The fund was set up to look after the pensions of America's truck-drivers. The weekly contributions of their employers soon mounted up to billions of dollars. From the start the fund was the Mafia's private bank.[4]

The Mafia's 'bank manager' was a young insurance executive, Allen Dorfman. His stepfather was Paul 'Red' Dorfman, a Capone gunman who was a friend of Jimmy Hoffa, the Teamsters' vice-president for Detroit.[5] Hoffa wanted to succeed the ageing Dave Beck as Teamster president. In return for the support of organized crime, which had immense power in many union locales across America, Hoffa dreamed up the pension fund. He cared for his Teamster members but also for himself, so he placed the management of the pension fund in the hands of young Dorfman. Hoffa duly received the corrupt backing of mob-controlled Teamster locals and became president of the Teamsters when Dave Beck was jailed. But Hoffa had sold his soul to the Devil. So had Allen Dorfman. Dorfman became a front man for the Mafia. In 1972 he was convicted of taking a $55,000 bribe in return for giving out pension fund loans, for which he spent ten months in jail. In 1982 he went on trial again for conspiring to defraud the fund, along with the Teamsters' crooked president of the day, Roy Williams, and the Chicago Mafia's pension fund watchdog, Joey 'the Clown' Lombardo.

A handsome man, a war hero and one-time gym instructor, Dorfman was an ideal front man for the mob. 'They are looking for the intelligent businessman, the wheeler-dealer type, like Meyer Lansky,' says Doug Roller, the Chicago Strike Force chief who prosecuted Dorfman. 'They want people who are very bright in financial manipulations. Organized-crime people don't have that ability. Joey Lombardo and the others are just not astute businessmen and they do not know how to manipulate funds.'

In the late 1950s Dorfman's mob masters ordered him to pilot the fund into Las Vegas. He handed out huge loans to casino owners at a time when no one else would lend them money. He made the fund's first Las Vegas loans to the Desert Inn crowd led by Moe Dalitz, not just for casinos like the Stardust but for a golf course, a hospital and an office block. Other casino loans went to Caesar's Palace, Circus Circus, the Fremont, the Dunes and the Aladdin. In all the truck-drivers of America lent hundreds of millions of dollars to Nevada casino owners. Not that anyone consulted the truckers.

In 1974 the fund made the loan which shows most clearly how the Mafia uses front men in Las Vegas. The beneficiary was an unknown 32-year-old lawyer named Allen Glick. A slight, bald wheeler-dealer who had risen from nowhere, Glick had minimal experience of casino management. In April 1974 he committed himself to buying the Stardust and Fremont casinos. He put down a deposit of $2 million but did not have the other $60 million necessary to complete the deal. If he did not come up with money fast he would lose not only the casinos but also his $2 million deposit.

Recently released federal trial papers state that in the same month of April 1974 Glick met Frank Balistrieri, the boss of the Milwaukee Mafia, to discuss the purchase. By the end of May Glick was granted a $62 million Teamster loan. He then signed a secret deal with Balistrieri and his son which gave them the option to buy 50 per cent of the shares of his casino holding company (the Argent Corporation) for a mere $25,000 at any time over the next fifteen years. This laughably low price for a half share in a major casino corporation was not enforceable in the courts but it was enforceable in the underworld. Balistrieri told Glick that without the Mafia he would not have got his loan and that henceforth the Mafia owned half of him. Now Glick had to fulfil his part of the deal. He hired Frank 'Lefty' Rosenthal, a notorious criminal gambler from Chicago, to oversee the casino operations. Rosenthal was also close to Tony 'the Ant' Spilotro, another diminutive mafioso who is regarded by law enforcement as Chicago's resident capo in Las Vegas. The Argent Corporation then hired a known slot-machine cheat, Jay Vandermark, to run its slot-machine operations.

In December 1974 Glick went to see Nick Civella, the boss of the powerful Mafia family in Kansas City. He was promptly granted another $25 million loan to refurbish the Stardust, taking his entire borrowings from the Central States Pension Fund to $132 million. Glick now employed more organized-crime nominees to the point that in 1975 and 1976 his casino corporation declared losses of more than $11 million. By mid-1976 Nevada's gaming authorities learned that the slot-machine takings at all four Glick casinos were being flagrantly 'skimmed'. Raids proved that between $7 and $12 million had been stolen from the machines. Vandermark, the skim's 'mechanic', fled to Mexico and disappeared. He is believed to have been killed, following the murder of his son. Both are thought to have been murdered by the Mafia to shut them up.

The skim money, from the tables as well as the slots, was going to at least four Mafia families. But Glick's usefulness was coming to an end. In April 1978 Carl DeLuna, a top Kansas City mafioso, ordered Glick to sell the Stardust and Fremont. In a conversation overheard by the FBI, DeLuna claimed that he told Glick, 'Do what you got to do, boy. Make your public announcement that you are getting out of this for whatever reason you want to pick, and get out.'

Perhaps Glick was being deposed because his wondrous rise and Rosenthal's criminal past were bringing too much 'heat' from both the Press and the FBI. In other FBI-intercepted conversations Kansas City mafiosi complained that Glick was stealing too much money for himself. In 1979 the Nevada authorities finally denied Glick the licence he needed to operate a casino.[6] Glick did not re-apply. In July 1979 he sold the Argent Corporation to Allan Sachs, an old Las Vegas hand and a close friend of the Stardust's former *éminence grise*, Moe Dalitz. The big wheel of Las Vegas fortune had turned full circle.

Doug Roller used Glick as a witness in his 1982 trial of Dorfman, Williams and Lombardo. 'Allen Glick is an amazing individual. For the entire period that he has been involved in Las Vegas he appears to have walked a fine line between organized crime and the government. Organized crime has not killed him and the government has not put him in jail. I think he went to the Central States Pension Fund because he had made a commitment to purchase the Argent Corporation without financial backing and therefore had to cut a deal. Part of that deal was organized-crime placement of officials who could then do what they wished.'

In 1980 an FBI raid on the Balistrieris' Milwaukee headquarters discovered the deal signed by Glick and the Mafia. In October 1983 fifteen organized-crime figures in five different cities were charged with skimming the profits from his casinos. Those now facing trial include the top bosses of Chicago, Kansas City and the Balistrieris from Milwaukee. Glick himself hasn't been charged and nor has Rosenthal but both are under round-the-clock protection from the federal government. Rosenthal knows only too well how working with organized crime can damage your health. In Las Vegas in

1982 his Cadillac was blown up with him inside it. Miraculously he survived. Allen Dorfman was not to be so lucky.

The 1982 trial of Dorfman, Roy Williams and Joey 'the Clown' Lombardo was over the sale of prime building land owned by the pension fund in Las Vegas. The conspirators were trying to sell the land for less than its market value to Nevada's US Senator Howard Cannon and his Las Vegas neighbours. Had this sale gone through the fund's pensioners would have been defrauded of their proper investment earnings. Dorfman, Williams, Lombardo and their underlings were all convicted. But now Dorfman faced trial in another court where he could not defend himself. The bosses of the Chicago outfit judged this urbane and witty man of 60 incapable of stomaching the rest of his life in jail. They could not run the risk that he might become a government informer in return for a light sentence. As a Jew Dorfman could not be a 'made' man but he knew many secrets that only a 'made' man should know. In January 1983, before the federal judge could sentence him, Dorfman was shot to death gangland-style in the car park of a Chicago hotel. As his Mafia master, Joey 'the Clown' Lombardo, once said in an intercepted conversation, 'Allen belongs to Chicago. Half of what Allen gets Chicago gets. Allen is meek and mild but the people behind him are not.'

For the first twenty-four years of legal gambling in Las Vegas no one running a casino was ever investigated. Organized-crime figures like Siegel, Lansky and Dalitz could walk in and do almost whatever they wanted. But in 1955 the Nevada State Gaming Control Board was set up to regulate the industry. Nowadays anyone who wants a key position in a casino is investigated to find out if they have any connections with organized crime. Only those that are 'clean' are then granted the necessary licence. There are, however, ways round this. When Frank Rosenthal first worked for Allen Glick he was employed as the casino's food and beverage manager, a post for which no licence was required.

In recent years members of most American crime families have been jailed for skimming from Las Vegas casinos but the cases have been brought by federal prosecutors not by the state of Nevada. Even when casinos are proved to have connections with organized crime the Nevada State Gaming Control Board rarely punishes the operators.

John 'Pete' Donohue worked for the board as an investigator until he left in disgust. 'My job was to investigate allegations of organized-crime infiltration into the casinos and into those casinos' operations all over the world. I found out that almost every known crew of organized crime was involved. They weren't only skimming the casinos. They were using them to wash their funds from illegal activity such as loansharking and narcotics.'

One service organized crime often performs for the casinos is collecting gambling debts which have been run up on credit markers (a kind of IOU) rather than cash. The debtors are often degenerate or compulsive gamblers who have been flown to Las Vegas on 'junkets'. They get on a junket by undertaking to gamble an agreed sum, say $5,000, win or lose. In return they pay nothing for their air flight, hotel room, food or entertainment. Of course they must eventually settle their losses which usually turn out to be heavy. Many losers do not have the money and try to escape their debts.

Pete Donohue found that junkets were tailor-made for the mob. 'We took the casinos' records of debts owed by junketeers and went back East to interview them. We found the markers were no longer in the hands of the people who had arranged the junkets but in the hands of the New York crime families. When the hotel was having a hard time collecting, the mob would take the markers off the hands of the hotel by paying the hotel 25c in the dollar and then they'd go to the victim. Now he would become a real victim because they would tell him, "We got your marker, you owe x amount of dollars, the juice on it is five points a week and you're gonna pay it every week." Now they are in the hands of the loansharks for the rest of their life.'

Donohue detected many other organized-crime abuses. Some involved the rule which allows casinos to 'write off' debts that have proved uncollectable. A mobster using an assumed name gets extended credit from a casino. He is given his gambling chips which he soon exchanges again for cash. He now walks out without gambling a cent. His debt may run into hundreds of thousands of dollars but it is never recovered. However, it may be written off if the Gaming Board casts a tolerant or blind eye over it. When debts are written off no state taxes are paid on them as casino 'winnings,' so the casino recovers much of its loss. The potential for fraud is obviously enormous where casinos or their employees are in collusion with organized crime.

Other abuses investigated by Donohue involved the provision of all the services without which a hotel-casino cannot operate, from the supply of linen to public relations contracts. The mob can inflate the costs of genuine services by millions of dollars and again compliant hotel executives will make sure the accounts are settled, some of which may be wholly fictional.

Donohue found that the Nevada State Gaming Control Board was reluctant to act on his reports of crimes committed outside Nevada either by casino operators or by mobsters acting in their name. He claims that both the board and its overseeing authority, the Gaming Commission, do not ensure a 'fair shake' for the gambling public. When the public loses nearly $2 billion a year in Las Vegas's ninety casinos, that is the least it deserves. He claims that some Nevada officials are soft on the casinos because, today as in his day, 'Almost everyone connected with the board ended up going to work for the very industry they were regulating just beforehand.' Nor do they close down casinos for malpractice because even a crooked casino offers up at least a few dollars whereas a closed casino yields no taxes at all. Donohue points out that none of the casinos which have been proved to have organized-crime connections have ever been shut down, even for a 24-hour period. The relationship between the casinos and the state regulators is so close, claims Donohue, that it verges on the corrupt. 'You just can't regulate it when they're feeding from the same pot.'

At the time of writing Nevada is forcing Allan Sachs to sell the Fremont and Stardust casinos which he bought from Allen Glick in 1979. For many years Sachs has been closely identified with the Godfather of Las Vegas, Moe Dalitz. Moe himself is still going strong. At the age of 84 he has applied for a licence for the Sundance Casino. He is expected to be 'grandfathered' into the licence because influential Nevadans love him so. If that happens it will not surprise Pete Donohue who says the state's entire mechanism for controlling the casinos and throwing out the mob is not up to the task. 'It's not working properly. It's a sham, a farce.'

18

The Mob, the Boardwalk and Atlantic City

There are few buildings worth preserving in New Jersey but the Marlborough-Blenheim Hotel in Atlantic City used to be one of them. By 1978 this blue palace with its three noble domes had graced the world-famous, ocean-side Boardwalk for seventy-two years. But state officials had no sooner declared it a protected historic site than they were persuaded that its façade was unsafe. In 1979 developers blew up the entire hotel. It collapsed in eleven seconds. It would still be standing today if the developers had not been a slot-machine corporation bent on building a $300-million casino.

For more than half a century Atlantic City, 110 miles south of New York, had been America's favourite playground. It was hailed as the 'Queen of Resorts' but by the 1950s the Queen was dying. In the age of cheap air travel holiday-makers preferred Florida, the Caribbean, in fact almost anywhere to Atlantic City. By the early 1970s there were few tourists, the city's population had fallen to 40,000 and young whites were leaving a largely black and Hispanic town which had few jobs to offer.

In the same decade, but for reasons which had nothing to do with the plight of Atlantic City, some New Jersey politicians were becoming increasingly covetous of Nevada's casino revenues. In a referendum in 1974 they asked New Jerseyans whether they wanted casinos to be legalized in their state. The voters said no but in 1976 the issue was put to them again, reworded so that casinos would be allowed only in Atlantic City. This weakened the anti-casino campaign, which had stressed the social pollution that goes with gambling and the damage it would do in middle-class, residential neighbourhoods. Such considerations counted for little in Atlantic City, especially when the casino lobby promised gambling would revive the resort. It would bring back the crowds, jobs would flow to the blacks and the poor and casino taxes would help both city and state care for their old and sick. Most voters believed the rhetoric and approved.

In the spring of 1978 New Jersey's governor, Brendan Byrne, rode in a triumphal cavalcade to Atlantic City's convention hall and signed the casino law. In passing Byrne told organized crime to: 'keep your filthy hands out of Atlantic City. Keep the hell out of our state.' These were bold but empty words, as Byrne himself should have known. New Jersey is perhaps the most 'mobbed-up' state in the Union. It is home territory for seven crime families and hundreds of mafiosi. Atlantic City has been a mob town since long before Nucky Johnson hosted the national crime syndicate meeting there in 1929.[1]

The governor should have listened to New Jersey's own top police expert on organized crime, Lieutenant-Colonel Justin Dintino, who voted against casino gaming in the state. 'I had spent a lot of time in Nevada studying their problems,' says Dintino, 'and I concluded it was not the kind of environment in which I would like to raise my children. When you legalize a form of gambling you create a whole new bunch of consumers and you create a whole new market for illegal enterprises. Every prediction the state police made before casinos were allowed in Atlantic City has come true. We knew there would be an increase in organized crime and there has been.'

On Memorial Day in May 1978 Resorts International opened Atlantic City's first legal casino in a renovated 1000-room hotel on the Boardwalk. It was chaos, mayhem, as gamblers rushed the doors. Roulette, blackjack, craps, baccarat: every table was jammed. There were queues at the change booth, at the giant lottery wheels and at all 900 slot machines. Over that weekend tens of thousands of people gambled in the casino. Resorts soon 'won' more than $1 million in a single day. In 1979 the casino grossed $232 million and made net profits of $41 million.

Atlantic City's missing visitors were flocking back. This was no surprise because, for the first time in the eastern USA, Americans could gamble in a casino without breaking the law. Fifty-five million people – a quarter of America's population – live within 300 miles of the Jersey shore. Day-trip gambling, a few hours' drive away, will always attract more people than a wearying flight to Las Vegas and a large hotel bill.

In three years seven more casinos opened on the Boardwalk and another by the marina. In 1983 all nine together 'won' $1770 million. A tenth casino opened in 1984 when the city's take should exceed that of all 130 casinos in greater Las Vegas. With more casinos due to open shortly, Atlantic City's gross revenues will soon overhaul those of all Nevada's 200 casinos. In 1983 Resorts International's casino won $6.2 million in a single weekend. The shabby old seaside town will soon displace Las Vegas as the gambling capital of the world. It is already back as America's number-one tourist attraction with more than 26 million visitors a year. Atlantic City's casino will never be exclusive, elitist joints for high-rollers only. Millions of their customers are senior citizens shipped in on subsidized bus trips but even if all the old folk in the north-east only gambled away their Social Security cheques an Atlantic City casino licence would still amount to a licence to print money.

In 1981 Resorts International temporarily lost its place as Atlantic City's most lucrative casino to the Golden Nugget 'Gambling Hall and Rooming House'. The Nugget is decked out in tribute to America's pioneers and prospectors. Gamblers are meant to feel they are back in the days of the Gold Rush but there never was a gold rush like this one. The owners, who operate another Golden Nugget casino in downtown Las Vegas, display the world's biggest gold nuggets (both found in Australia) amid the massed ranks of their clanking slot machines. The biggest payout from a single machine has been more than $1 million. This is not charity. It is good publicity and helps the casino win as much as £30 million in the peak month of July.

A few blocks away from the Boardwalk casino winnings have made little impact. At the northern end of the narrow coastal island on which Atlantic City is built the black and Hispanic neighbourhoods have continued to decay. The casinos have bought much of the land for development and their plans do not embrace the people who live there. The few blacks employed in the casinos either do menial work or they do not come from Atlantic City. The Puerto Rican croupiers are not recruited from the Puerto Rican ghetto at the north end of Pacific Avenue. They come direct from Puerto Rico's own casinos.

Luxurious condominiums and vacation apartments are being built in self-contained complexes on the Ocean but in downtown streets muggers lurk for stray visitors, prostitutes tout for clients on church steps and the last surviving cinema shows only blue movies. The population has continued to fall. Most of the 30,000 casino employees live out of town. Few of the promises which made New Jersey vote for casino gambling in 1976 have been fulfilled in Atlantic City. That may be the fault of the state rather than the casinos but the citizens are angry. In 1983 they voted in a black mayor, James Usry, to replace the white mayor accused of winning the previous election on Mafia money and only then by filling in hundreds of postal votes in his own favour.[2] Mayor Usry must now get the state to spend some of its huge casino revenues on his city rather than on the 7 million citizens of New Jersey as a whole. 'What we have here is a tale of two cities: the city that represents the casino interests and the city of the people who live here. We have to make the casinos the catalyst which will turn the place around but so far all we've seen is more casinos and more parking lots,' he says.

New Jersey takes hundreds of millions in taxes every year from the casinos' gross winnings so it is in the state's interest to ensure no one skims or steals. In Atlantic City security is oppressive. Video cameras, hidden and not-so-hidden, are everywhere, spying on gamblers and employees alike. Each casino has a surveillance room with dozens of video screens. Expert staff scrutinize everything that happens at the tables, the slot machines and even out on the Boardwalk. They try to spot card cheats and any accomplice croupiers. They also watch over the cage where millions of dollars are handled every day. A New Jersey inspector is always present in the cage with the power to check the takings at any time. In Nevada no state official has a right to be in the cage, which is one reason why organized crime has found it easy to skim. Whereas Nevada has only some 300 officials to watch over its 200 casinos, New Jersey has more than 450 employees policing only ten.

New Jersey investigates each corporation that wants to run a casino and roots out anyone connected with organized crime. A casino will only be allowed a permanent operating licence if the state considers both its owners and its employees 'clean'. New

Jersey would bar anyone who had ever been directly involved with Meyer Lansky but no Lansky aide would be foolish enough to seek a licence in his own name. Realizing this, New Jersey has vetoed people who have ever done business with anyone alleged to be a front for Lansky. Some people are bitter about the state's presumption of guilt by association and its tough procedures. New Jersey's victims include Clifford and Stuart Perlman, the brothers who made Caesar's Palace in Las Vegas the most famous entertainment venue in the world. They wanted to open another casino in Atlantic City but New Jersey refused them permission because of past real estate deals with men close to Lansky, a decision which later helped push the Perlmans to quit their beloved Caesar's in Las Vegas.

Atlantic City might still be waiting for its first casino if such ruthless standards had been applied to Resorts International. This corporation was granted a temporary licence to allow it to open its doors in 1976. Only then did state investigators dig up evidence which made the organization look less than wholesome. In 1965 when much the same company was called Mary Carter Paint, it had gained a lucrative casino licence in the Bahamas with the help of some unsavoury allies. One was an American, Wallace Groves, who had been jailed in the 1940s for a Wall Street swindle. Another was a white Bahamian lawyer, Sir Stafford Sands, who demanded and was paid exorbitant fees for arranging Mary Carter's licence for a casino on Paradise Island. Sands, for many years a Bahamian cabinet minister, was a notorious fixer whose conduct was later viewed by a commission of inquiry 'with considerable suspicion'. The committee did not, however, have the power to find anyone guilty.

In the 1960s Wallace Groves was running other casinos in the colony, including the Monte Carlo which employed many of Meyer Lansky's men in powerful positions. In 1966 Mary Carter Paint and Wallace Groves opened the Bahamian Club casino, which was also staffed by Lansky men. Many of these employees went to work in the Paradise Island casino when it opened in 1967. As a result of these dealings Mary Carter Paint had become closely involved with two men named Cellini. Dino Cellini was a man who, having been banned from the Bahamas in 1964, was now supplying croupiers to

Mary Carter's casinos from his croupier school in London.[3] Edward Cellini, Dino's brother, was given a three-year contract by Mary Carter in December 1967 as general manager of Paradise Island.

The Cellini brothers, natives of the staunch mob gambling town of Steubenville, Ohio, had been key men in Meyer Lansky's Cuban operations until the 1959 revolution. Mary Carter later parted company with them both but in Eddie's case far too slowly to satisfy the investigators working for New Jersey's Division of Gaming Enforcement. The Cellini connection, among many others charted in a 115-page report, so disturbed the state's attorney-general that in December 1978 he objected to Resorts International being granted a permanent licence. Resorts was saved only when the Casino Control Commission gave it the licence despite the objections. The commissioners were, it seems, satisfied that Resorts International had cleansed itself of Mary Carter's Augean past. They were also aware that if they were to shut Resorts International down because of Mary Carter's mob ties, Atlantic City's infant casino industry would have died a quick death, never to be reincarnated.

Having once cast a blind eye it now became difficult for New Jersey to keep any company off the Boardwalk, however bad its connections. Bally Manufacturing has long had a near-monopoly on gambling slot machines in America. In 1978 it applied for a New Jersey casino licence. This was granted on condition that its chairman and president, William O'Donnell, resign. His mob connections were too blatant even for New Jersey.

In 1963 O'Donnell had taken Bally over with only the financial support of business partners of Gerry Catena, who was soon to become joint boss of the Genovese crime family. Under O'Donnell's nose Catena became Bally's main distributor for New York and New Jersey. Another top Bally 'salesman' was – yet again! – Dino Cellini, Meyer Lansky's front man, to whom Bally paid a fat commission for selling its slot machines to the Mary Carter/Resorts International casino in the Bahamas in 1968. Bally's mob links were soon discovered by law enforcement, yet Nevada still allowed it to take a 70 per cent share of the state's slot-machine market in the 1960s. In 1974 Bally decided to do its own distributing in

Nevada for which it had to get a state licence. Nevada demanded some staff resignations but was happy to leave O'Donnell in charge. Five years later New Jersey forced him to resign. The Gaming Control Commission thought Bally without O'Donnell was clean enough to deserve a permanent licence. It now hovers at around third place in Atlantic City's casino profit league.

New Jersey's in-depth investigations, more rigorous than anything undertaken by Nevada, have made it difficult for the Mafia to take over the casinos through front men in true Las Vegas-style. Yet Justin Dintino believes that New Jersey has only kept the mob out of the front door. 'They aren't on the boards of the corporations owning the casinos, they aren't named as stockholders, but they *are* in the service industries. Remember, each casino-hotel has to use some 250 ancillary services to stay open. Services like food products, maintenance, laundry, linen and advertising all provide an excellent way for the mob to skim from a casino. All they need to do is to top up the charges for those services.'

Even before any Atlantic City casino had opened, in 1977 Philadelphia's Mafia boss Angelo Bruno held a crime-family meeting at which he ordered each high-ranking member to put up $500,000 for Atlantic City. According to federal witness Charlie Palermo 'Allen' (who admits to having carried out six murders for the Philadelphia Mafia), with this money they were going 'to take over all the bar supplies; they would supply all the linen, all the vending machines, all the meats and groceries going into the hotels'. If the hotels and restaurants wanted to have a good relationship with the labour unions, says Allen, 'They would have to buy off us.'

The Mafia is actually believed to have extorted money from Atlantic City's casinos before they were even completed. Building a casino these days can cost $300 million. Most of that money is borrowed and until it is repaid interest can pile up at a rate of $200,000 a day. For each day's delay in construction the owners have to pay another day's loan interest not to mention the revenue they are losing that they would have won had they been open for gambling. When a casino is built and open for business the same arithmetic applies. The owners cannot afford any shutdowns so they may not be able to resist the extortion demands any union boss dares to make.

Justin Dintino saw instantly how the Philadelphia Mafia was going to muscle in on the action. 'If I were an Angelo Bruno I would not be concerned about owning a casino, particularly when I knew the complex investigations that would involve. Organized crime does not like that kind of scrutiny. They can make all the money they need by controlling the peripheral activities. If I were Angelo Bruno trying to get in the back door, I would control the labour union that is organizing the casino employees and they have done that.'

By law Atlantic City's ten casinos have to be big hotels with a minimum of 500 bedrooms, so good casino business depends on the entire hotel staff: maintenance and garbage men, valets and laundrymen, room maids, porters, bell boys, cocktail waitresses, barmen, cooks and restaurant staff. If they all went on strike the casino would have to close. In Atlantic City 10,000 of these workers belong to Local 54 of the HEREIU, the hotel and restaurant employees' union. Before the first casino opened Local 54 'belonged' to the Philadelphia Mafia.

The HEREIU is the largest union in America's hotel and restaurant industry with some 400,000 members. A Justice Department report has claimed that many of the union's officials are 'syndicate controlled'. Since the 1970s several of Local 54's top officials have been creatures of Nicodemus 'Little Nicky' Scarfo, who seized control of the Philadelphia family in the civil war which has raged ever since Angelo Bruno's murder in 1980.[4]

Bruno sent Scarfo to Atlantic City in the 1960s to oversee the family's long-standing rackets on the Jersey shore. Scarfo moved into a house with his mother and took over Local 54. Robert Lumio, 54's secretary-treasurer until he died in 1981, was another 'made' man in the Bruno family. When Scarfo was charged with murder in 1979 the local's president, Frank Gerace, put up Scarfo's $10,000 bail. Another Philly mobster, Ralph Natale, was a HEREIU official until he was jailed on arson and drugs' charges in 1980. In 1984 Albert Daidone, 54's vice-president, was convicted of conspiring to murder another mob union boss, John McCullough of the Philadelphia Roofers' Union. Despite the local's appalling record a federal judge has told New Jersey that it has no power to oust organized crime figures from Local 54. The US

Supreme Court overturned that judgment in July 1984, but it is still not clear how New Jersey can keep mob unions out of casinos.

The Mafia's control of Local 54 was the subject of a Senate rackets committee hearing in June 1982. By this time Scarfo was boss of the Philadelphia family. In traditional Mafia style he cited the 5th Amendment and said nothing. More insight was provided by federal witness Joseph Salerno, who ran a plumbing company from Scarfo's headquarters in the 1970s. He became friendly with Scarfo and saw how the mafioso treated Bob Lumio. On one occasion Lumio came into Nicky's apartment and started telling him 'about an article in the Atlantic City paper that said Lumio and Scarfo were hooked up together with organized crime. Nicky read it and the more he read the madder he got. And he got real mad when Lumio started laughing about the article. Scarfo looked up and told Lumio, "Yes, I am your boss. I got you that job." '

When Scarfo told Salerno he would soon be getting a plumbing job from a contractor on the Playboy casino Salerno wondered if there might be any opposition from the plumbing union. 'Don't worry about union problems,' said Scarfo, 'never any union problems we'll have because we control the unions.' Salerno asked him about the mob's future in Atlantic City. 'Joe,' he replied looking out of the window across the Boardwalk's booming skyline, 'you see this. We'll own this city one day. That's what we're going to do.'

New Jersey has tried hard to keep the Mafia out of Atlantic City, to stop it from becoming another Las Vegas, but the Mafia is in there. Pete Donohue, the New York state trooper turned Nevada gaming investigator, believes things are as bad in Atlantic City as they are in Las Vegas. 'Before the first hotel opened organized crime had things like the napkins and the vending machines. Law enforcement thinks it's keeping the mob out of the gaming rooms. But what the hell's the difference? If the mob run the union, if they pick up the garbage and they put the milk on the table, they own you already. They'll skim you to death through *those* services. They're not going to go and cheat in the card games or on the tables, or skim from the cage. They don't need to!'

In 1983 Dintino told New Jersey's Commission of Investigation about the abuse of credit at Atlantic City casinos. He produced proof that top organized-crime figures were being 'comped' at most casinos (supplied with rooms, hospitality and entertainment for nothing as 'complimentaries') despite the fact that those same casinos were only too keen to throw out petty offenders. 'I find it rather unusual, given their elaborate security and intelligence systems, staffed in most part by former law-enforcement officials, that only prostitutes and card counters were being ejected. . . . It's obvious that there are no incentives on the part of the casino management to exclude organized-crime members or their criminal associates.'

Dintino's staff carried out a small random sample of 500,000 credit records incurred in 1982. Many 'made' members of the Mafia had been given credit of up to $55,000 and comped for as much as $7000. A Mafia contract killer was allowed to deposit $504,000 in cash at Resorts International. Dintino said the evidence strongly indicated the killer had walked out with the same amount later that day in other cash, thus laundering a fortune. Claiming that these abuses were only the 'tip of the iceberg', he pointed out the contrast between the laborious investigations that precede the granting of casino licences and the way 'we allow paid killers, convicted murderers, drug-traffickers and known loan-sharks to enter the casinos and receive preferential treatment.'

Dintino stressed that if any casino dared to exclude Nicky Scarfo it could suffer both physical and economic retaliation imposed by the labour unions he controls. 'Through Local 54's 10,000 members he has one hell of a hammer over the casinos. I wouldn't want to make him too mad at me. You would be inclined to comp him or allow him into the casinos. The fear a Scarfo brings to the casino overrides any sanctions that the state may impose.'

In February and March 1982 Scarfo was comped at the Tropicana, Claridge and Golden Nugget casinos. The hospitality added up to a mere $2400. It seems he required little more than a room and dinner with a few friends but comping is meant to be extended only to high rollers and regular gamblers who habitually lose. The casinos that comped Scarfo overlooked the fact that he has never been known to gamble at any Atlantic City casino.

A Scotland Yard detective on a recent visit to Atlantic City told the security staff at one casino that its surveillance cameras were all pointing the wrong way. He was right. They spy on the gamblers but who protects the gamblers against the casinos? Is anybody keeping out the real mobsters? They cast as big a shadow on the Boardwalk as the towers of those casino corporations who claim legal gambling in America can have a future without organized crime. It depends on your definition of organized crime. Shutting out men whose names end in vowels will not shut out the mob.

19

Sinatra – His Way

One man above all has come to be affectionately regarded as a symbol of the world of casino gambling: Frank Sinatra.

'Ol' Blue Eyes' draws more gamblers to America's casinos than any other entertainer. When he plays Las Vegas profits soar, not just in the casino where he is appearing but in every casino. One Las Vegas figure who worked with Sinatra for many years is Clifford Perlman, former joint-owner of Caesar's Palace and the inspiration of much of its success. From 1969 to 1982 Sinatra played Caesar's every year. 'I happen to like Frank Sinatra very much,' Perlman said. 'He is a warm, enormously charitable human being. He's rather diverse, as you probably suspect, but in the main he's quite attractive as a person. His presence at Caesar's was an important piece of our marketing, not just as a performer, but it was his appearances in a relaxed and informal way in the lounge, in the restaurants and at our various events that made the hotel even more exciting than it could possibly have been with him just as a performer.'

Recently Sinatra has signed a lucrative, exclusive deal with Golden Nugget Inc. which limits his appearances in Las Vegas and Atlantic City to Golden Nugget's two casinos. The man behind the company's astonishing growth is its president and chairman, Stephen Wynn. He has come to know Sinatra well and they appear together in the Nugget's television advertisements. Wynn believes that the secret of Sinatra's appeal is 'the lifetime of ups and downs, the music, all of it has come down to an identification he has with a wide spectrum of people. Part of it is the sporting life, the Guys and Dolls, the action, the guys that are down on their luck. Frank, I think, is popular with people that have taken a shot and missed a lot.'

It is unfortunate that the nickname 'Ol' Blue Eyes' is so near to the 'Baby Blue Eyes' by which George Raft addressed Bugsy Siegel, for Frank Sinatra has been dogged for years by allegations of Mafia connections and of a series of doubtful friendships. Many of the allegations were revived in 1980 when the singer sought a licence to become entertainments consultant to Caesar's Palace. In 1981 he faced questioning from the Gaming Board, which is the controlling authority of Nevada gaming, and from the Gaming Commission, an overseeing body made up of high-ranking figures including state senators. Public interest was so great that local television stations covered both hearings. Cynics felt that they were just a formality, a ritual to save Nevada's gaming face. They say Sinatra was bound to get his licence in a state where he is treated more like royalty than royalty, but at both levels his inquisitors tried to appear to be conducting a fair yet rigorous cross-examination.

At the heart of the disquiet are Sinatra's alleged friendships with notorious mobsters from New York and Chicago. Some of the most persistent allegations cannot be proved or disproved. The oldest goes back to Sinatra's early days, not long after he graduated from the saloon bars of his native Hoboken to join Tommy Dorsey's band. According to Sinatra's Nevada testimony he once bought a house in New Jersey where one of his neighbours was a Mr Willie Moore. Sinatra later found out Moore was really Willie Moretti, a sinister mafioso who in 1951 would be murdered by his gangland *compares*. It has been said that Moretti helped Sinatra's career by getting him singing engagements and contracts. Sinatra told Nevada that Moretti had never helped him and that the two men had never discussed any such help. He refuted the claim that Moretti had assisted him in getting out of his contract with Tommy Dorsey. When Gaming Board chairman Richard Bunker raised the story that 'one of the reasons you progressed was due to the efforts of some members of organized crime' Sinatra's response was 'ridiculous'.

Another recurring story is that Sinatra was a friend of Lucky Luciano's. Sinatra is alleged to have flown to Havana in 1947 carrying an attaché case with $2 million for the Mafia's exiled boss of bosses. Sinatra admitted he had met Luciano on Havana on that trip but said that it was through a Chicago newspaperman. 'I just met him in a bar and shook hands and that was it.' They never met again. Sinatra refuted the story of the attaché case: 'If you can find me an attaché case that holds $2 million I will give you the $2 million.' He said he had not the slightest idea how his name and address were on Luciano's person when he was once searched by Italian officials.

Sinatra knew another mobster: Joseph Fischetti, alias 'Joe Fish'. Joe Fischetti was Al Capone's cousin. Two of his brothers – Rocco and Charlie – were notorious Chicago mobsters and Joe himself had his own page in the Federal Bureau of Narcotics' 'Mafia' book in the late 1950s. The FBN claimed he was an associate of Chicago crime bosses Paul Ricca and Tony Accardo and that he controlled extensive Mafia gambling interests in Florida. Sinatra testified that he and Joe were 'just friends. I was fond of him and he was fond of me.' Sinatra said they had never had any business dealings: '. . . he was just a social acquaintance, a dear friend. I liked him and it was mutual.' Of Joe's brothers Sinatra said that he had 'just met them vaguely'.

Sinatra had to face tougher questions about his relationship with a far bigger Chicago mobster, Sam 'Momo' Giancana.[1] A gunman during Prohibition, Giancana was chosen as boss of the Chicago outfit in 1959 and took over all its gambling rackets. In 1961 Sinatra became the 50 per cent owner of a Nevada casino hotel, the Cal-Neva Lodge at Lake Tahoe. Twenty years later Richard Bunker asked him if Giancana had ever had a hidden interest in the Cal-Neva and if Frank Sinatra might have been his front man. The entertainer rejected the suggestion.

In July 1963 Giancana stayed at the Cal-Neva with his girlfriend, the beautiful Phyllis McGuire of the McGuire Sisters singing group. One night a fight broke out over Phyllis between Giancana and another man. Stories go the rounds that Sinatra joined Giancana in beating the man to pulp but Sinatra told the Gaming Board that he was in Los Angeles that night. The Cal-Neva's manager, Eddie King, called him up asking what to do about Giancana because the staff had just broken up 'one helluva fight'. Sinatra testified that he told King to get Giancana 'off the property. Just get rid of him.' Sinatra claimed he had never invited, entertained or even seen Giancana at the Cal-Neva. However, Phyllis McGuire told Nevada investigators she recalled Sinatra being present at the Cal-Neva on some occasion when Giancana was staying there.

During the Gaming Commission hearings Senator Dodge asked Sinatra whether he had wanted to get Giancana off the property because he knew 'this guy was an undesirable and could be getting you into trouble?'

The entertainer replied, 'Of course.'

Sinatra's admission to Senator Dodge that he knew Giancana was an 'undesirable' and that any connection between the Chicago mobster and himself would 'of course' get him into trouble is in conflict with the claim that Sinatra maintained a friendship with Giancana over many years. The Nevada hearings did not explore that friendship, which was a strange omission. One person who could have enlightened Sinatra's gentle inquisitors was Judith Exner who, as Judy Campbell, knew Frank Sinatra, President John F. Kennedy and Sam Giancana very well. She had met both the mobster and the politician through Sinatra.

Judy Campbell had known Sinatra socially for years. She was married and divorced before she first dated the entertainer. She soon realized he had a bizarre line in friends. 'Frank had gotten his group together in the early sixties and put a show on in Las Vegas with Dean Martin, Peter Lawford, Joey Bishop and Sammy Davis. They were making a picture at the time, *Oceans 11*. The show was such a success they took it to Florida. I went down there with some friends to see the show. It was at a party for the closing night that I was introduced to Sam Giancana by Frank Sinatra.

'Sam had known Frank for many, many years,' says Judith, who saw the two men together on many occasions. She also saw Sinatra with Joe Fischetti and another Chicago mobster Johnny Formosa. Her impression was that Frank always treated people from the underworld with great respect.

Judy recalls how in 1962 Sinatra appeared at the Villa Venice, a restaurant club outside Chicago, at Sam Giancana's request. 'It was a place that you wouldn't ordinarily find a name like Frank Sinatra.' Not only did Sinatra appear there but he also brought along his friend Sammy Davis Jun. The Villa Venice was another subject for discussion in Nevada in 1981. Sinatra said he had entertained there but that he didn't know whether Giancana had anything to do with the club. 'He never asked me to entertain there. An agent asked me.'

The interest in Sinatra's appearance at the Villa Venice arose because Giancana had exploited the booking to attract high-rolling gamblers. Former FBI agent Bill Roemer was assigned to an investigation into the Villa Venice when Sinatra and Sammy Davis were appearing there. 'Giancana refurbished the Villa Venice on the Northwest Side of Chicago and brought in these top entertainers. Now he made a lot of money from that but he also set up a concert hut alongside and put in a casino there. That thing went full blast as high rollers came in, attracted by the Sinatra–Dean Martin–Sammy Davis appearance. They would watch the entertainment and then spend the rest of the night at the casino, gambling away hundreds of thousands of dollars.'

At the Nevada hearings Sinatra refuted any suggestion that he had appeared at the Villa Venice for a low fee as a favour to Giancana. A contract was produced to show he had appeared there for seven days for a total fee of $15,000. This was stated to be his going rate at the time. As for the gambling, all Sinatra could recall was that: 'On the fourth night I heard some rumours about a dice game, and it didn't affect me so I didn't pay any attention to it.' In Nevada Sinatra was vague in recollecting whether he ever saw Giancana during his Villa Venice shows – 'I might have' – but Giancana's daughter Antoinette has recently revealed that she saw the entertainer hug her father on each of the many occasions that the mobster entered his dressing room.

Perhaps the trickiest questions Sinatra had to answer in Nevada were over his three appearances at the Westchester Premier Theatre in 1976 and 1977. The Westchester Theatre was located at Tarrytown in Westchester County, just north of New York City. The management's declared aim was to attract top-line entertainers to a luxurious new concert hall, convenient for well-heeled suburban patrons who did not want the misery of driving into Manhattan for a night out.

The truth was that the theatre was planned as a bankruptcy fraud from the time it opened in 1975. Mobsters from the Gambino crime family put up the initial capital, then hid behind front men who sold the stock to unsuspecting members of the public. It was fitting that the Westchester was built on a swamp. Even on the landfill contract the mob inflated the cost and left behind a disaster.

Soon after the theatre was completed the surrounding parking area sank six feet, leaving the loading dock high, dry and out of reach. From the moment Diana Ross performed the theatre's first shows its ticket revenues, bar sales and souvenir takings were being looted by the mob.

When Jerry Donnellan became stage manager at the Westchester he noticed that a bizarre crew of non-theatrical heavies were running the place. 'Fellows in $800 suits were selling popcorn. Whenever a big-name entertainer was on stage the guys in the front rows looked like 500 years of good behaviour. It was wall-to-wall shoulders, fellows with no necks dragging their knuckles on the ground, refrigerators on casters accompanied by ladies who were obviously not their daughters.'

New York state trooper Pete Donohue worked the Westchester in his undercover role. 'The mob was using it as a "dump site" for all kinds of rackets, stolen jewellery and paintings. I bought millions of dollars of Rumanian money there, at 10 cents to the dollar.'

When Frank Sinatra made the first of his three week-long appearances the theatre was largely controlled by mafiosi belonging to the Genovese as well as the Gambino crime families. By this time, says Donnellan, 'there was so much comping, free seats, dinners and drinks, that the place could not have made a profit even if it had sold out every night. The entertainers were being paid 50 per cent above the going rate.'

Sinatra was getting $30,000 a show: $360,000 for each series of twelve performances. The mobsters were making their money on top by 'scalping' (pocketing a proportion of the profits) from shows by superstars like Shirley Bassey, Tom Jones and, most lucrative of all, Dean Martin and Frank Sinatra. In total the mobsters looted $9 million. The theatre went bankrupt and seven of the fraudsters were later sent to jail. One of them was Louis Pacella, also known as 'Louis Dome' or 'Dones'. At the Nevada hearings Sinatra said he knew Louis Pacella 'very well'. He was a good friend. 'He was the first man to invite me to perform at the theatre . . . . He explained it to me and I said, "well, we will see what we can do about it." ' Sinatra's engagement calendar was not completely full so he went ahead and appeared at Westchester.

Asked if Pacella had 'the type of background that one might be aware of', Sinatra said, 'I know what you are saying, Mr Chairman, but I can't attest to that because I have never been present if he had any form of activity. I have never been present. He had a restaurant in New York and I visited it very often. I liked it. It was good food. I became fond of him and that was the extent of my friendship with him.'

When asked if he was aware that Pacella was convicted of not reporting some of his income from the Westchester, Sinatra responded tetchily, 'I am well aware of it.'

Sinatra could not possibly have been unaware of it. In 1979 his friend pleaded guilty to skimming $50,000 from Sinatra's final series of Westchester concerts in May 1977. In return for booking Sinatra Pacella was paid 'under the table' cash skimmed from ticket sales and the sale of Sinatra souvenirs at a time when the theatre was already in bankruptcy proceedings. Pacella was sentenced to two years in jail and fined $5000 for evading income tax on the $50,000.

Pacella's hoodlum activities were nothing new but Nevada did not ask Sinatra whether he was aware of the serious offences publicly attributed to his friend seventeen years earlier. In 1963 and 1964 Joe Valachi identified Pacella as a Genovese family soldier before the Senate Rackets Committee. The committee displayed Pacella's photograph and listed his alias and his main criminal activity (gambling) in its Genovese family chart. All this was published in the give-away volumes of the committee's hearings which also incorporated the FBN's 'Mafia' book entry on Pacella. The FBN stated, although Pacella had only once been arrested, that he 'was engaged in large-scale distribution of pure heroin'.

The Pacella restaurant, which Sinatra liked to patronize, was presumably the 'Sepret Tables' on the East Side of Manhattan. In 1979 Pacella denied owning it although he had formerly described it as 'my place'. At his trial FBI and DEA agents testified that Mafia informers had told them Sepret Tables was a rendezvous for top mobsters and a 'drug hang-out for organized-crime figures'. FBI informers had also identified Pacella as a Shylock or extortionate moneylender.

Sinatra says he was unaware of anything nefarious about Pacella but the restaurateur's criminal side was well known to the former Los Angeles Mafia boss Jimmy Fratianno. He was on the inside of the Westchester Theatre scandal. 'Sinatra got there through Louis Dones. Louis Dones went to the Westchester Theatre, he says, "Lookit, I can get you Sinatra but I've got to get a piece of the proposition." So they went along with it. So when Sinatra got there Louis Dones used to run it: he got a piece of the scalping, he got a piece of the T-shirts, he got a piece of everything. See, Louis Dones is a "made" guy with the Genovese family. The Westchester people got Sinatra and they got him three times through Louis Dones. Now Louis Dones went to the grand jury and refused to talk about Sinatra and he did fourteen months for it, so you know there's something he could say and he don't want to say.'

The grand jury had been empanelled following Pacella's tax conviction to investigate criminal allegations against other people over Westchester. His silence in response to the question, 'Do you know an individual by the name of Frank Sinatra,' was particularly odd because at Pacella's own trial his lawyer had been only too keen to impress the jury with the strength of the two men's relationship: 'You will find that Frank Sinatra and Louis Pacella were very, very, very close and dear friends. In fact the evidence will show to you that they were brothers, not because they shared the same mother and father but because they shared love, admiration and friendship for many many years.'

In Nevada Sinatra had to answer questions about a notorious photograph taken backstage at the Westchester in 1976 after one of his performances. In the photo Sinatra is surrounded by leaders of the Mafia including Carlo Gambino, then the most powerful crime boss in America, his under-boss Paul Castellano and Los Angeles boss Jimmy 'the Weasel' Fratianno.

Sinatra explained his side of the story. 'I was asked by one of the members of the theatre – who he was doesn't come to me, I don't think it is that important – he told me Mr Gambino had arrived with his grand-daughter, whose name happened to be Sinatra, a doctor in New York, not related at all, and they'd like to take a picture. I said, "Fine."

'They came in and they took a picture of the little girl and before I realized what happened, there were approximately eight or nine men standing around me and several other snapshots were made. That is the whole incident that took place.' Sinatra said he had never met Gambino before or since (Gambino died a few weeks later). He said he only knew one of the men in the photo, Tommy Marson, a neighbour of his from Palm Springs. 'I later found out that I was introduced to somebody named Jimmy, and I found out later it was this fink, "the Weasel".'

Chairman Bunker told Sinatra: 'certainly one takes the opportunity to review the background of all of the people in that picture, save and excepting yourself, and it is quite a Who's Who of What's What in the area of organized crime.'

When Bunker confronted Sinatra with other incidents involving Jimmy Fratianno Sinatra angrily countered, 'For the record, I wish that we didn't have to discuss Mr Fratianno because he is a confessed murderer, a perjurer and I would rather not discuss him involved with my life.'

Bunker gently came back, 'I can appreciate what you're saying. It is in the public record and Mr Fratianno has received a great deal of acclaim as a very credible witness.'

Fratianno flatly contradicts Sinatra's account of how the photo came to be taken. 'He said he was gonna take a picture with somebody's niece and he says, all of a sudden eight men were around him. Well that's a lot of baloney. He wanted to take a picture with Gambino and he offered Gambino to come in the back, he wanted to meet him. And he goes to the Gaming Board and he just lied about these things. He said he didn't know who was there. He knows me, he knows Gambino, Tommy Marson, Paul Castellano. *He* knows who they are. He knows just as much about this as I do.'

When the members of the Nevada Gaming Commission voted on whether Sinatra should get a gaming licence they backed him four to one, with only Senator Dodge dissenting. Sinatra's friends regard that decision as a vindication of his past. Stephen Wynn says: 'He defended himself admirably on those "fast-lane personality" allegations. He was licenced and found to be suitable. The president of the United States doesn't seem to be bothered very much by Mr Sinatra's alleged associations because I don't think he believes them any more than I do.'

Sinatra was Ronald Reagan's master of entertainments for his inaugural gala in 1981. The president reinforced their friendship by writing a testimonial to the Nevada Gaming Commission on the singer's behalf. Frank, he said, was 'an honourable person, completely honest and loyal'. Asked about Sinatra's cronies and associations, the president responded, 'We've heard these stories about Frank for years. We just hope they're not true.' With the FBI's investigative resources at his command the president of the United States should have rather more than hope to go on.

Other people are not impressed either by Sinatra or by Nevada's licensing decision. It was, they say, a foregone conclusion. The state called no witnesses who might have damaged Sinatra's cause. Judith Exner says she 'absolutely refused to appear because there wasn't any question that he was going to get his licence'. At the outset Jimmy Fratianno was not asked to testify. By the time he *was* asked 'the Weasel' felt he had been gratuitously abused by one of Sinatra's witnesses so he refused to appear.

Fratianno may soon have another opportunity to take on Sinatra. In 1984 New Jersey's Division of Gaming Enforcement announced its intention to put all entertainers earning more than $50,000 from one casino through its licensing process. If this happens it would mean that Sinatra, whose annual Golden Nugget earnings in Atlantic City alone run into millions of dollars, will have to explain his connections all over again. If he were to refuse to submit himself to this scrutiny his only alternative would be to kiss the Queen of Resorts goodbye for ever. They don't have end-of-the-pier shows any more.

Fratianno poignantly sums up 'Ol' Blue Eyes'. 'He likes "made" guys. He likes to be around them. He likes to have pictures taken with them. Look at all the publicity: Giancana, Lucky Luciano, the Fischettis, Gambino, myself! He thrives on the stuff, I'm telling you. Of course he ain't gonna tell that to the president. I don't know how he covers that up.'

20

On the Waterfront

Organized crime has been the curse of American industry for nearly a century. In the early 1900s New York employers hired hoodlums, known as goons, to break the heads of workers who dared to strike or picket. This provoked the unions to hire their own goons to fight those hired by the employers. Some union leaders were more interested in money for themselves than wage rises for their members and would foment strikes to force employers to pay them 'kick-backs' or bribes. On pocketing a fat wad of notes they would order the strikers back to work, often without having gained anything on their behalf. If anyone cried corruption the bosses would tell their hired hoodlums to beat them up.

Gangsters on both sides became a permanent feature of America's industrial battlefield, so much so that only a crime supremo, Arnold Rothstein, could end New York's six-month garment industry strike in 1926.[1] In the early 1930s Dutch Schultz, the New York bootlegger and numbers gambling boss, forcibly took over the city's waiters' and cooks' union and extorted $1 million a year from its members. Union bosses no longer had to hire gangsters. They were gangsters themselves.

In the 1930s Chicago hoodlums took over Hollywood's most powerful movie union, the International Alliance of Theatrical Stage Employees and Moving Picture Operators (IATSE). They extorted millions from compliant movie moguls, anxious to buy labour peace and gain an advantage over their strike-paralysed competitors. Alert investigators from the Internal Revenue Service broke open the conspiracy and jailed Joe Schenk, chairman of Twentieth Century-Fox, for tax evasion. Six leading Chicago gangsters (including the outfit's boss, Paul Ricca and Johnny Roselli) were also jailed for extortion.

Hollywood has never made a movie about that disgraceful episode in its own history but it did immortalize another pack of labour racketeers in the Marlon Brando film *On the Waterfront*. The baddies were the thugs who ruled the New York docks in the 1940s and 1950s. They did it through the International Longshoremen's Association (ILA), which is still the main dockers' and stevedores' union on the Atlantic coast. The story of its chronic corruption was exposed by Malcolm Johnson in hundreds of articles in the *New York Sun* and in his book, *Crime on the Labor Front*. The movie owed much to Johnson's revelations about a mob union which perpetuated appalling working conditions instead of fighting to abolish them.[2]

'The Port of New York, the greatest in the world, is an outlaw frontier,' wrote Johnson. 'Murder on the waterfront is commonplace. Organized crime and racketeering add millions of dollars annually to the cost of the port's shipping. Pier facilities, representing an investment of almost a billion dollars, are controlled by ex-convicts and murderers.' In Johnson's day New York Harbor contained 1,900 working piers along its 755-mile length. In 1948 20 per cent of America's imports and exports, worth more than $7 billion, passed through the port. ILA gangsters orchestrated $140 million-worth of thieving. They also controlled smuggling, especially of narcotics, and bled their own 45,000 members through gambling and loansharking rackets on the waterfront.

Johnson exposed the loading racket through which union gangsters extorted millions from trucking companies using the docks. No merchandise going in or out escaped this levy but the victim companies just passed the cost on to the unknowing American consumer. Steamship and stevedoring companies also had to bribe the union bosses for labour peace. They gave in to the racketeers' demands just to stay in business and alive. The City of New York, which owned most of the large piers, did nothing.

The payoffs went into the pockets of the ILA bosses. Rank-and-file members got nothing. On the contrary they suffered the humiliation and exploitation of the 'shape-up', the biggest single cause of gang rule on the waterfront. In effect longshoremen were hired not by the employer but by the union which nominated the hiring bosses. Each hiring boss ruled his own pier. Usually a thug himself, he dictated which longshoremen would earn enough money to feed their children and which would see them starve.

Whenever a ship needed loading or unloading longshoremen would shape up by forming a semi-circle at the pier entrance around the hiring boss. He would call out the workers of his choice, usually picking only those who gave him part of their earnings. On most piers if you did not kick back you did not get hired. As Johnson commented:

> Everything about the shape-up lends itself to graft and corruption, fear and avarice. Through this antiquated system of hiring, the criminal gangs find it easy to place their own men in key jobs. . . . The shape-up fosters fear. Fear of not working. Fear of incurring the displeasure of the hiring boss. Under the terror of the shape-up the longshoremen have learned from bitter experience to bow to the system, to keep their mouths shut.

The shape-up had once been commonplace in docks all over the world but it lived on longest in New York. Pitting one starving man against another it was a daily reminder of hoodlum power in the union. Even when the port was busy there was only enough work for one longshoreman in five. ILA bosses made no effort to reduce membership and so reduce their unemployed. On the contrary, they kept the books open so that dues would keep pouring in. This arrangement suited the employers because, with so many men fighting for such little work, wages were kept low.

New York's longshoremen earned far less than those in San Francisco who belonged to another union. The ILA paid no strike, sickness or death benefits. Few members earned more than a meagre $2000 a year while Joe Ryan, their Irish-American president, paid himself a tidy $25,000. All New York's politicians knew the union was corrupt yet none dared campaign against it because Ryan and his thugs were themselves political princes who could make or break politicians with their campaign funds and block votes.

Mobsters kept control over the ILA by using violence both against reform rebels and against each other. Joe Ryan's most brutal ally was Johnny 'Cockeye' Dunn, a ferocious young thug who ruled sixty downtown piers for ten years by murdering more than thirty rival gangsters. Dunn was to die in Sing Sing's electric chair in 1949 for killing a disobedient hiring boss, but a few years earlier he would have thought such a fate inconceivable. During the Second World War Naval Intelligence had craved his help in securing the waterfront against sabotage. The deal had been set up by the Mafia's boss of bosses, Lucky Luciano.[3]

While a clutch of Irish gangsters, of whom Dunn was only marginally the most brutal, controlled the transatlantic piers on Manhattan's Westside, the Brooklyn waterfront was ruled by an equally violent clan of Italians. Life in Brooklyn's pierside communities was a throwback to the New Orleans of the 1890s. Like old-time padrones, in controlling all waterfront jobs the Mafia's union bosses controlled the economic and political life of an entire community. Ultimate power lay with the Anastasia brothers. In the 1930s Albert Anastasia led the Italian chapter of Murder Inc. and became known as its lord executioner.[4] In 1951 he murdered his way to become boss of one of New York's five families. This strengthened his brother, Anthony 'Tough Tony' Anastasia, who was president of Local 1814, the biggest ILA branch in Brooklyn. Across the bay the New Jersey piers around Hoboken and Newark were controlled by Vito Genovese who became Mafia boss of bosses in 1957 with the murder of Albert Anastasia.

Organized crime thus ruled the biggest port in the world, untroubled by the police or any other authority but in 1953 public outrage forced New York and New Jersey to set up a Waterfront Commission to fight the gangsters. The commission did away with the shape-up and the hiring boss, founded work information centres and tried to reduce the number of surplus longshoremen looking for jobs that did not exist. For those in work wages rose.

The commission ended many of the waterfront rackets because it had the power to licence or disbar anyone working on the piers. It could also prohibit criminals with serious convictions from holding union office. However, barred mobsters soon found their way round the rules by giving themselves highly paid 'no-show' jobs for which no licence was needed. One crew of convicts, burglars and bankrobbers set up a new ILA local, 1826, which was technically outside the commission's jurisdiction. Local 1826 was a Genovese family wedge to undermine the commission which was so outraged that in 1960 it won new powers to expel Genovese henchmen Barone, Rago and Vanderwyde from the port for ever.

The blacklisted hoods were not dismayed. They just set sail for Florida. Anyway old ports like New York were shrinking because of old-fashioned facilities, traffic problems and – not least – the extortionate cost of doing business with the mob. New ocean terminals and container ports were being built where America was booming: in the South. Shipping and transport companies were drawn to such ports because, initially, they had weak unions and no organized crime. But mobsters can spot new areas of growth as quickly as anyone else. They saw the revolution taking place in American shipping and they also knew that in America's most flourishing port there was no Waterfront Commission to stand in their way.

Miami has lost much of its glamour in recent years but it is still the nerve-centre of America's fastest growing state. In the last twenty years the 'Gold Coast' counties of Dade, Broward and Palm Beach have boomed, with the aid of good money and bad.[5] Miami has become the economic capital of Latin America and its port now handles a lot more than bananas. In 1964 its facilities were transformed from a few piers off Biscayne Boulevard to a huge new transatlantic seaport on Dodge Island. There, in the shadow of Caribbean cruise liners and container ships, the wiseguys from New York Local 1826 moved in.

Joey Teitelbaum was one of the first people to find out they had hit town. Joey is short but stocky, with arms like Popeye when the spinach goes down. His glasses make him appear timid but they conceal a fiery temper and the conviction that he has not been put on this earth to be pushed around. His family have been in Miami shipping for generations. In the 1960s he was working for Eagle Inc., the family steamship and stevedore concern which took care of the ships, cargo and crews of many shipping lines. Eagle's longshoremen were ILA members but their local was not mob-controlled. Their checkers, the men who check cargo on and off ships and in and out of warehouses, were not unionized.

In 1966 Joey and his father were visited by the mob invaders from New York. They told the Teitelbaums that the ILA was organizing the port's checkers. Fred Field, the union's international organizer and its third highest ranking officer, introduced them to George Barone (one of the Genovese front men expelled from the New York piers), whom Field described as president of the checkers' union. Joey's father asked Field, 'What checkers' union are we talking about?'

Field replied, 'Local 1922, the new one that we just formed. You people will sign a checkers' contract.'

The Teitelbaums refused so Field pointed to Joey and said, 'Listen, you! Is there some place we could talk? I understand you're a bright little boy.'

'Sure, let's go fishing,' suggested Joey. A few days later he hired a fishing boat and sailed around Miami with Freddy Field and another man called Benny Astorino.

'Benny wore his coat the whole time we were on the boat,' Joey remembers. 'At 110 degrees he refused to take it off. The whole day he walked around in an open boat wearing this coat. Later I found out he was packing a gun.' As Fred Field sat at the other end of the boat Astorino told Teitelbaum that Field and his group were 'here to stay. The checkers' union was in Miami. It was a way of life.' But with Dodge Island opening up Joey could become Field's partner. He could bring Joey a lot of business provided that Joey put up $3000 to show good faith. When the fishing trip was over Joey talked through the proposition with his father. They resolved not to sign the checkers' contract and not to hand over $3000 to Freddy Field.

But the Teitelbaums were not the masters of their own fate. They made most of their money from loading, unloading and storing cargo off ships belonging to major navigation lines. One of these corporations now called Joey up with what amounted to an ultimatum: 'Sign the contract or we're going to have to get someone else to handle our ships. We've got ships in New York, Boston, Philadelphia and there's no way we're going to let our operation stop because you won't sign . . .' It dawned on Joey that mobsters ruled ILA locals not only in Miami but in all the Atlantic ports. They could simply destroy any company whose executives did not do as they were told. Organized crime had some of the world's biggest shipping lines by the throat.

'It was right after this,' recalls Joey, 'that Freddy Field called me and said, "Are you ready to sign or do I have to break your balls?" I told him I wasn't signing.

'When I got home that evening my wife was waiting for me outside, really upset, and I asked her what was wrong. She said, "Someone called me and said that we were a nice family and I was a nice lady. He said he wouldn't want to see our daughter have an accident on the way home from school. Sign the contract!"

'So my wife told me, "Joe, sign the contract!" And we signed. But we refused to pay off.'

Joey now realized he was dealing not with just a few maverick crooks but with the Mafia. His ILA extortioners were commanded by Doug Rago, a 'made' man in the Genovese family. Joey never met Rago but dealt with his underling, Barone, who now dumped his New York buddies on Teitelbaum's payroll as checkers. They did no work. Where Joey had previously employed only one checker he was now paying for six. 'They started ghosting. They were on the payroll but they were never there! We didn't even know who half these people were but we were told every week to make a cheque out in their names, and we did.' Phantom checkers were soon costing Joey tens of thousands of dollars a month but when he complained they were bankrupting Eagle he was told that three other Miami companies were paying even more.

Joey and his father were still refusing to put cash directly in the pockets of the ILA officials. The gangsters took their revenge by ordering Eagle's big customers to take their business elsewhere. The firm was dying. Joey tried to attract new business with the purchase of a 90-ton crane for handling containers. He and his wife had bought it by mortgaging their home. Barone's boys promptly slashed its tyres and hydraulic hose. He was still sore because Joey was not paying. The message was clear: if Joey wanted to stay in business he had to make peace with Barone.

'So we made a deal,' says Joey. 'I began to pay. Suddenly life became very easy on the docks. The more you paid the more contracts you got.' For every hour he used his crane he paid $15 to the mob. He paid $200 a week for labour peace to ensure he never had a strike on his hands. He paid $2000 to handle a passenger boat. Whenever Joey was awarded a contract to service a cruise liner he not only paid the mobsters their usual cash demands but he also had to give them $600 Caribbean cruise tickets.

As well as servicing other people's ships the Teitelbaums were building up their own small cargo fleet. Joey had contacts all over the Caribbean and if his containers were damaged he used to get them repaired cheaply in Latin America. The mob now forced him to give that work to a Miami yard which soon charged him $113,000 for doing no repairs at all. Containers had to be repaired there even when there was nothing wrong with them. 'They would say a container had a dent in it. I'd tell them it was only a small dent and we could live with it. They'd say, "We don't care. You have to put a patch in it." Then I had to pay for a welder and a foreman, and an inch-square patch would cost me $1000.

'The mob became so powerful that they controlled every pencil or toothpick delivered to the dock. If you didn't pay the longshoremen wouldn't load. They wouldn't even allow your truck on the dock. They controlled the laundries, the vendors and the checkers. Theft was rampant. You could not accuse a man of stealing. If you did everybody walked off the dock. Thievery became a way of life on the waterfront.

'Their control was so enormous that they would pick up the telephone in Miami and call the local ILA president in Mobile and say, "Joey Teitelbaum has a ship going into Mobile. You're not to unload it." No labour would show up. Everyone who moved on the dock worked for them. From Searsport, Maine to Galveston, Texas – every port on the East Coast of the USA.'

In 1975 Joey's life became even more enmeshed by Mafia dealings. For years he had been supporting a Catholic orphanage in Honduras. In September a hurricane devastated that country and Joey and his wife despatched a container filled with food, clothing and medical supplies to the orphanage. Joey was already convinced that his Honduran partner was thieving large sums of money from the business but when he heard that the man had stolen the entire consignment intended for the orphanage something in him finally snapped. In a moment of intense anger he contracted a hit man to murder the thief. The hit man turned out to be an FBI informer who had entrapped him and tape-recorded their incriminating conversations.

It had taken six years for law enforcement to find out that New York mafiosi ruled Dodge Island. For another three years state and federal agents had been trying to get Joey to talk. In September 1975 when they charged him with attempted murder he could no longer refuse them. 'They told me they wanted "in" on Dodge Island, and I told them, "I walk from the other one."

'They said, "it's a deal." So a deal was made and they said, "How far can you take us?"

'I said, "How far do you want to go?"

'They said, "All the way to the top."

'I told them, "Hang on for the ride." '

Joey now infiltrated three FBI agents into his operations. They worked undercover, one as his brother-in-law, another as his cousin. Soon they were making payoffs themselves. In 1976 Joey's extortioners offered to help him expand into other southern ports like Savannah where he 'bought' the contract to handle ships belonging to Zim-Israel Navigation for $15,000. The FBI gave him the money which he paid up front to the ILA bosses in Miami. Joey also agreed to give them a large percentage of his profits. Now he needed a representative in Savannah which gave him the chance to place an FBI man in the heart of the racket. The undercover agent made payments of $7500 directly to Local 1922's secretary treasurer, Bill Boyle, transactions which he recorded on a tape-machine hidden on his body.

Joey himself went 'wired-up' into these payoffs but in the middle of this deal the ILA mobsters discovered that someone was walking around Dodge Island with a tape-recorder. They searched Joey but found nothing. By chance he had taken the machine off his body minutes before. He pretended to be insulted. They then found out that a shipping company had hired a theft investigator who was walking round Dodge Island wired-up. Joey was once again a trusted man.

A week later an FBI man strapped a recorder on Joey's thigh to immortalize another $1500 payoff to Bill Boyle. Before the mobster's eyes the recorder slipped down Joey's trousers and crashed on the floor. 'They said, "What's this?"

'I said, "Oh my God, my portable pacemaker!" So I took the money out of my pocket and gave it to him and said, "You count the money, I've got to go to the doctor, get my pace-maker checked." And I ran out.' Joey was lucky. His extortioners knew he had suffered a heart attack not long before. He was even luckier that they knew nothing about heart surgery or pacemakers.

The FBI told Joey they still had to have this payoff confirmed on tape. The next day he went back to Boyle wired-up once more to ask him if he had got the $1500. Boyle nodded. A nod was not what Joey needed. 'Listen,' he shouted, 'do I speak English or don't I? God dammit! Did you get the fucking $1500 dollars?'

Boyle said, 'I got the $1500.' The FBI had their confirmation – Joey had nudged Bill Boyle to convict himself.

Through Teitelbaum and other witnesses the FBI were able to prove that waterfront corruption embraced every southern port and went well beyond the ring of New York gangsters in Miami. Excluding the checkers, most southern longshoremen are black as are their union leaders, several of whom took part in the Mafia's conspiracy. As Joey kicked back more money to expand into Mobile one of his undercover FBI employees taped payoffs to the black president of that city's ILA local. Joey himself recorded payoffs to black union bosses in Miami and Jacksonville.

In sixteen months the FBI monitored more than fifty payments adding up to $53,000 from its own agents and Teitelbaum. By the end of its Miami operation in 1977 it was able to prove that millions of dollars were being paid every year to organized crime. The corruption had penetrated many shipping lines. Their top officials were taking payoffs from union hoodlums who would then 'sell' the lines' stevedoring contracts to people like Teitelbaum. In 1979 eighteen union officials and shipping executives were convicted of taking part in the criminal conspiracy that had been strangulating America's southern ports. Barone was jailed for fifteen years, Boyle for twelve, Vanderwyde for ten and Field for six.

The FBI called its investigation UNIRAC, short for 'union racketeering'. It was far from over. When Teitelbaum had bought his way north to Savannah he had been told that just as George Barone controlled all America's southern ports, all the ports from Virginia north to Maine 'belonged' to Anthony Scotto. With this lead the FBI expanded UNIRAC up to New York where more undercover agents, informers and telephone wire-taps proved that despite the Waterfront Commission organized crime and corruption in New York were once again as rampant as they had been back in the 1950s.

In 1979 and 1980 as a result of the FBI's efforts New York's leading waterfront racketeers were convicted of extorting millions from stevedoring and shipping companies. Each of the port's segments – Brooklyn, Manhattan and New Jersey – was shown to belong to a different Mafia princeling.

In Brooklyn the prince was Anthony Scotto who had become president of Local 1814 in 1963 when 'Tough Tony' Anastasia died. Nepotism is one thing but in Scotto's case keeping it in the family had a double meaning: 'Tough Tony' was his father-in-law. When Tony's brother Albert was murdered in 1957 Carlo Gambino had become boss of the Anastasia crime family. In 1963 Scotto, aged 28, swore allegiance to Gambino, who in return made him a member of what was now the Gambino crime family. The wise old don also gave him Local 1814 and thus secured the loyalty of the surviving Anastasias. Young Scotto was now launched on a spectacular career.

As early as 1969 the Department of Justice publicly named Scotto as a 'made' member of Gambino's family. Despite this known pedigree – or perhaps because of it – Scotto soared high in New York's social and political circles. He lectured at universities on labour relations. He became a leading Democratic Party fund-raiser. When President Carter visited New York in 1978 Scotto was one of only six labour leaders chosen to lunch with him.

All this time Scotto was extorting huge sums from waterfront corporations. In return for large bribes he sold labour peace. At his bidding longshoremen would either work properly or walk off a pier and bring a business to its knees. Executives of stevedoring companies also paid him to bring them new business. Just like the boys in Miami, Scotto told the biggest shipping and transport lines where to place their loading and repair contracts. Invariably those contracts would go to those stevedoring firms who paid him bribes.

Scotto's speciality was fraudulent compensation claims. A change in the law in 1972 meant that workers claiming injuries at work could choose their own physician. Scotto's longshoremen promptly conspired with crooked doctors, lawyers and compensation experts to concoct huge claims. McGrath Services Corporation saw its compensation payouts soar from $230,000 in 1972, to $616,000 in 1973 and a staggering $1.4 million in 1974. On the verge of bankruptcy the company's chairman began paying Scotto monthly bribes. Over three years he paid him $210,000 but it was money well spent. Successful insurance claims against McGrath fell to $883,000 in 1975 and were less than $400,000 thereafter.

Scotto rose fast in the Gambino family where he was already a capo and in the ILA hierarchy, where he became its vice-president for legislative affairs and then in 1979 its national organizer, replacing the convicted Fred Field. As number three in the union and still only 45 Scotto looked set to become its national president when the somnolent Thomas Gleason finally stood down. He was climbing higher in American political life than any other mafioso had done. His prestigious standing in the labour movement was the perfect cover and came unstuck only because several businessmen who were giving him bribes became government witnesses. In 1979 he was convicted of racketeering and tax fraud and jailed for five years.

Just as Scotto ruled Brooklyn's waterfront for the Gambino family, so on Manhattan an old-time mafioso, Michael Clemente, ruled for the Genovese. Born in 1908 Clemente had been a labour racketeer for forty years. In 1953 he had been convicted for taking payoffs from the same McGrath Services Corporation which Scotto extorted twenty years later. Clemente was jailed for five years and banned from union office but he remained the most powerful mobster in the union. His prosecutor told a Senate sub-committee in 1981 that Clemente 'exercized control' not only over brother-mobsters like Scotto and the wiseguys in Miami but over the ILA president Tommy Gleason. In 1980 Clemente was convicted of extorting $1.5 million from shipping and stevedoring companies and jailed for twenty years.

The New Jersey waterfront is now New York Harbor's only area of growth but UNIRAC proved that this too is ruled by the Genovese family under a Clemente protégé named Tino Fiumara. A young firebrand, Fiumara has a taste for violence which has won him rapid promotion in the Mafia. Allegedly a killer, Fiumara's power goes far beyond the waterfront in the New Jersey locals of other unions. He may now find it difficult to wield that power. In 1979 he was jailed for twenty years for extortion. In 1980 he got another twenty-five years for shaking down the waterfront.

Today Manhattan's Westside piers are almost dead. Where racketeering, exploitation and murder once terrorized a helpless workforce and its employers alike, homosexuals now stroll hand in hand as the sun sets over the Hudson River. The old bars where union bosses ran their rackets, counted their take and ordered hits, now cater to the black-leather brigade. But the Port of New York remains one of America's life-lines and it is still controlled by the mob.

The UNIRAC investigation is law enforcement's greatest triumph against organized crime. Yet many of the jailed mobsters have simply been replaced by other men in the same huge conspiracy. The ILA's continuing reluctance to take convicted mobsters off the payroll provoked one senator to accuse Tommy Gleason of running a rehabilitation programme for felons by putting them in high international office.

There is no sign that the Mafia's waterfront rackets are any weaker than they were in the 1970s. Their political clout may be even stronger. When Tony Scotto needed character witnesses at his trial he called some of America's leading public figures: Governor Carey of New York (for whose 1974 election campaign Scotto raised $1 million), former New York mayors Lindsey and Wagner, and Lane Kirkland, president of America's biggest labour organization, the AFL-CIO. As one New York politician told *Crime Inc.*, 'In America nothing is black and white. There are only varying shades of grey.'

Down in Miami Joey Teitelbaum now runs a flourishing shipping company. He refused to enter the government's witness protection programme. He did not see why he should be forced to live under a false identity thousands of miles from his home, cut off from the shipping business he knows and loves. He has moved off Dodge Island up the Miami River to a site bought by his grandfather in 1937. 'I operate very pleasantly without a union. I have my own ships, my own cranes and my own equipment. I don't have any gangsterism or extortion, no payoffs and I have bigger and better contracts than I ever had.'

Joey's extortioners are now in jail but in a few years they will be out again. In the meantime their relatives and sidekicks have taken the jobs they were forced to quit. Hit men still stalk Miami looking for the chance to carry out the Mafia's contract on Joey. As soon as his role as an FBI informer was exposed Joey and his family were put under twenty-four-hour protection by federal marshals. Once the trials were over the marshals were withdrawn. The government refused to pay for them any more. Now Joey has to pay for his own round-the-clock protection and wherever he goes a bodyguard goes too.

'I run that dock of mine with an iron hand. No gangsters are gonna run it for me. I run it myself: win, lose or draw. I'm not ashamed to tell you I've run gangsters off this dock with a pistol. If they ever come back they had better come looking to kill me, because I'll kill them first.'

Whatever the cost Joey thinks it is better to spend money on bodyguards to protect him against the mob, than to have to pay the mob not to kill him or destroy his business. 'What a helluva way to live! I don't believe this country was founded on people having to pay for the right to work. If the American people don't stand up and fight gangsters they will ruin you. They will bleed you dry. They will take it all.'

21

The Mob Keeps on Trucking

Organized crime realized a long time ago that in the vast country of America one industry governs the fate of all the others: transportation. Because almost everything has to be moved by road the truck-drivers are among the nation's most powerful workers. They keep America moving but they could also bring it to a standstill, which is why more than fifty years ago the mob expanded its labour rackets from the waterfront on to the nation's highways. Once again its Trojan horse was a union: the International Brotherhood of Teamsters.

In labour history there is no greater scandal than the bloody saga of the Teamsters, America's biggest union. It began in 1898 when drivers of horse-drawn wagons in Detroit formed the Team Drivers' Union. Five years later they merged with the Teamsters' National Union of Chicago to form the IBT, 50,000 members strong. The new union was baptized in violence but the violence came from goons hired by employers, such as those who ran Chicago's meat-packing houses. By 1933 most of its 125,000 members drove motorized trucks. By 1939 the socialist, Farrell Dobbs, had boosted membership to 400,000 by recruiting all over the central states and the far west. Dobbs was the first organizer to see that the Teamsters' future lay with the long-haul, 'over-the-road' (inter-state) truckers and the warehousemen who handled their loads.

By the 1960s the Teamsters was much more than a truckers' union. Among its 2 million members were factory workers, nurses, teachers, airline pilots and police officers. Only 500,000 worked as truckers and warehousemen. Attorney-General Robert Kennedy described it as 'the most powerful institution in this country, aside from the government itself'. Today Teamster bosses are courted by US presidential aspirants. The union always used to back Democratic candidates but when it endorsed Republicans Richard Nixon and Ronald Reagan both men went on to the White House. In 1980 the Teamsters were the only big union to back Reagan, which gave them some clout when he was elected. No politician dares attack the Teamsters at any level without first weighing up the votes and the funds he will lose. This is a sorry state of affairs when for at least thirty years the Teamsters' national organization has been controlled and abused by organized crime.

Recent television dramatizations have compressed the Teamsters' story into a personal struggle between Jimmy Hoffa and Robert Kennedy.[1] This is a fascinating but distracting theme. Hoffa led the union during the ten years of its greatest expansion. He was an outstanding leader, a ruthless negotiator and a fine orator. He was charming, witty, approachable, tenacious and inspiring – not that he displayed these virtues in his encounters with Kennedy. The two gladiators had very different starts in life: one privileged, the other deprived. In most ways the union boss was just as good an American as the attorney-general. The trouble with Hoffa was that he had sold his soul to organized crime.

He was born in 1913 in the small mining town of Brazil, Indiana of Dutch pioneer stock. His father worked for a drilling company but died when Jimmy was 7 years old. Jimmy's mother took the family to Detroit where she worked in factories making car parts. Jimmy left school at 14 and by the time he was 16 he was working as a night warehouseman for the Kroger grocery chain. He emerged as a courageous spokesman for his workmates, winning them a pay rise, and taking them into the Teamsters' union. Hoffa became a full-time Teamster organizer and led a strike against his old employers. In a twenty-four-hour battle with strikebreakers Hoffa was beaten up six times and arrested eighteen times. Although short he was brave and tough and always led from the front. He often had to have his head stitched up after fights on the picket line. In 1937 he switched to organizing the over-the-road car-haulers who transported finished automobiles across America. Again Hoffa excelled and was made chairman of the central states drivers' council. In 1945 he was elected president of Detroit Local 299 and in 1947 he became president of the union's regional organization, Joint Council 43. This confirmed him as Michigan's most powerful Teamster and a national figure in the union.

In 1952 Dan Tobin, the union's international president for forty-five years, stood down. At this point Hoffa did a deal with an old Teamster warhorse named Dave Beck. Hoffa did not run against him for president and in return Beck named Hoffa as one of the union's vice-presidents. In 1956 investigators working for Robert Kennedy, then chief counsel to the Senate rackets committee, gathered enough evidence to show that Beck had embezzled $350,000 from union funds for his own ends, such as developing his ranch-style home in Seattle. Beck was jailed for five years and forced to quit the presidency. Hoffa was elected in his place in October 1957 at the union's convention in Miami. He won by a landslide but the delegates at such conventions (which only happen once every five years) are largely full-time officials and business agents who do not truly represent the feelings of ordinary working Teamsters. An influential proportion of the delegates were either mobsters or their nominees.

Hoffa's ten-year battle with Robert Kennedy had already begun. In 1958 Kennedy accused Hoffa of being controlled by gangsters, which Hoffa of course denied. He was outraged by Kennedy's investigations and the criminal trials he instigated. Some writers have alleged that he took the argument as far as joining with the Mafia in the conspiracy which led to the killing of President John Kennedy on 22 November 1963.[2] Certainly JFK's death ensured that his brother's term as attorney-general would soon end, ridding Hoffa and the Mafia of their most tiresome enemy. Not long after the assassination Hoffa told a reporter, 'Bobby Kennedy is just another lawyer now.' In fact he remained attorney-general under President Lyndon Johnson until August 1964 when he had finally nailed Hoffa. In two trials that year the Teamster boss was convicted of tampering with a jury and of improperly obtaining $2 million in loans from his union's pension fund. In March 1967 he finally went to jail and was forced to pass the presidency to his faceless Detroit underling, Frank Fitzsimmons.

Hoffa would not be freed until Christmas 1971 by which time Bobby Kennedy had long been dead. Hoffa later called their conflict a 'blood feud' and a 'disastrous mistake'. The feud's legacy was that Hoffa's own days were numbered. He shuffled around America working for penal reform but his real campaign was to recapture the Teamster presidency. In 1975 he drove to a restaurant near Detroit for a meeting but was never seen again. His body was never found, which is why it took another seven years for him to be declared legally dead.

No one has ever been charged with Hoffa's murder but there is no doubt that he was killed by the Mafia. They had made him Teamster president. When he went to jail he was too tainted to be their front man any more. When he came out he became a troublesome liability. When he refused to slip into obscurity on his $1.7 million pension they decided he had to die.

Hoffa's forty-year affair with the Mafia is a textbook example of how organized crime takes over a union to extort members, employers and the public. The alliance was born in Detroit in the 1930s when the young union organizer came up against a problem. If company bosses used goons to break union men's heads, to kill and maim, how were union men to defend themselves?

In Detroit's motor plants at that time racketeers ran rampant at the employers' invitation. One man who saw them in operation was Vincent Piersante, later chief of detectives in the Detroit Police. 'When I came out of college I went to work for Ford's. There was no union. If you joined a union you kept it a secret. If they found out you would be fired. All kinds of things went on in the non-union shop. The mob was running the food concession, the lunch wagons. I later found out they were given the concession in return for protecting the children of the original Henry Ford. The mob ran bookmaking and numbers gambling in the plants. Even the security guards were big, muscular ex-convicts. It was like living in the middle of the underworld.

'It was still the Depression years and a job was hard to come by. You were completely intimidated by the fact that you could be laid off for any reason whatsoever. One of the bosses used to come round every pay day and ask for a "loan" of $10 or $20. If the loan was not made the employee would get laid off. The working person was helpless. Who would you report this kind of crime to? Certainly not the security force. You felt you couldn't report it to anyone.'

The security or 'service' force worked directly under Ford's personnel director, Harry Bennett. Under Henry Ford II both Bennett and the mob were ousted from the Ford plants. The

Detroit motor industry later recognized the United Auto Workers' Union as the authentic voice of the workforce.

The UAW refused to work with organized crime and kept itself clean but Hoffa had no such qualms. He harnessed Detroit's Teamsters to the former bootlegger Santo Perrone in order to crush any trucking companies who dared resist union demands for recognition, higher wages and better conditions. It was a cynical alliance for the mafioso Perrone had smashed another union's attempts to organize the city's steelworkers. Perrone himself ran a non-union steel-hauling business whose drivers Hoffa never tried to unionize. With friends like this Hoffa soon got what he wanted. Every non-Mafia trucking company in Detroit was forced to recognize the Teamsters.

As a young cop in the late 1930s Vincent Piersante first encountered Hoffa when he had to confiscate a baseball bat he had brought along as a weapon on a picket line. For decades Piersante watched him rise in league with organized crime. 'Hoffa made no bones about being friendly with these people. They used him and he used them. Organized-crime groups in any society are part of the power structure. It's a lot easier to accomplish your goals, even your legitimate goals, with them on your side.'

In Teamster circles there was nothing odd about Hoffa's alliance with the underworld. In America's industrial cities the mob was the union. In Cleveland a 23-year-old thug named Jimmy Fratianno helped the Teamsters win strikes. 'The secretary-treasurer would call me and say, "Jimmy, bring me ten guys." I would get $15 for each guy I brought to the picket line. I'd give them each $5 and I'd keep $10 for myself. Other guys would bring in men from their neighbourhoods so maybe we'd have 150 tough guys on the line, guys that could use their "dukes". At that time you could fight and the cops would do nothin'. They'd just make sure you ain't got no clubs. I threw acid on cars, put sugar in engines and the Teamsters would win the strike. The union did good for the working class, they always got them good money, but it was the mob that started the Teamsters from the ground floor in the 1920s. They're the originators.'

In the 1940s Hoffa's ambition took him far beyond Detroit. In each Mid-Western city – Cleveland, St Louis, Kansas City – he allied himself with the mobsters who ruled the big Teamster locals. In Chicago his backer was Paul 'Red' Dorfman, a Capone gunman who ran the Wastehandlers' Union for Tony Accardo and the Chicago outfit. Dorfman introduced Hoffa to Teamster moguls like mafioso Joey Glimco, who ran the city's cab-drivers' local. These men would be happy to back Hoffa for president providing he gave them something in return. His gift turned out to be money in bigger lumps than the Mafia had ever handled.

In 1949 Hoffa had set up a welfare fund for Michigan Teamsters with contributions from members and employers. He seems to have cared as much about the mob's welfare as the truckers' for in 1951 he switched the fund's management to the Chicago arm of an insurance company run by Red Dorfman's wife and his stepson, Allen. Dorfman Jun. knew nothing about insurance but Hoffa soon put an even bigger fund in his care, the Central States Health and Welfare Fund. In eight years the Dorfmans 'earned' $3 million in commission, twice as much as any major insurance company would have charged. At least half of Dorfman's take went to the Chicago crime outfit.

In 1951 Hoffa devised the biggest fund of all: the Central States, Southeast and Southwest Areas Pension Fund. This cumbersome name was concocted to embrace the pension interests of some 300,000 Teamsters in more than twenty states. Hoffa wanted to provide monthly pensions for members aged 57 or over who had worked continuously for twenty years. This time the employers paid all the contributions. In a few years the fund's assets reached $½ billion.

Hoffa put this fund, just like the others, in Allen Dorfman's hands and the mob's pocket. In return Red Dorfman gave Hoffa the contact that would win him the presidency. His big obstacle was that few Teamsters in the eastern states knew much about him. Red Dorfman was close to a New York labour racketeer named Johnny Dioguardi who was also a capo in the Genovese family. He asked Johnny 'Dio' to make sure Hoffa was the choice of Joint Council 16 which ran Teamster affairs in the city. Hoffa helped Dio rig the vote by creating seven phantom New York locals and giving them all to Dio. These 'paper locals' had no members, served no industry and had no territory but they did have votes on the Joint Council. Dioguardi handed them out to brother mobsters who took over the council and duly voted for Hoffa as Teamster president at the 1957 convention.

Hoffa made a similar deal with Joint Council 73, in northern New Jersey across the Hudson River from New York, where the kingmaker was another Genovese mafioso, Anthony Provenzano. Jimmy already had the Mid-West in the bag but now all over America the message went out to the mob that he was their man. Even down south in New Orleans and Florida the godfathers knew that Hoffa would not only recognize their power as the union's regional warlords but would soon be handing them their share of the honey from the central states pot.

The fund now became the Mafia's own giant bank as Allen Dorfman began a twenty-year career investing its billions on their orders. Most pension funds are impeccably administered by out side insurance corporations. Prudential Life, for instance, looks after the fund for Teamsters in the western states. Hoffa's decision to hand the Central States Fund to a mob stooge should have outraged the employers who constituted half its trustees, but it made no difference to them if the fund was cherished or looted. As for the truckers slogging their way across America, they were too busy working to realize that fraud on an unprecedented scale was about to be committed in their name.

Hoffa's first duty was to tell Allen Dorfman to reward his staunch Mafia friends in Detroit. The sum of $500,000 was lent to a company owned by two old allies, Anthony and Vito Giacalone. Hoffa sponsored loans to other Detroit mafiosi and made Dorfman buy a bank in Florida which would be used by mob financiers including Meyer Lansky to send Las Vegas skim money out of the country.[3]

In 1960 Hoffa and the mob made the fateful decision that the fund should invest heavily in Las Vegas casinos. At that time no reputable bank or pension fund would lend to casinos which were considered both bad risks and bad for the image. Four Teamster loans went to the Desert Inn crowd led by Moe Dalitz.[4] The venerable organized-crime figure later borrowed another $18 million to build the La Costa Country Club near San Diego, California. This health spa and golfers' paradise, which hosts the prestigious Tournament of Champions every year, became notorious as a mobsters' hang-out, an Apalachin in permanent session, hosted as often as not by Allen Dorfman who bought one of the hundreds of luxurious villas on its 3,000 acres.

In 1965 the fund lent more than $20 million to another Las Vegas impresario, Jay Sarno, to build Caesar's Palace. Sarno was later seen with 'Fat' Tony Salerno, New York's biggest Mafia loan-shark, and Jerry Zarowitz, a convicted sports fixer who was running the casino at Caesar's under Sarno's ownership. When the hotel changed hands in 1969 Zarowitz received $3.5 million from the sale, even though he was not a stockholder. One year later FBI agents raided Caesar's and found another $1 million in cash in safe-deposit boxes in Zarowitz's name. Inevitably he was suspected of skimming the money from the casino on behalf of organized crime.

In 1966 the fund made a loan of $5.5 million to complete the Landmark Hotel in the interests of the Kansas City Mafia and its boss Nick Civella. The man who fixed the deal and took a finder's fee was Roy Williams, Kansas City's Teamster boss, who was later described in a federal report as being 'under the complete domination of Civella'. By the late 1960s the fund had lent nearly $100 million to eleven Las Vegas casinos and other Nevada gambling houses. Later it would lend more than that sum to one man, Morris Shenker, Hoffa's defence lawyer and the owner of the Dunes Hotel.

Las Vegas notables such as Shenker and Hank Greenspun, publisher of the Las Vegas *Sun*, assert that the fund has never lost any money by investing in casinos. When a casino has defaulted the fund has simply taken over the property and rearranged the loan for the new buyer. But such loans have often been handed out at low rates of interest, costing the fund and its pensioners many millions of dollars over the full repayment period. Also finders' fees, which are legal when paid openly to outsiders who match lenders with borrowers, were being paid covertly and corruptly to Hoffa and Dorfman. Countless other fees, amounting to as much as 10 per cent of the loans, were being secretly kicked back to organized crime. The aim of most of the Las Vegas loans was to parcel out casinos to the crime families of America. Each family thus acquired the underworld 'right' to skim from the profits of the casino or casinos it controlled through the loan. In this corrupt climate no one seems to have bothered about the best interests of America's truck-drivers, in whose name the loans were being made.

The bent investment decisions of Hoffa, Dorfman and the Mafia kinked the fund into a dangerous dependence on real estate. Most American pension funds put no more than 5 per cent of their assets into property, preferring the relative safety of stocks and bonds. By the late 1960s the Teamsters' fund held a staggering 73 per cent of its assets in property such as golf courses, cemeteries and even a dog and cat home. Even had it lost nothing by investing in casinos, it lost heavily in other ventures and its growth fell far behind that of other pension funds.

Sadly for Hoffa he would lose control of the gangsters he had embraced in his rise to power. By the time he went to jail in 1967 he was a burden, not an asset, to the mob. Frank Fitzsimmons, the man he chose as his caretaker-successor, was their puppet, not their partner as Hoffa had been. 'Fitz' had no independence, no flair and little intelligence. He loved the job and its $125,000-a-year salary, three official homes, private jet and visits to the White House. In return he let the mob run riot throughout the union.

Hoffa, meantime, languished in Lewisburg Penitentiary. He still had many supporters in the union, particularly among the rank-and-file who never saw Fitz as anything other than Hoffa's 'shoeshine boy'. To appease them President Nixon signed Hoffa's parole papers in December 1971. Only when he came out did Hoffa realize that his enemies, including Fitz, had insisted on a proviso banning him from union activities until 1980.

Hoffa never stopped fighting to get this condition lifted. Charlie Allen, the Mafia hit man who is now a federal witness, has recently revealed to the Senate rackets committee that Fitzsimmons' treacherous refusal to step down made Hoffa so angry that he contracted Allen to murder his rival.[5] In his autobiography published in 1975 Hoffa charged Fitz with 'selling out to mobsters and letting known racketeers into the Teamsters' and 'making vast loans from the billion-dollar Teamster pension fund to known mobsters'. Hoffa vowed that 'when the conditions on my commutation are lifted – as I am certain they will be – I *will* be back as president of the Teamsters'.[6]

Maybe the mob had read the proofs for by the time that book was published Jimmy Hoffa was missing, presumed dead. On 30 July 1975 he drove to the Red Fox Restaurant in Detroit's northwest suburbs to meet Anthony Giacalone, his old Mafia buddy from the 1930s who had kept in close contact with him after he came out of jail. For months Giacalone had tried to get Hoffa together with Anthony Provenzano, the most powerful Teamster official in New Jersey. Back in 1957 'Tony Pro' had been one of the mafiosi who had made Hoffa president. In 1975 he would have tried to talk him out of fighting Fitzsimmons.

Neither Giacalone nor Provenzano met Hoffa that day. Both had sound alibis. Giacalone was at a health spa not far from the Red Fox while Tony Pro was playing cards 650 miles away in a New Jersey union hall. Government investigators identified Charles 'Chuckie' O'Brien as the man who drove Hoffa from the restaurant. O'Brien had been raised from infancy by Jimmy Hoffa and his wife and in 1975 he was a Teamster official. One story says Hoffa was taken to a house nearby where he was murdered by gunmen from New Jersey. O'Brien reappeared, but not to tell the tale.

By the time reporters caught up with Tony Pro he was sunning himself at his Florida home. He told them Jimmy was his 'dear, dear friend'. He hoped nothing had happened to him and he offered to do anything to help. Despite this 'friendship', Pro said he had not seen Jimmy since November 1970. He did not point out that their last encounter had been in Lewisburg Penitentiary where he had been incarcerated for extortion. In jail the two men had fallen out and become sworn enemies. According to Charlie Allen, who was in Lewisburg with both men, Provenzano found out in 1975 about Hoffa's plot to kill Fitzsimmons. Allen claims that Pro also found out Hoffa was plotting to kill him too.

A few months after Hoffa's disappearance federal investigators were convinced that he had been killed by mobsters from within Provenzano's New Jersey empire. The main suspects were Provenzano himself, his Teamster sidekicks Salvatore and Gabriel Briguglio, and two other racketeers from New Jersey and

Philadelphia. They were all called before a grand jury in Detroit but no one was charged. Pocket-sized 'Little Ralphie' Picardo, another New Jersey racketeer who later turned government witness, was told at the time that Hoffa's body had been stuffed in a 55-gallon oil drum and destroyed in a car-crusher. Another story said he had been smelted and his ashes were now rotating in a hub-cap somewhere on America's freeways. Charlie Allen claims Tony Pro told him that 'Jimmy was killed, ground up in little pieces and dumped in the swamps.'

Ralph Picardo worked as a union organizer under Provenzano. He is convinced the Mafia killed Hoffa because his popularity among ordinary Teamsters might eventually have won him back the union presidency and thus upset the Mafia's cosy deal with Fitzsimmons. 'Hoffa was a man who wouldn't be dictated to. He was his own man, regardless of the fact that he invited organized crime into the Teamsters.' Jimmy Fratianno agrees. 'They didn't want him to run, they were happy with Fitzsimmons, so that's the reason they killed him.'

With Hoffa gone, the Teamsters under Fitzsimmons lost direction as a force for improving the lives and working conditions of its members. Even the National Master-Freight Agreement was ignored. This agreement with the employers guaranteed basic rates of pay and conditions for 500,000 Teamsters throughout the trucking industry. One employer who saw it collapse was Bob Kortenhaus who runs a trucking firm in New Jersey. He negotiated with Hoffa and Fitz in turn. 'Hoffa was a man of his word. He may have embezzled pension monies but the men on the job got their just due. They were always paid their correct hourly rate. But when Hoffa went to prison Frank Fitzsimmons could not control all the warlords in the various areas and the Master-Freight Agreement fell apart.'

In New Jersey Teamster bosses were taking payoffs from employers to turn a blind eye when their members were being underpaid. The same officials set their own relatives up in trucking firms, which then made 'sweetheart' contracts with the union. This meant that they paid low wages and no health or welfare contributions and thus undercut legitimate operators like Kortenhaus who were paying the full rate. Some of these companies got away with employing no Teamster members at all, thanks to their blood brothers in the union.

Kortenhaus still suffers because he will not do business with the mob. He owns one of the largest trucking fleets in New Jersey yet he cannot move in or out of Elizabeth, the largest container port in the world which has 50,000 containers passing through every week. It is on Kortenhaus's doorstep but without a 'sweetheart deal' he says his trucks would be held up for hours by pier officials. With such a deal they would be in and out in minutes.

Bob Kortenhaus says his rivals regard the payoff as 'the cost of doing business in New York. We've lost lucrative contracts because we won't pay off. It's my right and privilege to do business without fear or favour in the all-American way. I don't have to pay off anyone. I'm not a policeman but I am going to fight for my rights.'

Kortenhaus can afford these sentiments because his depot falls outside the area of Anthony Provenzano's Teamster local – 560. Today 560 has 10,000 members working for more than 400 companies in the New Jersey–New York area. 'If I was with 560 they would have put me out of business.' Kortenhaus admits. In the 1960s he met Tony Pro and recalls his suave veneer. 'He'd like you to believe he had a lot of influence and powerful contacts. He portrayed himself as a very macho person. He had a bodyguard by the name of Buttercup, a 6 ft 5 in, 275-pound gorilla who drove him around and used to intimidate people.' According to some of his accomplices Tony Pro's menacing air often turned into homicidal violence.

He was born in Manhattan's Lower East Side in 1917. He became a truck-driver at the age of 18. A man of 5 ft 7 in, he displayed a talent for prize-fighting, a hot temper and unrelenting ambition, characteristics which soon recommended him to the Mafia. He fell in with the Luciano (Genovese) crime family, which he later joined. In 1950 he slipped across the Hudson River to New Jersey to organize Local 560. In the next ten years he became president of 560 and of northern New Jersey's Joint Council 73. In 1960 Jimmy Hoffa made him one of only sixteen Teamster international vice-presidents. It was his reward for helping Hoffa into the top job.

Local 560 is based in the coincidentally named Union City, a rundown town of 50,000 souls, most of them Cuban these days. In recent years its only claims to fame have been corrupt politicians and the doings of Tony Pro and his blood-brothers. Local 560 has a disproportionate importance in America's economic life because it operates in the industrial heart of greater New York. This part of the 'Garden State' is a grim landscape of garbage mountains, chemical fumes, poisoned waterways and bleak highways. Some New Jerseyans know that beyond this wasteland is a beautiful state, but most of its 7 million inhabitants never see it. They live in the most concentrated nexus of organized crime and corruption in America, on show at their worst in Local 560.

No sooner had Tony Pro moved in on the local in the 1950s than he was extorting payoffs from trucking companies by threatening them with industrial unrest. He bled one firm of $17,000, for which he was jailed in 1966 and served more than four years. What frightened his victims was not just his methods. It was the man himself.

He ruled Local 560 with a blend of outward charm and inner brutality. In 1961 he had felt threatened by the popularity of another 560 official, Anthony Castellitto. Provenzano's underlings clubbed Castellitto about the head and strangled him. One of the killers was Sal Briguglio whom Pro rewarded with the lucrative union job of business agent. Fourteen years later Briguglio would be a prime suspect in Jimmy Hoffa's disappearance.

When Tony Pro was jailed in 1978 the main witness against him was Ralph Picardo. 'Tony was a ruthless, self-educated, cunning schizophrenic. He was brilliant at times but he always treated ambitious people as rivals, even when their ambition was directed to his benefit. That's why he had them killed.' There are plenty of stories to illustrate this. For example in 1963 Provenzano had faced a rare threat from the rank-and-file. At a union meeting Walter Glockner openly challenged the appointment of yet another gangster to the 560 payroll. He was set upon by union thugs and ejected. The following morning Glockner was shot dead outside his home.

Ralph Picardo started his working life as a truck-driver in Newark, New Jersey, where he fell under the influence of Sal Briguglio. Briguglio brought him into the Genovese family. 'My energy was to be solely devoted to their well-being. I belonged to Briguglio. I had become a member for life. There was no turning back.'

Ralph joined the Teamster Local 84 as an organizer and was soon taking kick-backs from companies keen to buy labour peace, pay low wages and sack surplus drivers. Tony Pro had created Local 84 for just such deals. Whereas Local 560 was bound to enforce national wage agreements, 84 was bound by none. It was a cut-price local. Ralph's drivers could be paid only $7 an hour when 560 drivers had to be paid $12. Companies would pay huge kick-backs just to be allowed to deal with 84, not 560.

One of Picardo's most rewarding rackets concerned Seatrain Lines which in the early 1970s was one of America's biggest container transportation firms. It operated from a spacious terminal on the Hudson River where ocean-going ships unloaded hundreds of containers at a time. With such a company Ralph first had to knock their managers into such a frenzy of distraction that they would run to the underworld for help. His goons sabotaged their trucks. They put graphite in the oil so that engines seized up. They undid locks so that containers would fall off tractors. They turned refrigeration units from cool to freezing to destroy certain kinds of merchandise. If a container held food they switched on the heating to make it rot. Once Ralph destroyed a cargo of coffee beans by turning on the fire hoses. Ships missed their sailing times when he disrupted their loading.

Sabotage, theft and slowdowns would soon bring even big international shipping companies to their knees. 'British companies were very receptive to paying,' recalls Ralph. 'As a matter of fact they volunteered to pay. They came to *me*.' Seatrain's managers became desperate. When Ralph offered them an uninterrupted service and an end to sabotage they were in the mood to pay anything.

Seatrain paid Picardo $500,000 through a consulting company set up just to receive such kick-backs. Picardo would bill Seatrain for the work of dozens of fictitious employees and the company would duly pay him their wages. Picardo also enabled the company to avoid millions of dollars in Teamster pension and welfare contributions by leasing hundreds of non-union drivers to Seatrain through his own company. While working as a Teamster organizer Picardo was also selling advice to the employers on how to do truckers out of their rights.

Not surprisingly companies found it easier to pay than fight. They passed the cost on to the customer, the consumer or the insurance company. Some executives even used to inflate the payoff and keep a chunk of it for themselves, becoming as corrupt as their extortioners. They knew they were dealing with the Mafia, otherwise they would not have paid. They also knew that Picardo was giving most of what they paid him to Briguglio and Tony Pro. These men took their cut and put what was left into the Genovese family pot. Picardo estimates that labour racketeering in the New York area adds 30 per cent to transportation costs. 'The racket is a huge conspiracy to make money from one person: Joe Public. All these costs are always passed on to the public.'

Picardo's hopes of advancement in organized crime were not helped when he was imprisoned for killing a man who had brutally robbed his mother. But Ralph's mob career really ended when he fell out with his Mafia overlord, Tony Pro. Ralph alleges that Provenzano once threatened to murder him and dump him in a grave already dug for him at Joe Celso's notorious chicken farm in Jackson, New Jersey. Picardo claims he later saw the grave when he visited the farm on other mob duties. He was convinced it was a graveyard for Genovese family victims. New Jersey police later dug up the farm and found several bodies but no one was ever charged with these murders.[7]

Eventually Picardo's sponsor, Sal Briguglio, was murdered, a ritual which the Genovese family performed to maintain discipline in the New Jersey locals. Briguglio had, of course, been one of that ritual's greatest exponents. 'All Mr Briguglio did was carry out Tony's orders. He did what he thought was best for the whole family. He was the only one that had any brains amongst the whole group, brains *and* brawn. Ruthless, crafty, cunning. He was brilliant. I liked him and that's why I was so loyal to him,' says Picardo. The shooting took place in March 1978 outside Umberto's Clam House in Mulberry Street in the heart of New York's Little Italy.

Today Tony Pro is in a Californian jail, doing life for the murder of Castellitto and twenty years for extorting Seatrain. He may spend the rest of his life inside. His repeated convictions might indicate that law enforcement has destroyed his power. Far from it. In or out of prison he has ruled 560 for over twenty years. Whenever he has been jailed he has simply installed another of his relatives to look after the shop.

In 1961 Tony brought his brother Salvatore 'Sam' Provenzano into 560's hierarchy. When he went to jail in 1966 he handed three of his union jobs to another brother, Nunzio. He also promoted Sam to the presidency. In 1975 Tony reappointed himself secretary-treasurer and made Nunzio president in place of Sam. Jailed again in 1978 Tony gave the secretary-treasurer's job to his 23-year-old daughter, Josephine. When Nunzio was convicted of racketeering in 1981 Sam came back as president. Tony has also given his brother-in-law and nephew union jobs. In 1984 Sam Provenzano, who replaced Tony as a Teamster International vice-president, was sentenced to three years in jail for a pension fund fraud. Another case of keeping it all in the family.

When law enforcement publicly asserts that Tony Pro is a member of the Genovese family many of his members seem to adore him all the more. Despite disqualification from union office he has been paid a handsome union salary for all his prison years. He received 'back-pay' of $223,000 to cover his first four-year jail term. Now he is back inside he is on a 'half-pension' worth more than most Teamsters earn for a hard year's trucking. Of Provenzano and his crew Picardo says, 'They all started out as common criminals. They become more sophisticated criminals as time goes on but none of them has any concern or compassion for the union member himself. They treat his dues and his pension and welfare payments as their own money, their own private bank.'

Not surprisingly Tony Pro's daughter Josephine disagrees. An engaging and personable young woman, she thinks 560 members adore her father. They don't care if what the papers say about her father is true or untrue. All they care about is how he treated them. 'Look what Tony did for me,' Josephine claims they say to themselves, 'he gave me pensions, eye-glasses, dental care, welfare payments. He saw me on the street and took me in a bar. We had a drink. He remembered my wife's name. He asked me how my daughter was, the one that had concussion in the hospital.' She went on: 'There is something about the man you can't understand until you're like one of the guys from 560. Those people go wild about him. To them there can be no higher recommendation than that I am Tony's daughter. And I am so proud to be my father's daughter.'

Those Teamsters must be remarkably thick-skinned if what Josephine says is correct. One scam for which he did not go to jail cost them a lot of money. It surrounds his homes in Sunny Isles, Florida. In the 1970s two developers named Romano borrowed more than $7 million from union funds to build a block of luxury apartments near Miami. At the same time Pro bought two luxurious houses from the Romanos for $64,000 below market price. This looked like his kick-back for getting them their loans. The project was a catastrophe. The Romanos pocketed $1 million themselves and then could not meet their obligations. The loss to union funds currently stands at well over $2 million.

Robert Stewart, the US attorney for northern New Jersey, became so appalled by 560's chronic corruption that he resorted to civil law to remove all power from its crooked leaders. He cited the 1970 RICO Act, which stands for Racketeer Influenced and Corrupt Organization. This enables prosecutors to charge organized-crime figures with carrying out crimes in the course of a continuing criminal conspiracy. The law can be applied in criminal courts, as it was against the Cleveland Mafia but Stewart applied it in the civil courts.[8]

For fifty-one days Stewart paraded Local 560's grotesque past and present before US Judge Ackerman. It had been the umbrella outfit for what Ackerman summed up as 'a multi-faceted orgy of criminal activity': hijackings, extortion, gambling, payoffs, kick-backs, loansharking, counterfeiting and murder. He described 560's history as 'a shameful horror story'. The union had become 'a Provenzano group fiefdom'. In 1984 Ackerman resolved to 'use a judicial scalpel to excise this malignancy'. He found that 560 was a 'captive labor organization' within the meaning of the RICO statute' and judged the Provenzano crew unfit to run the local. This was the first time an American civil court had taken a major racketeering operation out of the Mafia's clutches. Outside trustees will now run 560 for as long as it takes to restore union democracy.

The battle against the Provenzanos is not over. They will remain a corrupting force in Teamster affairs in the many other locals they control through Joint Council 73. The tenacity they have displayed for more than twenty years is not going to end just because 560 has been taken away from them. If ever New Jersey runs short of Provenzanos there will always be other folk to take their place. That is the essence of the Mafia. As Ralph Picardo says, 'it will never end. That's why they call it "our thing". Something that will survive as long as man is on earth.'

The story of Local 560 shows organized crime's penetration of the Teamsters at its clearest. Yet that kind of corruption and racketeering has flourished in dozens of locals across America. In recent years the Department of Justice has jailed many Teamster bosses for racketeering. Five leaders of New Jersey Local 945, another Genovese family fiefdom, defrauded its funds and caused several banks to collapse. Rudy Tham, boss of San Francisco Local 856, was jailed for embezzlement, partly on the evidence of the renegade Los Angeles mafioso Jimmy Fratianno. Frank Sheeran, boss of Local 326 in Delaware, has been jailed for ordering murders, bombings and arson. Sheeran is allied to the Mafia families of Philadelphia and north-east Pennsylvania.

Mafiosi running a trucking company in Detroit extorted $130,000 from their drivers in health and welfare payments which the company should have been paid. Also in Detroit Richard Fitzsimmons, Frank's son and himself an offical of Local 299, was jailed for taking $105,000 in kick-backs. John Nardi, a capo in Cleveland's Mafia family, was a top official in Local 410 at the same time as he ran gambling and drugs rackets. Nardi was blown to pieces in his union car park in 1977.[9] A Justice Department report written that year claimed organized crime was running eleven Teamster locals in Ohio alone. In New York organized-crime figures are even behind the main Teamster local at Kennedy Airport.

The Teamsters' national leaders have, if anything, acted even more corruptly than the hoodlums running the locals. Frank Fitzsimmons never made any attempt to get rid of his mob connections. Why should he bother when, despite them, US presidents and their Secretaries of Labor paid him homage? He died of lung cancer in 1981 but for the Mafia it was 'business as usual'. A few weeks later at the Teamsters' convention Roy Williams was elected president, even though it had long been public knowledge that he was owned by the Kansas City Mafia. The delegates even gave him a pay-rise, increasing his salary by a third to $225,000 a year. Williams's elevation had been assured by the boss of the Kansas City family, Nick Civella, who had nurtured him for thirty years.

Williams was felled by the continuing catastrophe of the Central States Pension Fund. When Hoffa had gone to jail in 1967 he told all concerned that Dorfman was 'the guy in charge while I'm gone'. Fitzsimmons did not challenge Dorfman as he bent the fund even more to the will of organized crime. In 1974 he lent $12 million to Bally, the slot-machine corporation which at that time was deeply involved with the Genovese family. Interest on the loan was fixed far below the going rate. He lent more millions to Alvin Malnik, a Miami lawyer alleged to be fronting for Meyer Lansky. One of the Malnik loans was on a country club and was interest free for forty years. Loans to another country club, La Costa, headed by Moe Dalitz, soared to $97 million. Allen Glick was lent an even bigger sum on his Las Vegas casinos, courtesy of the families in Chicago, Milwaukee and Kansas City.[10]

The law caught up with Dorfman in 1972 over a loan he had made to a textile firm. The borrower, George Horvath, convinced a jury that Dorfman had extorted a $55,000 bribe in return for the loan. Dorfman served ten months in jail. In 1975 he faced trial alongside the Chicago mafiosi, Tony 'the Ant' Spilotro and Joey 'the Clown' Lombardo for defrauding the fund of $1.4 million lent on the fraudulent hoax that they were going to manufacture pails in New Mexico. Just before the trial the main witness was gunned down and all the defendants were acquitted.

In the mid-1970s alarm at what was happening to the fund turned to outrage. Dissident pressure groups, such as PROD (Professional Drivers' Council for Safety and Health) and TDU (Teamsters for a Democratic Union) were making a political impact. The fund had to write off $100 million in bad debts. Low interest rates on many loans had cost it another $100 million. It had exaggerated the value of its real estate holding by $200 million. The fund's notional value of $1.4 billion was much inflated. The fears of hundreds of thousands of Teamsters that they might never get their pensions was to cause a crisis of confidence in America's entire pension system. The Department of Labor finally acted in 1977, forcing the fund's trustees to surrender their control by threatening to take away its tax-exempt status. Independent managers – a leading life assurance company and a firm of investment specialists – were now appointed to try to reverse the consequences of twenty years' criminal abuse.

In a little over two years the independent managers boosted the fund's assets from $1.6 million to $2.2 million and doubled its rate of return, partly by reducing the fund's dangerously high real estate holdings. But by 1984 the managers were discovering the true cost of the Las Vegas loans. The Aladdin casino went bankrupt still owing the fund $36 million. The Stardust, in the middle of a massive skim scandal, was having great difficulty finding a new owner willing to take on nearly $100 million of pension fund loans (originally borrowed by Allen Glick) which still have to be repaid.

Organized crime, meanwhile, has been trying to find ways of interfering with the managers and destroying their independence. Allen Dorfman and Roy Williams were at the forefront of those efforts. Their crimes would never have been discovered if it had not been for an armoury of bugs and wire-taps in Dorfman's office and in mobsters' hang-outs. Some of the 400,000 conversations they recorded showed how the Teamsters tried to block a law 'deregulating' the trucking industry which would weaken the union's chokehold on employers. In 1979 Williams and Dorfman devised a scheme to sell land owned by the fund to Nevada's Senator Howard Cannon at a knock-down price. In return the racketeers wanted Cannon to campaign against the new law. The land was a prime building plot next to the senator's Las Vegas home which he and his neighbours wanted to buy to ensure that it would not be used to build a high-rise tower.

In the bad old days Dorfman could have done the deal at any price he dreamed up and no one would have complained. This was no longer possible, however, because the fund's independent managers, Palmieri and Company, would sell only to the highest bidder. Dorfman and Williams met Cannon in Washington and offered him the land at $1.4 million but Palmieri had received another bid of $1.6 million. If that bid were accepted Williams and Dorfman would not be able to deliver their side of the alleged bargain.

Enter Joey 'the Clown' Lombardo. On the tapes this mafioso is heard deciding to fly two messengers to talk to the higher bidder and persuade him to withdraw. That bidder happened to be the rich but hapless Allen Glick, owner of four Las Vegas casinos until the Mafia told him to quit. The messengers dined with Glick at La Costa (where else?) and talked him into withdrawing. There were no threats. None were necessary – Glick knew whom he was dealing with – but there was a hitch. Glick had a partner, Fred Glusman, who refused to back down. He broke with Glick and put in his own bid at $1.6 million so Glick went to see him. He told Glusman, 'Don't fight City Hall.' This time Fred understood the message and withdrew.

All this dithering and delay upset Cannon and his neighbours and their bid fell apart. The land was eventually sold for $1.6 million but not to Cannon's group. By May 1979 the hoods were in disarray. On the tapes Dorfman is heard recounting how he had chastized Williams. 'I says, when this commitment was arranged, Roy, you sat in the same fucking room. You made the same fucking commitment I made. Now the property's gone. Fuck it, let it go. But I'll tell you something. I don't give a fuck if you have deregulation shoved up your fucking ass.'

Deregulation became law and Cannon did not fight it. In December 1982 Dorfman, Williams and Lombardo were all convicted of attempting to bribe a US senator and conspiring to defraud the fund. Dorfman raised $5 million bail to stay free until he was sentenced. He would have been safer in prison. In January 1983 the multi-millionaire mobster was shot dead. It was the one thousand and eighty-first mob killing recorded in Chicago since 1919.[11]

Lombardo was jailed for fifteen years. Roy Williams was sentened to fifty-five years but he spent ninety days in a prison hospital convincing doctors he suffered from emphysema. He gave up the Teamster presidency and its $225,000 salary. Now free on bail he will probably never serve another day in jail. He is the third Teamster president to be convicted of federal crimes in twenty-five years.

In April 1983 his successor was chosen: Jackie Presser, the Teamster mogul of Cleveland. He has a reforming air but his track record is not impressive. He inherited the post of Teamsters' international vice-president when the law forced his father Bill to resign over his criminal record. Bill Presser's mob connections stretched back to the 1930s. He was an inveterate racketeer, with convictions for strong-arm tactics in the vending-machine business, obstructing justice, contempt of Congress and taking payoffs from employers. Yet he was still being paid $173,000 a year from Teamster funds when he died in 1981.

At that time his son Jackie was picking up nearly $300,000 for a batch of Teamster jobs. Jackie Presser has never been charged with any offence but he has done little to oust the Mafia from the northern Ohio locals for which he has long had responsibility as vice-president and now president of Joint Council 41. In his own Local 507 one organized-crime figure was paid $109,000 in the 1970s for a 'no-show' job. Presser's uncle, David Friedman, has received $165,000 for doing no work whatsoever. In 1983 Friedman was sentenced to three years in jail but Jackie Presser's own role is now under federal investigation. He will have to convince the investigators that he was unaware these men were 'ghost' employees getting paid for doing nothing. This may be difficult when he was Local 507's treasurer at the time.

Now he is the boss of what is still America's biggest union Presser can put to the test the view he expressed to author Steven Brill in 1977. The job was not a throne, he said, 'it's an electric chair . . . If you're totally honest and if you try to clean up the union so the government won't get you, the other guys – the hoods – will get you. Just like they got Hoffa when he threatened them. So that's a death chair either way.'

In June 1984 two American newspapers revived a story that Presser has been an informant for the FBI since the 1970s. If this is true it may explain his absence from the trials which have brought down so many Teamster bosses in recent years. It must also complicate the investigation into Local 507.

The Mafia's bosses must now be debating what to do about Presser if he is an FBI informer. If they decide he is . . . it may only be a matter of time before they apply their code of Omerta.

Might Jackie Presser go the same way as Jimmy Hoffa, Allen Dorfman and countless Teamster officials who have found out too late that you cannot make 'sweetheart deals' with the mob and then try to break off the engagement?

22

The Chokehold on New York Construction

Manhattan is once again the most dynamic construction market in the world. Every Sunday the *New York Times* real estate section hails the rebirth of another part of the city, a new skyscraper tower topped out, another 50,000 office jobs created with the redevelopment of just one block. It makes exhilarating reading. The very heart of capitalism is pumping out confidence. This is indeed the golden door beside which Liberty lifts her lamp.

And yet that monumental skyline, America's most photographed horizon, is being renewed courtesy of racketeers, extortioners and killers. In the concrete canyons the Mafia and their front men levy their own unrelenting tolls. They control dozens of New York construction unions. When they order their members to black a contractor, walk off his site or cut off his supplies the victim can do little but pay off or go out of business.

The most powerful construction union in New York is Teamster Local 282. It has only 4000 members but they have a stranglehold on the industry because they alone are permitted to drive trucks on and off the city's building sites. If 282's monopoly were exploited for the good of its working members it might be a legitimate industrial weapon. Under John Cody, however, it was far from legitimate. Cody was Local 282's president until 1982 when he was sentenced to five years in jail for racketeering, extortion and evading taxes on more than $160,000 which he had extorted in payoffs.

John Cody, now in his sixties, is an old-style hoodlum. A heavily-built Lower East Sider he left school at 15 and spent most of his early manhood in reform school and prison, convicted of assault, robbery, gun-toting and two serious burglaries. All this was ideal training for the tough world of New York labour relations. In Local 282 he has many fans who praise his rough and tough leadership and turn a blind eye to his abuse of office.

Cody's strength came not from honest industrial muscle but from his connections with the Gambino crime family. Don Carlo Gambino, the boss of bosses, was an honoured guest at the wedding of Cody's son. Gambino died in 1976 and was succeeded as boss by his brother-in-law, Paul Castellano. In 1980 Paul's son Philip set up a concrete business and immediately won a huge sub-contract for sewer construction on Staten Island, the Castellanos' home territory. Teamster dissidents were not surprised to discover that, courtesy of Cody, Philip Castellano's company was not paying union rates to its Local 282 drivers. They were not getting their full fringe benefits which, at $5.61 an hour, amounted to a lot of money. But what ordinary truck-driver is going to argue with an employer named Castellano?

Cody used his mob power to good effect against non-mob companies facing the relentless urgencies of the New York construction industry. Jim Abbott is an FBI agent who went undercover to gather evidence of organized crime's role in this brutally competitive world. He knows from the inside that 'in erecting a large building everything has to be like a well-oiled machine. You have to have certain people come in, pour the concrete, figure it out, do duct work and so on. It all has a logical sequence. If any one of those trades are held up or subverted the entire project is held up, so they have you by the throat financially.'

Cody controlled the fate of every company bringing concrete into Manhattan. His power went beyond the trucking concerns back to the quarry owners who excavate sand and gravel on Long Island. He could destroy a cement manufacturer by telling the quarry owners not to supply him. The quarrymen would not disobey Cody in case their mining permits were withdrawn by the local politicians whom he controlled. At every phase of the sand, cement and concrete business Cody had the industry by the throat. Largely because of Cody and his mob sidekicks concrete costs 70 per cent more in New York than in any other north-eastern city.

In just ten years reserve naval officer Tom Gallagher had become the largest concrete supplier in eastern Long Island. By the late 1960s he was delivering huge loads from his plant in Suffolk County to major contractors in New York City. In 1968 he was asked to do $4000 worth of work on a house which, he later found out, belonged to John Cody. Gallagher did the work but it took him two years to get the money from Cody. When Cody handed over the cheque he simultaneously demanded $3,000 of it back in cash. Gallagher refused.

Cody was furious. He ordered the big New York contractors not to buy cement from Gallagher and sent city pickets down to Gallagher's rural plant to stop his supplies of raw materials getting in. Gallagher survived but found out that Cody was also forcing local contractors not to use him and recruiting his workers into Local 282. As non-union drivers they used to deliver up to eight loads a day. As 282 men they delivered only two loads. With his output slumping Gallagher finally realized that Cody had him beaten. The mobster had destroyed his business. Gallagher shut it down, went into liquidation and spent the next two years paying off debts. He had lost almost $1 million but he had also brought in the FBI and would later testify in the trial which sent Cody to jail.

Gallagher would probably still be in business had he handed Cody that $3000. 'Let's face it, if John Cody wakes up in the morning and he doesn't like you, you can't work that day. Some way or another he can stop any operation he wants to. He has almost total power in New York City.' Having taken a firm stand himself Gallagher has no respect for fellow-contractors who give in and pay men like Cody. 'There are a lot of people involved. I blame not so much Cody but the whole system which allows one man to control the whole thing. We're strong in protecting the working man which is fine, but when it gets to the point that one man uses the power of the union to represent himself alone, we're doing it wrong.'

Tom Gallagher's story is just one personal tragedy but it is repeated thousands of times over in the lives of business people who have no option but to give in. For every man who has the courage to go to the FBI hundreds dare not. As Jim Abbott put it, 'People who are from New York have their families here, they've grown up here, their roots are here. It's very unlikely that they would go to the FBI or the police and say, "Look, this illegal thing is happening here." If they survived – if they weren't killed – they'd be out of a job. At best they would have to leave New York and leave all their roots. It's very entrenched.'

Cody forced some companies to give his chauffeurs no-show jobs. They would drive him around while contractors paid their wages. One builder gave a $500-a-month apartment to Cody rent free for him to house his young mistress. In return Cody guaranteed him no union trouble on his building sites. Cody took $160,000 in payoffs from a real estate broker who had sold 282's pension fund a golf course and 1600 acres of land for $6.5 million. This corrupt deal is causing the fund heavy losses.

As Cody went on trial in 1982 he showed his strength by bringing New York construction and its 50,000 workers to a standstill. The excuse was the contractors' refusal to hire hundreds of extra 282 members as security guards on building sites. The union claimed the guards were needed to defend its members against minority protesters complaining about the shortage of construction jobs for blacks and Hispanics. The only unrest which had occurred to justify such a move were fisticuffs between some 282 members and an organization called Black Economic Survival. It later emerged that a Black Economic Survival leader had been given $3000 by Vincent Di Napoli, one of the most powerful mafiosi in the Bronx. The whole affair looked like a classic Mafia shakedown: create the problem and then extort a huge payoff to 'solve' it.

Vinnie Di Napoli is the obese owner of four dry-wall construction companies. He is also a capo in the Lucchese crime family and manages to control both sides of the business through his power over a cluster of construction unions. His front man used to be Teddy Maritas, president of New York's 27,000-member Carpenters' Union. Maritas was an outgoing showman, a prominent charity fundraiser and a campaigner for Ed Koch when he was elected mayor of New York in 1977. In a conversation taped without his knowledge Maritas boasted that he had raised $100,000 for Koch. Other tapes show that he thought of himself and his union as the property of the Genovese family although he did business for all the families.

Jim Abbott's undercover work was with an informant who ran a heating, ventilation and air-conditioning company. Calling himself Jim O'Brien Abbott claimed he had served a five-year jail term in Atlanta Penitentiary in order to gain the trust of the labour racketeers he was trying to gain evidence against. He set up a company called James Rico Construction Consultants offering advice on labour problems. Jim told employers how to 'cover' a job. 'Coverage' is a term for paying off union leaders to stay away from a construction contract. Abbott estimates that coverage can save more than $3 million on a $10-million project. Of that $3 million a large chunk is kicked back to the union bosses and thus to organized crime. The contractor saves the rest. (Abbott later shopped the union bosses who were taking the payoffs.)

Usually the contractor only wins a job because he has put in a low bid knowing he will not have to pay full labour rates, unlike his straight competitors. Abbott recalls how a contractor got a job to build two McDonald's hamburger outlets. He tendered at around $1 million, knowing that Rico Consultants would 'cover' his labour costs. His straight competitors bid around $1.4 million, as low as they could if they wanted to make a profit. The McDonald Corporation understandably chose the lowest bid. They did not ask the contractor how he could bid so low. No doubt the same level of 'coverage' goes on over the construction of Manhattan's latest towering rivals to the Empire State Building which can cost $100 million to erect. Federal investigators have not yet managed to infiltrate one of these giant projects with an undercover agent.

Another way in which organized crime creams off millions of dollars on a single project is by bid-rigging. In Britain contractors often secretly orchestrate their tenders for public works so they all come in at the same inflated level. Whoever gets the job takes a rich profit and stands aside next time for his 'competitors'. It is the same in New York except that the bid-rigging 'club' is run by the mob. The club is indestructible for it operates where the crime families not only control the unions but also own the construction companies.

Jim Abbott and the FBI successfully penetrated one bid-rigging operation in which all the mob contractors bar one inflated their bids on a job. 'His price was inflated but the others were ridiculously inflated so he was sure to get the job, at which point everybody else would take their kick-backs out of the profit. But what happened on this particular project was that a Mr Molinari, who was not a member of the club, underbid the club's chosen bidder by $1 million. Molinari was awarded the contract so Mr Maritas and Mr

Di Napoli had to explain to him that he could not accept this job because wiseguys were involved.'

Maritas was heard on an FBI tape telling a jumpy Molinari, 'Nobody wants to hurt you. You're being nice [but] we're going to have to meet people. . . . You know, you took $1 million out of people's mouths.' Molinari now had a choice. He could do the job anyway and pay off Maritas and Di Napoli with thousands of dollars. He could withdraw from the job so that it would go to the bidder nominated by the mob. The alternative, in Abbott's words, was that 'he would have gotten hurt. . . . Needless to say, Mr Molinari withdrew.'

At this point, however, the FBI declared its hand and the ring of Mafia racketeers and their front men was put on trial. At first there was a mistrial but it revealed enough of the FBI's damning evidence to alarm Di Napoli and his mob masters. They feared that in the retrial the prosecutors might call some of New York's highest mafiosi such as Tony Corallo, the boss of the Lucchese family. To a don like Corallo appearing as a subpoenaed witness is like going on trial himself. He would not be pleased at suffering this indignity. There was only one way out – everyone would have to plead guilty at the retrial.

Not surprisingly this scheme did not appeal to Teddy Maritas who clung to the illusion that he might be acquitted. With his social standing and political respectability he had a lot to lose by pleading guilty. He told his Mafia associates he would be pleading not guilty. In March 1982, only a week before the retrial, Maritas disappeared. A few days later, under a bridge on the edge of the city, his wallet was washed up, still containing $200 and his credit cards. Federal prosecutors had just warned him he was likely to be murdered. Characteristically Maritas had boasted that he would 'take his chances'. As Jim Abbott says his 'untimely death is a classic example of what happens when a front man puts his own interests ahead of La Cosa Nostra figures. He paid the ultimate price.'

In the last few years New York prosecutors, notably the Brooklyn strike force, have won convictions against racketeers not just in the cement truck-drivers' and carpenters' unions but in those of the labourers, hodcarriers, the boilermakers, electricians, plumbers, painters, sanders and blasters, and tapers and plasterers. 'There is no construction in the City of New York,' says Jim Abbott, 'no matter how large or small, that could not be strangled by organized crime. They have an absolute chokehold. If they desired to do it they would stop the city.'

23

One Big Octopus

Organized crime exists to make money. If money can be made by honest means even mafiosi will stoop to them but to the Mafia there is really no such thing as 'legitimate' business. However straight a Mafia-owned company may seem to be, its success depends on some form of extortion being applied against its suppliers, its competitors or its customers. The basic skills were learned long ago in one of organized crime's staple rackets: loansharking.

John Vitale was a compulsive New Jersey gambler who lost \$250,000 in Mafia-run poker games during the late 1970s.[1] To pay for his habit he passed bad cheques and then turned to Mafia loansharks. He had known this species of predator since he was a teenage crook. 'You'll find loansharks in candy stores, bars, taxi companies – any small business where there's a steady flow of people, where they can get to know lots of regular customers. No matter where you go in America there are loansharks. They make their fortunes out of "vig" which is the slang term for extortionate interest. The rates vary but I got into deep trouble over a loan of \$1500 on which the vig was \$5 on each \$100 each week. After one week the interest on that \$1500 was \$75. Pay back that loan in a week and the interest wouldn't feel very heavy. Leave it for a few months at compound interest and you owe a fortune.

'I had not borrowed this money for myself. I vouched for someone else who just took off, left town. That was twelve years ago and I have never seen the man again. The loansharks didn't get back in touch with me for a couple of months. When they did the note stood not at \$1500 but \$4500. They held *me* responsible for the entire debt which I had to pay back week by week but because the note was now "delinquent" the loansharks were adding interest daily. It just kept on piling up. By the time I paid them back \$6000 I still owed \$4,000. I could no longer meet the payments so I went underground. I split.

'Eventually my sister took them $500 so we could start talking terms again. I came out of hiding but now they wanted to rip my head off. I wasn't home ten minutes when there was a knock at the door. It was Benny the loanshark and his boys. It seems that a few weeks earlier he had been driving his new Cadillac around town and thought he saw me in another car. He smashed his Caddy into my lookalike and put the guy into hospital. For this Benny was charged with attempted murder so he was pretty mad by the time he caught up with me. His boys smacked me a few times for being an asshole but we worked out a new deal. Then I ran out of money once more. They invaded my house, smashed up my car and harassed my wife so I went underground again.

'Eventually I was arrested for fraud and went to jail but by then the FBI had me on film and tape talking with these guys. The FBI gave me a deal over my cheque offences when I agreed to testify against the loansharks. I told them to talk to another of the loansharks' victims but he was too frightened to speak. In front of his two kids the Shylocks had cut his throat – not to kill him but to teach him a lesson and get their money. He was so scared he went out and borrowed $2000 from a church pastor in New Jersey, paying *him* back by working weekends as the church handyman for two years. He knew these guys had been dead serious. They wanted their money and if they didn't get it he was gonna die.'

One man who knows the loansharking business both as a borrower and a lender is Joey Cantalupo. 'Loansharking is a primary source of income for all organized-crime families,' he says. 'The boss of a family hands many millions of dollars to his "made" men to put out on the streets. He might lend a soldier $100,000 at ½ per cent a week. He doesn't care what the soldier does with the money so long as every week he gets his ½ per cent. The soldier now lends the money on at a far higher rate, maybe to a businessman who's got so many bank loans he can't get any more.

'One time Joe Colombo lent money to an individual who fell behind on his weekly interest payments but, instead of coming in the first week and telling Joe he didn't have the money, the man just didn't show up. He let three weeks go by and then he came into my father's real estate office and told Joe, "I ain't got the money."

'Colombo was embarrassed: "You come in after three weeks to tell me! Hey, boys! Take him downstairs. Just tell him what it's all about!"

'They would take the guy down to the basement. Boom! Boom! Boom! Punch him around a little bit. He would come up, his face all swollen, and he'd be escorted out of the office. (Imagine – this is happening in a respectable place of business!) You could be sure that guy would be back within the hour to hand over all his back payments.

'The owner of a trucking company borrowed $100,000 from Joe Colombo, Carlo Gambino and my father at 2 per cent a week. This meant he had to pay them $2000 cash every week before he even started paying back the principal. I used to collect the money from this man. He paid $2000 a week for a year and a half, which added up to $156,000, and yet he still owed the $100,000 he had originally borrowed.

'I became a Shylock myself because I figured I could borrow say $10,000 at 1 per cent a week and lend it out at 3 per cent, which would give me a profit of $200 each week. Eventually I ran up Shylock tabs totalling $80,000 on which I was paying the Shylocks $1600 each week. But some of the guys I was lending money to never paid me back. When I went back to the Shylocks and told them I had been beaten out of the money they said I was responsible. They didn't care who beat me. I had to pay them back with interest.

'Once I borrowed $10,000 at 2 per cent a week from Allie Boy Persico, who's the under-boss or *consigliere* of the Colombo family. It was for a client of mine but when I took him the money he said he didn't need it after all. Now I couldn't just take the money back to Persico because I'd look like a jerk, so I kept it for a week. And then I started spending it. I paid him back some of the money but I still had to pay him $150 a week interest on the rest for more than a year and a half. Now somehow Persico found out that I had kept the money myself. I was called down to his club on President Street in Brooklyn. As I walk in who was there but my buddy Michael Bolino, who's a "made" member of the Colombo family, Allie Boy Persico and an enforcer.

'Allie Boy is sitting down and as I go to shake his hand he gets up and grabs me by the collar and starts punching me in the face. "I want my fuckin' money back and I want it now." And as I'm falling to the floor with blood coming out of my face Michael Bolino comes over and picks me up and takes me outside and washes my face off.

'Now I could not raise my hands to this man because of his position. These "made" men can hit you with a bat, do anything they want but if you raise your hands to them you're gonna be dead. I owed Funzi Tieri's driver, Johnny Russo, $22,000 so he spat on my face. He's a little piece of nothing. If I'd have spat on *him* he would have drowned. But whatever his abuse, God forbid you ever touch him. You'd never see your family again.

'Shylocks won't usually kill you because if you're dead they know they're going to lose their money but they will abuse you. One guy owed Russo $33,000. He's three times the size of Russo but Russo went up and punched him in the face. This guy was walking out the house with his wife and daughter and Russo said, "I want my fuckin' money", calls his wife a "dirty fuckin' whore" and his daughter a "cunt", but the guy couldn't do anything.'

Most people who borrow money from loansharks are not crooks, just people who need cash in a hurry or small businessmen who are over-extended at the bank. To get money from loansharks they put up their business as collateral but because the interest is so high they often cannot repay the loan and forfeit their business to organized crime.

Cantalupo says that the borrower may be a successful businessman who just wants money to launch a good idea. 'The loanshark may put up $100,000 at 2 per cent a week but when he sees your business is flourishing he'll say, "I don't want the money back. I want 20 per cent of the business." This not only gives the loanshark a good income, it also gives him a legitimate income which helps him out when the tax man wants to know how he can afford his lavish lifestyle.'

Thousands of businesses have fallen prey to the Mafia either because their owners defaulted on loans or because loansharks just decided to muscle in. The lesson is simple. Once you borrow from mafiosi they will keep taking your money whether you owe them any or not. When you go to a loanshark you accept not only his rates of interest but also, tacitly if not explicitly, his methods of collection. At first the loanshark appears benign. He is careful not to make you feel like a victim – indeed he may act like your saviour. He is only an extortioner by another name, however, and his ultimate sanction is that of the extortioner: violence to you and your family. The threat does not have to be voiced. Even if it is you are unlikely to run to the police because you feel you have placed yourself outside the law's protection by going to the loanshark in the first place. And Shylock victims do not have to be criminals to know how the mob deals with informers.

It was the out-and-out extortioner rather than the loanshark who tyrannized the straight folk trying to make a living in New York's garment centre in the 1920s and 30s. Manufacturers found armed men walking into their premises demanding to be made partners. In the 1926 garment strike both employers and unions hired gangsters to defend their interests.[2] Out of the gang hired by the unions sprang the most notorious extortioners in the history of organized crime: Louis 'Lepke' Buchalter and Jacob 'Gurrah' Shapiro. From the night of 15 October 1927 when they murdered their former boss, 'Little Augie' Orgen, the squat pair of 'L & G' terrorized the garment centre.

The 1929 Wall Street Crash devastated the fashion business and knocked the bottom out of fur prices. New York's biggest furmakers hired Lepke, Gurrah and their strong-arm boys to eliminate competition by forcing all fur companies into a price-fixing cartel. In return L & G extracted fees from each cartel member. The mobsters were soon extorting $10 million a year from rabbitskin makers. They took over employers' associations and labour unions in the rest of the industry, emerging as owners of some of the centre's largest firms, including America's biggest coat-front company. As every suit had to have a coat front the pair had taken effective control of the industry through this one move. Rackets' investigator Victor Herwitz recalls that they did not need to buy their way into any business. Their reputation for violence sufficed. 'Lepke would come in and say, "You don't have to put us on your payroll, nothing will happen to you." Businessmen told us that the most frightening thing in the world was to hear Lepke and Gurrah saying nothing was going to happen.' According to mob mythology Shapiro won his nickname because no one dared disobey his uncouth order to 'gurrah!' (get out of here).

In 1936 L & G were sentenced to two years in jail for racketeering in the skin trade. Gurrah was jailed but Lepke won a retrial and fled. Special Prosecutor Tom Dewey launched a huge 'Get Lepke' campaign. The racketeer replied by unleashing a team of gunmen to kill all potential informers such as Lepke's reluctant partners in dress and trucking companies and any garment centre people seen talking to detectives. This mass slaughter earned the killers the title 'Murder Inc.' They were mostly Jews, like 'Pittsburgh Phil' Strauss and 'Tick Tock' Tannenbaum who had worked as professional killers for years. Their pedigree was Siegel and Lansky's 'Bug and Meyer' gang which was active in the Castellamarese wars, when they worked closely with mafiosi like Albert Anastasia. It later emerged that Lepke had despatched the hit team which killed Dutch Schultz in 1935. Some of Murder Inc.'s most spectacular hits were of its own members.[3] Even so it is unlikely that the gang carried out anything like the 1000 slayings mob mythology has attributed to them.

By 24 August 1939 Dewey had whipped up such a hue and cry about Lepke that the gangster suddenly surrendered in person to the FBI's director, J. Edgar Hoover in the heart of New York City. Lepke assumed that Hoover would give him a far easier time than Tom Dewey, now New York's DA. But for once Hoover co-operated with Dewey and Harry Anslinger of the Bureau of Narcotics. Anslinger brought a case against Lepke for heroin smuggling and had him jailed for twelve years. Dewey then successfully prosecuted him for extorting millions of dollars from the baking industry. He now faced more than forty years in jail. In February 1940, however, Lepke was appalled by an even worse prospect.

A Murder Inc. assassin named 'Kid Twist' Reles just arrested for murder had turned informer.[4] Other hit men followed his example, putting many Murder Inc. killers on trial. Lepke was tried for the murder of Joe Rosen, a garment industry trucker whom he had forced out of business in 1932. He later had him killed to stop him talking. Lepke was convicted and electrocuted in Sing Sing on 4 March 1944. He remains the only top mobster in the history of American organized crime ever to be legally executed. His partner, Gurrah Shapiro, convicted for a second time of extorting the garment industry, died in jail.

Lepke, Gurrah and Murder Inc. have long since expired but their legacy, inherited by the Mafia, remains to this day. As Joey Cantalupo says, 'The garment centre is run by Italian–American organized crime. Each family has interests in this vast industry and they use Jews as "pillowheads" or fronts.' Ten of the mafiosi caught at the Apalachin summit owned garment companies. Today the crime families own clothing factories, trucking companies and clothing retailers from New York to California. They also control the garment unions. One man who knows how the mob have stitched up the industry from both ends is the president of a warehousemen's union, Local 20408, Matthew Eason.

Eason is a mountain of a man: black, 6 ft 5 in and 300 lb. He looks even bigger these days as he strides through the garment centre in a bulletproof vest. Whenever he walks around 'Fashion Avenue' he takes two armed bodyguards with him. Such precautions are wise. Eason put his life in permanent danger when he chose to work with the FBI rather than the mob.

In 1978 200 employees of one of the garment industry's biggest trucking firms, Interstate Dress Carriers (IDC), were looking for a new union to represent them. Mostly blacks and Hispanics, they were employed through a temporary labour agency at low wages with sub-standard fringe benefits. They had discovered that the Garment Workers' Union, the ILGWU, by far the biggest in the industry, did not want to recruit them.

Before he could recruit these workers to his union Matthew Eason had to win the legal right to represent them. IDC tried to buy him off through a Teamster official named Tony Di Lapi. 'He came to me with several other "gentlemen" – I use that term loosely – and made me an offer I couldn't refuse. I had been forewarned that I should walk away from organizing this company or else certain unpleasant things would happen. A lawyer told me these were bad people who would think nothing of handing me my head.'

Di Lapi told Eason he was rocking the boat. He should take a payoff and forget about IDC. It later became clear that Di Lapi's Teamster local and the Garment Workers' Union had a deal not to organize IDC. By stopping these workers from joining any union they were saving the company millions of dollars. At that time

Eason had no idea Di Lapi belonged to the Lucchese crime family. He had innocently stumbled into a Mafia republic.

Eason was not prepared to go along with the plot so he went to the FBI who wired him up. He met Di Lapi several times and recorded their conversations. He also met the man running IDC, Sidney Lieberman, who gave him $2000 to drop his plans to unionize his workers. The FBI charged the conspirators but in July 1979 a key potential witness, Lieberman's cousin Judith, was shot to death with her husband. She was Interstate's secretary-treasurer and may have known a lot about the company's crooked dealings with the mob. However, Eason's evidence was enough to send Lieberman to jail for one year and Di Lapi for ten.

In the middle of his undercover dealings Eason had led a strike of his would-be members within both IDC and another giant trucking company, Consolidated. At Consolidated the strikers were confronted by the time-honoured goonery of America's labour wars: baseball bats, iron bars, knuckle-dusters, knives and guns. Strikers were stabbed and Eason himself was clubbed with an iron pipe. Yet he still established his right to represent those workers. How he can build on this breakthrough will be dictated by the crippling curbs on his activities. His movements are necessarily furtive. To stay alive he makes no advance appointments. As we followed him around the garment centre he met union members who had not seen him for six months. How safe can they feel belonging to a union whose leader only dares appear in a bullet-proof vest, flanked by armed bodyguards?

IDC is now under new ownership but this one successful case has not seriously weakened the mob's power in the garment industry which, according to Eason, is 'deep-rooted and widespread. It's one big octopus.' By owning some of the biggest garment trucking companies and controlling the Teamster locals to which the truckers belong, organized crime dominates an industry which today employs 250,000 people and has an annual turnover of $14 billion. 'Whoever controls the trucks controls the garment centre. Nothing moves without your consent. You have it by the throat.'

That feeling is shared by garment manufacturers like Bud Conheim, a maker of ladies' high-fashion clothing since 1955. 'Don't cheat on your trucker unless you want big trouble. It would be better to cheat on your *wife* than cheat on your trucker. I can have all kinds of trouble. Things don't get delivered or they get damaged. The ability to move the merchandise is the heart of the business, it's the pump that keeps the whole industry going.

'Nobody's a free agent in trucks. You have two choices: you use the truck line you're married to or you truck yourself. You can complain to your trucker about lousy delivery and high prices, you can bitch and you can moan, and the guy might make the deliveries better for you, but you can't say, "I'm gonna get XYZ to truck for me because he runs a real snappy service and we're gonna use him instead" because there is no XYZ service. And XYZ would take his life in his hands to service you so he doesn't do it. The territory is all carved up.'

The presiding power in garment trucking is Tommy Gambino who owns Consolidated along with his brother Joseph. They are both sons of Carlo Gambino. Tommy is also the son-in-law of Tommy Lucchese, now dead, whose own crime family has dominated the garment centre, with the Gambinos, for thirty years. Cantalupo says of the Gambino brothers, 'These people actually go to work every day. They oversee everything and play the part of Mr Nice Guy.'

Tommy Gambino has consistently denied having anything to do with organized crime. In 1981 he was named the industry's 'Man of the Year'. Lieutenant Remo Franceschini of the New York Police looks at the issue from another angle. 'The name Gambino instils fear in a lot of people so the Gambinos avoid a lot of problems that an everyday businessman cannot avoid: union disputes and strong-arm tactics for instance. Tommy Gambino did not get established in the garment area on his own. He was established through his father and his father's underlings. The association doesn't stop just because Carlo died.'

For three years investigators working for State Senator Franz Leichter dug up an encyclopaedia of dirt on 'the return of the sweatshop' in New York's garment industry. In 1982 they produced evidence that the Gambino and Lucchese families controlled dozens of garment trucking companies and scores of garment manufacturers. There are now 3000 sweatshops in New York, where Chinese and other impoverished immigrants work in appalling conditions for less than $2 an hour. Many sweatshops have been set up by mob-owned trucking companies. They supply the machinery, the orders and, of course, the trucking without which the sweatshops would collapse. Mafia loansharks have been only too willing to supply the necessary start-up capital. According to Senator Leichter the result is that 50,000 New Yorkers suffer 'a form of labour exploitation which we thought had been outlawed for more than fifty years.'

Organized crime has used the same octopoid methods to dominate other industries vital to America's cities, such as garbage collection. In our throw-away society it is big business, worth $120 million in New York alone. Huge areas of the states of New York and New Jersey are shared out among mob-owned garbage companies according to a system of 'property rights'. Individual customers – factories, shops, schools, municipalities and private householders – have no say over who takes away their rubbish, no matter how bad the service. Cartels of garbage companies, known as trade waste associations, are often no more than clubs of mafiosi and Mafia front men. Occasionally a mob garbage man steps out of line and tries to take customers away from other gangsters. Retribution is certain. As Colonel Justin Dintino of the New Jersey State Police explains, 'The individual who continues to play hardball finds that he is no longer on this planet.' Three such careless garbage operators have been murdered in recent years. As in the garment centre the Mafia completes the circle of its control by dominating the union, in this case Teamster Local 945 to which most garbage truckers belong. But even if you insist on removing your own garbage you still need the Mafia – they own most of New Jersey's mountainous waste dumps.

In 1983 New Jersey won convictions against a trade waste association dominated by the Genovese crime family. The cartel had forced up charges by simply eliminating competition. One children's hospital had tried several times to change its garbage removers but each time was forced back to the company to whom the hospital 'belonged' under the property rights system. The hospital's administrators were then punished by having to pay far higher charges. The case against the racketeers was made largely by an organized-crime accomplice who turned federal witness. Only one clean operator dared testify: Clem Pizzi.

Clem still has a few trucks but he sold out of the garbage business in 1980. 'Through the trade waste association the industry has been controlled by a select few. The cartel operators are scum. The independent just makes a living at the risk of having his trucks set on fire or even being murdered. The threat of violence is always there. They're destroying the good clean operators who are being forced to sell out but if you have mob connections you'll make a fantastic profit.'

Clem advises businessmen not to try and change their garbage man: 'You have no choice. You look at who's picking up the stop next to you, and who's picking up the stop on the other side and then you call the same guy, because that's all you're gonna get.' In New York's garment centre Bud Conheim met with just this response. On his first day in business he complained to the garbage collector about his charge of $275 a month. The collector told Conheim that if he didn't like it he could always take it out himself.

Conheim said, 'What if I want to call another garbage guy?'

'Just try it,' said the collector.

Inevitably, Conheim learned he was 'married' to this garbage man just as he was married to his trucker.

The rate of profit extorted by the mob through its grip on this industry was laid bare in 1982 when the city of New Brunswick put its garbage contract out to tender. Naively assuming the market was competitive it expected several bids. Only one came in: for $1.2 million – twice as high as the city fathers had expected. The outraged burghers decided New Brunswick should collect its own garbage. Today its service costs just $700,000, $500,000 less than the city would have paid to the trade waste cartel.

It took four years to bring New Jersey's garbage racketeers to trial. Fifty-five were convicted but the mobsters who ran the scam were sentenced to only two years at an open prison. Odder still, they were only kept inside over weekends and were allowed out during the week. Such feeble punishment is hardly likely to cast the Mafia out of the garbage industry.

The Mafia extorts Americans not only over what they wear and throw away but also on what they eat. In 1934 a *New York Times* editorial on the Fulton Fish Market said that, 'if there is any downward scale of ignominy in the [racketeering] profession, the man who preys on the city's food supply must stand very near the bottom'. Those were the days when 'Socks' Lanza – Lucky Luciano's runner – ruled the fish market.[5] Fifty years on the same market, through which $350 million worth of fish is sold every year, is still ruled by the Genovese crime family. In the words of Dan Bookin who prosecuted the present leaders of the Fish Market conspiracy it is, 'the most extreme example of an industry dominated by organized crime. Those who work there feel they live under two governments – one in Washington and one on the street. . . . The worst crime is that businessmen in the market believe the government of the streets – the Mafia – is the more powerful.' What is even more frightening is that this belief is held only six blocks from the Federal Courthouse where Bookin put the racketeers on trial.

In 1979 Department of Labor investigators began to probe the wealthy lifestyle of officials of Local 359, the same Seafood Workers' Union through which Lanza had controlled the market, in and out of jail, until the 1960s. Three years later the investigators had won convictions against more than twenty mobsters and a dozen fish wholesaling companies.

They found out that the Neptune of the Fish Market was now Carmine Romano, who at 6 ft 1 in and 300 lb oozes all the menace of an amphibian Jaws. From his social club in the heart of the market Romano, a 'made' man in the Genovese family, ran a protection racket against the market's seventy major wholesalers. In the mid-1970s organized theft had risen so dramatically that they ran to Romano for help. The mobster instantly created a security force known as the Fulton Patrol. Almost overnight all the pilfering stopped but it cost the wholesalers more than $700,000 in fees to Fulton Patrol.

Romano and his henchmen extorted a further $300 each year from wholesalers for the rental of cardboard union signs. The excuse was that small mom and pop companies who employed no union members would show they were compensating Local 359 for lost dues by displaying this sign. These payments never went to the union's working members though. The $12,000 extorted in this way each year went to union officials in increased expenses. Every Christmas Romano demanded goodwill payments from every market trader. These were spent on his own indulgences such as card-gambling. He placed large union deposits in a bank which gave him and his cronies $10,000 worth of colour TV sets in return for opening new accounts. The bank could afford these incentives because it was paying lower interest rates than other banks offered. This deal was strictly against American union law.

Fulton Fish Market was rife with dozens of other rackets which the investigators had no time to plumb but it is clear that Mafia-owned fish shops and restaurants get their supplies for next to nothing while every other consumer pays inflated prices. Since the fish racket has been going on for most of this century New Yorkers no longer feel any pain as they pay off the mob with every mouthful of red snapper.

Carmine Romano is now in a maximum security prison serving a twelve-year term but he has got off lightly. In the course of the investigation it became clear that few wholesalers dared take the opportunity to cast out their extortioners. They reminded federal agents that they would still have to make a living long after these trials were over. However successful this investigation they knew that the Mafia would still control the market. In 1981 one fish-market worker who had testified was shot five times as he walked past Local 359's offices.

Miraculously he survived but the lesson got home to everyone else who might have felt like talking. One terrified wholesaler, subpoenaed before a grand jury, refused to speak. When asked about Carmine Romano Alec Messing broke down in tears and grovelled, 'I am very sorry. . . . I want to answer your questions. However, I am afraid of what will happen to my wife, my children, my grandchildren and my business. Threats have been made against me if I answer your questions truthfully. . . . I don't want to go to jail. . . . but if you insist I have no choice. . . . I am frightened to death. You see pictures in the newspapers, on the television, where they do people in. People get in their cars and it explodes. I beg you, don't send me to jail.'

Messing was jailed for ninety days. He paid a $60,000 fine rather than give evidence. He never testified. He is still in business. And the rackets go on and on. Wholesalers like him simply hand the cost of paying off on to the retailers and the ultimate victims: the public.

In fact the public always pays in the end. As Bud Conheim commented, 'I've never put a percentage on what it costs us but those extra costs of doing business are part of my life. Nobody gets a break because this organization, this unseen government, collects its taxes from everybody. It's more efficient than the US government. We all have to increase our prices to cover the cost of this aggravation. We run our business the best way we can under *laissez-faire* capitalism and it works in spite of it. Maybe it's a testimony of how strong the capitalist system is here that it can sustain a parasite this long and stay this strong.'

No reader will be surprised to learn that pizzas in America are even more 'mobbed-up' than fish. From Toronto to Miami, from New York to Chicago and Arizona, thousands of pizza parlours are owned by organized crime. The pizza business, although an extreme example, shows how pervasive Mafia infiltration can become in one industry. When he owns a pizza parlour – or indeed any restaurant – a mobster has the means of showing enough profit to appease the inquisitors from the IRS. The pizza parlour may in reality be losing money but the mobster can over-declare its profits in order to launder illegal earnings through the tax system. Owning a pizza parlour also gives him a veneer of respectability, however thin, in the wider community. He can now pass himself off as legitimate in church, business and political circles where such considerations count. They also count at school. It is important for a mafioso's children to be able to tell their friends what Daddy does for a living. Saying that he kills people would not go down well.

A pizza parlour is of course an ideal place to employ young bloods from Italy, be they illegal aliens employed at rock-bottom rates (as in the old *padrone* system) or legal immigrants for whom sought-after 'green cards' are easily acquired because the pizza parlour owner promises to give them a job. What they really do, once they are in America, may be along traditional Mafia lines. As Colonel Dintino says, 'They can be used to import narcotics, they can be inducted into the ranks of the American Mafia and, because they have no fingerprints on file and are unknown to US law enforcement, they're a perfect force for contract murders.'

Like any other business front, a pizza business provides a useful cover for further criminal ventures. Dozens of people – heroin wholesalers, loanshark victims, burglars, truck hijackers – can come in and out of any fast-food venture every day without arousing the suspicion of neighbours or local police. And there is always the consolation that if the business loses its charm you can set it on fire. In every state where there is a heavy concentration of mafiosi pizza parlours have been 'torched'. In New Jersey Sicilian immigrants have seen their restaurants go up in flames. The fires may be acts of competition, extortion or vengeance but law enforcement suspects the owners of torching their own premises in order to make fraudulent insurance claims. Arson for profit is an increasingly popular Mafia racket.

Joey Cantalupo knows how the Mafia controls pizzas wholesale as well as retail. 'When a new shopping mall opens one of the crime families will get the sole concession on pizzas. They'll open up a shop, run it for a year and then sell it. It may have cost them $50,000 to start but they could sell it for $250,000. In the pizza business you buy your cooking and salad oils from a company that's run by the crime family. The same with the mozzarella cheese, the tomatoes, the anchovies, all your ingredients, and of course the wine. Now, if you are a legitimate businessman and I agree to sell you this pizza business, I will do so only on the understanding that you continue to buy these products from suppliers within the crime family.

'I had an uncle who owned a fast-food restaurant called Eddie Arcaro's in a big Brooklyn shopping centre. Two doors away is an Italian delicatessen selling mainly cold food but also pizza. So my uncle thinks that he would like to sell pizza in Eddie Arcaro's because there's a tremendous demand in this big shopping mall and a lot of money to be made. But Funzi Tieri, the boss of the Genovese family, found out so he tells me to get hold of my Uncle Sal and take him to meet the owner of the delicatessen, who happens to be related to Tieri. So this guy tells my uncle, "We don't want any competition with the pizza so be a nice guy, Sal, and don't put pizza in the restaurant."

'As we were driving away my uncle got very upset: "Who the fuck do these people think they are? They think they are going to tell me what I can and can't do."

'I said, "But Uncle Sal, you're talking about Funzi Tieri and you're going to get yourself in trouble."

'The next day Funzi comes back to the office and asks me what my uncle has decided. I said, "Funzi, he didn't decide yet. I don't know what he's going to do."

'And Funzi turns to me and he says, "If your uncle thinks he's going to put pizza in Eddie Arcaro's he's better off putting pizza in Scarpaci's! – and he points to Scarpaci's, the funeral parlour across the street – "Because that's where he's going to wind up!"

'I go back and tell my uncle what Funzi has said. My uncle gets so nervous that he sells out from Eddie Arcaro's. He was so fearful he got out of the business.'

The mob does not stop at intimidating small-time restaurant owners. It takes on major corporations too. In 1964 Jerry Catena, who later became joint boss of the Genovese family, tried to market a brand of detergent. The giant Atlantic & Pacific supermarket chain thought the product sub-standard and refused to stock it. Jerry and his brother Gene were incensed. In the next few months five A & P supermarkets were fire-bombed to destruction. Early in 1965 two A & P store managers were shot to death gangland-style. New York's US attorney was sure the Catenas had ordered the killings. Jerry was called before a grand jury and the terror campaign ended as suddenly as it had begun. Astonishingly no one was ever charged.

One way to bypass recalcitrant supermarket chains is of course to buy your own supermarkets. The New York families own a dozen in Queens and Brooklyn while across the East River they control some of Manhattan's most famous restaurants. But it is in the meat business that the Mafia's pretence at legitimacy is most blatant. Organized-crime figures own more than twenty New York meat companies. Gambino family boss Paul Castellano is one of the biggest meat and poultry wholesalers in the entire New York area. Castellano is so big that even giant legitimate success stories like Frank Perdue (whose Perdue chickens turn in gross revenues of $430 million a year) do business with him. As Joey Cantalupo puts it, 'Sure Castellano's meat business is legal and it generates millions of dollars a year, but where did the money come from in the first place?'

This food empire generates an insatiable appetite for all kinds of products, whatever their origin. In one case chicken suppliers in far-off states were defrauded of $1.3 million by Peter Castellano (Paul Castellano's brother) and other Mafia sidekicks. In 1960 mobsters controlling a wholesale meat company called Murray Packing used to buy chickens and sell them on to Castellano at cost price. In 1961 Murray suddenly increased its orders but stalled on its payments to the suppliers. By the time the suppliers realized what was happening Joe Pagano, the 'made' man who was Murray's president, had cashed $745,000 worth of company cheques in nine days but the chickens had flown off to Castellano. In 1964 the fraudsters were convicted. Castellano was jailed for five years. Pagano served six, apparently for insulting the judge's intelligence by claiming he had lost the $745,000 in floating crap games at places he could not recall with players he could not remember. In 1970 he bought his freedom, paying a mere $75,000 to Murray's creditors in final settlement.

In the 1970s two brothers associated with the Gambino family, Vincent and Joseph Falcone, approached gullible cowmen offering to market their surplus milk as mozzarella cheese for city dwellers' pizzas. In three separate scams the Falcones built up the farmers' trust, then increased their wholesale orders and sold the mozzarella on to New York cheese shops part-owned by relatives of Carlo Gambino. When the farmers came to their senses, stopped supplies and demanded payment the Falcones went bankrupt. Farmers as far away as Vermont and Wisconsin lost $2 million.

Not every Mafia business is destined for such a 'bust-out' or planned bankruptcy. Such scams are easily detected and somebody may go to jail. Mobsters usually own 'legitimate' businesses to stay *out* of jail. That is why Al Capone used to say he was an antique dealer. Lucky Luciano preferred the humbler calling of waiter. Meyer Lansky claimed he was a car mechanic. Frank Costello gave his occupation as public relations consultant for a brand of Scotch whisky. Carlos Marcello, boss of New Orleans, still says he is a tomato salesman. All mobsters must have a legitimate job description. It would not be the thing to admit to the calling of extortioner, loanshark, pimp or murderer on their income tax returns.

Among long-standing mob enterprises in New York are dry cleaners, juke-box suppliers, car dealerships, furniture and furnishing stores, liquor importers, travel agencies and bowling alleys. Appropriately Aniello della Croce, the Gambino family's current under-boss, is on the board of a company that services sewers.

Joey Cantalupo worked inside the empire that is the respectable face of organized crime in Brooklyn for fourteen years. 'All these businesses are fronts or "covers". Every legitimate business that you can draw a cheque from you can show to the government: "I'm making $300 a week here, $500 there." Now you don't have to worry about income tax evasion on your crooked money. You can live lavishly and in the open. Every "made" man has to have a tax cover. He has to "show" money. Take Michael Bolino. The Colombo family invested a Shylock loan in a flourishing baker's business. The baker is still paying off the loan and Mike is put on the books. Once a week he goes to the baker's, puts on a smock, throws a little flour around him to show he gets dirty, so he doesn't feel so bad about collecting his cheque every week to show a legitimate income.

'Now all these businesses make money by feeding off each other. Take the Colombo family. They once lent money to a big catering-hall owner and in return took a piece of his business. Once you own these halls you get the wedding receptions, the photography that goes with the weddings, the wedding favours and gifts, the invitation cards, the limousine hire – ten or fifteen different businesses all stemming out of catering halls.

'The same with the funeral business. One big funeral parlour owner is in trouble so the Colombos and Gambinos help him out and become his partners. Now we're in there we're involved with the casket-makers. The old bronze caskets used to cost $7000 but even the fibreglass ones cost $750. They're sold to the grieving widow at twice the price paid by the funeral parlour. We do our own embalming, we got the florists and whenever there's a big crime family funeral we get the business.'

However legitimate the mob become there is always room for a little old-fashioned extortion. In 1960 Paul Gambino suddenly set up a knife-grinding business. He had no experience – at least not in this kind of knife-grinding – and his employees provided a shoddy service. Yet out of fear dozens of New York butchers switched to his company, deserting their regular knife-grinders who, it turned out, were northern Italians with no Mafia connections. Facing huge losses the legitimate knife-grinders approached Paul Gambino and paid him $177,000 to get out of the business. Added to his knife-grinding profits this smart little shakedown had 'earned' Paul Gambino $500,000 in just three years.

The 1960s also saw an astonishing takeover by the Genovese capo, Johnny Dioguardi, of much of New York's kosher meat and bagel business. Another long-running food scandal was the mass marketing of tons of meat which had been condemned as diseased. Racketeers bought this 'beef' on the pretence that it was heading for mink farms. They then laced it with formaldehyde to prevent it decaying any further and sold it for human consumption. Millions of unsuspecting New Yorkers chomped their way through hamburgers made from the rotten and poisoned carcasses. It later turned out that much of the meat was kangaroo from Australia.[6] In the 1970s the Mafia muscled in on the strategically important field of one of America's biggest industries: energy. Along the entire Appalachian coal field – from New York State all the way to Georgia – organized-crime figures have been buying coal mines. Were their concern to free America from dependence on foreign oil we might be hailing the mob for its patriotism but it is another story of rip-off and spoliation. They bought one of Pennsylvania's biggest coal concerns only to close it down, sell its equipment and go bankrupt, leaving the state with a $10 million obligation to 'backfill' excavations and compensate workers for industrial injuries. In another case a bank lent $35 million against the value of coal in a mine offered as collateral. Later it found out that the mine's reserves were worth only $300,000.

Organized-crime men have also bought mines to beguile greedy investors with partnership schemes. Bursting to get long-term tax breaks, well-heeled Americans have rushed to buy even marginal chunks of the energy business. It may be years before they realize that the mine they now part-own along with scores of other suckers was worked out long ago. Meanwhile the mob has conned ten times more money out of the tax dodgers than it paid to buy the mine.

Organized crime has also moved into the fashionable business of uranium mining. In the 1970s a New York public electricity company lent $76 million to a New Mexico entrepreneur who claimed to have 'discovered' uranium. The electricity company anticipated that its investment would secure enough uranium to guarantee Long Island citizens cheap electricity for decades. No uranium has yet been delivered. All that has come from the $76 million investment is a dead-end highway in New Mexico leading to a flooded hole in the ground. Long Islanders can now look forward to paying more, not less, for their light and heat for the rest of this century.

Sunbelt states like New Mexico, Arizona and Texas are ripe for all kinds of scams and frauds because massive federal funding is available to boost employment and match the region's rapid population growth. But even as it moves in on boom businesses such as oil organized crime does not forsake its old rackets. Mafiosi from New York have taken part in New Mexico's garbage industry, even winning contracts to cart waste away from missile sites. They are infiltrating Indian reservations where the locals can make their own gambling laws overruling those of the state. The Mafia has tried to talk Indians into letting it operate slot machines and racetracks on the reservations, to draw palefaces deprived of legal gambling in their own communities.

The Mafia's deep penetration of America's business community can be seen most clearly in the growth of Medico Industries. This Pennsylvania conglomerate was founded in 1938 by five brothers named Medico. The Pennsylvania Crime Commission has identified three of the brothers as members of the Buffalino crime family. Until his death in 1972 William (Bill) Medico seems to have been the company's driving force so it is significant that in 1957 Russell Buffalino, the local Mafia family's future boss, arrived at the Apalachin summit in a car owned by Bill Medico. James Osticco, another family member, drove there in a second Medico car. The link became even clearer when Osticco said that he worked as Medico Industries' transportation manager.

Further investigations showed that Bill Medico had bootlegged his way through Prohibition and had been arrested for murder. It is unclear whether this background was a drawback or an advantage to Medico Industries but over the years it has grown to embrace companies which make paint, asphalt and electric carts, sell contracting equipment and lease cars. It also owns large property holdings. Medico Industries' greatest break came in 1968 when it won US army contracts to produce tank parts and 600,000 missile warheads for use in Vietnam. The deals were worth at least $8 million. There have been unsubstantiated allegations that the Medicos won the contracts through the intervention of a corrupt US congressman.

Russell Buffalino's chauffeur has testified in the federal court that for twenty years until 1975 he drove the Mafia boss to the Medico plant on Thursdays, Fridays and Saturdays to read the newspapers. The rest of the week Buffalino was doubtless too busy running ten garment firms in Pennsylvania and New York City.

However the money is made organized crime's game remains the same. In Cantalupo's words, 'You get in all the legitimate businesses you can, make it legitimate, but you still have on the side all your illegal businesses still bringing in incomes. And it's more and more money, more legitimate things and more illegal things. It's just a vast, vast empire.'

24

New Scams for Old

So long as pornography was the largely literary pursuit of Bohemian intellectuals sheltering in Paris organized crime took no commercial interest in it. Indeed the older Dons abhorred porn as degenerate and would not traffic in it. They likened it to narcotics but, as with narcotics, when they saw what kind of profits could be made from the market they lost their moral qualms.

Today pornography is the Mafia's biggest growth industry, worth $6 billion a year.

Organized crime has taken over the erogenous zones of most American cities. New York's 42nd Street and Times Square, Chicago's South State and Rush Street areas and Boston's 'Combat Zone' all contain sex shops, peep shows and porno movie houses run by the mob. In Washington the White House is only a hooker's saunter away from 14th Street's vice while on 9th Street, staring the FBI building in the face, are two branches of Doc Johnson's Love Shops, a sex-aids chain which has even reached London's Soho.

The Doc Johnson operation ought to turn the stomach of any FBI man who has probed the porn racket for it is just one element in the huge empire of Reuben Sturman, probably America's richest pornographer. In 1980 Sturman was arrested for his alleged part in a pornography distribution racket that stretched from coast to coast. He was among fifty-eight people charged after a massive two-year-long FBI investigation codenamed Miporn (for 'Miami Porn'). Undercover agents had set up a porn business in Miami enabling them to buy stocks of hard-core video cassettes and magazines wholesale and meet America's top pornsters at trade conventions. On St Valentine's Day 1980 400 FBI agents arrested the fifty-eight pornographers in thirteen cities. It would have been fifty-nine but 66-year-old Mickey Zaffarano realized that FBI agents were coming up to his Times Square office to arrest him and, rushing to destroy the print of a brand-new blue movie, he died from a heart attack. Zaffarano was a capo in the Bonanno family who had made millions from producing and distributing porn from Hollywood to London so his death deprived the FBI of one of its biggest prizes. There was an even bigger disappointment twenty-one months later when one of the FBI undercover men was caught shoplifting. This caused the trial judge to throw out the charges against Sturman and thirty-six other porn merchants. Fortunately twenty-one had already been convicted, including several top mafiosi who, with Sturman, have cut up America's huge porn pie.

Sturman's relationship with the Mafia is indirect. From his Cleveland headquarters he runs Sovereign News, the major distributor of pornography in America's West and Mid-West. He also dominates the eastward flow of porno films and magazines produced in California. This huge empire has made the former used-comics' salesman a multi-millionaire and brought him a delightful home in the lush Cleveland suburb of Shaker Heights. What intrigues law enforcement is how he runs this empire in happy co-existence with the company that controls the huge eastern US market, Star Distributing of New York.

Star's boss and vice-president is Robert Di Bernardo, who New Jersey Police say is a capo in the DeCavalcante crime family. When I met Sam DeCavalcante, the family's boss, in his Florida home he denied any involvement with pornography. But the handsome 'DeeBee' was among those convicted in the Miporn case and jailed for shipping obscene films across state lines. Star sells porn to fifty countries and monopolizes porn distribution in greater New York. One porn man who does business with Star is Al Goldstein. The incorrigible publisher and editor of *Screw Magazine*, Goldstein turns Manhattan cablevision viewers insomniac with his *Midnight Blue* sex romps.

When Goldstein started *Screw* in 1968 legitimate distributors refused to handle it because they rightly feared being arrested for obscenity. The previous year Goldstein had been writing soft-core material for some Star publications which he dubbed 'masturbation magazines'. This connection encouraged him to show *Screw*'s first issed to Di Bernardo hoping he would agree to handle it. He was unlucky. 'He said it was too dirty. He's always seemed to me to be a prude, puritanical, a Nixon supporter. He's asked, why am I attacking the church, the FBI, the police. He said, "Just sell sex." If he's organized crime I've never seen it in terms of guns or violence but not being naive I know there must something outside the normal marketing situation. In any other venture there would be other people bidding for my product but no one has come to take *Screw* away from my present distributor.' Goldstein's distributor in Cleveland is Reuben Sturman.

'DeeBee's a nice man,' says Goldstein. 'He's twice lent me $15,000 when I could not meet a payroll but he has no piece of my company. He makes his money from distribution. He'll go and pick up the little crumbs like *Screw* which big news-dealers won't handle. Now if there is a Mafia – and I don't know concretely that there is – then the Mafia goes in the grey areas where corporate America is afraid to go. When people say, "Is the Mafia exploiting you?" I see all capitalism as predatory. I'm a capitalist. Everyone exploits everyone. As for Di Bernardo, he is a lovely, sweet man and I'm glad to be his friend.'

Goldstein's portrait of Di Bernardo is hard to reconcile with the image he has in law-enforcement circles. They believe that he presides over the porn business for all the eastern crime families and mediates in their territorial disputes. This market has recently proved as violent as any other Mafia fiefdom. In January 1982 in Brooklyn unknown assailants gunned down two porn merchants. The younger man was killed, the other survived. The hit men also killed an innocent woman at whose door the intended victims Joseph Peraino Jun. and his father, a massive man nicknamed 'Joe the Whale' – had sought refuge. The Perainos belonged to a family shoal hooked up with the Colombo crime family. For three years Joe the Whale's brother Anthony and the latter's two sons had been the biggest Mafia success story in Hollywood's mob-riddled history.[1]

Their rise to riches began with a remarkable stroke of luck. In 1971 Louis 'Butchie' Peraino was the part-owner with a former Brooklyn barber named Gerald Damiano of a porno film company. Louis put up $22,000 for a movie Damiano brilliantly titled *Deep Throat*. The now remorseful Linda Lovelace starred in a lewd little screenplay about a girl for whom satisfaction could only come orally because she had been born with her clitoris in her oesophagus. On that initial $22,000 investment *Deep Throat* has now grossed an estimated $100 million worldwide. An astonishing 300,000 video tapes of the film had been sold by the end of 1981. Mafia custom would dictate that at least half *Deep Throat*'s takings must have flowed down the even deeper, indeed bottomless, throat of the Colombo family. The Perainos were soon handling another porn moneyspinner, *The Devil in Miss Jones*.

Louis and his brother Joseph C. Peraino used some of the profits they were allowed to keep for a triumphant assault on Hollywood. From 1973 to 1976 they ran an independent movie company called Bryanston Distributors. Among some twenty feature films Bryanston either financed or distributed were Andy Warhol's *Frankenstein*, *Return of the Dragon* (with Bruce Lee) and the outrageously profitable *Texas Chain-saw Massacre*. Bryanston acquired those three films for less than $1 million and netted some $30 million in two years. By 1975 Louis Peraino was ambitiously hiring some of the industry's most commercial producers. Within two years of its foundation it was by far the most successful independent company in Hollywood where the Perainos, with their quaint Brooklyn accent, were well liked. Yet, as one producer half jokingly told *Los Angeles Times* reporters, when you negotiated with them you did not know whether you were negotiating for your picture or your life.

In 1976 Bryanston suddenly collapsed, owing $750,000 in taxes and millions more to film-makers who had never been paid their share of the profits. The company's accounts were so devious that they accorded the makers of the *Texas Chain-saw Massacre* $5734 for their 35 per cent share of its gross earnings of $25 million. There is a slight chance that Bryanston was in real financial difficulties but there are inevitable suspicions that here was a model mob bust-out. The company had lost money in some production ventures but nowhere near as much as it had made in distribution profits on other movies. What finished Bryanston off was the zeal of a US attorney in Memphis who in 1976 tried the Peraino brothers and their ever-present father Anthony for transporting obscene material (*Deep Throat*) across state lines. Joseph was acquitted but Louis and Anthony were both sentenced to short terms in jail.

While Louis was free on bail appealing against sentence he and brother Joseph were scooped up in the FBI's Miporn sting and charged with interstate shipment of hard-core video cassettes. After the collapse of their Hollywood empire the brothers had returned to their porno careers. Among the 'lewd, lascivious and filthy' videos they were handling in 1979 were the *Confessions of Linda Lovelace* and *Hot and Saucy Pizza Girls.* Louis Peraino was jailed for six years and Butchie for three. Reuben Sturman had no such problems, despite his handling of equally lewd material. When the Miami judge dropped all the charges against him the public were deprived of the chance to learn what it was Sturman had discussed with the likes of Michael Zaffarano and Joe Peraino at a Las Vegas porn convention in January 1978. It is unlikely to have been the artistic virtues of the lewd videos he distributes such as *Jewish American Princess No. 8*, *Mr Footlong No. 3* or *Three in a Tub*.

25

Banks, Wall Street and Three-piece Suits

'Money makes the blind see and the lame walk.' The old Italian proverb ought to be updated with the tag '. . . and the Mafia take over banks'. The time-honoured Mafia habit of hoarding illegal monies in mattresses or in the cellar has been overtaken by an increased respect for the virtues of banking. Or rather a realization that banks can be abused, manipulated and defrauded just like any other business.

In 1965 a 32-year-old Swiss citizen named Sylvain Ferdmann was loading his bags into a car at Miami Airport when he dropped a receipt acknowledging the deposit of $350,000 in a numbered bank account in the International Credit Bank of Geneva. One of the men whose signature attested to the deposit was John Pullman, a Canadian citizen resident in Lausanne. In 1931 Pullman had been jailed for fifteen months for bootlegging. His greater claim to immortality in the Valhalla of organized crime, however, is his fifty-year working friendship with the Mafia's financial brain, Meyer Lansky.[1]

Ferdmann's lost receipt was handed to federal investigators who believed they had stumbled on a five-year-long skimming operation from Las Vegas casinos. Every month 'bagmen' or couriers working for Lansky would pick up satchels full of undeclared casino takings and take them to Miami. The bagmen included Ferdmann, Pullman and even a 'bagwoman', Ida Devine. They were shifting at least $1 million each month. Much of it was distributed among the Mafia crime families of America but a hefty chunk went out of the country, via mob-controlled banks in Miami and the Bahamas, where Pullman, Devine and two other Lansky couriers were listed as directors of the 'Bank of World Commerce'. Much of this money ended up in the International Credit Bank in Geneva.

The ICB was founded in 1959 by a Hungarian refugee named Tibor Rosenbaum. A pious rabbi and a tireless worker for the resettlement of European Jews in Israel, Dr Rosenbaum was also a reckless land speculator. In the 1970s he barely survived a series of scandals which cost Israel tens of millions of dollars that it had deposited with the ICB and sent one of its leading public officials to jail. Lansky and his Mafia friends got their money out just before ICB crashed. Ferdmann's position as one of the bank's proxy directors should have given them advance warning.

The Swiss authorities had been warned by the FBI about both Rosenbaum and his American underworld investors as early as 1967. In a top-secret report written in March 1968 Swiss security police were jumping with alarm at the FBI's investigation into 'the destination of certain Jewish–American funds originating with the American underworld as the profit of either gambling, prostitution or narcotics. There is no doubt that the aforementioned bank is in close contact with certain underworld heads as proven both by American police investigations and by our own.' The secret report listed the transatlantic activities and Swiss trips of Lansky, Ferdmann, Pullman, two other Lansky bagmen and a dozen more notorious American mobsters including Joe Adonis, Lansky's long-time Mafia *compare*.

The ICB affair provided a rare glimpse into the relationship between the clandestine world of Swiss banking and American organized crime. Lansky was shown to be the mastermind laundering tens of millions of Mafia dollars every year. Once he had magicked them into Switzerland they could be re-exported to America and invested in impenetrable corporations fronted by unknown mob lawyers. Thus organized-crime figures have acquired huge pieces of real estate in Florida, New York, California – wherever there are attractive, safe investments. Law enforcement can do little to stop them for usually these purchases go wholly unnoticed.

A curious spin-off from the ICB affair was the revelation of the subsidiary role played by the Miami National Bank, then the sixth biggest bank in Florida but deep in debt to the Teamsters' Central State Pension Fund because of loans arranged by Jimmy Hoffa and Allan Dorfman.[2] Lou Poller, the bank's president, was in contact with Pullman and Joe 'Doc' Stacher, another notorious Lansky sidekick who emigrated to Israel. One of the bank's owners was

Sam Cohen who, as joint owner of the Flamingo casino in Las Vegas, served four months in jail for his part in skimming $30 million of its takings.[3] There can be little doubt that the MNB, now free of all taint, was used in the 1960s as a Mafia laundry.

Lansky devised the basic techniques for washing illegal money through the world's financial system. No doubt today organized crime regularly smuggles far larger sums out of America and back again through Switzerland, the Cayman Islands, the Bahamas, Liechtenstein, London, Hong Kong – any financial centre that swears secrecy and asks no questions. The string of zeros such money movements involve are a long way from the grubbing extortion and Shylocking of the mob on the streets of Brooklyn, Chicago or Philadelphia and go to show how diverse its operations are.

On a more modest scale small banks all over America are prey to organized crime through Mafia-run union locals. Pension and welfare fund deposits can make a bank's books look healthy, allowing it to lend a lot more money, but if those funds are suddenly withdrawn the bank can get into difficulties. In the 1970s the hoodlums who controlled Teamster Local 945 – the union for New Jersey garbage workers – placed $1.3 million in local banks. The banks paid low interest on the deposits to the detriment of the garbage-truckers whose pensions and welfare the union was meant to be protecting. In return the bank gave cheap personal loans to the union's leaders, their relatives and their mob masters. One bank lent nearly $4 million to some of America's top mafiosi including Carmine Galente, then boss of the Bonanno family. Another bank lent over $130,000 to Mafia loansharks. One loanshark got a $2500 loan the day he walked out of jail on forged release papers. The predictable happened. The union funds were soon withdrawn, many loans were never repaid and four banks went bust.

Both in America and Italy the Mafia appears to have played some part in the troubles of the more prestigious Vatican Bank. That story – of intertwining conspiracies involving the papacy's former investment overseer Archbishop Marcinkus, the jailed Sicilian banker Michele Sindona, his friend Banco Ambrosiano chief Roberto Calvi, found hanged under Blackfriars Bridge in London, and the Italian masonic lodge P2 – is still being unravelled.

On Wall Street Mafia fraudsters are easier to spot, but little has been proved about their manipulation of stocks and shares. This is partly because complex 'paper' fraud is the most difficult crime to prove and the least understood by juries. Another problem is that while organized crime may be up to all sorts of stock exchange scams, so are scores of 'legitimate' WASP brokers. Nevertheless it is known that in the 1960s one top mafioso, who specialized in robbing banks, infiltrated his son into Wall Street's second biggest brokerage firm. By 1976 the son had concocted a multi-million-dollar securities fraud.[4]

Other Mafia offspring have been employed by firms of New York brokers to handle the investments of Mafia-controlled unions. Some racketeers' relatives have formed their own brokerage firms and bought seats on New York's Stock Exchange. At this point they can make big money by 'churning' a union's investments: repeatedly selling its stocks and shares and buying others so they can claim their legal percentage charges each time. They thus skim millions from the fund to the detriment of the union's working members and without committing an obvious crime. The rewards are then split up among the crime family.

The shadowy genius of Meyer Lansky may have been behind the activities of Yiddy Bloom, one of his long-time side-kicks who pleaded guilty in 1978 to floating the stock of the Magic Marker Corporation up from $6.50 a share to $30 during a ten-month period in 1971–7. Magic Marker made a well-known brand of pen. A Philadelphia-based conspiracy (including Magic Marker's then president) forced up the company's value by buying its stock in hundreds of names through accounts all over America, creating the appearance of genuine, widespread demand. The conspiracy was cemented with high sales-commission payments, loans and bribes including free vacations in Florida. When the price looked as if it was about to peak the conspirators sold their stock to gullible investors who watched helplessly as the stock they had bought at $30 a share tumbled to $7 in four months. These luckless citizens – many of them retired – lost millions of dollars. Yet few of the twenty conspirators later convicted suffered anything more than probation and a modest fine. Only Yiddy Bloom and one other man went to jail (for a year less good behaviour) which must have signalled to the mob that frauds are worth it, even if you get caught.

Such scams require too much organization for the average mafioso, however, even the mighty Carmine Lombardozzi. Now ranked by the New York Police as a capo in the Gambino family he has been known as 'the King of Wall Street' for twenty years. Also known as 'the Doctor', Lombardozzi does not suffer the headaches of stock manipulation. One convicted trafficker in stolen stocks and bonds, Ed 'the Paperhanger' Wuensche, told the Senate rackets committee in 1971 that Lombardozzi was the biggest man in a business involving 500 'fencers' (handlers of stolen securities) across America. 'Carmine had more young Wall Street clerks under his thumb who were trapped either because of indebtedness, gambling or otherwise, and if he said, "Go get me XYZ" [a certain stock] they darn well went in and got it because they were afraid of losing their lives." Such stolen stock certificates (and the thieves have included stockbrokers as well as their clerks) are too risky to sell on the open market but mobsters deposit them with banks as collateral for loans. They can then default on the loan without risking their own assets.

In 1982 the rich towns of Broward County north of Miami, with their plush restaurants and department stores, fell victim to a plague of credit card frauds. Counterfeit cards were produced by the thousand by a small team of mafiosi who had become the third largest credit card manufacturers in the New York area after Citibank and Chase Manhattan.

Broward County detectives went to see US postal investigators in New York and found out that the scam was headed by Paul Vario, a capo in the Lucchese family with a criminal record mammoth even by Mafia standards. The counterfeit gang used to go through the garbage of leading stores to find discarded carbon copies of genuine credit card transactions. On these slips, of course, were the names and numbers of each cardholder. The counterfeiters would emboss these real details on 'virgin' white cards on to which they would press the appropriate card logo. The entire process was achieved with astonishing ease and speed on silk-screen printing presses, laminating machines and hot-striping machines identical to those on which Visa, Mastercard and

American Express cards are made. The Mafia probably stole the machines but they could have bought them legally for $100,000 and made that money back in a week.

Mafia couriers would then fly into Florida with cases full of the counterfeit cards which they distributed to scores of criminals. Each card could be used for weeks before the person whose details had been counterfeited would be sent his statement and realize something was wrong. In that time the counterfeit cardholder would spend right up to the credit limit. Blessed indeed was he who had a counterfeit American Express card on which there was no limit.

Broward County is riddled with 'made' men and associates of all the northern crime families. Some winter in Florida, some reside there permanently. They have built an entire Mafia business community almost as pervasive as in parts of Italian Brooklyn. These people now used the counterfeit cards to pay for meals in their own restaurants, to buy liquor from their own liquor stores and rent cars from mob-controlled car-hire companies. They also sold cards to freelance thieves but these included undercover detectives who discovered that many store-owners were no better than their crooked customers. When the undercover men told storekeepers the cards were counterfeit some merchants would run off a few sales slips for their own use. A shoe-shop owner, for instance, used the slips to 'buy' some of his own stock. He would pocket the proceeds of the 'sale' but still have the shoes to sell again.

The credit card racket in Broward County was broken up but the same fraud was being operated all over America at the same time. Just a few sheets of counterfeit cards can yield millions of dollars for organized crime, losses which are borne by the companies issuing genuine cards, their insurers, and by the public in increased card charges. Whatever the advances in credit card security – fingerprint checks, hidden coding, holograms and more complex designs – the Mafia will soon crack them. They already have their people inside credit card companies and banks duplicating lists of cardholders and spilling the latest security beans. In the land of plastic money they might as well have their own mint.

Organized crime may also be involved in computer crime but no major case has yet been proved. In Silicone Valley near San

Francisco organized crime has got no further than stealing millions of silicone chips. The robbers have no clear link with the Mafia and appear to be more interested in sales to the Russians. Major banking and commercial fraud perpetrated with the aid of computers seems to be restricted at present to college graduates and high-school dropouts. When such folk fall into the clutches of Mafia loansharks God help the world's banking system!

'All the mob is doing is changing,' says former undercover cop Pete Donohue. 'Now they're in three-piece suits. They've taken the kids out of the traditional family and they've put them through the finest colleges. They've made them lawyers, accountants, business types and everything but they are still controlling the scenario. They've gone legitimate but they don't have the same competition as the legitimate businessman. They still have the edge.'

26

The Political Fix

The stretch of northern New Jersey across the Hudson River from New York has a grim reputation. It is grim to look at and grim to live in yet it is home for 4 million people. Its air is polluted by heavy industry and the fumes of millions of vehicles on its dense network of highways. Its rivers have been killed by poisonous chemicals dumped by big business. The latest mortality statistics have won it the title of America's 'cancer corridor'. But over the last forty years a worse cancer has destroyed some of its biggest cities: political corruption.

The mob makes so much money from both legal and illegal business that it can buy up the political hierarchies of entire cities and counties. In some New Jersey communities the corruption is as bad today as it was in Becker's New York or Capone's Chicago. And, as State Police Colonel Justin Dintino says, 'When organized crime controls the local political structure it can make even more money because it can operate openly. The politicians will intercede if you face arrest for gambling, loansharking, prostitution, whatever. Since the politicians control the police department you become immune from arrest.'

Often the politicians are greedier than the mobsters. In the 1960s none was greedier than Hugh Addonizio, the portly, bald mayor of Newark, the largest city in New Jersey. A contractor whom Addonizio was extorting once asked him why he had quit Washington after seven terms as a US congressman. 'Simple,' he replied, 'there's no money in Washington but you can make a million bucks as mayor of Newark.'

Evidence of Addonizio's graft emerged after the 1967 riots when Newark's black population took to the streets for four days in an ill-articulated protest about the city's rampant corruption. As a result, for the first time in recent history a major American city was in flames. Twenty-six people were killed, 1000 were injured and another 1000 arrested. Damage to property was put at $10 million. A subsequent commission of inquiry found 'a widespread feeling that Newark's government is corrupt'. The commission's investigators were repeatedly told that there was 'a price on everything at City Hall'.

Newark's blacks felt shut out of legitimate careers because white organized crime was running City Hall. But black criminals felt equally frustrated because the Mafia also controlled the city's crime. These two furies combined to make civil disorder, verging on revolution, inevitable.

A grand jury, empanelled to investigate these allegations, was told of the direct relationship between the mayor and the Mafia. Much of the evidence came from an engineer named Paul Rigo who, despite threats to his life, explained how the mob and public officials bled contractors and citizens of thousands of dollars. In his diary Rigo had encoded scores of payoffs he had made in his role as intermediary for a racket embracing almost all of Newark's top officials. Businessmen could only win public-works contracts by paying 10 per cent of their value to Newark officials through the mob. Rigo testified that in 1964 Newark's director of public works had told him, 'I am going to take you to the man who really runs this town.' It turned out to be a leading Genovese family mafioso, 'Tony Boy' Boiardo. When Rigo protested about a demand for 10 per cent of the value of a sewer contract Boiardo said, 'There is a lot of mouths to feed in City Hall. You pay me the 10 per cent. I take care of the mayor. I take care of the council. I take care of anybody that has to be taken care of down there. . . . Everybody in Newark pays 10 per cent or they don't work in Newark.'

Rigo duly paid $30,000 to the mob on the $300,000 sewer contract but when the grand jury started its investigations Addonizio became its prime target. The mayor now had to avoid direct contact with Boiardo but he still wanted his payoffs. Henceforth Rigo was ordered to act as Boiardo's bagman, delivering the payoffs to Addonizio and other officials on behalf of all the city's contractors. In 1970 the testimony of Rigo and many other witnesses, with an avalanche of supporting paperwork garnered by US Attorney Fred Lacey and his assistant Herbert Stern, helped jail Addonizio for ten years on extortion charges.

By then two top New Jersey mobsters had been convicted of other crimes: Sam DeCavalcante, head of New Jersey's only homegrown Mafia family, and Angelo 'Gyp' DeCarlo, a Genovese capo. In both their trials over-zealous defence counsels demanded the release of government evidence which would not otherwise have been disclosed. The evidence turned out to be 3200 pages of unauthorized FBI wire-taps and bugs in transcript form. The DeCavalcante and DeCarlo tapes showed the appalling extent of corruption in New Jersey. The mafiosi had close links with police, mayors, even US Congressman Cornelius Gallagher and Senator Harrison Williams, both of whom were later convicted and jailed for federal crimes.

The DeCarlo tapes also revealed how the Mafia had secured Addonizio's election as mayor in 1962. He was the Mafia's nominee but the plan was upset when another Italian announced he also wanted to run for mayor, which would have split the Italian vote. The tapes disclosed DeCarlo's frantic negotiations to eliminate either horse. He was heard telling Addonizio's challenger, 'I don't care if it's you or Hughie as long as it's an Italian.' The problem was solved when the mob levied $5000 from Newark's illegal bookmakers as a bribe to make Addonizio's rival withdraw.

In June 1970 Addonizio was defeated by a black candidate, Kenneth Gibson, who thus became the first black mayor in the north-east states. He promptly fired the police chief who, according to the DeCarlo tapes, was also a mob nominee. Mayor Gibson found the city treasury empty, the blacks bitter and the whites in flight. He remains in office today, having himself been acquitted on charges of corruption, but Newark has not yet recovered from the Addonizio years when the Mafia had a licence to loot and pillage. As Lieutenant Freddie Martens of the New Jersey State Police explained. 'Newark is a textbook example of what happens when organized crime corrupts a political administration. Until the 1950s this was one of the major industrial centres of the north-east United States. But the corruption and the consequent riots made it too expensive to do business. The economic base of the city has been destroyed and Newark is left struggling for its survival.'

Paddy Carr is a detective with the Essex County Prosecutor's narcotics squad. Born and raised in Newark he has seen it decline in twenty-five years from a thriving business community with plenty of jobs to a dying city. 'It's a total slum. Everyone has run away to the suburbs and now they're moving their businesses out too, first big employers and then small. Newark's streets have turned into a jungle. At five o'clock not even the downtown shopping areas are where any man would want to take his wife.

'Organized crime is behind the whole thing. People say they ought to run the government because they are the only ones who make any money but they only take from a community. They give nothing at all. When they've done corrupting the city they're in they just move to somewhere more lucrative.

Now more than 60 per cent of the city's population is black or Hispanic but even though Newark has a black mayor the blacks still feel alienated. 'The people distrust the police and they distrust City Hall,' says Paddy Carr, 'so they end up running their own street justice. They don't report crimes. Many times muggings happen right in front of them and they won't say anything. That comes from seeing generations of people with power using it for their own gain.'

Today Italian-American organized crime is no longer running Newark but it still bleeds the community through its share of the city's multi-ethnic narcotics' market. The total collapse of Newark's economic and social life has left it a dead-end city where nothing can be revived. In Paddy Carr's words, 'We've lost the war on drugs.' [1]

From 1969 until the mid-1970s the US attorney's office in Newark under Lacey and Stern successfully prosecuted scores of corrupt local politicians and broke the power of the Democratic Party machines which ran Essex, Hudson, Union and Bergen Counties only for themselves and organized crime. Today the efforts of both federal and state police have made New Jersey rather cleaner than it used to be. Colonel Dintino claims, 'We've cut the umbilical cord between organized crime and political corruption.' But the Mafia never gives up. Its main aim in corrupting politicians is to ensure its rackets go on undisturbed by the police. When politicians turn out to be incorruptible the mob reverts to corrupting the police directly.

Joe Delaney is police chief of Paramus, New Jersey, a dormitory town of 150,000 citizens. Delaney affectionately sums up Paramus by joking that its name is the Red Indian word for 'shopping mall'. A proud Irish-American, sandy-haired, slim and resplendent in his much-emblazoned uniform, Delaney became a national hero in 1983 when he refused to apologize to the Soviet Union over the arrest of a diplomat's wife for shoplifting. In the 1970s Delaney deserved many more Brownie points for his work against America's biggest internal enemy. He played the part of a deeply corrupt detective on the Mafia's payroll.

In 1974 Joe was a lieutenant in the Paramus force and the chief of a special narcotics squad for all Bergen County, an area with 900,000 inhabitants. In three months the squad made 180 busts and seized large quantities of barbiturates, methadone and heroin. Delaney's successes brought him to the attention of a low-level mafioso named 'Bugsy' La Salle who told him he could become a rich man if he could get drugs and gambling charges dropped against a local bookmaker. Delaney informed the county prosecutor who told him to play along and see who they could pick up for bribery. Joe was paid $2000 and told the bookmaker he was in the clear.

In mob circles La Salle bragged of the fix and catapulted Delaney into the affections of the New Jersey chapter of the Gambino family. He was embraced by its ageing don, Anthony Carminati ('Tony C') and by Butch Miceli who, say the New Jersey Police, had been a professional killer and was now Carminati's right-hand man. Delaney's entrée was made easier when a Gambino soldier named Vincent 'Waxy' Toronto told his bosses he had been in the army with Joe and had played baseball with him back in Brooklyn. Toronto had simply made these stories up to look big in the eyes of his masters.

By now, wired for sound and recording all his dealings with his friendly neighbourhood mobsters, Delaney fixed whatever cases they wanted dropped. In quick succession he appeared to crush charges brought over bad cheques, cocaine, burglaries and gambling. In return he received a total of $40,000. In fact all these cases were being shelved to build up his credibility. His paymasters became convinced that as president of all New Jersey's narcotics officers he could fix police and prosecutors throughout the state. He impressed them even more when he gave prior warning of a gambling raid in another state. He appeared so powerful and so corrupt that the Mafia took him on a tour of prospective illegal gambling premises and offered him $400,000 a year for protection. Naturally he feigned interest but all the time he was wearing a belt full of radio microphones, transmitting his conversations to a nearby office block known as 'the Plant' and to unmarked police cars a few streets away.

In March 1975 Joe went visiting Butch Miceli at his neat, swimming-pooled, suburban home. Although the detective was wired for sound 'Butchie was smart. He had six televisions in his house and every time I walked in he would put on a TV. I thought he was just being cautious, that he didn't want anyone to hear in case I was wired, but he must have noticed that when I had been to see him previously this TV had gone a little out of whack. It seems that the frequency of my radio mike was very close to the frequency of Channel 7. So this night I go in to do a $30,000 deal but he doesn't talk anything about the deal. He brings me into the kitchen, turns on the television, goes right to Channel 7. It starts to waver so he says, "There's something wrong with the set, let's go into the den." In the den the same thing happens, so he says, "Let's go into the living room." The same thing. Then he calls upstairs to some guy, "Put on Channel 7." The same thing.

'Now I *know* something is wrong and I'm starting to sweat. I figure this guy knows I am wired. I was afraid the next thing would be that my voice would come out of the TV. He walks out of the room and I'm certain he's going to come back with a baseball bat and hit me over the head and that's the end of the case. I had a gun on me and I almost had it out when he came back in. So I said, "Well, maybe there's a big antenna round here, you've got a ham radio operator in the neighbourhood, maybe that's your problem." And he kept looking at me with a cocked eye, thinking something else naturally. But because I was so close to his boss Carminati he wasn't going to risk frisking me or shaking me down. But nor was he going to do the deal. So no deal and out the door I go.

'When I got back to the Plant I found that I had sweated so much I had burned my chest. The people listening in said I was very calm but I had been scared skinny. I thought: for sure I am dead. They say this guy had killed forty-two people. I said, "Let's end this case. No way am I going back in there. This guy knows I'm wired."

'Then a guy from the state police comes up within the hour and built a little black box that was identical to Channel 7. He drove around the neighbourhood that night knocking out every TV set on Channel 7. Fortunately only three blocks away there's a ham radio operator with a 60-foot antenna. He had to take down his antenna, TV repair men made a bundle and Butchie accepted me again.

'These guys think that everyone can be bought for a price. They'll pay whatever price that is. Here was I taking home $22,000 a year and they were offering me $400,000 and I knew from Miceli that I wasn't the only one. I could see how some policemen go the other way. But talking to Butchie and Tony C. I realized they owned politicians and judges too: "They're good people," they'd say, "They're *our* people", meaning the Mafia had bought and controlled them. This gave them tremendous influence here in Bergen and in many other counties.'

In May 1975 Delaney's undercover role came to an end when twenty mobsters were arrested including Miceli, Carminati and leading members of the Genovese family for whom Joe had also appeared to fix cases. 'I didn't feel good,' Delaney recalls. 'Usually when you make a big case there's exhilaration, euphoria, but I had become very close to these people and I knew they probably wouldn't hesitate to kill anybody, including a cop. After the arrests my wife and children were taken to a safe place and I was shifted from hotel to hotel but we made sure these people knew there were thousands of hours of tapes and eighty-two state police officers involved so there was no point in killing me. I told the prosecutor I wanted to be home, so eventually I came out of hiding.'

All the mobsters were convicted but the outcome of the investigation was to dismay Delaney. After four years' preparation and 2000 hours of tape-recordings none of them served more than two years in jail. 'When these organized-crime figures go on trial they all show up in wheelchairs or on crutches. Suddenly they have bad hearts or livers and are about to die. Of course after the case they're all very healthy again. They must go to Lourdes and get cured. Even Butchie Miceli walked away, without his crutches. This guy had multiple sclerosis. Found a cure the minute they said, "Probation!" Great cure.'

Delaney feared that once again mobsters had escaped lightly because of the intimate relationship between organized crime and politics. Without the judiciary in this case being in any way corrupt the American legal system has developed reflex mechanisms for rich crooks with smart lawyers to talk their way out of jail before their racket empires slip out of their hands.

In the 1980s even more New Jersey politicians have been convicted of conspiring with the mob to extort money over contracts to build old folks' homes, apartment blocks, high schools, shopping malls and medical centres. The cost of the payoffs was simply added to the cost of these projects so the public, as usual, paid in the end. A state senator has been convicted of labour racketeering in conjunction with Teamster Locals 560 and 945 (both Mafia-dominated),[2] while one small-town mayor was found guilty of evading tax on the proceeds of two go-go bars he owned with a mobster. Another mayor has been accused of protecting illegal gambling and handing some of his take to a loanshark to lend at extortionate rates on the streets. Even the president of New Jersey's Republican Bar (the party's chief legal spokesman) has been convicted of bribing a state trooper to get charges dropped against a top mobster's son. The good news from New Jersey is that the state police are going after crooked politicians and putting them in jail. Other states are probably just as corrupt but they leave their politicians alone.

When Joe Delaney was playing the role of the corrupt cop leading members of the Gambino and Genovese families told him they were pouring huge sums into politicians' pockets so they would vote in legalized gambling in Atlantic City. Delaney asked them, 'Why would you want to spend money on legalized gambling? You guys have already got illegal gambling.'

Tony Carminati responded, 'Hey, if they pass it, we got the legal and we got the illegal!'

Within ten years Carminati's words came true. In March 1984 the FBI charged Mayor Michael Matthews of Atlantic City with extortion and revealed he had confessed to selling his office to organized crime. As mayor of the only place in America outside

Nevada where casino gambling is legal Matthews was a certain target for the Mafia but what shocked even New Jersey's cynical citizens was the eagerness with which the Prosecution says he succumbed. It claims that in December 1981, while he was preparing to run for election, Matthews accepted $125,000 from an official of Local 54 of the Hotel, Restaurant and Bartenders' Union. The official was Frank Lentino who handed the money over on behalf of the Philadelphia crime family led by Nicky Scarfo. In return Matthews agreed to push through any mob business demanded by the Scarfo fraternity.[3] The crime family then arranged for Matthews to receive other large contributions. When the election took place in May 1982 Matthews' resources were so much greater than his black opponent's that he could not fail to win. Even so there had to be a runoff for which the Scarfo organization allegedly gave him a further $25,000.

Matthews now appears to have favoured mob-backed companies seeking public contracts or inside information on land deals. Sadly for the conspirators the Philadelphia family's front man, Lentino, had been taken in by an FBI agent calling himself Bannister who claimed to represent a major Washington investment group keen to buy city-owned land on which to build a casino. Over two years Bannister wormed his way into Lentino's confidence and madc 300 tape-recordings of Lentino and Matthews conspiring over payoffs.

The tapes reveal that with a member of Scarfo's mob they devised a scheme which would give each of them 1 per cent in the new casino, valued at $200,000 a head. All Matthews had to do was make sure Bannister's group got the land. In November 1983 Bannister paid $10,000 to Matthews, which he had demanded to speed the sale, and a further $15,000 to Lentino to spread around the crime family. The sale never went through because in December 1983 the FBI revealed its hand to Matthews. He allegedly confessed his role and agreed to go wired-up into meetings with Phillip Leonetti, Nicky Scarfo's nephew and his right-hand man in Atlantic City. But Matthews, fearing for his life, changed his mind. The FBI showed him no mercy. They raided his office and charged him with extortion and conspiracy. The only man who should now fear a mob rubout more than Matthews is Frank Lentino who, according to Mafia custom, is due for extermination for bringing Bannister into their inner circle.

Organized crime does not stop at corrupting local politicians. It also has friends on the national scene. Congressman Cornelius Gallagher, who represented Hudson County in Washington for many years until he was jailed for tax evasion, was no mere machine politician. In 1963 President Johnson considered him as his vice-presidential running mate. Tall, handsome, a foreign affairs expert with a fine civil liberties record, Gallagher appeared to be the kind of East Coast Catholic Johnson needed to recapture the lustre of the Kennedy years. In the end Johnson chose Hubert Humphrey so Hudson County's mob overlord, 'Bayonne Joe' Zicarelli, never did have a friend only an assassin's bullet away from the presidency.

But other Mafiosi have had influence in the White House. Usually they shelter behind union leaders in their control like Teamster president Frank Fitzsimmons who was courted by President Reagan. Sometimes they are union leaders themselves like Anthony Scotto, who rose to hold the third most important position in the Longshoremen's union. Scotto was embraced by President Jimmy Carter when he went to New York to win over the city's Democratic leaders. No one seems to have told the president that his Justice Department had named Scotto as a 'made' member of the Gambino family as far back as 1969.[4]

The tongue-tied attitude which American political leaders often display towards organized crime is caused by fear not of physical reprisal but of an electoral backlash. They are afraid that assailing the Mafia in public could alienate millions of Italian voters. The man who made that fear real was himself a Mafia boss: Joe Colombo, creator of the Italian-American Civil Rights League.

Joey Cantalupo was working with Colombo when he dreamed up the League. 'In the late 1960s we were forever being harassed by the FBI. Outside my father's real estate office, where Joe Colombo and I worked, the FBI were always watching you, taking your pictures, following you everywhere. This made it hard for Colombo to conduct his illegal business because all his mobster friends did not want their pictures taken. There came a point where Joe Colombo Jun. got picked up for melting down silver coins, so Joe Snr. said. "This harassment has to end. I am going to form the Italian-American Civil Rights League', and he started it right there in Cantalupo Realty.'

Colombo won the support of many of New York's 1.6 million mostly working-class Italian-American people. Few had any love of organized crime but they fully supported Colombo's brash attacks on the WASP establishment: 'The president is knocking us down, the attorney-general hates our guts. They're prejudiced against Italian-Americans.' Eighty years after the New Orleans massacre it looked as if generations of pent-up anger against the 'dago-wop-guinea-greaseball' style of abuse could be harnessed by this demagogue into a political force as powerful as the anti-defamation organizations of American Jews. According to the league's chant, the Italians were now 'Numero Uno'.

With his star quality Colombo became a frequent guest on TV talkshows. At the time *New York Magazine*'s organized-crime expert, Nicholas Pileggi wrote that Colombo was 'repeating in 20th-century New York what the Honoured Society has been pulling in Sicily since the 17th century. He has managed to convince thousands of honest men and women that whoever defames the Honoured Society also defames them.'

According to Cantalupo, himself a captain in the league, the Mafia boss approached all the crime families saying, 'We're going to make a stand against the FBI.' He then signed up all the top people who owed him favours: politicians, lawyers, judges. Soon 50,000 people had joined at $10 per head a year. All the time he was mouthing the cause of Italian-Americans' civil rights, however, he was stealing their contributions in what was just another Mafia fraud.

Colombo made trouble for the FBI as Cantalupo recalls. 'We started to picket FBI headquarters in New York: 10,000 people walking around the building all night long. Now *we* were harassing *them*.' For a while Colombo had the G-men on the run. In July 1970 Attorney-General John Mitchell gave in to the league's pressure by ordering the FBI not to use the words 'Mafia' and 'Cosa Nostra' in its press releases. Although Mitchell himself would soon be disgraced and jailed over Watergate neither the FBI nor the Justice Department has ever again used the term Mafia.

The league also brought Hollywood to heel in 1971 when it tiraded against *The Godfather*, then still in production. The movie got into serious trouble as soon as league leaders branded it defamatory of Italian-Americans. Producer Al Ruddy recently told *Los Angeles Times* reporters, 'There were no overt threats but I couldn't get locations. So I called Joe Colombo and I told him I wanted to sit down and talk to him about it and he said, fine.' To overcome his problems Ruddy appeared at a league press conference to announce that, due to its representations, he was removing all references in the script to 'the Mafia' or 'La Cosa Nostra'. Ruddy says, 'The league helped me in one enormous sense only, that suddenly any real resistance to the film faded.' League leaders then found suitable homes to film in but Ruddy denies they influenced the casting.[5]

Colombo's greatest stunt was the annual Unity Day rally at Columbus Circle. In 1970 Italian shopping streets and markets closed down as 100,000 people gathered in Manhattan around the statue of the only Italian to whom Colombo would by then have deferred. Cantalupo recalls 'dozens of politicians on the podium alongside Joe saying, "What a wonderful thing this is. We have to rid the Italian people of this stigma of the Mafia. Why should every Italian be crucified just because of some organized crime?' But what was really in those politicians' minds were the votes of all the people attending the rally.

'Buses would come in from Rhode Island, planeloads from Florida. We had shows at Madison Square Garden and Felt Forum. Frank Sinatra and all the Italian singers would come and perform for this man.' Leading non-Italian politicians also wanted to be seen supporting the league. Governor Nelson Rockefeller beamed for photographers as he became an honorary member of the league and shook the hand of Colombo's son Anthony. On his lapel the governor sported a badge that said it all: 'Italian POWER'.

'Unfortunately Colombo let the power go to his head,' says Cantalupo. 'He saw all these people out there looking at him, like he was a Caesar, and he just loved it. But it was bringing heat, not only on the Colombo family but on all the other crime families. So Carl Gambino and Joe Colombo and my father went to a meeting where Joe was asked to step down, get out of the picture, because we didn't need the heat. "Put someone else in as head of the league – a politician, a judge, an entertainer."

' "No," says Joe, "I want this. This is *my* baby." '

One of Colombo's reasons for hanging on was that the league was coining so much money. 'Joe was obsessed with the fact, at $10 a head the subscriptions were bringing in millions of dollars. I have no doubt there was skimming. When you're dealing with thousands of memberships it's simple to skim money off the top, to forget about $1000 worth of subscriptions and go and spend it.'

The other Mafia bosses were jealous of his new source of wealth. They saw him opening up league offices beyond his own territory in their own domains. Most of all they were vexed by the 'heat', the massive publicity he was attracting. Meanwhile the FBI was planning its revenge, stepping up its undercover operations, and the IRS was ready to nail him for evading tax on the league's income. Sooner or later Colombo would also have to deal with the growing strength of the rebels in his own crime family, led by 'Crazy' Joe Gallo.

Colombo had many enemies when he arrived at the league's Unity Day rally at Columbus Circle on 28 June 1971. As he stood on the podium preparing to make his speech a young black claiming to be a photographer forced his way to the front and shot Colombo three times in the head. The band played on as the gunman, James Johnson, was himself promptly killed by a Colombo supporter. Women screamed and men prayed as Joe was driven off in an ambulance to Roosevelt Hospital where supporters mounted a candlelit vigil. The mighty Don Carlo Gambino came to pay his respects. Mob watchers speculate that Johnson was put up to the job either by other crime family bosses (notably Gambino), or by Joe Gallo or even by the FBI, but nothing was ever proved. Johnson may have been just another crazed loner. As for poor Joe Colombo, he never recovered. He lingered on paralysed and brain-damaged for seven years until he died in 1978. By then his league was little more than an outrageous memory.

Until the shooting Joe Colombo had wielded huge, quasi-legitimate power. He could do this only because generations of mafiosi have invested their criminal wealth in outwardly legitimate enterprises and laundered themselves in the process. Under cover of respectability they have befriended scores of politicians, judges and other public figures. In many American communities mobsters and politicians tend to share the same views on local issues. In

1981 Senator Cannon of Nevada introduced a bill in Washington to exempt gambling profits from taxes. Cannon's perception of the best interest of his state happened to coincide with the best interests of the Mafia which has exempted itself from gambling taxes for decades.[6]

One of the current US senators for Nevada is Paul Laxalt, a former state governor. Laxalt is one of President Reagan's closest advisers whom Reagan wanted as his vice-presidential running mate until some of the sources of his campaign funds became known. In 1980 he took contributions from Frank Rosenthal, the Chicago mob's front man in Las Vegas, from Allen Glick, and from Moe Dalitz, the notorious organized-crime figure who happens to be one of Laxalt's old friends. To questions about these and other unsavoury donors Laxalt responds that in his home state, 'We do up front and out in the open what a lot of other states do in the back room under clandestine conditions.' Laxalt, himself a former casino owner, has openly espoused causes of which organized crime would approve. He has condemned what he calls 'overly aggressive' federal investigators in Nevada and tried to curb the FBI, the IRS and the federal strike force in their work against mobsters and racketeers in Las Vegas.[7]

In 1971 Laxalt met Allen Dorfman, the Mafia's front man who handed out Teamster Pension Fund loans to Las Vegas. Laxalt subsequently wrote to President Nixon urging him to free Jimmy Hoffa from jail. According to the *Wall Street Journal* Laxalt's letter said that he had 'worked closely' with 'Al Dorfman' who was not 'the criminal type so often depicted by the national press'. In 1983 after a spell in jail for taking kick-backs and another conviction in the Senator Cannon case, Dorfman's days in organized crime came to a sudden and predictable end.[8]

Even a member of Reagan's Cabinet has been subjected to a mass of allegations about his organized-crime connections. Until he was named as secretary of labor Ray Donovan was unknown, but he had earned Reagan's affection as chairman of his 1980 presidential campaign in New Jersey and by raising $600,000 in election funds. At the time Donovan was a partner in Schiavone, one of America's fastest-growing construction companies, specializing in tunnelling contracts for the New York subway.

As Ray Donovan faced Senate nomination hearings in January 1981 evidence surfaced that Schiavone had given a no-show job to the chauffeur of a union boss in return for labour peace. Since Donovan was in charge of Schiavone's labour relations he had overall responsibility for such a deal. He told the senators he did not like paying the 'ghost' employee but his staff had told him that a collective bargaining agreement stipulated that a 'working Teamster foreman' had to be paid, whether or not there was work for him to do and whether or not he showed up on site.

The Teamster boss in question, Harry Gross, was described in the Senate as a 'notorious shakedown artist and extortionist'. It was clear that if his chauffeur had not got the no-show job Schiavone's $400 million Manhattan tunnel project would have been subject to strikes, pickets and sabotage. Donovan recalled the time when Gross had threatened his life saying, 'My friend, keep your headlights on high beam when you get in your driveway at night.' Yet he was unrepentant about the no-show job before the senators: 'If you call that extortion I think it is totally incorrect. We did not buy labour peace. . . . We have never been extorted. We are not extortable.'

Donovan acquitted himself before the Senate and became Reagan's secretary of labor, but dozens of other allegations were still being investigated by a special prosecutor two years later. Teamster union racketeer 'Little Ralphie' Picardo claimed he had often collected payoffs from Schiavone in return for labour peace. Another convicted mobster holding a job in the Blasters' Union said that Donovan had been present in a restaurant when a similar payoff was made. When the allegation became public a Schiavone executive had the nerve to call the restaurant and ask for its records to be destroyed.

All the stories indicated that no-show jobs for mob minions were the rule on Schiavone jobs rather than the exception. None of the allegations against Donovan were substantiated and the entire investigation was shelved. But it was proved that Schiavone had given a lot of work to a subcontractor named William Masselli who was a 'made' member of the Genovese family. Donovan recalls meeting Masselli but says he had no idea he was in the Mafia. Schiavone gave Masselli's company large loans to buy construction equipment. In return Masselli lavished hospitality on leading Schiavone executives. The mobster has since been jailed for hijacking meat trucks and for trafficking in cocaine. His son Nat was murdered by mobsters not long after he had given evidence to the special prosecutor investigating the Donovan allegations.

Ray Donovan has kept his Cabinet post. Indeed he has stayed in office longer than most of Reagan's original choices. Of all the allegations on which he has been grilled by Senate, Press and special prosecutor Donovan told *Crime Inc.* they just go to show that 'Where there's smoke, there's smoke.'

The smoke around Donovan, Laxalt and, most of all, Frank Sinatra signals that in the United States of America the Mafia is rarely more than two steps away from the White House. Even though there is no evidence that these men would abuse their access to President Reagan on behalf of any mobsters they may have known, the fear must be that people in such positions might do so in the future.

27

Can the Mafia Survive?

At midday on 11 July 1979 a van emblazoned with the words 'Happy Time Complete Party Supply' drew into the Dadeland Shopping Center south-west of Miami City, Florida. The van was stalking a leading Colombian drug-trafficker named German Jimenez Pannesso and his accomplice, Juan Hernandez. The pair had just walked into the Crown Liquor Store when two men climbed out of the van, came in the store behind them and opened fire with .45 calibre MAC-10 machine-guns. Pannesso and Hernandez died instantly. Their bodies were so perforated that a policeman said they looked like Swiss cheese. The killers ran out of the store, sprayed mesmerized bystanders with more fire, jumped into the van and drove off. Dumped nearby, the van contained an armoury of automatic weapons. It had been reinforced with enough steel plating to withstand a siege, portholes had been cut in the bodywork and a rack of bulletproof vests installed for extra protection if the rear door had to be opened in a shoot-out. Three men who had been inside were later identified by their fingerprints but no one was charged with these murders.

The Happy Time Party van is now a 'black museum' piece in the care of Dade County Public Safety Department. On 18 March 1983 *Crime Inc.*'s camera team were filming this war wagon when they were called to Miami's south-west outskirts. As they arrived police frogmen were pulling a heavy blanketed object out of a canal. On the bank detectives unwrapped the shroud. Out tumbled a grotesque, bloated corpse: male, handcuffed at the wrists and chained at the ankles. The mouth had been sealed with masking tape and there was one gunshot wound in the head. Anywhere else in America this murder would probably have been attributed to the Mafia but in south Florida the police knew instantly that this was just another statistic in the incessant carnage inflicted by Hispanic drug merchants on each other. They later discovered that the dead man was

Rodriguez Seferino, a 38-year-old Cuban involved in the illegal manufacture of quaaludes. This murder too is unsolved.

For Dade homicide police such killings are everyday affairs. They handle nearly 600 murders a year; 40 per cent of the dead are Latin-Americans involved in the drug trade. Most of those dumped in remote areas are Latins, often Cuban but usually Colombian. The Colombians kill women too, shot in their apartments, hog-tied in the boot of a car or trussed up like chickens, put in a box and dumped on the roadside. Unlike the Mafia these 'Cocaine Cowboys' have no worries about their public image and they have no qualms about who they kill. Most of the murders spring out of deals that have gone wrong, rows over fake cocaine, squabbles over money. Some stem from feuds originating back in Bogota or Medellin – Colombia has a homicide rate almost twice as high as any other country. But in one way or another all these south Florida killings are the outcrop of a brutal battle for supremacy in a highly lucrative and ferocious racket. Drugs are south Florida's biggest business. Miami in the 1980s is Chicago, the Roaring Twenties and Prohibition all over again, writ even larger.

In the Dade County morgue, where all drug murders are brought, Deputy Medical Examiner Charles Wetli showed us another casualty of America's drug bonanza. 'This 21-year-old man was found dead in a motel near Miami Airport. When I arrived he was lying face down, in complete rigor mortis, very stiff. He'd been dead for several hours but his temperature was still forty degrees centigrade, a very high fever. Water and towels were scattered all round the room, typical of heatstroke victims or people who've overdosed on cocaine. His passport showed he was Colombian, just arrived in Miami. He had an air ticket to California. His suitcases were empty.

'Back in our office we X-rayed his abdomen and found numerous foreign objects scattered throughout his gastro-intestinal tract. When I performed the autopsy I opened his stomach and found thirty-three packets of cocaine and another twenty-six in the rest of his body. The cocaine was packed in plastic containers which had been wrapped many times with the tips of surgical gloves and then tied. One of these had broken open and the cocaine it contained killed him.' The smuggler had swallowed these tiny packets one by one, intending to pass them through his body and pluck them out of his faeces. 'The cocaine inside all the packets weighed 550 grams and was 85 per cent pure. Had he lived to retrieve it he would have sold it for $25,000 to $30,000 to a wholesale dealer.'

Dr Wetli has seen a dozen such deaths. Another sixty smugglers suffering the same catastrophe have been taken straight from the airport to hospital for emergency operations. Astonishingly all of them survived. What drives Colombians to take such risks is partly the poverty of their lives at home and partly the outrageous profits to be made in America's cocaine market. In the early 1980s a farmer in Peru or Bolivia was selling the 500 kilos of coca leaves needed to make 1 kilo of cocaine for a few hundred dollars. The leaves would then be converted into a coca paste to be smuggled into Colombia and processed into cocaine. Now worth some $20,000 this kilo of cocaine would be smuggled into America where its value immediately rose to $60,000. It would then be cut (divided and diluted with other substances) and cut again, down to a purity of only 12 per cent for 'retail' consumption. By this time the original kilo of pure cocaine would have yielded between $1 and $2 million.

At the time of writing the figures may have fluctuated but the profit margins are still colossal. All the middlemen, mostly Colombians, make fortunes but the boy in the morgue was probably on his first run and never made a peso. He lay unclaimed by his family in Colombia, who may still have no idea what happened to him even years after his excruciating death. The same goes for many Latins murdered in Miami. World-weary homicide cops say there are few 'who-dun-its' in their town. Most of them are 'who-is-its'.

Dr Wetli believes that America's huge cocaine hunger, which is what provokes such slaughter, is founded partly on a myth that coke is non-addictive. Yet 36 per cent of people entering drug rehabilitation programmes are cocaine addicts, as are 1 million of America's 5 million regular coke-users. Today it is snorted not only by super-rich showbusiness stars and fast-rising business executives whose addiction may cost them $50,000 a year. It has also seeped down to street level where cocaine that is only 5 per cent pure may be bought for as little as $10 a 'bag'.

In 1982 President Reagan, realizing that there was no business like 'snow' business, launched a much-publicized war on the drug smugglers. His administration set up the South Florida Task Force to co-ordinate the efforts of the agencies already fighting but losing the drug war. The task force was soon claiming credit for the coke-busting successes of those agencies, much to their chagrin. In March 1982, for instance, Miami Airport customs seized 3,748 lb of cocaine, packed in twenty-one boxes from Colombia marked 'blue jeans' and worth $1 billion on the streets. In November the media circus flew into town with Ronald Reagan. At a local airforce base, surrounded by heaps of confiscated drugs, weapons and currency, he vowed to 'break the power of the mob in America'. The mob Reagan seems to have had in mind was not the real mob – the Mafia and its allies – but alien Hispanics running amok in Miami.

Reagan's war was a desperate measure to combat a desperate disease. In the late 1970s south Florida was overflowing with marijuana and cocaine from Latin America. In 1980 Peter Bensinger, chief of the DEA (Drug Enforcement Administration), estimated that up to 25 tonnes of cocaine had been smuggled into the USA in 1978, worth a staggering $16.2 billion at street level. Almost all of this came from coca plant leaves harvested in Peru and Bolivia but processed in and trafficked through Colombia. Bensinger's upper estimate of the marijuana sold in America was 16,400 tonnes, of which 70 per cent came in from Colombia and 25 per cent from Mexico. For all the efforts of America's own marijuana growers, Colombians controlled the market in two of the three main illegal drugs consumed in the USA. Most of this was coming in through Florida but no matter how many agencies would now be yoked together in the task force – DEA, customs, coastguard, FBI, IRS (Internal Revenue Service), ATF (Bureau of Alcohol, Tobacco and Firearms), even the navy and air force – they would not be able to seal off Florida's 8000 miles of irregular shoreline. For a few months the traffic did fall off but only in Florida. The smugglers simply switched their routes to other states, from Louisiana to New York. They would return to Florida when the task force was pared down and the politicians had lost interest.

America's drug and customs agencies usually estimate that they seize 10 per cent of all the illegal drugs in circulation but even this modest claim withered in the late 1970s. In 1978 the street value of heroin, cocaine and marijuana seized by the agencies was a mere $3.2 billion compared to an estimated $50 billion profits 'earned' from the drugs in circulation. Much of that $50 billion was banked in Florida. In 1979 every other state had a net outflow of cash that had to be replaced through the federal reserve banks but in Florida the reserve banks had a $3.2 billion surplus. In other words Florida's commercial banks were taking in huge deposits of cash which could only have come from sales of cocaine and marijuana.

The money was being carried into the banks in bags, boxes and suitcases by casually dressed young men who refused to show any identification. Bemused bank tellers would have to count cash deposits of as much as $950,000, mostly in $20 bills. Liberace's old joke about buying the bank he used to laugh all the way to was a joke no more in Miami. The new drug millionaires were not all Hispanics. Some were Anglos: either opportunist college boys from California and the north-east states or members of the deep south's own 'good old boy' crime network known as the 'Dixie Mafia'.

Much of their drug money was instantly transferred to accounts in Switzerland, Panama, the Bahamas and the Cayman Islands. Having been washed through the system it was then brought back into Florida. In Dade County, which includes Miami and its satellite towns, 40 per cent of all real estate transactions above $300,000 were being made by offshore corporations. In Broward County, which includes Fort Lauderdale, foreign investment accounted for 25 per cent of all real estate deals. These included not just lush homes and private estates, where the Latin drug kings were living, but also property investments – apartment and office blocks, shopping malls and warehouses. Some Cocaine Cowboys bought private piers with dock facilities for ocean-going vessels. These were sealed off from the outside world by high walls, electronically operated gates, the most modern alarm systems and the inevitable armed guards. Any quantity of cocaine or marijuana could then be smuggled in by sea and the authorities could do little about it.

Drug money has so boosted property prices and land values that south Florida has discovered a new addiction. Without it the economy of Dade, Biscayne and Palm Beach Counties would collapse. In 1979 Charles Kimball, a tenacious investigator of real estate transactions on Florida's Gold Coast, told US senators: 'If we were to cut off the narcotics money coming into the state we would precipitate a substantial real estate recession.' Kimball advocated the strongest possible action against drug money but said it had inflated the price of most Florida property by thousands of dollars. Blocking it off would mean that innocent people, who had bought property at the drug-inflated price, would suffer as prices tumbled.

The presidential onslaught on the drug merchants would have no such impact. South Florida's property prices have held up as the region's drug money surfeit has continued. Towards the end of 1983 so much cocaine was coming into Florida that the wholesale price fell to less than $20,000 a kilo. As the task force agencies seized ever larger amounts the Cocaine Cowboys were smuggling even greater quantities past them. No matter how many Latin traffickers are jailed or murdered others are always ready to take their place. As one Florida official put it, 'Colombians are like Dixie cups. You use them once and throw them away.'

Every year the government sells dozens of boats and planes seized from the drug-smugglers. Vessels worth hundreds of thousands of dollars are auctioned off: freighters, shrimpers, lobster boats, racing boats, luxurious yachts, even one-time navy minesweepers. The planes are usually Piper Aztecs or Cessna jets and are kept on private airfields until their owners face trial. Some convicted traffickers have had the nerve to buy back their own planes and fly them again on the drug route from Colombia to the Everglades.

Some gangs use aircraft as big as DC-7s which carry 15,000 lb of marijuana on each flight. The profit margin is so huge that if they are apprehended on the ground in Florida the pilots coolly abandon both the plane and its load. In 1981 Senator William Roth was so outraged by the repeated undetected penetration of American airspace by planes the size of DC-7s that he maintained with some justice, 'If these illegal drug-traffickers can do it, why can't some terrorist with a bomb-laden plane do the same thing?'

Some gangs have even acquired their own landing strips in Florida. The pilots, who are usually white Americans, earn up to

$60,000 a flight. One gang that called itself 'The Company' had remarkable connections with the Colombian army delivering marijuana to their aircraft in military trucks. Colombian officers were only too keen to take payoffs. One general was invited to dinner by fifty top suppliers who ceremoniously agreed over the cigars to give him a bribe of $1 million.

By the late 1970s Colombia's economy was being upset by the drug trade as much as Florida's. Six per cent of the country's 30 per cent inflation rate was caused by drug money but the state was also piling up huge foreign exchange reserves. In 1982 Colombia had a new president, Belisario Betancur, whose government resolved to fight the drug menace. The move was partly made to appease the USA but it was also a belated attempt to challenge the economic and political power of the *narcotrafficantes*. Their response was predictable. On 30 April 1984 the minister of justice, 38-year-old Rodrigo Lara Bonilla, was machine-gunned to death. Since Bonilla's assassination the Colombian government has destroyed many cocaine-processing laboratories and forced the smugglers to set up new labs in Florida. This shift has not reduced the amount of money the Cocaine Cowboys are making in Florida, however, where some gangs have bought machines to count the notes.

To get into the money end of the traffic rather than just seize cocaine, DEA undercover agents set up an investment company in Miami in 1981. The company, Dean International, wormed itself into the business of advising Colombian drug syndicates how to launder their profits out in Florida. In eighteen months the agents transferred $19 million in drug money to banks in Colombia, Panama and Japan. They handled a staggering $1 million in a single day. As business got bigger and their commissions grew they had to show wealth by moving into grander offices and driving around in luxury cars. Their designer-bejeaned, Gucci-shoed patrons were so beguiled that they offered the undercover men the chance to get into the drugs business themselves. The agents refused but further ensnared their clients by introducing them to other agents posing as buyers.

This sting, codenamed Operation Swordfish, penetrated Colombian syndicates which had smuggled in 18,000 lb of cocaine, 90 lb of heroin, hundreds of tonnes of marijuana and millions of dosages of methaqualone tablets. The conspirators despatched money to eight countries in the Caribbean and Europe and to eight cities across the USA. In October 1982 Dean Investment closed its doors and sixty people were arrested, among them several prominent Floridians: a plastic surgeon, two bank vice-presidents and three attorneys (one a prosecutor). At the same time the DEA seized cocaine with a street value of $60 million, a methaqualone laboratory, twelve bank accounts, fifteen cars, two houses and a block of apartments. It was a triumph for the undercover men, especially since much of the evidence had been gathered on video and sound-recording devices hidden in Dean's plush premises. At one point the video tapes show the agents and the smugglers counting hundreds of thousands of dollars in small dollar bills.

A separate operation convicted Eduardo Oroczo in 1982. A remarkably brazen Colombian money-launderer, Oroczo deposited $97.4 million in one New York bank in three months, much of it in million-dollar chunks. Oroczo, who claimed to be a coffee-broker, used to bring in the cash packed in suitcases, briefcases and cardboard boxes. He would give instructions for the money to be wired to Swiss and Caribbean banks. He was later jailed for eight years and fined $1 million, but the exported money could not be recovered and the drug dealers whose money it was were not troubled.

To crush all the drug-dealers and their front men would require dozens of Dean Investment-style stings and far more government agents than Americans are willing to pay for. Besides, as the business manager of The Company told US senators, 'As long as you have 30 million people smoking marijuana who don't feel it is any worse than beer, whiskey or cigarettes, they are going to smoke it. As long as there is a demand there will be a supplier.'

The parallels with Prohibition are obvious but just as Florida's drug trade has exceeded Prohibition in the amount of crooked money it has generated, it has also outdone it in terms of public corruption. George Ray Havens is chief investigator for the state's attorney in Dade County and has the responsibility in greater Miami for probing wrongdoing among local police forces. In nearly twenty years spent working for law enforcement in south Florida Havens has seen the idea of what constitutes a 'big' drug seizure change from a few cigarettes of marijuana to 20 tonnes of the stuff. In the same period the number of detectives working on narcotics has risen from 2 to 500. Local prosecutors now spend nearly all their time on drug cases while other crime – including Mafia organized crime which is rampant – is not investigated. Even so many of the drug-dealers go unpunished. 'They are making so much money that in many cases they've bought the very people meant to be enforcing the law. They've bought policemen, judges, prosecutors and they're buying the criminal justice system.'

Havens says it is not unusual for police officers, paid between $25,000 and $30,000 a year (including overtime) to arrest an eighteen-year-old carrying $500,000 in cash. To the eighteen-year-old that money may not mean very much – losing it would be part of the risk of doing business – but it is a strong-willed policeman who can resist pocketing the $500,000 in return for the simple favour of releasing the dope-dealer. The cop might easily rationalize this crime by thinking that if he were to put this man in jail there would soon be another Colombian on the streets in his place.

In 1983 Havens was told that some police were retaining seizures of cocaine to use or sell. To test the allegation he arranged for 5 lb of high-grade cocaine to be left in a house and then leaked its whereabouts to the suspect officers. As investigators lay in wait the policemen drove up, broke into the house and took the cocaine, which was worth over $7 million on the streets. It was clear the men did not intend to report their find so they were arrested. 'Professionally our people were elated at arresting these corrupt officers but personally it was embarrassing to stand in a residential neighbourhood, remove a badge from an officer's shirt, handcuff him and take him to jail.

'I was disgusted. I say, why have we come to this? But you stop and think. Policemen are human beings. Here's a man who has an opportunity to make twenty-five times his salary – maybe more than his lifetime's earnings – in fifteen minutes.'

Because of their control over most of America's cocaine and marijuana supplies Hispanics have soared in the ethnic league table of organized crime. Colombians rule these markets not just in Florida but as far north as New York. In ghetto strongholds such as New York's Jackson Heights they are able to deliver the coke straight to the consumer, keeping far more of the profit than would come from selling to Anglo-American wholesalers in Miami. The Colombians may lack the established political connections necessary to insulate a criminal organization from prosecutorial zeal but they can easily buy that in Miami and in greater New York from Cubans with deeper roots in the community.

America's drugs explosion is changing the balance of power in organized crime. Not only Hispanics but also criminals from many lower economic groups have taken this opportunity to climb the 'queer ladder of social mobility', as sociologist Daniel Bell once described crime in America. The ethnic succession theory is based on the historical fact that the Irish crime syndicates of the nineteenth century were supplanted by Jewish gangs who were in turn ousted by the Italian Mafia. Therefore, the argument goes, it is only a matter of time before the Mafia crime families are replaced by groups from other, poorer communities. In some ways this theory trips up over the blacks, who were running their own gambling and narcotics syndicates, independent of both Jews and Italians, from the 1910s to the early 1930s. They were then knocked out of those markets by Jewish and Italian gangs. By the late 1960s blacks were back in strength, not just as narcotics' consumers but as large-scale importers and wholesalers. Their breakthrough came in the Vietnam War which enabled black criminals to make connections with dealers marketing opium from the Golden Triangle region of Thailand, Burma and Laos.

No one exploited this connection better than Frank Lucas, leader of the 'Country Boys'. In the 1960s Lucas, a sharecropper's son from North Carolina, broke into the heroin market serving blacks in Newark and other north New Jersey cities. He built his organization around five of his own brothers. At first he bought heroin from New York's crime families, who in turn acquired it through their French and Italian connections. They would sell him 1 kilo of heroin for $40,000, he would cut it three times and sell it on the street for millions of dollars. But his most useful contact was to be another black from North Carolina, Ike Atkinson. A twenty-year army veteran, Atkinson had served in Bangkok where he owned a bar and kept up his contacts. Using Atkinson as his supplier, Frank Lucas built a monopoly pyramid over all phases of importation, production and distribution. He would buy 1 kilo from Atkinson for $4,000, cut it five times and sell it for $316,000. In the early 1970s he cut at least 800 kilos of pure heroin, yielding him and his brothers the lion's share of its street value of $240 million. The Mafia did not get one dollar.

In many ways the Country Boys resembled a Mafia crime family. The gang was based on blood relationships. According to the Country Boys themselves their southern traditions gave them a solidarity which most northern-born black gangs seem unable to build. Their violence against outsiders and fringe members was another strength and similarity. They killed as many as twenty associates whose loyalty was suspect. But by 1974 Lucas was carelessly flaunting his immense wealth. He bought large farms back home in North Carolina and lost millions in Las Vegas casinos without a whimper. About this time mafiosi, whose heroin business had suffered when Lucas started supplying the Harlem market, informed on him to the police. One of his own men turned government witness and helped put him in jail for seventy years. By 1982, however, Lucas was free again. He had agreed to turn witness himself against more than 100 black traffickers. Omerta was not part of his code.

One Harlem heroin king who briefly outlasted Frank Lucas was Leroy 'Nicky' Barnes. Known also as 'Mr Untouchable' because of his untroubled criminal career, Barnes was the leading member of a 'council' of seven black heroin dealers who divided up Harlem between them. They worked together to reduce the cost of bulk narcotics' purchases, eliminate competition and murder suspected informants. With other council members Barnes would often recite the 'oath of brotherhood', pledging 'to treat my brother as myself'. In 1978 Barnes was sentenced to life imprisonment for heroin-dealing. Five years later he also turned government witness and testified against five other council members (on the grounds that one of them had been making love to his girlfriend while he was in jail). If Barnes and Lucas are typical of black American organized-crime bosses, it seems unlikely that they yet have the discipline and organization to supplant the Mafia.

Yet they may not be typical. Other black crime bosses have stayed silent, however many years they spend in jail. In the late 1970s Frank Usher controlled much of Detroit's immense illegal drug market, the second biggest in America. He ran his business on Mafia lines with several tiers of employees between himself and the pedlars on the streets. In twenty months he and his most trusted henchmen carried out at least eleven murders to maintain discipline and control over the enterprise. As if to highlight his respect for the Mafia Usher called himself Frank 'Nitti', after the Sicilian who succeeded Al Capone as head of the Chicago crime syndicate. Usher, however, went well beyond the Mafia in one way. Women were an integral part of his organization: on his orders they carried out murders and on his orders they too were murdered. Usher was an equal-opportunity employer.

Since 1974, when the anthropologist Francis Ianni published *Black Mafia*, a study of black, Puerto Rican and Cuban crime organizations in America, many researchers have found evidence of emerging crime groups. Most of the studies have been based on ethnic gangs, for race is the bond holding most gangs together. California state investigators have targetted two groups among its Mexican population: the Mexican Mafia and La Nuestra Familia. Both originated in California's prisons where young inmates are recruited into the fraternities, undergoing Mafia-like rituals. On release they join with the rest of the brotherhood on the streets. One racket they kill each other to control is the extortion of many thousands of illegal Mexican immigrants.

In America's western and south-west states Mexicans control much of the heroin market because Mexico is where most of the region's heroin supplies come from. In the 1970s the Herreras, a large blood family from the state of Durango, operated a coast-to-coast heroin syndicate from Chicago. They grew so big, particularly in their own minds, that they made a Bonnie and Clyde-type feature film starring themselves gunning their way to riches!

Californian prisons have also spawned enduring black and white prison gangs: the Black Guerrilla Family and the Aryan Brotherhood. California has also suffered from organized crime among Israeli immigrants. New York police believe 1,000 Israeli criminals are now active in the city, specializing in narcotics, insurance frauds and the extortion of other Israelis who have built up successful straight businesses. In Detroit rings of Chaldean Arabs (Christians from Iraq) specialize in arson for profit: burning down their own stores and claiming the insurance. They follow in the tradition of Lebanese Christians, known in America as Syrians, who for fifty years have worked closely with the Mafia in cities such as Detroit and St Louis.

In New York and on the West Coast long-established Chinese gangs are slaughtering each other once more over gambling and protection rackets in their own communities and the Hong Kong and Singapore heroin routes. In Hawaii and California members of the 100,000-strong Japanese crime organizations known as the Yakusa, have built business empires on profits from drugs, prostitution, gun-smuggling and extortion. In other states immigrants from India have formed crime groups, dubbed the 'Patels' by American police because most of the criminals bear that name. The most intriguing combines, however, have been formed by new Russian immigrants as soon as they enter the USA. American authorities believe the newcomers are reconstituting gangs that have worked together for years in the Soviet Union. Washington fears that they are only allowed out of Russia either because Moscow has had enough of them (and where better to dump them than America), or because they are really working for the KGB.

The only major emerging crime groups not based on one race or immigrant sector are the motorcycle gangs. The Hell's Angels, the Outlaws, the Bandidos and the Pagans have each built near nationwide organizations around 'chapters' and 'mother clubs'. Within each chapter bikers bear titles such as president, vice-president, treasurer and sergeant-of-arms. Today these four gangs, with scores of smaller outfits, form the biggest criminal organization in America with more than 7000 full members and many more hangers-on, including some of the lawyers and front men who look after their business affairs. In 1983 renegade bikers and one-time biker women, known as 'old ladies', mesmerized Washington senators with horrific tales of drugs, rape, forcible prostitution, wife-selling and murder. Some of the witnesses have claimed that Mafia families hire bikers as musclemen and contract killers.

Ethnic successionists argue that, with all this tough and relatively young competition, the Mafia has to be on the way out. Even the family bosses must wonder sometimes whether soon there will be any room left for their ageing group of Italians, only 3000 or 5000 strong, who spend much of their time killing each other. The crime families are also losing manpower because some 'made' men's sons are opting out of family life. A few prefer to work as legitimate businessmen, others become college professors. With no experience of poverty or deprivation they lack the appetite for the grubbing, violent life of the street racketeer. Other sons, however, become lawyers or stockbrokers, jobs where they are well placed to serve the crime families as they turn themselves into quasi-legitimate corporations. In this sense the Mafia is climbing the ethnic ladder and may quit the streets, not out of weakness but because its members can make more money from white-collar crime.

There is evidence that the Mafia is withdrawing from at least some street activities. Economist Peter Reuter has recently tried to establish on a scientific basis who really does control bookmaking, numbers gambling and loansharking in New York City.[1] He concludes that many blacks and Hispanic numbers operators control their own banks and pay no tribute or protection money to the Mafia. Many substantial black and Hispanic bookmakers never turn to the Mafia for back-up or layoff finance, nor do they fear its violence. In Puerto Rican neighbourhoods non-violent competition among numbers operators is so fierce (and profit margins are so low) that there can be no controlling cartel, Mafia or otherwise.

The Mafia, Reuter argues, may be surviving largely on its reputation.

> 'The Mafia, like the rest of the world, has come to recognize that there is no such thing as bad publicity. Their reputation for violence gives them a great deal of power in the underworld. That reputation is in part sustained by the newspapers. That's no conspiracy. Newspapers report what we're interested in reading about and organized crime is still one of the best entertainment stories of our time.'

Reuter maintains that it is the Mafia's reputation, based not on its real power today but on its past strength, which enthrones it as the king-pin organization of the underworld. It is the only arbitrator to whom underworld figures turn when they want a dispute resolved peaceably. 'When a dispute arises a bookmaker has to have somebody who, for a fee, can sit down and represent his interests and only mafiosi seem to have that power.'

The key factor here is the Mafia's reputation for enforcing its decisions, ultimately by violence. To quote Reuter again:

> 'If the Mafia says that I shall pay $10,000 to the other person, then I run some serious risk of having damage done to me if I don't pay. But one thing that bothers me in my research is that sometimes nothing happens to the people who don't pay. My guess is that the Mafia's getting old and lazy. Eventually people will decide the Mafia isn't what it used to be, but that could be a long time after they have lost most of their powers.'

In terms of violence the Mafia's American bloodstock may be failing but killers are not hard to find. In the words of Pete Donohue, an organized-crime fighter of thirty years' standing, 'Those Mustache-Petes who run the families can still call Sicily, get a guy sent over, bring him in through Canada, have him come in to whack you tonight and be back in Sicily at the weekend. What do the cops know about that kind of a hit?' Raw young Sicilians may prove themselves to be just what a family needs, not just for a few contract killings but as full-time members. A transfusion of native Italian blood has recently rejuvenated several American crime families, particularly the Gambinos. Many young Sicilians are willing to serve family apprenticeships in America and they cede nothing to Hispanics or blacks in criminal skills.

The Mafia's future may not look so good to many 'made' men jailed because of the legal tools available to federal and state investigators since the early 1970s. Electronic surveillance laws authorizing telephone wiretaps and listening devices have meant that police and prosecutors can now prove criminal acts which formerly would have gone undetected. They can keep up with new developments inside the crime families and prove connections between the Mafia and its front men. Unlike the sensational but unauthorized FBI wiretaps of the 1950s and 1960s this evidence can be introduced as evidence in trials.

Another blow for the Mafia has been Witsec, the government's witness security programme, which has encouraged hundreds of criminals inside the Mafia or on its fringes to turn public witness. They can do so without suffering the fate of earlier informers. Unlike Abe Reles of Murder Inc. today's canaries do not have to fly as well as sing.

Organized-crime strike forces, US attorneys and some state prosecutors have used another new law to knock out the Mafia's bosses: the RICO statute, Title 18.[2] Crimes that until 1971 might have brought only a few years in jail can now send top mobsters down for life. Under RICO a life sentence really can mean life, which in turn helps persuade more racketeers to turn federal witness: blacks like Barnes and Lucas but also Mafia associates like Ferritto and Zagaria, and even 'made' men like Fratianno. It becomes the kind of offer they cannot refuse.

In the last five years hundreds of mafiosi have been jailed, including many family bosses: Carlos Marcello of New Orleans; Joe Bonanno, exiled founder of one of the New York families; Colombo family boss Carmine Persico; Russell Bufalino of Pennsylvania; Eugene Smaldone of Denver; and the entire leadership of Cleveland and Los Angeles. Frank Tieri of the Genovese family was convicted but died before he could be jailed and Nick Civella of Kansas City died before he could be tried. Now Boston's Mafia hierarchy awaits trial. The Ballistrieris of Milwaukee, and Cerone and Aiuppa of Chicago face serious charges of skimming from Las Vegas casinos, while the doyen of Chicago's collective leadership, Tony Accardo, is on the verge of going to jail for contempt of the US Senate unless he dies of old age first.

The latest leader to be indicted is Paul Castellano, 68-year-old boss of New York's Gambino family. In March 1984 he was charged with being the leader of a 'racketeering crew' and with murder. He and twenty underlings were accused of a total of twenty-five murders in addition to bribery, drug-trafficking, loan-sharking, prostitution and exporting stolen cars. If convicted on all counts 'Big Paulie' could go down for 270 years!

Not every mob watcher is impressed by these triumphs. Professor Robert Blakey is the lawyer who drew up the RICO statute and the laws on electronic surveillance and witness protection. He believes that spectacular convictions of Mafia bosses only do for the mob what a lion does to a herd of zebras: 'cull the old, the sick and the lame'. They do not affect the basic strength of the families which, he says, will not be broken until the civil RICO law is applied. This would confiscate all family assets acquired with the proceeds of crime: businesses, investments, even private homes.

But the bitch that bore the Mafia is in heat again. In the 1960s and early 1970s Europe's heroin market was dominated by the 'French Connection' – Corsicans who monopolized the traffic in heroin made from Turkish opium. The Sicilian Mafia was unable to break this monopoly, hence the direct connection between the 'French' and the New York families. This axis was destroyed in 1973 by massive seizures in New York and Turkey's destruction of its opium poppy fields at America's request. The main source of heroin for the USA then became South-East Asia. By the mid-1970s it was Mexico. By 1980 Iran, Pakistan and Afghanistan had taken over. Today opium gum harvested in those countries is reduced to a morphine base and transported to Europe where the Sicilian Mafia controls most of the trade. Much of the morphine is shipped to Palermo and other Italian cities where it is refined into 90 per cent pure heroin for onward smuggling into the USA.

Recent trials in Italy and the USA have proved that heroin has revived the ancient alliance between America's mafiosi and their Sicilian cousins. Some spectacular cases have involved those Gambino second cousins, born in Sicily but living in New Jersey. In 1979 a bulky package was left unclaimed at New York's Kennedy Airport. Suspicious DEA agents opened it up and found tins of heroin disguised as talcum powder. The agents realized a corrupt Alitalia cargo-handler was involved and persuaded him to turn informer. In March 1980 he revealed that the Italian end of the gang was about to ship 40 kilos of heroin from Milan to Brooklyn in boxes of records. The heroin had cost them $4 million but they planned to sell it in America for $100 million. The shipment was intercepted in Milan and in 1983 sixty of the conspirators were tried in Sicily. Two New Jersey-based Gambino brothers were sentenced in their absence to twenty years in jail. They were tried in person in America for the same conspiracy but a different verdict was returned and they were acquitted. Italy is unlikely to ask for their extradition so these convicted drug-traffickers are free to bleed and enslave the addicts in the ghetto with yet more planeloads of heroin.

DEA agents at Kennedy Airport are well aware that any kind of airfreight from Italy may contain this rich cargo, worth twenty times the same weight of gold. Recent seizures include 10 kilos hidden in tins of olive oil, 20 kilos in furniture and over 50 kilos in espresso coffee urns destined for a Brooklyn store. In April 1984 charges were brought against the owners of a clutch of pizza parlours who happened to be members of the Bonanno family. New York police and federal agents rounded up forty people said to be responsible for importing 750 kilos of heroin, worth $1.65 billion. They sent some of the heroin across America in pizza boxes and some of the profits back to Sicily through New York brokerage houses and banks in Bermuda and Switzerland. The Sicilian mastermind of the conspiracy, Gaetano Badalamenti, was arrested in Madrid.

Such seizures and arrests are usually announced with trumpets. The attorney general flew into New York just to attend the news conference on the pizza parlour charges, but no heroin had been seized and the trade itself was barely disturbed. The DEA says that New York's crime families now import 85 per cent of America's heroin, amounting to 4.4 tonnes and worth many billions of dollars. Half a million Americans are addicted to what the Mafia now monopolizes. Thus the Mafia is responsible for much of the street crime committed by addicts who can only pay for their habit with the proceeds of muggings, stick-ups and burglaries. This exposes the nonsense in the minds of many people who exonerate the Mafia by saying it is only responsible for 'victimless crime' whereas the real enemies of society are street punks and muggers. Street crime and organized crime are inseparable. They are two sides of the same coin.

America could smash the new Palermo connection only by persuading the opium-growing states of south-west Asia to destroy their poppy fields. As America's influence over Iran and

Afghanistan is minimal at present this is unlikely to happen. Until it does Sicilian-processed heroin will probably continue to flood America. By itself the island can do little to challenge the Mafia's ever-increasing power. It still operates its traditional rackets, which are stronger now than they were 100 years ago, but the heroin trade has boosted its income by $600 million a year. This money is laundered into legitimate businesses and investments like the high-rise buildings that now ring Palermo. The city booms even though unemployment is higher than almost anywhere else in Italy. Awash with crooked money, western Sicily suffers more than 100 Mafia murders each year. Most of the dead are other mafiosi but executions of anti-Mafia fighters are commonplace: magistrates, judges, police chiefs and politicians including the president of Sicily's Parliament. Even Palermo's most outspoken journalists have been gunned down.

In 1982 General Carlo Alberto Dalla Chiesa was appointed prefect of Palermo. He decided that his aim was to crush the Mafia. As he had played a considerable part in crushing the Red Brigades he seemed to be a man who would carry out his promises. In September 1982 a motorcycle drew up beside the general's car, a pillion passenger raised a Kalashnikov and machined-gunned Dalla Chiesa and his wife to death. In remorse the Italian Parliament belatedly passed an anti-Mafia law which gives the state powers like those enshrined in America's RICO and electronic surveillance statutes. Many Palermitans have been so outraged by the slaughter that they have dared to demonstrate in public against the Mafia. Even the Pope spoke out against it, albeit in muted terms, on a visit to Palermo. The city now has a woman mayor, elected partly on an anti-Mafia platform.

Inevitably some years must pass before Sicilians will know if these developments can smash a 700-year-old tradition. In Sicily even optimists must be pessimistic. In the 1970s the island's bravest and most successful anti-Mafia policeman was Boris Giuliano, chief of Palermo's flying squad. In 1978 he broke open the heroin connection between Palermo and the Gambino crime family in America. Giuliano was much admired by visiting American detectives to whom he would show the sights of his city. He once took an American drugs agent to the Piazza Marina and pointed to the spot where Lieutenant Joe Petrosino of the New York police was gunned down in 1909. Half in jest he told his visitor to take care. Seventy years after Petrosino's murder Giuliano walked into a Palermo bar to have a cup of coffee. A moment later he was shot dead.

As for the state of the Mafia in America, add the giant income it now makes out of heroin to its huge earnings from other criminal rackets; add also its massive holdings in thousands of outwardly legitimate businesses and its investments in stocks and shares; take into account the fortunes it has piled up in overseas banks; now consider whether it is realistic to believe the crime families are on the verge of destruction.

If Hispanics, blacks and any other races are making billions out of organized crime, it is not at the expense of the Mafia but because America's organized crime industry is growing so fast that there is room for everybody. Today more than 2 million Americans use heroin on a daily or weekly basis, at least 5 million use cocaine every month while 30 million use marijuana at least once a month. In 1980 one estimate put the retail value of all America's illegal narcotics' consumption at between $68 and $90 billion. As almost all of this money amounts to clear untaxed profit, narcotics-traffickers make more money out of America than do its top 500 industrial corporations. Even if blacks and Hispanics were soon to control all their own narcotics, gambling and prostitution rackets why should the Mafia worry? It would still be making billions if it serviced only the illicit needs of America's whites.

Crime Inc.'s witnesses hold different views on the Mafia's future. Jimmy Fratianno, the self-styled 'Last Mafioso', thinks its days are numbered. 'It will be a long time before they can destroy it but now that they know what it is they've got a good chance. If they can get more guys like me, people that are really involved, to help the government then sooner or later it will go down the drain. This thing is no good. If I knew when I joined what I know today they'd never have got me in the organization. As Johnny Roselli used to say, you need this like you need a hole in the head.'

Joey Cantalupo, in contrast, thinks the Mafia will grow and grow. 'There is such a beautiful future for organized crime in America. It just keeps getting bigger and bigger and bigger: bigger than IBM, Xerox and everybody else put together. It has no end.'

Ralph Picardo says that all law enforcement has done is to knock off the Mafia's present leadership, only for some other Mafioso to take over. 'It will never end. That's why they call it "Our Thing" – something that will survive as long as man is on earth. People love it. People love for it to be around them. They idolize it, they idolize its leaders, like they are some kind of God. And they're not. They are lower than the lowest slime on earth.'

Professor Robert Blakey, director of the Notre Dame University Institute on Organized Crime, is the man who drew up the three federal laws which are now being applied so successfully against organized crime (the RICO statute, and the laws governing electronic surveillance and witness protection). Blakey regards the Mafia as the only enduring criminal organization of all those groups that have ever been active in America. 'The single strongest group happens to be people of Italian descent. The Sicilians put it together in the 1930s when they beat every single group and it is still together in the 1980s. There are emerging groups. Many of them have Mafia characteristics but only the Mafia has the cohesion, the wealth, the access to violence, the access to lawyers and to political corruption. That's a fact.'

For *Crime Inc.* we interviewed ten men who have testified in open court against the Mafia. At the time of writing five are living under new identities in varying degrees of comfort. Jimmy Fratianno, now in his seventies, is a rich man for the first time on the proceeds of a book on his life, *The Last Mafioso*. He is philosophical about Mafia vengeance. 'I just take my chances, go some place where they can't find me, just live as long as I can. It's better than being dead. You know, when they find you: "Bye-bye Baby!" What are you gonna do? But let them find me. If I had stayed on with them I *would* have been dead already, right? So every day I'm still living I beat them!'

Joey Cantalupo is struggling to make ends meet. He lives far from the streets of Brooklyn where he worked as an FBI informer and where he would certainly be killed if he dared to return. He no longer receives support from the government and jobs are hard to find. Still, he has no regrets. 'I know I'm a rat but what am I a rat against? I'm a rat against the bad people in this world. When I hurt those men who corrupt and hurt millions of people I did something good.'

Ralph Picardo, John Vitale and Herbie Gross are scattered across America. They are all careful. They sit facing the door in bars and restaurants and they don't give out their phone numbers, yet one day they may bump into an old *compare* and suddenly it will all be over. Gerry DeNono is still in jail, awaiting parole on two murder convictions. Even with a new identity there are few places Gerry can hide in America's prison system.

Garment union leader Matthew Eason still dares move among his members on New York's 7th Avenue only if he has the protection of a bulletproof vest and two bodyguards. On the Miami waterfront Joey Teitelbaum goes everywhere armed and protected but he has no intention of running from the mobsters he put in jail. Ray Ferritto, bitter about what he sees as the treachery of the Cleveland Strike Force, is living openly in his home town, even though, he says, it is 'only a matter of time before they get me'. In Paramus, New Jersey, police chief Joe Delaney runs a clean force, busts Russian shoplifters and takes target practice every week on the police range. Joe believes the Mafia won't try to kill him because it would create too much heat.

Despite the witnesses, the electronic surveillance and the RICO law the Mafia will continue to do business in America, no matter what law enforcement tries to do. In the words of writer Nic Pileggi, the mafioso has always been:

> . . . far more at home in the US than he ever was in the impoverished villages he came from. He is, in a sense, ideally suited to New York's eat-thy-neighbour business morality. He has become the perfect conduit for the kinds of vice America's law-abiding citizens insist upon enjoying. . . . He has filled the gap between the letter and the spirit of unrealistic, unenforceable and unpopular laws, and to consider him an aberration rather than a reflection of America today, is like blaming congenital obesity on an ice-cream manufacturer.

Why, then, do cops, agents and prosecutors bother to fight

organized crime? Former New York state trooper Pete Donohue has stalked the Mafia from the streets of Manhattan to the casinos of Las Vegas and the Sunshine Belt of Arizona, New Mexico and southern California. For years he risked his neck working undercover with New York's crime families. Once a mafioso held a shotgun to his belly and threatened to disembowel him from the groin up. Who would run that kind of danger for a cop's pay? 'You don't work organized crime for a cop's pay. Any cop who works *any* cop's job for the pay is a goddam nut. You work organized crime because you really believe somebody's got to be on the right side. Somebody's got to do something about what's happening in this society.'

Although in semi-retirement Donohue still fights organized crime, digging up dirt on Mafia front men who try to silence the Press and television by suing anyone who dares expose them. 'Do I think we're winning? No. We've lost. And we're losing bad. But somebody's got to try.'

BIBLIOGRAPHY

I recommend the following books, in addition to those mentioned in the notes.

Brashler, William, *The Don: The Life and Death of Sam Giancana* (Harper & Row, New York, 1977).

Brill, Steven, *The Teamsters* (Simon & Schuster, New York, 1978).

Chandler, David, *Brothers in Blood* (E. P. Dutton, New York, 1975); republished as *The Criminal Brotherhoods* (Constable, London, 1976).

Cook, Fred J., *The FBI Nobody Knows* (Macmillan, New York, 1964).

———, *Mafia!* (Fawcett, Greenwich, Conn., 1973).

Cressey, Donald, *Theft of the Nation* (Harper & Row, 1969).

Demaris, Ovid, *Captive City* (Lyle Stuart, New York, 1969).

———, *The Last Mafioso* (Times Books, New York, 1981).

Eisenberg, Dennis, Dan, Uri and Landau, Eli, *Meyer Lansky: Mogul of the Mob* (Paddington Press, New York, 1979).

Exner, Judith, *My Story*, as told to Ovid Demaris (Grove Press, New York, 1977).

Fried, Albert, *The Rise and Fall of the Jewish Gangster in America* (Holt, Rinehart, New York, 1980).

Gambino, Richard, *Vendetta* (Doubleday, New York, 1977).

Giancana, Antoinette, and Renner, Thomas, *Mafia Princess* (William Morrow, New York, 1984).

Goddard, Donald, *Joey* [Joey Gallo] (Harper & Row, New York, 1974).

———, *Easy Money* (Popular Library, New York, 1978).

———, *All Fall Down* (Times Books, New York, 1980).

Hoffman, Paul, *Tiger in the Court* (Playboy Press, Chicago, 1973).

Hougan, Jim, *Spooks* (William Morrow, 1978).

Ianni, Francis, with Elizabeth Reuss-Ianni, *A Family Business* (Russell Sage Foundation, New York, 1972).

Ianni, Francis, *Black Mafia* (Simon & Schuster, 1974).

Jennings, Dean, *We Only Kill Each Other* (Prentice-Hall, Englewood Cliffs, New Jersey, 1967).

Katcher, Leo, *The Big Bankroll* (Harper & Bros, New York, 1958).

Kefauver, Estes, *Crime in America* (Doubleday, 1951).

Lewis, Norman, *The Honoured Society* (G. P. Putnam's Sons, New York, 1964).

Maas, Peter, *The Valachi Papers* (G. P. Putnam's Sons, 1968).
McPhaul, Jack, *Johnny Torrio* (Arlington House, New York, 1970).
Meskil, Paul, *Don Carlo, Boss of Bosses* (Popular Library, New York, 1973).
Messick, Hank, *The Silent Syndicate* (Macmillan, New York, 1967).
———, *The Secret File* (G. P. Putnam's Sons, 1969).
———, *Lansky* (G. P. Putnam's Sons, 1971).
———, *The Mob in Show Business* (Pyramid Books, New York, 1973).
Messick, Hank, and Goldblatt, Burt, *The Mobs and the Mafia: An Illustrated History of Organized Crime* (Crowell, New York, 1972).
Nelli, Humbert, *The Business of Crime* (Oxford University Press, New York, 1976).
Pasley, F.D., *Al Capone* (republished by Faber & Faber, London, 1966).
Pennsylvania Crime Commission, 1980 Report: *A Decade of Organized Crime* (St David's, Pennsylvania).
Peterson, Virgil, *Barbarians in Our Midst* (Little Brown, Boston, 1952).
Powell, Hickman, *Ninety Times Guilty* (Harcourt Brace, New York, 1939).
Reid, Ed, *Mafia* (Random House, New York, 1952).
———, *The Grim Reapers* (Henry Regnery, Chicago, 1969).
Reid, Ed, and Demaris, Ovid, *The Green Felt Jungle* (Trident Press, 1963).
Rogovin, Charles (director), *Task Force Report on Organized Crime* (US Government Printing Office, Washington, 1967).
Talese, Gay, *Honour Thy Father* (World Publishing, New York, 1971).
Teresa, Vincent, and Renner, Thomas, *My Life in the Mafia* (Doubleday, 1973).
Turner, Wallace, *Gamblers' Money* (Houghton Mifflin, Boston, 1965).
Zeiger, Henry, *Sam the Plumber* (Mentor, New York, 1971).
———, *The Jersey Mob* (Signet, New York, 1975).

NOTES

Chapter 1

1. On organized crime, the Bruno family and Atlantic City's casinos, see Chapter 18.
2. See Chapter 18, pp. 217–19.

Chapter 3

1. Quoted in *Brotherhood of Evil* by Frederick Sondern Jr (Farrar Straus and Cudahy, New York, 1959).

Chapter 4

1. See Chapter 14, pp. 161–2.
2. In this book the words Mafia and La Cosa Nostra are used as interchangeable terms, describing the same organization. To explain FBI Director Hoover's adoption of the term La Cosa Nostra, see Chapter 14, pp. 166–7.
3. See Chapter 20, p. 232.

Chapter 5

1. On the Mafia in business, see Chapter 23. See also *Vicious Circles* by Jonathan Kwitny, the masterwork on the Mafia in the marketplace (W. W. Norton, New York, 1979).
2. On the Mafia and labour unions, see Chapters 20–22.
3. On the Italian American Civil Rights League, see Chapter 26.
4. The 'Blackie' to whom DeNono is referring was Sam 'Sambo' Cesario, an ex-convict and syndicate gambling boss aged 53, who was clubbed and shot to death in front of his wife on 19 October 1971.

Chapter 6

1. From *Lords of the Levee* by Lloyd Wendt and Herman Kogan (Bobbs-Merrill, New York, 1943).

Chapter 7

1. Clarence True Wilson, general secretary of the Board of Temperance, Prohibition and Public Morals of the Methodist Episcopal Church, quoted in *Prohibition: A National Experiment*, the September 1932 volume of *The Annals of the American Academy of Political and Social Science, Philadelphia.*
2. From a pamphlet quoted by Andrew Sinclair in *Prohibition* (Faber and Faber, London, 1962).
3. *Ibid.*
4. See Chapter 8, p. 78, for how John Torrio exploited the near beer racket.

Chapter 8

1. On the Five Points gang and its origins, see Chapter 13, pp. 133–5.
2. Quoted in *Chicago Gangland* by James O'Donnell Bennett, a slim paperback published by the *Chicago Tribune* 1929. See also John Landesco's article on 'Prohibition and Crime' in the September 1932 volume of *The Annals*, above, and *Organized Crime in Chicago* (part III of the Illinois Crime Survey, 1929, republished as a Midway Reprint by University of Chicago Press, 1968).

Chapter 10

1. Loftus's role as the first policeman on the scene and the man who questioned Frank Gusenberg on his deathbed only emerged in 1983 when I requested the St Valentine's Day Massacre (unsolved murder) investigation papers from the Chicago Police Department, through Ron Koziol of the *Chicago Tribune*. This elementary inquiry, which no one else appears to have made since the Massacre, revealed that the Loftus role has been wrongly attributed to a Detective Clarence Sweeney for the last 55 years. Sweeney himself appears to have been the source of this myth, recycled in an otherwise excellent biography of Capone by John Kobler (Fawcett Publications, New York, 1972).
2. Mark Haller, Department of History, Temple University, in 'Bootleggers and American Gambling 1920–1950', Appendix 1 to the Commission on the Review of National Policy Toward Gambling (1976). In citing Professor Haller's data, I do not wish to imply that he agrees with my interpretation.

Chapter 11

1. See Chapter 20, p. 232.
2. For an explanation of 'policy' or numbers gamblings, see Chapter 16, pp. 181–7.
3. For the background to the Robert Kennedy–J. Edgar Hoover row over the FBI's bugs, see *Kennedy Justice* by Victor Navasky (Atheneum, New York, 1971).
4. For more on Giancana's relationship with Sinatra, see Chapter 19.
5. On the Villa Venice, see Chapter 19, pp. 225–6.
6. On Las Vegas and the Chicago Outfit, see Chapter 17.
7. See Chapter 20, p. 232.
8. On Lansky and Cuba, see Chapter 17, pp. 193–4. On Lansky as the mob's money man, see Chapter 25.
9. On the Outfit and Teamsters' Union pension and welfare funds, see Chapter 17, pp. 204–8 and Chapter 21 pp. 251–4 and 264–6.

Chapter 13

1. From *The Gangs of New York* (Alfred A. Knopf, New York, 1927).
2. See Chapter 4, p. 33 and Chapter 15, p. 169.
3. On Hoover and organized crime, see Chapter 14, pp. 164–7.
4. On Capone's tax problems, see Chapter 10.
5. On racketeering in the fish market and the garment centre in the 1930s and today, see Chapter 23.

Chapter 14

1. In writing this account of the collaboration between the Mafia and US Naval

Intelligence in World War II, I have relied heavily on Rodney Campbell's masterly analysis of the Herlands Investigation in *The Luciano Project* (McGraw-Hill, New York, 1977).

2. On the origins of the Top Hoodlum Program, see Chapter 11, p. 110.

Chapter 15

1. On Dalitz, the Cleveland Syndicate and Las Vegas, see Chapter 17, pp. 200–2.
2. On numbers and policy gambling, see Chapter 16, pp. 181–7.
3. On the impact of black and Hispanic organized crime on the Mafia in recent years, see Chapter 27, pp. 325–39.
4. 'Barbut', spelled in a bewildering variety of ways including 'Barboute', is a dice game much loved by Greeks.
5. The 'continuing criminal conspiracy' law under which the Cleveland Mafia leaders were charged is Title 18 of the Organized Crime Control Act 1970, otherwise known as the RICO statute. RICO stands for Racketeer Influenced and Corrupt Organization. The statute does not refer to the Mafia, La Cosa Nostra or any other criminal organization by name. However, the Mafia is one of the law's primary targets.
6. For a brief examination of emerging organized crime groups in America, see Chapter 27.

Chapter 16

1. On nineteenth-century organized crime, see Chapter 3, pp. 27–8 (on New Orleans), Chapter 6, pp. 60–62 (on Chicago), and Chapter 13, pp. 132–5 (on New York).
2. On Tammany Hall, see Chapter 13.
3. On Schultz and Hines, see Chapter 13, pp. 147–8.
4. On the Mafia's role in illegal street gambling today, see Chapter 27, pp. 338–9.
5. As note 4. See also Peter Reuter and Jonathan Rubinstein, *Illegal Gambling in New York* (US Department of Justice, 1982), and Peter Reuter, *Disorganized Crime* (MIT Press, Cambridge, Massachusetts, 1983).
6. On the 1919 World Series fix, see Chapter 13, p. 140.

Chapter 17

1. Fratianno is referring to the October 1977 murder of Richard Schwartz, Meyer Lansky's stepson. Schwartz was gunned down in broad daylight outside his restaurant in south Florida, apparently because he had murdered Craig Teriaca four months before. Teriaca, the son of an organized crime figure, died in what seems to have been a drunken argument with Schwartz, not in an organized crime hit. Schwartz's relationship to Lansky did not protect him from being murdered in revenge.
2. This operation is described in greater detail in Chapter 25, pp. 302–4.
3. On Laxalt and Dalitz, see Chapter 26, p. 322.
4. For further material on the Fund, see Chapter 21.
5. On Jimmy Hoffa, see Chapter 21.
6. For some insight into Nevada's licensing procedure, see Chapter 19.

Chapter 18

1. See Chapter 13, p. 142.
2. See also Chapter 26, pp. 316–18.

3. The story of Mary Carter Paint and Dino Cellini is told in part in the report of the Bahama Islands Commission of Inquiry into the Operation of Casinos (HMSO, London, 1967).
4. See Chapter 1.

Chapter 20

1. See Chapter 13, p. 141.
2. *Crime on the Labor Front* (McGraw-Hill, New York, 1950).
3. See Chapter 14.
4. On Murder Inc., see Chapter 23, pp. 280–1.
5. See Chapter 27.

Chapter 21

1. Good written accounts, from different standpoints, of the Hoffa–Robert Kennedy struggle include Kennedy's own book, *The Enemy Within* (Harper & Bros, New York, 1970); *The Fall and Rise of Jimmy Hoffa* by Walter Sheridan (Saturday Review Press, New York, 1972); and *Hoffa, The Real Story*, by Jimmy Hoffa as told to Oscar Fraley (Stein and Day, New York, 1975).
2. The strongest advocate of this view is Professor Robert Blakey, who, with Richard Billings, wrote *The Plot to Kill the President*, subtitled 'Organized Crime Assassinated JFK – The Definitive Story' (Times Books, New York, 1981). A fine analysis of Hoffa's possible role in John Kennedy's assassination – and an excellent study of Hoffa and the Teamsters – is contained in Dan Moldea's *The Hoffa Wars* (Paddington Press, New York, 1981). Bringing the CIA into the plot with the Mafia is *Conspiracy* by Anthony Summers (Gollancz, London, 1980).
3. See Chapter 25.
4. On Dalitz and Las Vegas, see Chapter 17.
5. See Charles Allen's testimony in Volume 1 of the 1982 hearings of the Permanent Subcommittee on Investigations concerning the HEREIU (Hotel and Restaurant Employees Union).
6. See Hoffa & Fraley, *op. cit.*
7. For a lighter view of Celso's chicken farm, see Chapter 5, p. 57.
8. See note 5, Chapter 15.
9. See Chapter 15, pp. 170–1.
10. See Chapter 17, pp. 205–7.
11. See Chapter 17, p. 208.

Chapter 23

1. For Vitale on illegal gambling, see Chapter 16, pp. 187–188.
2. See Chapter 13, p. 141.
3. See Chapter 17, p. 195.
4. See Turkus and Feder, *Murder Inc.* (originally published 1951, republished by Manor Books, New York, 1974).
5. See Chapter 14, pp. 155–6.
6. For a brilliant account of Mafia meat racketeering, and much else, see Kwitny, *Vicious Circles*.

Chapter 25

1. On Lansky, see Chapter 17.

2. On Dorfman and the Teamsters' Pension Fund, see Chapters 17 and 21.
3. On the Flamingo skim, see Chapter 17, pp. 198–9.
4. See Kwitny, *op. cit.*

Chapter 26

1. Today Newark has 10,000 drug addicts out of a population of only 425,000. It has the highest addiction rate in New Jersey and the highest number of overdoses. According to the latest US census information, Newark has the worst poverty rating of all American cities with a population of more than 100,000 – 32 per cent of the population fall below the US poverty line. It also has among the worst housing and educational levels in the nation.
2. On Anthony Provenzano, see Chapter 21, pp. 255–63, Chapter 22, p. 285, and Chapter 25, pp. 304–5.
3. On Scarfo and Atlantic City, see Chapter 18.
4. On Scotto, see Chapter 20, pp. 242–3.
5. As quoted in an excellent series of articles on the Mafia in pornography and Hollywood, by Ellen Farley and William K. Knoedelseder Jr, published in the *Los Angeles Times* in June 1982.
6. See Chapter 17.
7. The clash between the philosophy of Nevadans and the role of federal law enforcement is examined in Chapter 17, pp. 201–3.
8. See Dorfman references in Chapters 17 and 21.

Chapter 27

1. See Reuter, *op. cit.*, note 5, Chapter 16.
2. See note 5, Chapter 15.

Index